岸本斉史

...ese days, I often hurt my
...sts when I wake up in the
...rning. When I sit up, I put
too much weight on one hand
and end up twisting it. You're
not too aware of things when
you've just woken up. So,
everyone please be careful when
you wake up in the morning.

—*Masashi Kishimoto, 2005*

Author/artist Masashi Kishimoto was born in 1974 in rural
Okayama Prefecture, Japan. After spending time ...rt college,
he won the Hop Step Award for new mang... ...ts with his
manga **Karakuri** (Mechanism). Kishimoto ...ded to base his
next story on traditional Japanese culture ...is first version of
Naruto, drawn in 1997, was a one-shot ...ory about fox spirits;
his final version, which debuted in **Wee... Shonen Jump** in
1999, quickly became the most popular ninja manga in Japan.

NARUTO VOL. 29
The SHONEN JUMP Manga Edition

This graphic novel contains material that was originally published in
English in **SHONEN JUMP** #63-64. Artwork in the magazine may have
been slightly altered from that presented here.

STORY AND ART BY MASASHI KISHIMOTO

Translation/Riyo Odate, HC Language Solutions, Inc.
English Adaptation/Ian Reid, HC Language Solutions, Inc.
Touch-up Art & Lettering/ Sabrina Heep
Design/Sean Lee
Editor/Joel Enos

Editor in Chief, Books/Alvin Lu
Editor in Chief, Magazines/Marc Weidenbaum
VP of Publishing Licensing/Rika Inouye
VP of Sales/Gonzalo Ferreyra
Sr. VP of Marketing/Liza Coppola
Publisher/Hyoe Narita

Printed in the U.S.A.

Published by VIZ Media, LLC
P.O. Box 77010
San Francisco, CA 94107

SHONEN JUMP Manga Edition
10 9 8 7 6 5 4 3 2 1
First printing, May 2008

www.viz.com

THE WORLD'S
MOST POPULAR MANGA

www.shonenjump.com

SHONEN JUMP MANGA EDITION

NARUTO

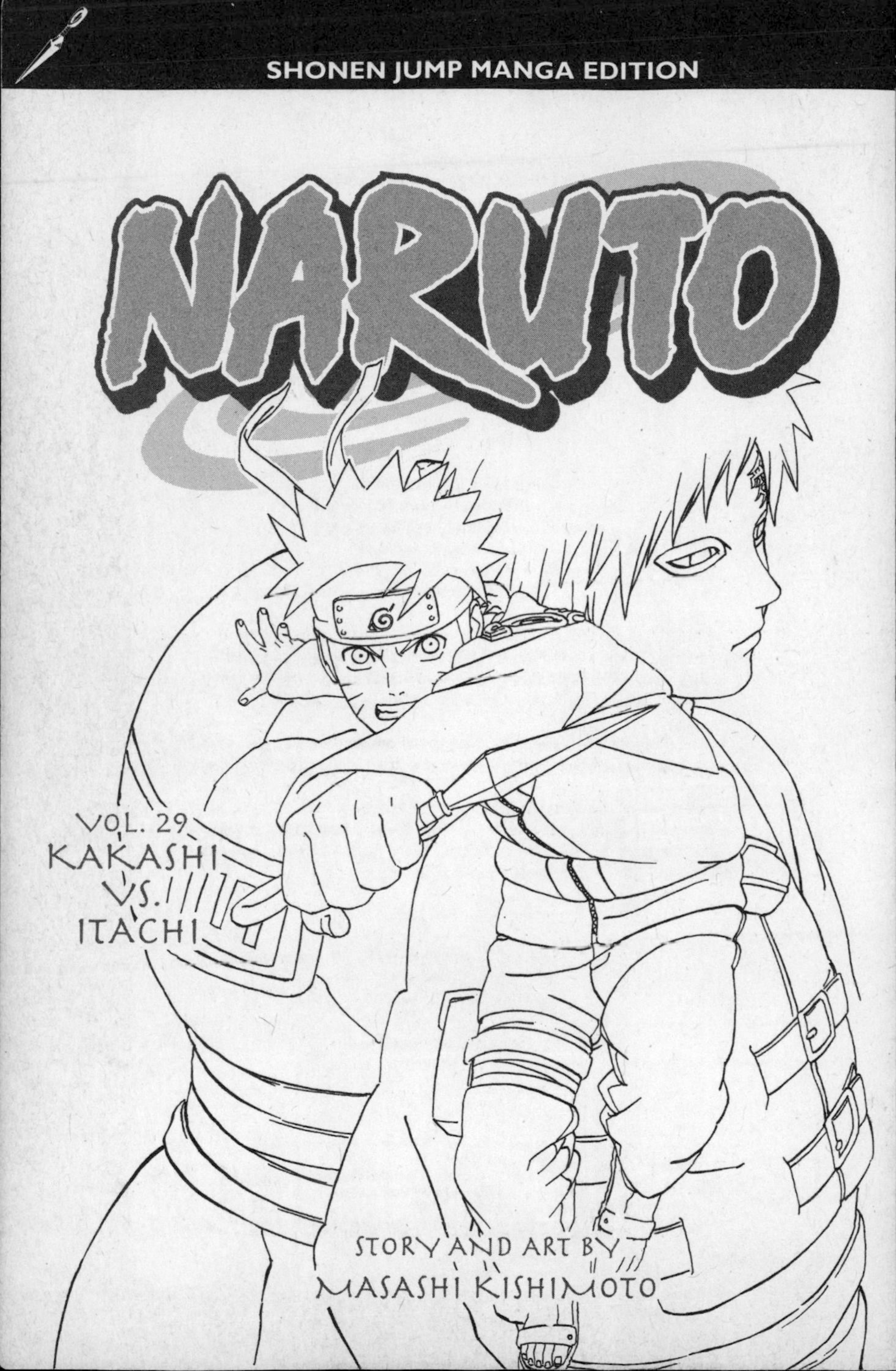

VOL. 29

KAKASHI VS. ITACHI

STORY AND ART BY

MASASHI KISHIMOTO

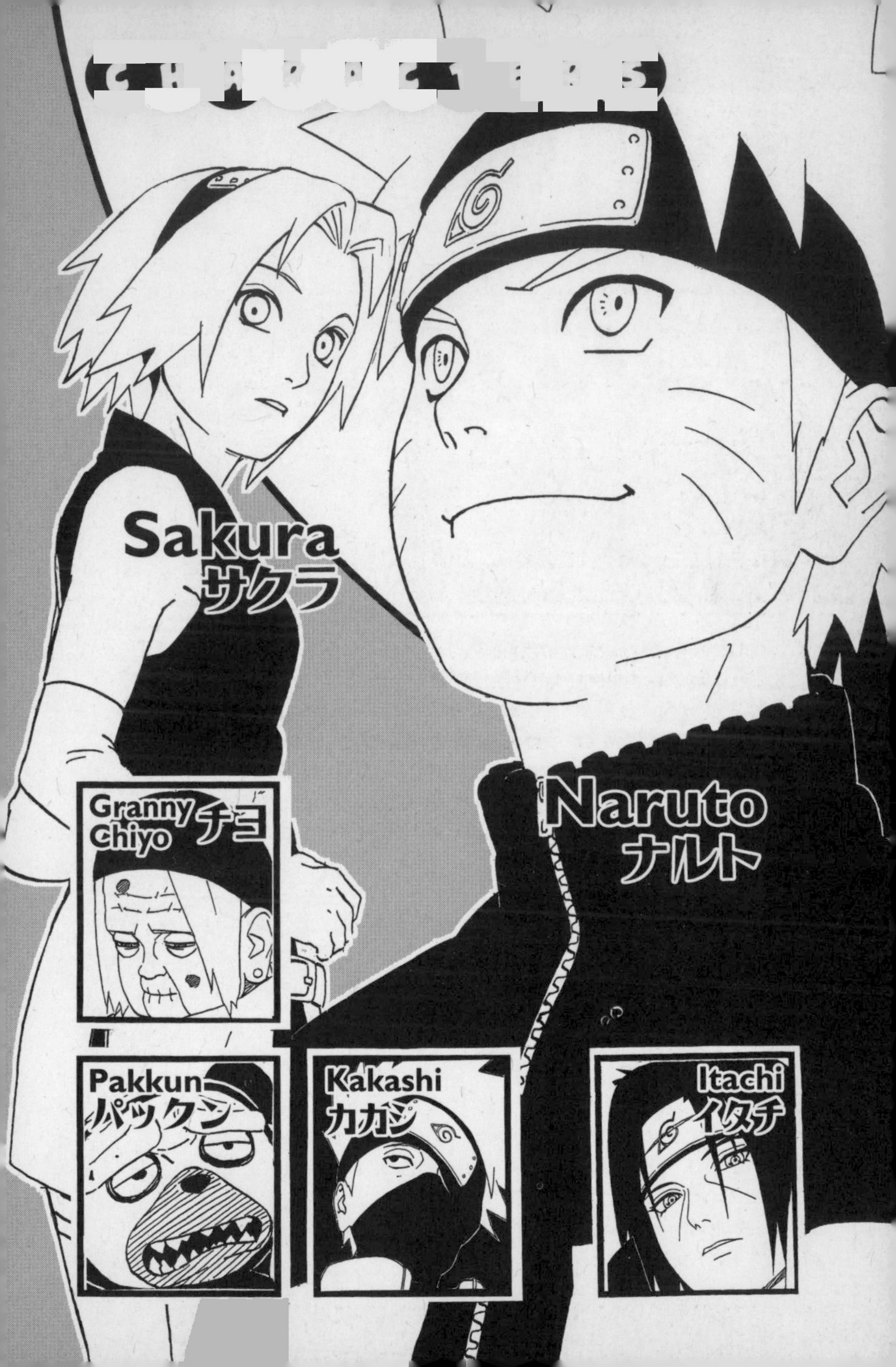
Sakura
サクラ
Naruto
ナルト
Granny Chiyo
チヨ
Pakkun
パックン
Kakashi
カカシ
Itachi
イタチ

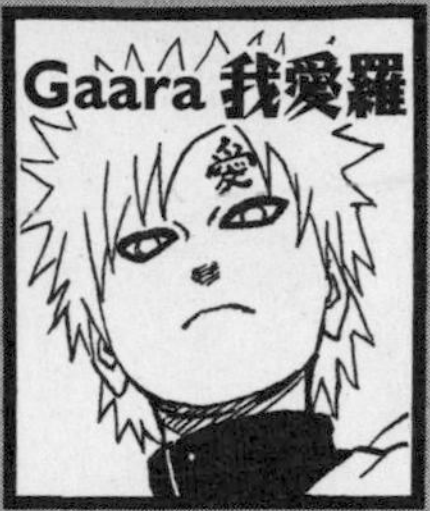
Gaara 我愛羅
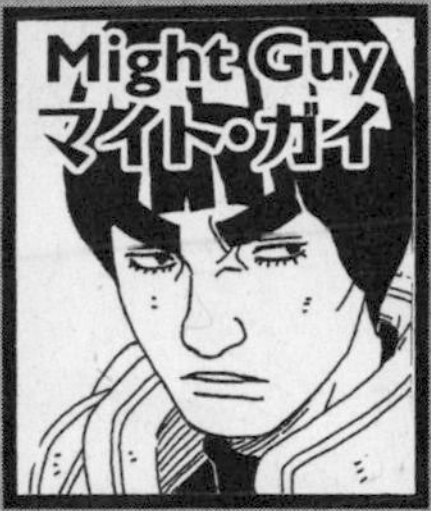
Might Guy
マイト・ガイ
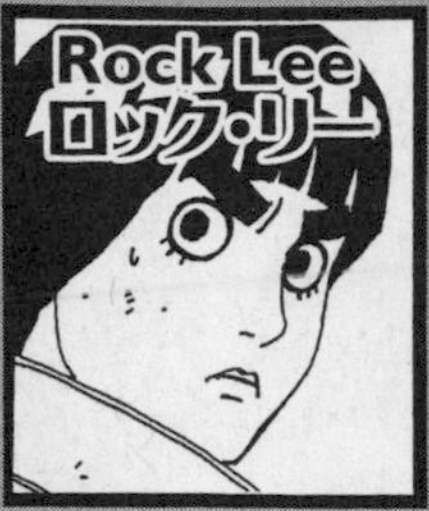
Rock Lee
ロック・リー
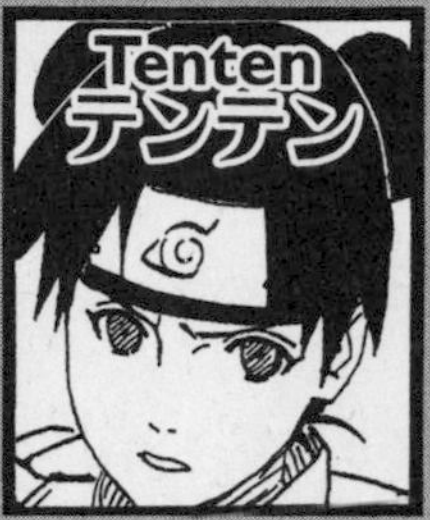
Tenten
テンテン
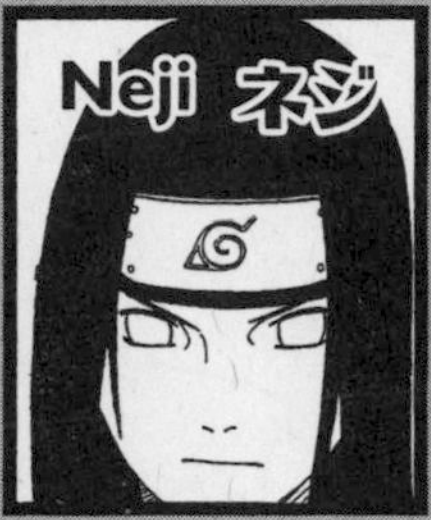
Neji ネジ
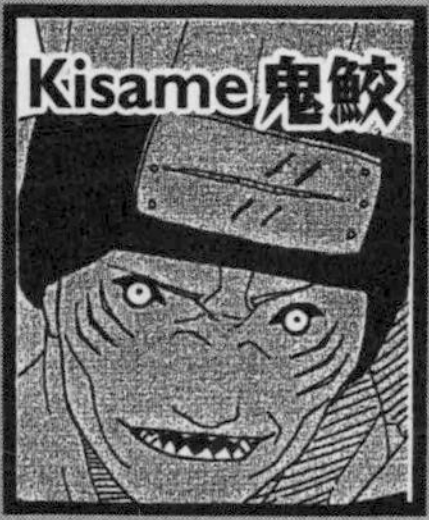
Kisame 鬼鮫

The Story So Far...

Naruto, the biggest troublemaker at the Ninja Academy in the village of Konohagakure, finally becomes a ninja along with his classmates Sasuke and Sakura. Right in the middle of the Chûnin Selection Exams, Orochimaru and his henchmen launch *Operation Destroy Konoha*, which ends when the revered leader of the village, the Third Hokage, sacrifices his own life to save his people.

Tsunade, one of the Three Great Shinobi of Konoha legend, becomes the Fifth Hokage. Sasuke, succumbing to the allure of Orochimaru's power, leaves the village with the deadly Sound Ninja Four. Naruto fights valiantly against Sasuke, but can't stop him.

Two years pass following that battle, and Naruto and his comrades train and mature. The mysterious Gaara becomes Kazekage and falls into the hands of the secret society of the Akatsuki! Naruto with one team and Lee with another set out for the village of Sunagakure to save him!!

CONTENTS

NUMBER 254: SIBLINGS...!! 7

NUMBER 255: APPROACH...!! 27

NUMBER 256: ENEMIES!! 47

NUMBER 257: KAKASHI COMES THROUGH 67

NUMBER 258: GUY VS. KISAME!! 87

NUMBER 259: THE POWER OF ITACHI...!! 107

NUMBER 260: KAKASHI VS. ITACHI!! 127

NUMBER 261: JINCHŪRIKI HOST...!! 147

NUMBER 262: NARUTO CHARGES ON...!! 167

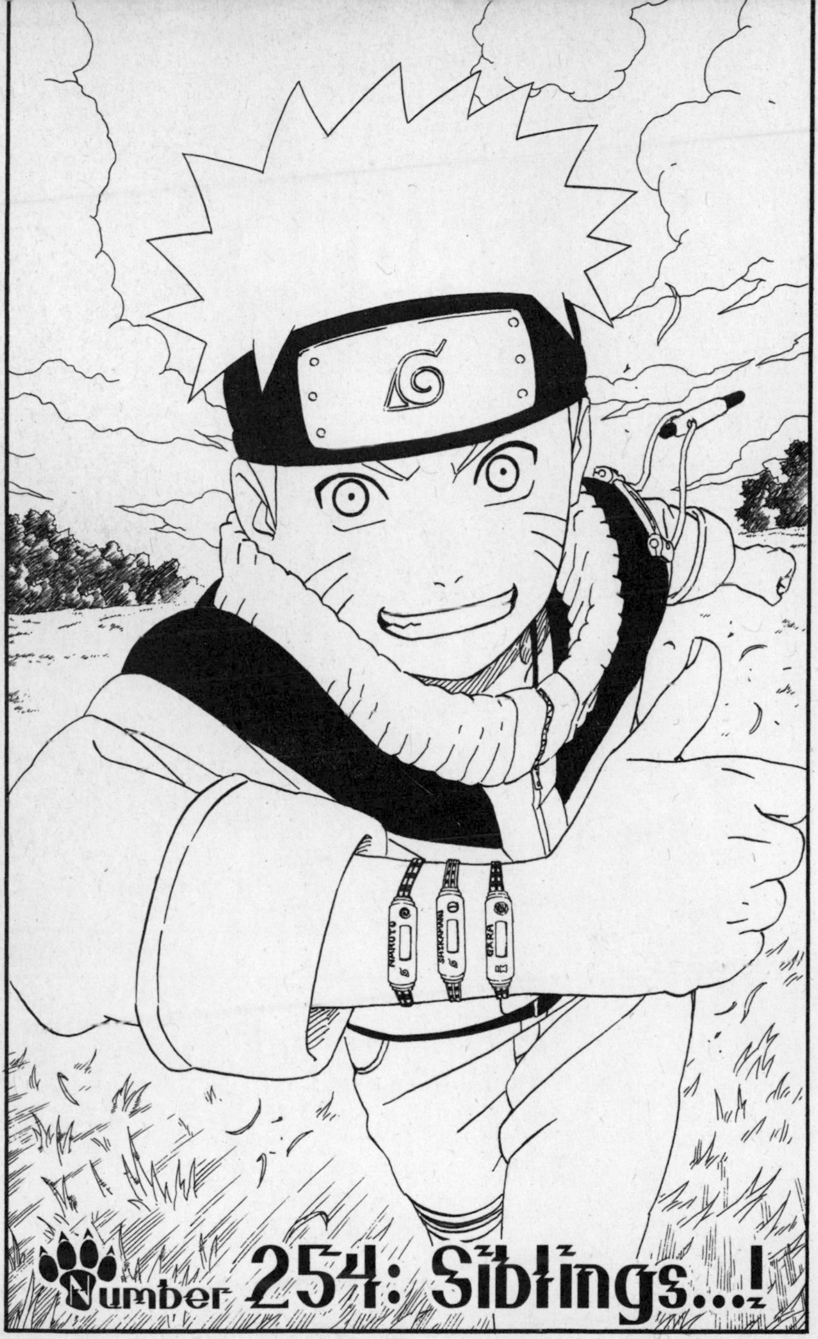
Number 254: Siblings...!

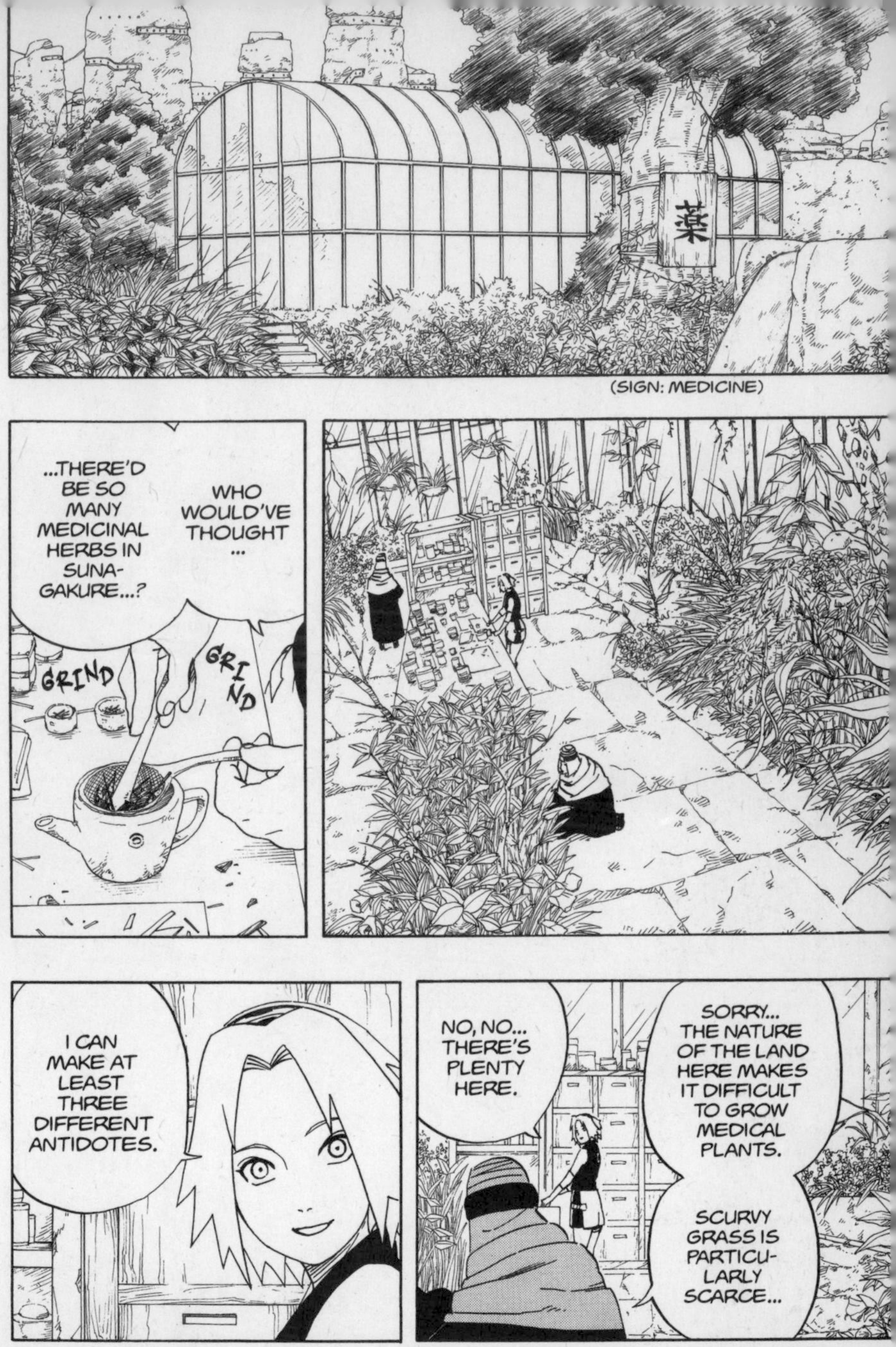
(SIGN: MEDICINE)
WHO WOULD'VE THOUGHT...
...THERE'D BE SO MANY MEDICINAL HERBS IN SUNA-GAKURE...?
GRIND
GRIND
SORRY... THE NATURE OF THE LAND HERE MAKES IT DIFFICULT TO GROW MEDICAL PLANTS.
SCURVY GRASS IS PARTICU-LARLY SCARCE...
NO, NO... THERE'S PLENTY HERE.
I CAN MAKE AT LEAST THREE DIFFERENT ANTIDOTES.

READ THIS WAY

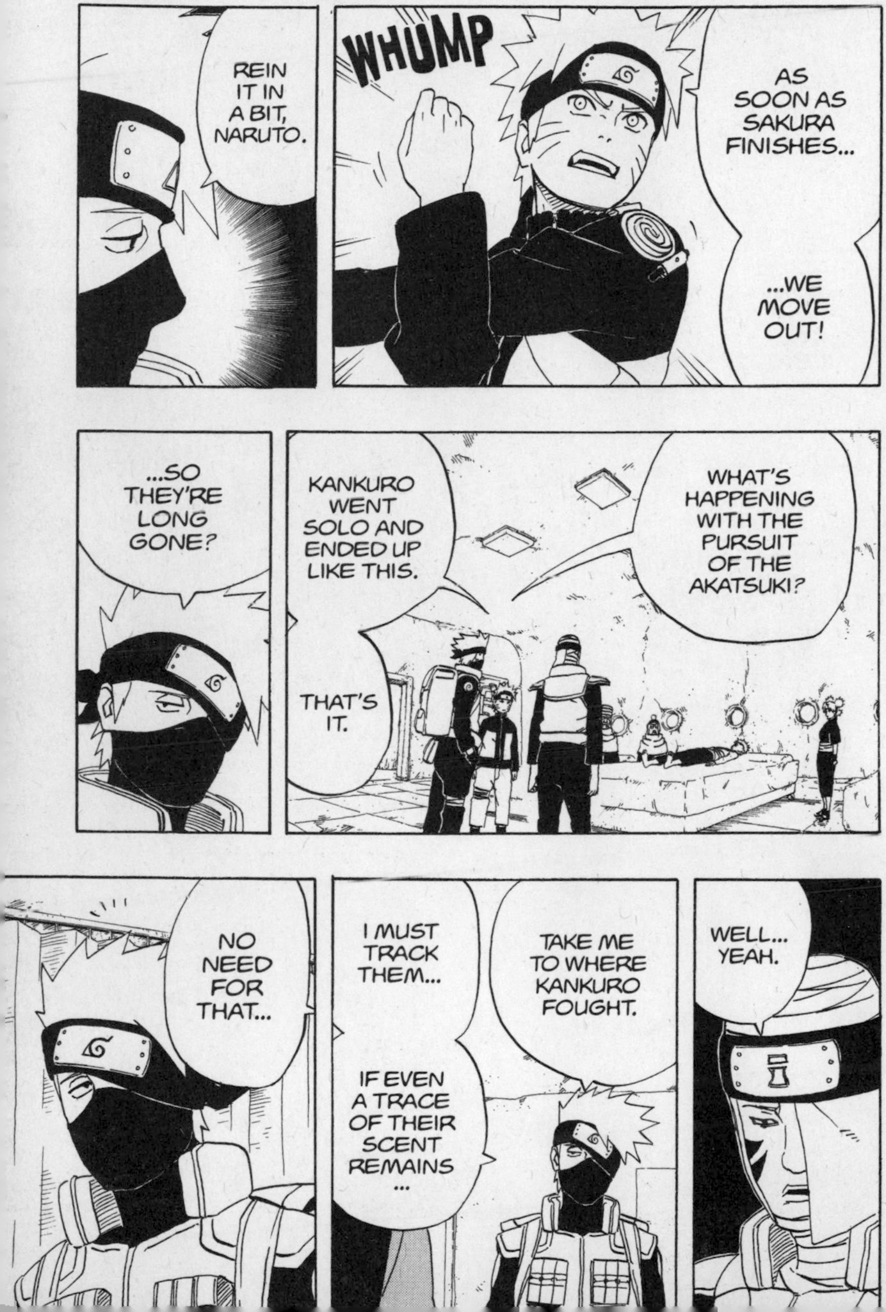
WHUMP
AS SOON AS SAKURA FINISHES...
...WE MOVE OUT!
REIN IT IN A BIT, NARUTO.
WHAT'S HAPPENING WITH THE PURSUIT OF THE AKATSUKI?
KANKURO WENT SOLO AND ENDED UP LIKE THIS.
THAT'S IT.
...SO THEY'RE LONG GONE?
WELL... YEAH.
TAKE ME TO WHERE KANKURO FOUGHT.
I MUST TRACK THEM...
IF EVEN A TRACE OF THEIR SCENT REMAINS ...
NO NEED FOR THAT...

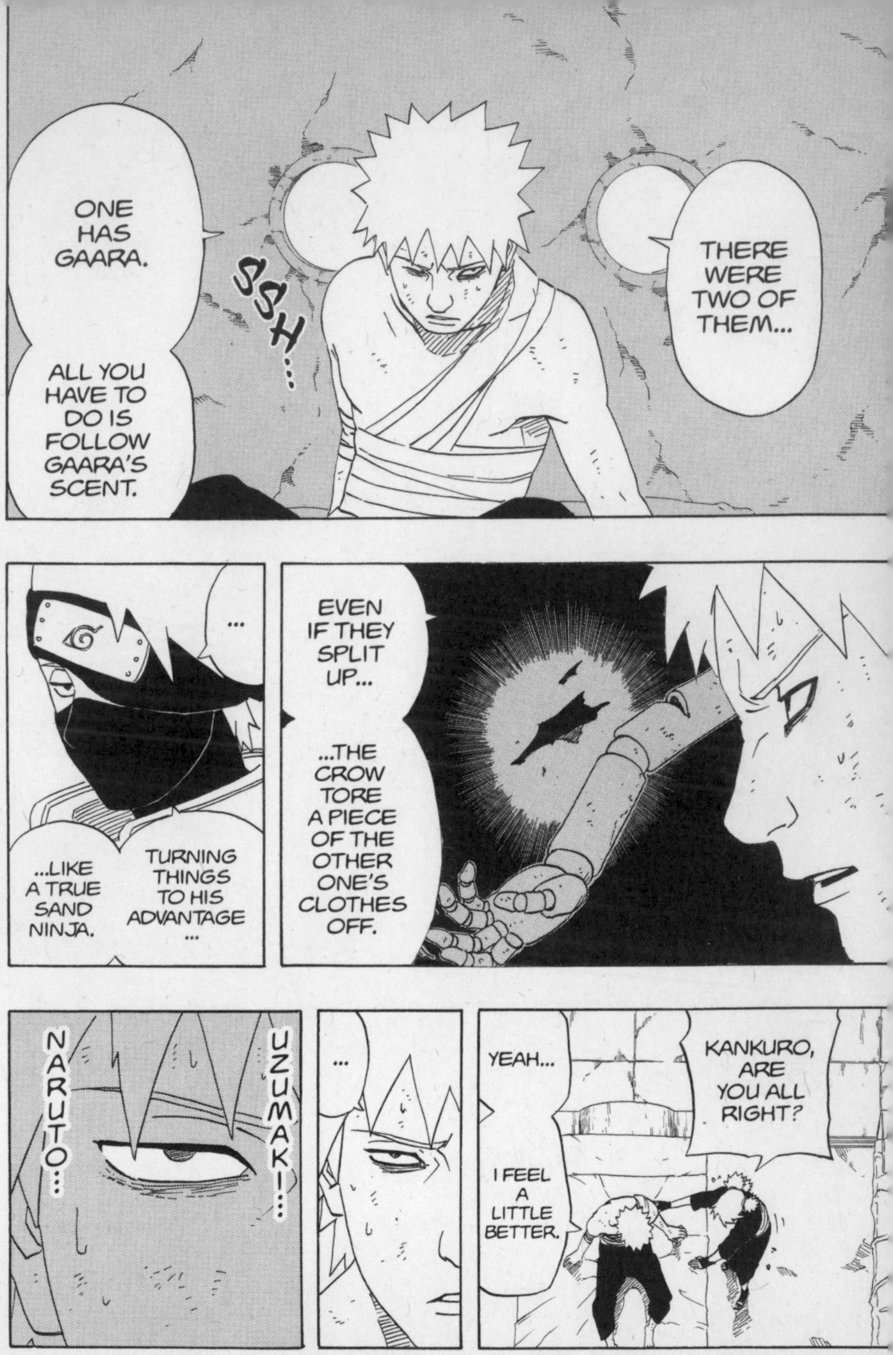
THERE WERE TWO OF THEM...
SSH...
ONE HAS GAARA.
ALL YOU HAVE TO DO IS FOLLOW GAARA'S SCENT.
EVEN IF THEY SPLIT UP...
...THE CROW TORE A PIECE OF THE OTHER ONE'S CLOTHES OFF.
...
TURNING THINGS TO HIS ADVANTAGE...
...LIKE A TRUE SAND NINJA.
KANKURO, ARE YOU ALL RIGHT?
YEAH...
I FEEL A LITTLE BETTER.
...
UZUMAKI...
NARUTO...

READ THIS WAY

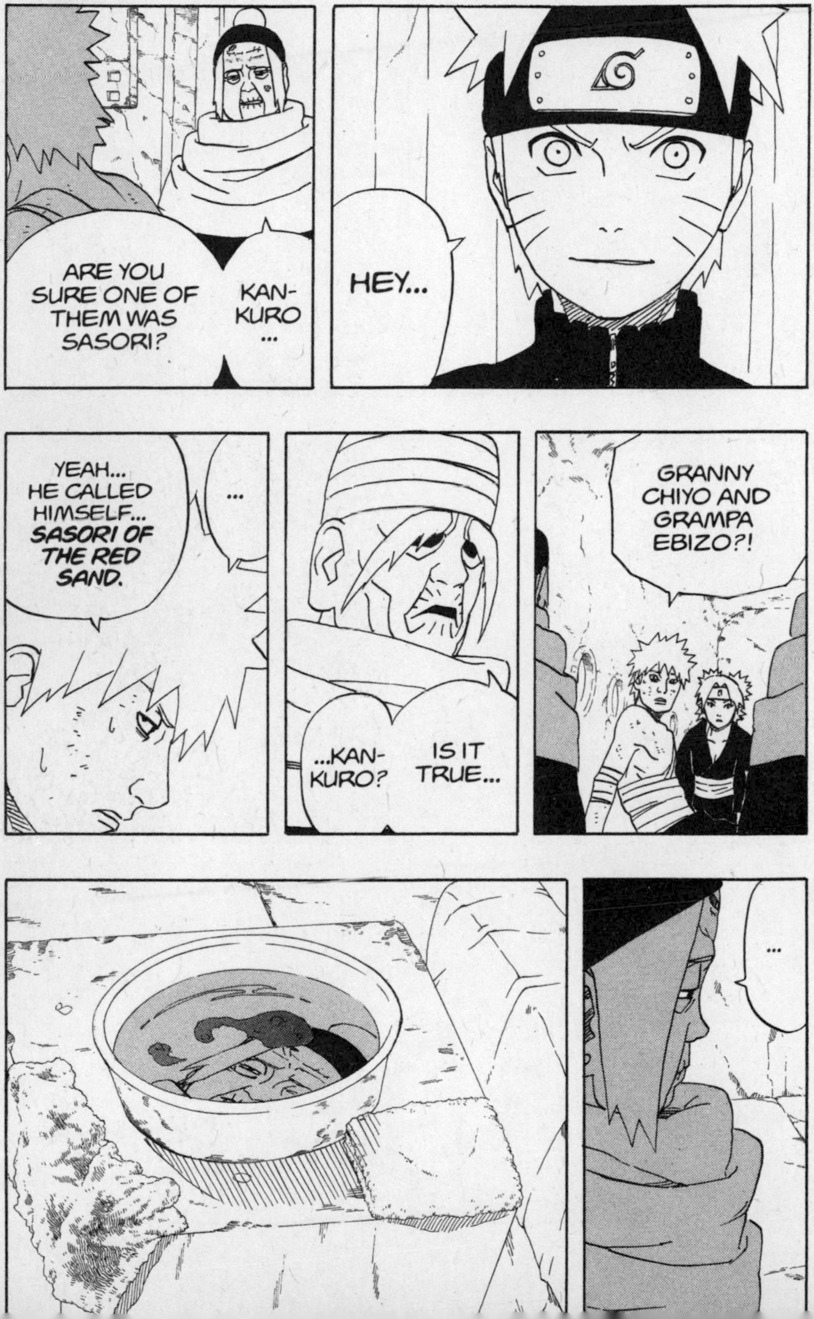
HEY...
KAN-KURO ...
ARE YOU SURE ONE OF THEM WAS SASORI?
GRANNY CHIYO AND GRAMPA EBIZO?!
IS IT TRUE...
...KAN-KURO?
...
YEAH... HE CALLED HIMSELF... SASORI OF THE RED SAND.
...

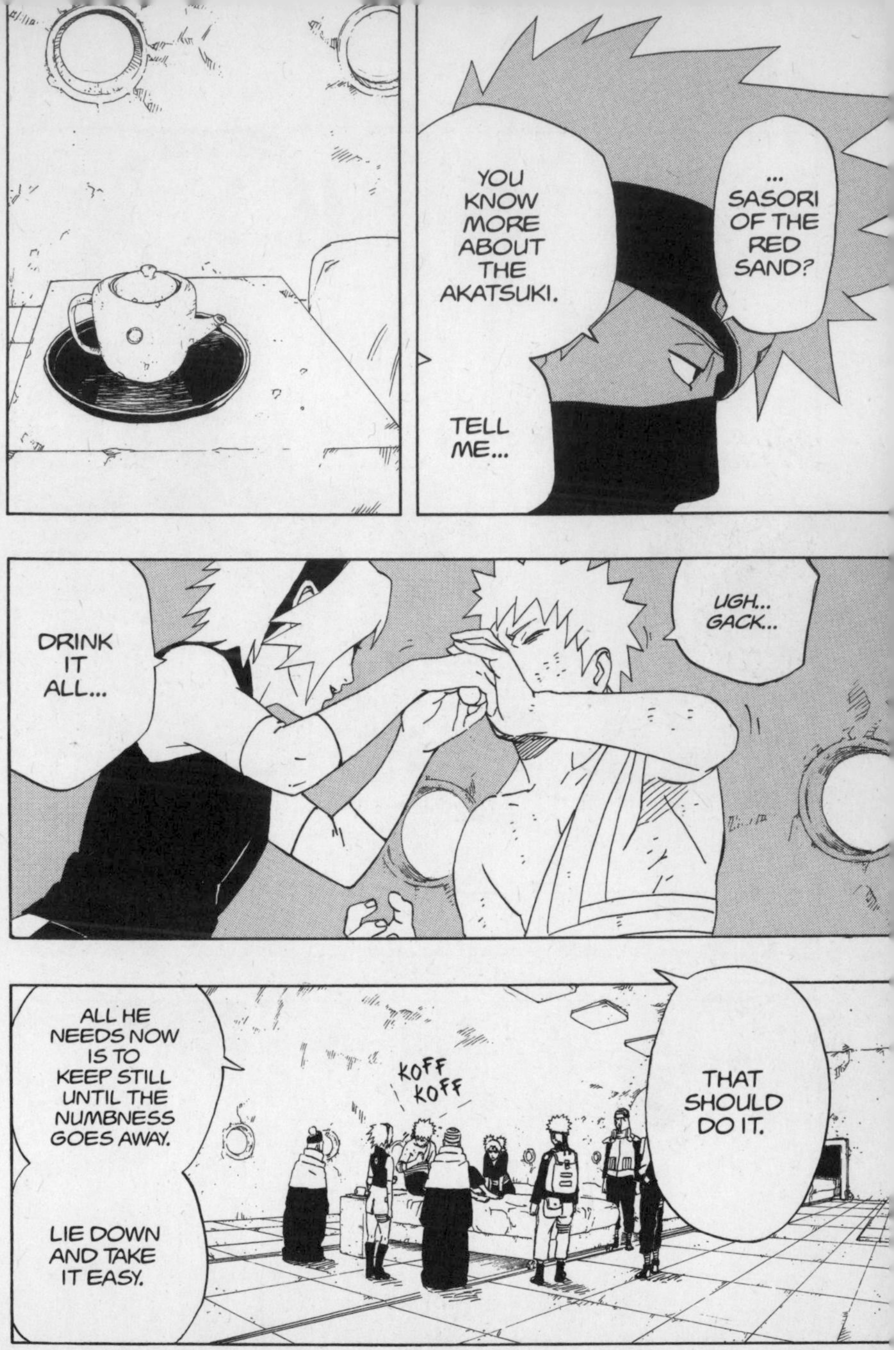

... SASORI OF THE RED SAND?
YOU KNOW MORE ABOUT THE AKATSUKI.
TELL ME...
UGH... GACK...
DRINK IT ALL...
THAT SHOULD DO IT.
KOFF KOFF
ALL HE NEEDS NOW IS TO KEEP STILL UNTIL THE NUMBNESS GOES AWAY.
LIE DOWN AND TAKE IT EASY.

READ THIS WAY

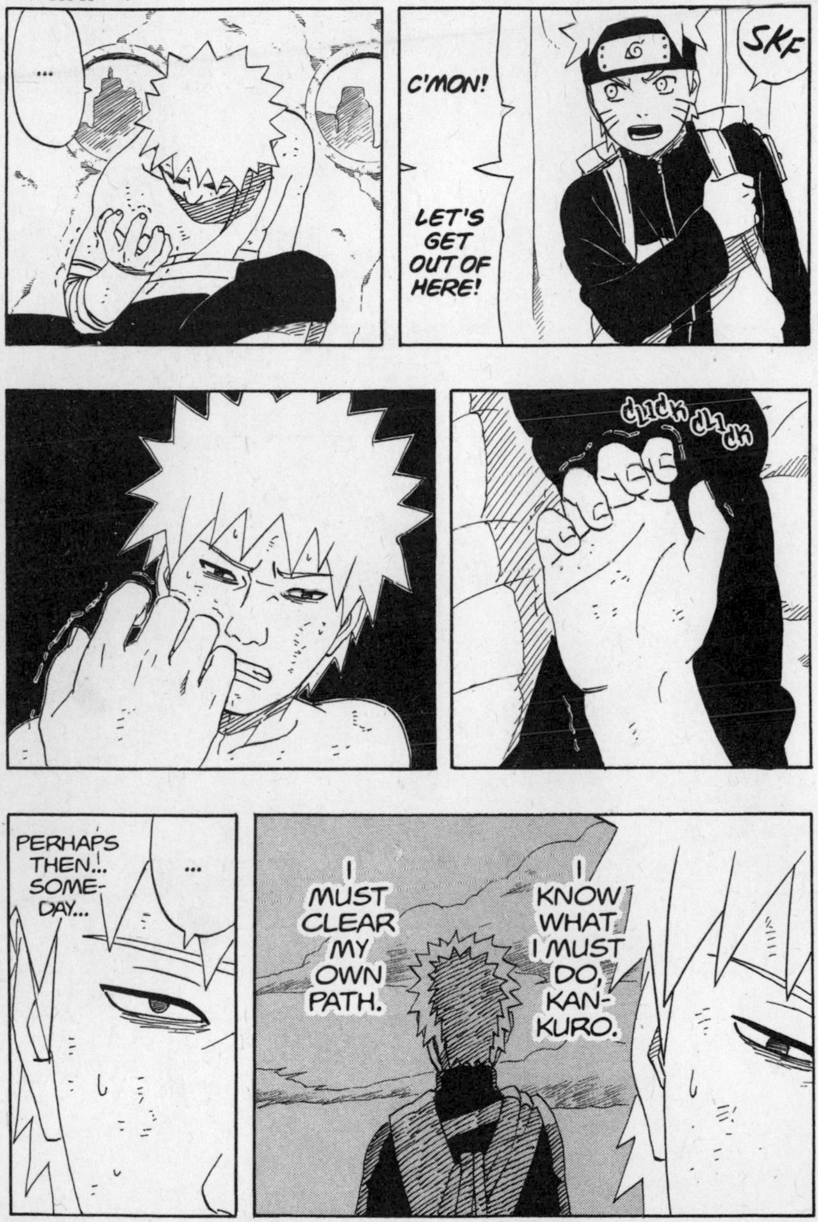
SKF
C'MON!
LET'S GET OUT OF HERE!
...
CLICK CLICK
I KNOW WHAT I MUST DO, KAN-KURO.
I MUST CLEAR MY OWN PATH.
...
PERHAPS THEN... SOME-DAY...

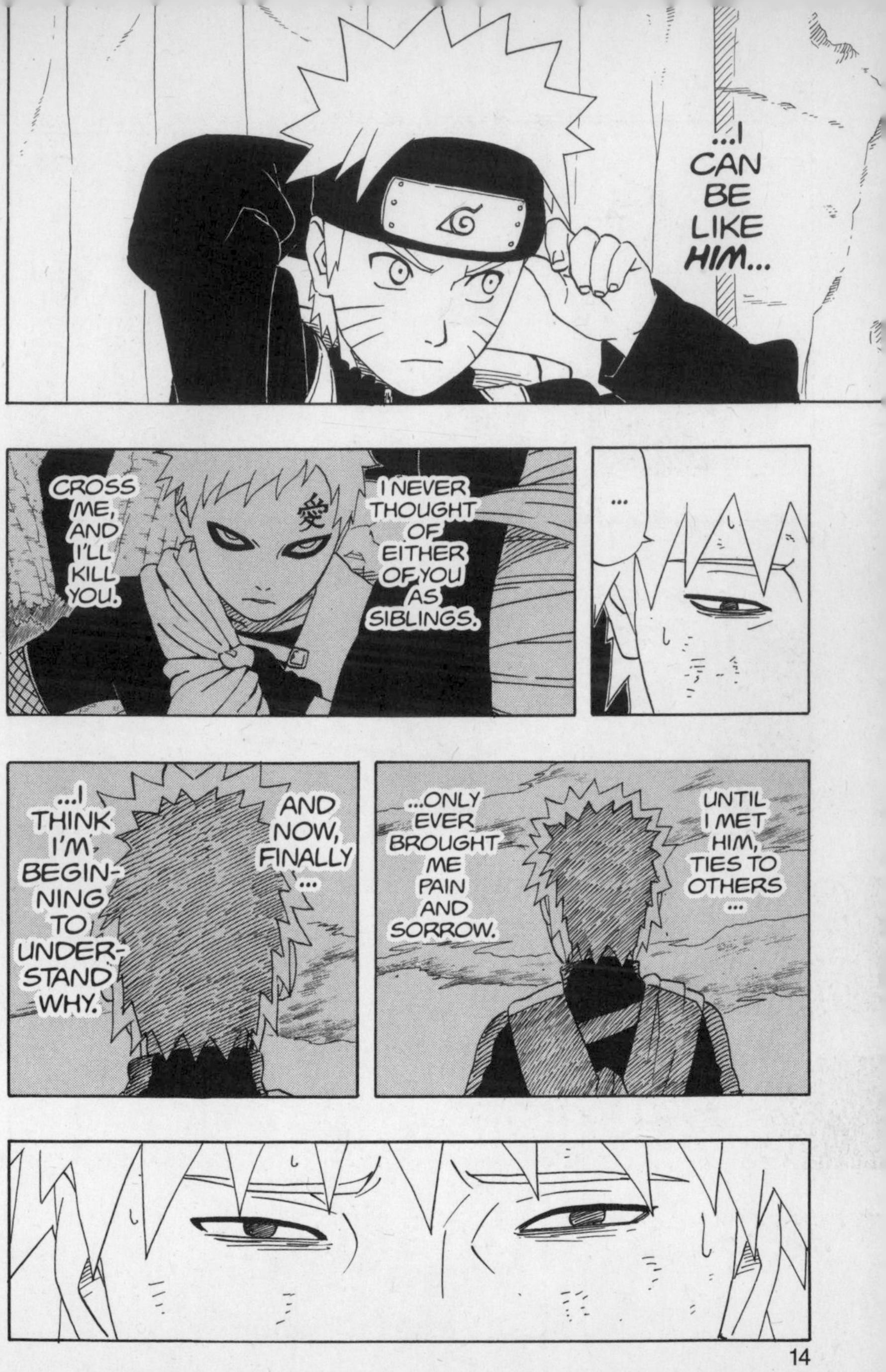
...I CAN BE LIKE *HIM*...
...
I NEVER THOUGHT OF EITHER OF YOU AS SIBLINGS.
CROSS ME, AND I'LL KILL YOU.
UNTIL I MET HIM, TIES TO OTHERS...
...ONLY EVER BROUGHT ME PAIN AND SORROW.
AND NOW, FINALLY...
...I THINK I'M BEGINNING TO UNDERSTAND WHY.

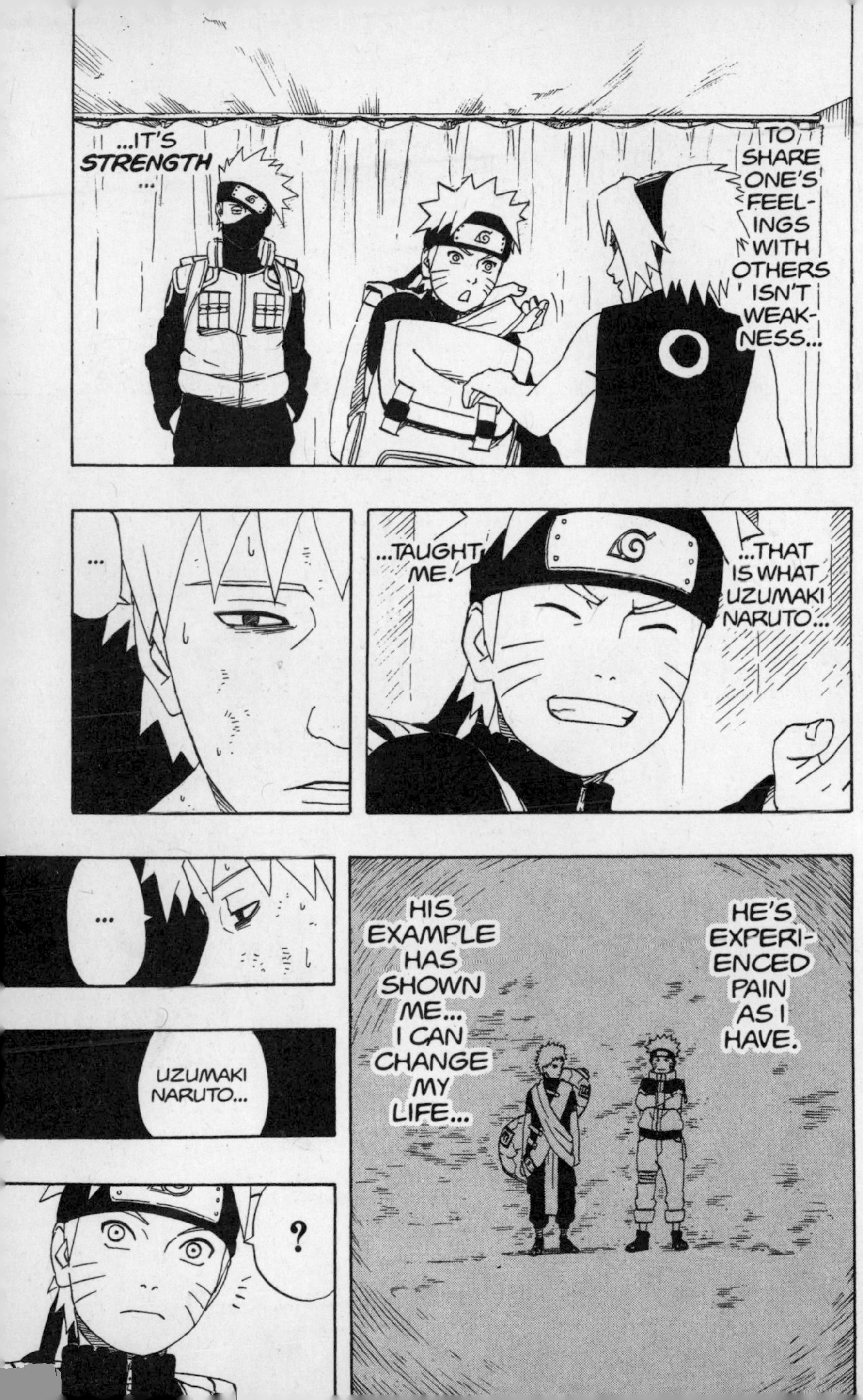
TO SHARE ONE'S FEELINGS WITH OTHERS ISN'T WEAKNESS...
...IT'S STRENGTH...
...THAT IS WHAT UZUMAKI NARUTO...
...TAUGHT ME.
...
HE'S EXPERIENCED PAIN AS I HAVE.
HIS EXAMPLE HAS SHOWN ME... I CAN CHANGE MY LIFE...
...
UZUMAKI NARUTO...
?

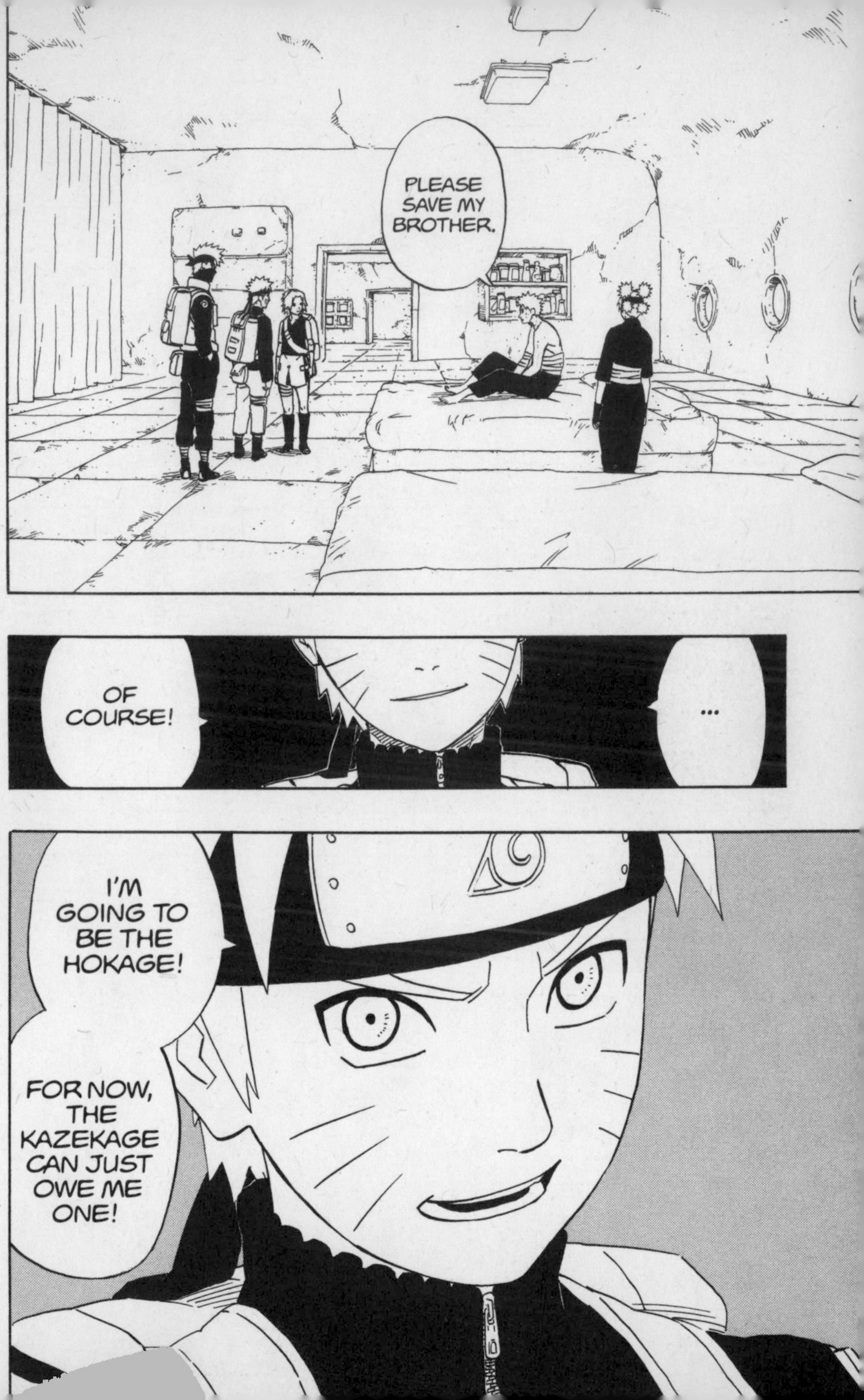
PLEASE SAVE MY BROTHER.
...
OF COURSE!
I'M GOING TO BE THE HOKAGE!
FOR NOW, THE KAZEKAGE CAN JUST OWE ME ONE!

READ THIS WAY

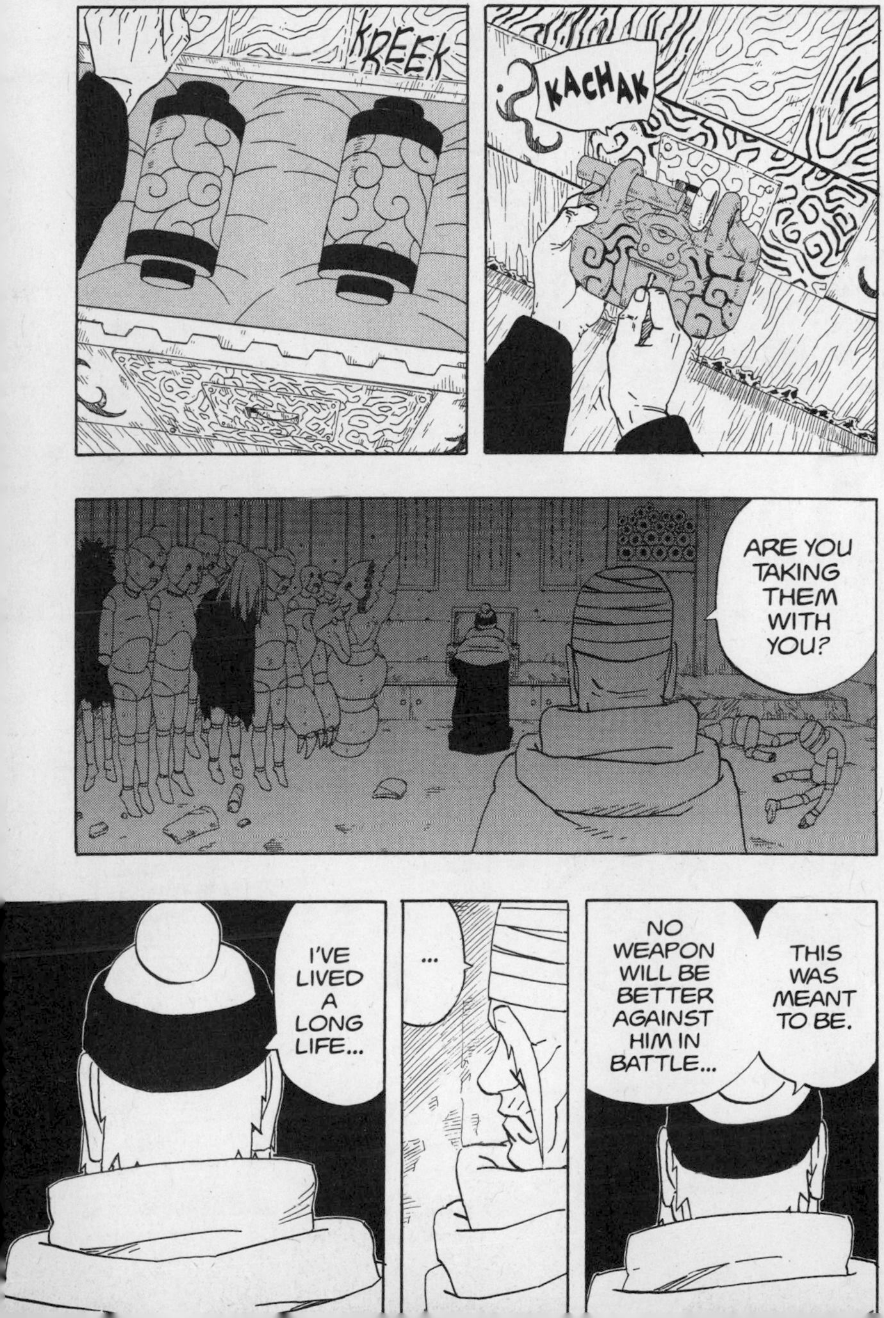
KACHAK
KREEK
ARE YOU TAKING THEM WITH YOU?
THIS WAS MEANT TO BE.
NO WEAPON WILL BE BETTER AGAINST HIM IN BATTLE...
...
I'VE LIVED A LONG LIFE...

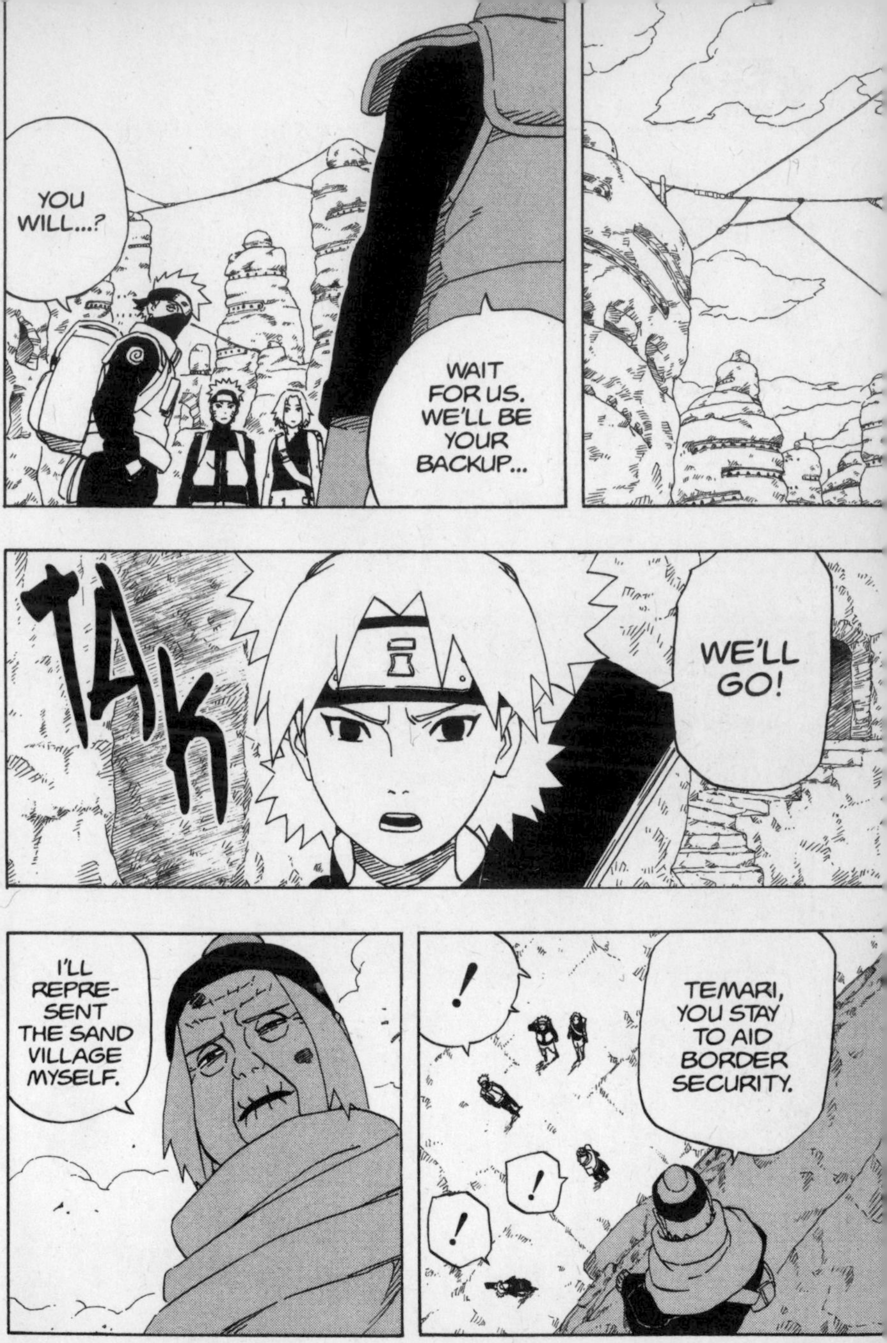
WAIT FOR US. WE'LL BE YOUR BACKUP...
YOU WILL...?
WE'LL GO!
TAK
TEMARI, YOU STAY TO AID BORDER SECURITY.
!
!
!
I'LL REPRE-SENT THE SAND VILLAGE MYSELF.

READ THIS WAY

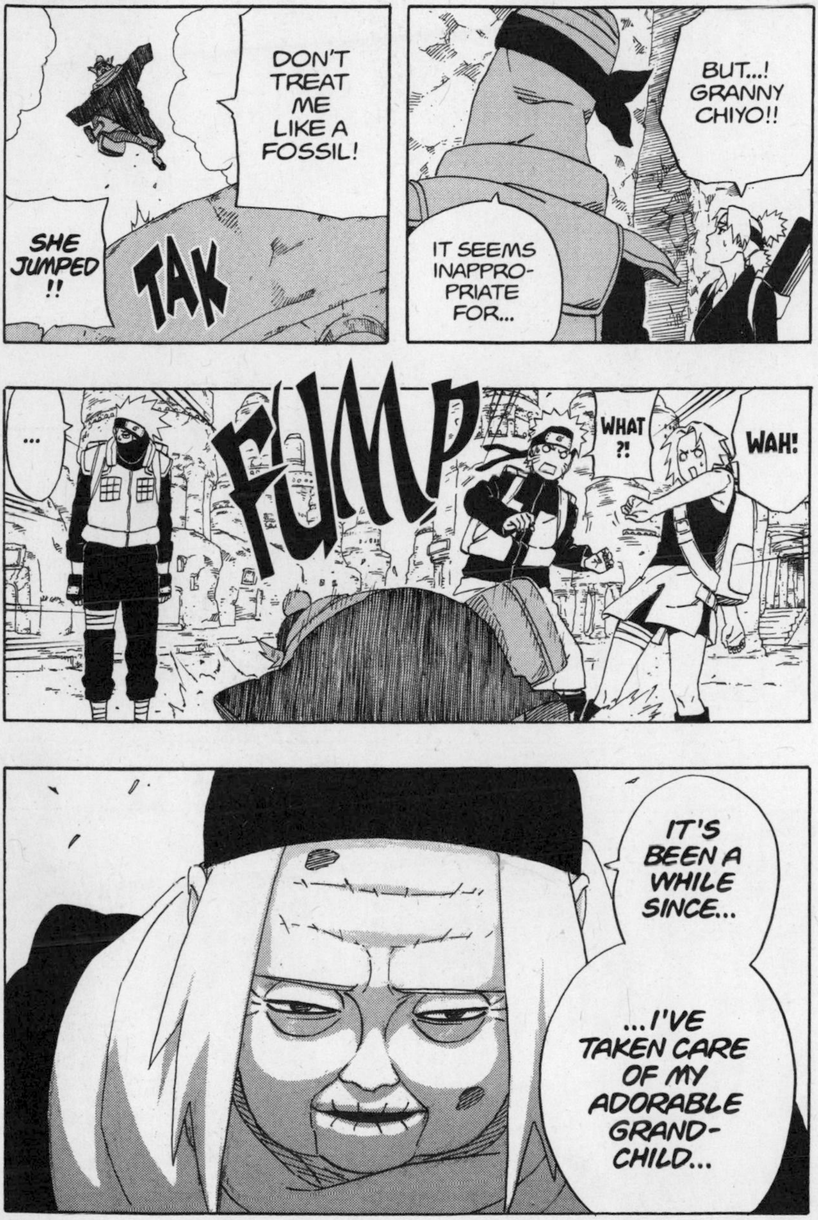
BUT...! GRANNY CHIYO!!
IT SEEMS INAPPROPRIATE FOR...
DON'T TREAT ME LIKE A FOSSIL!
TAK
SHE JUMPED!!
WAH!
WHAT?!
FUMP
...
IT'S BEEN A WHILE SINCE...
...I'VE TAKEN CARE OF MY ADORABLE GRANDCHILD...

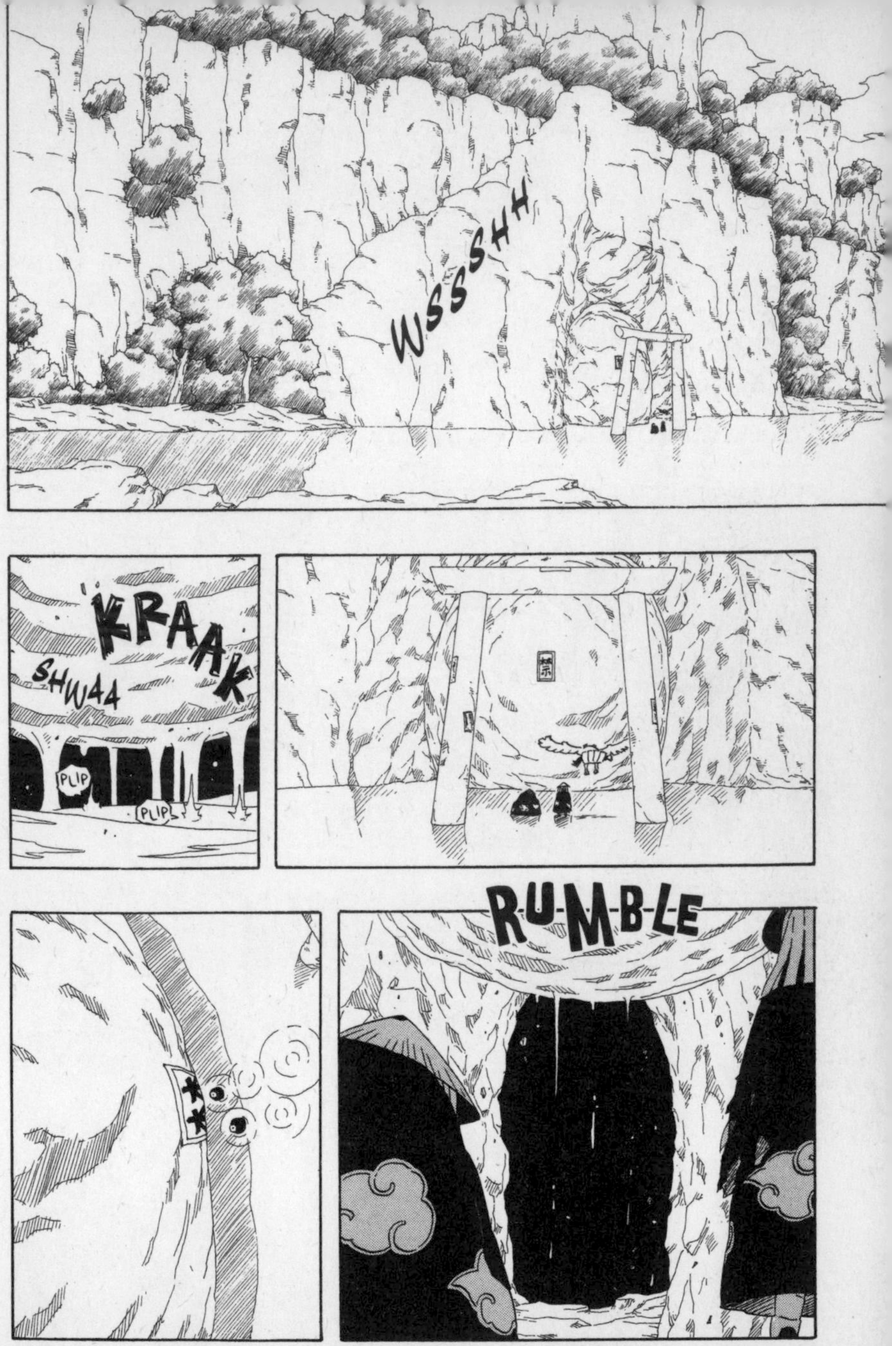
WSSSHH
KRAAAK
SHW44
PLIP
PLIP
RUMBLE

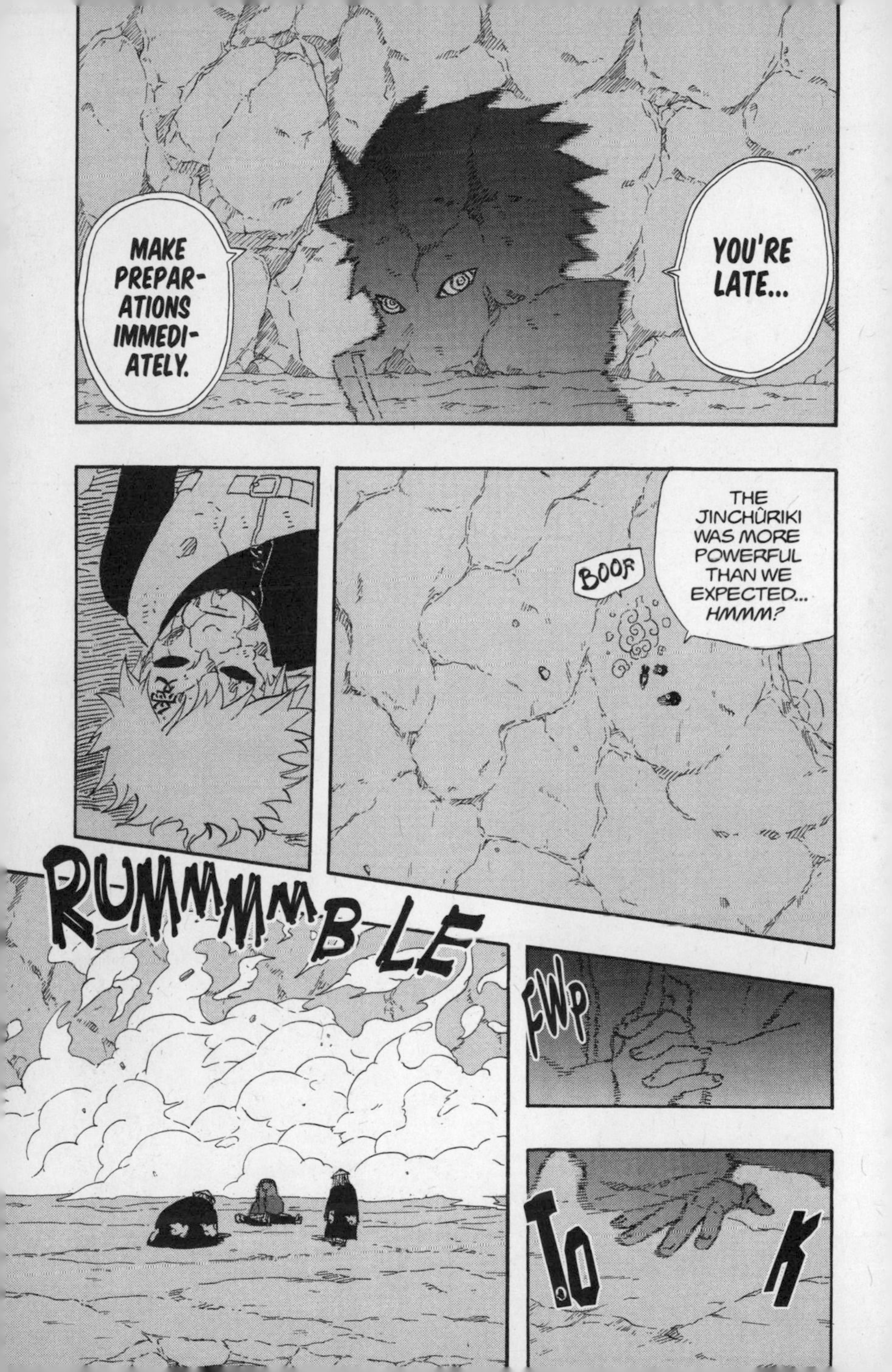
YOU'RE LATE...
MAKE PREPARATIONS IMMEDIATELY.
THE JINCHÛRIKI WAS MORE POWERFUL THAN WE EXPECTED... HMMM?
BOOF
FWP
TOK
RUMMMMBLE

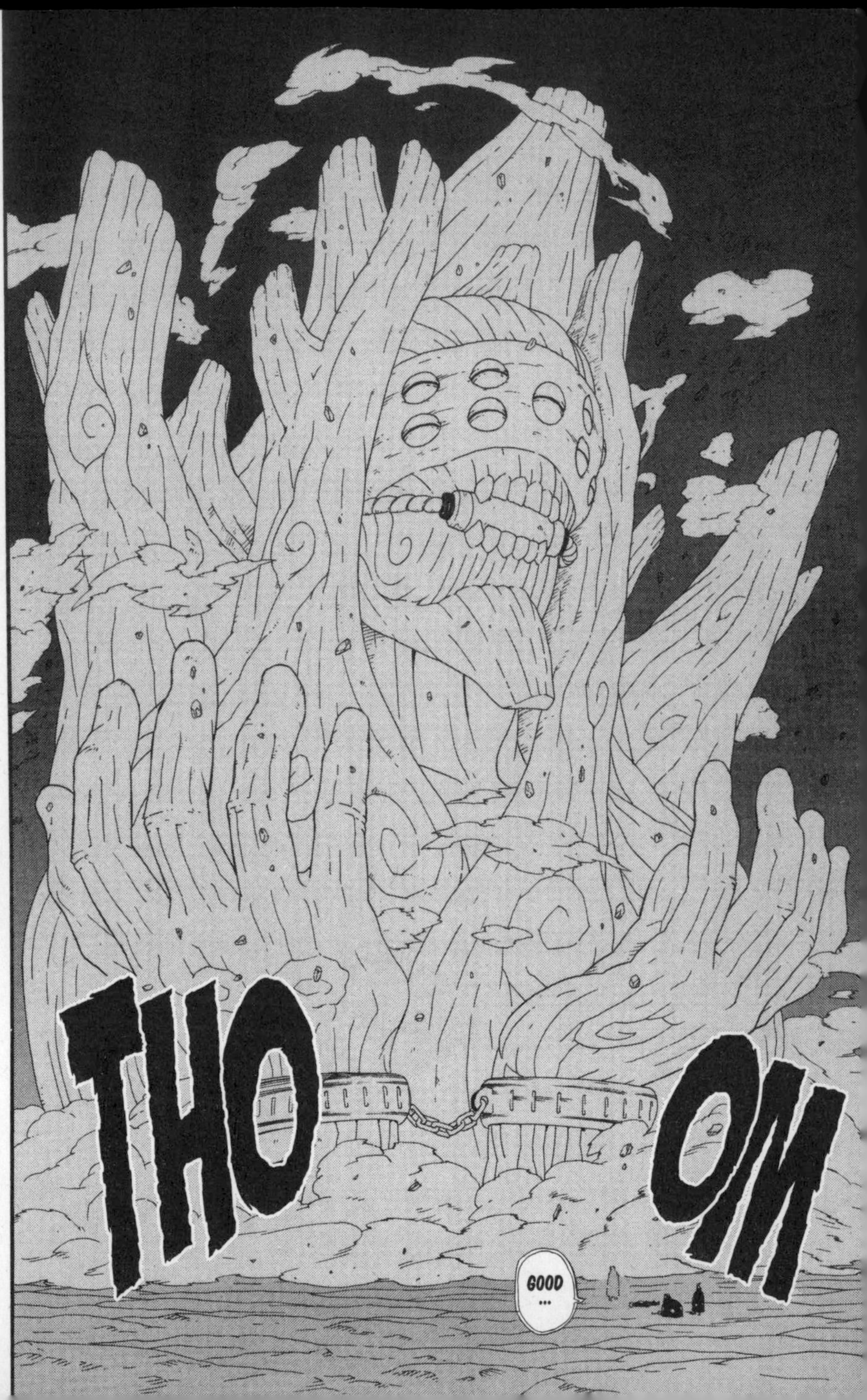
THO-OM
GOOD...

READ THIS WAY

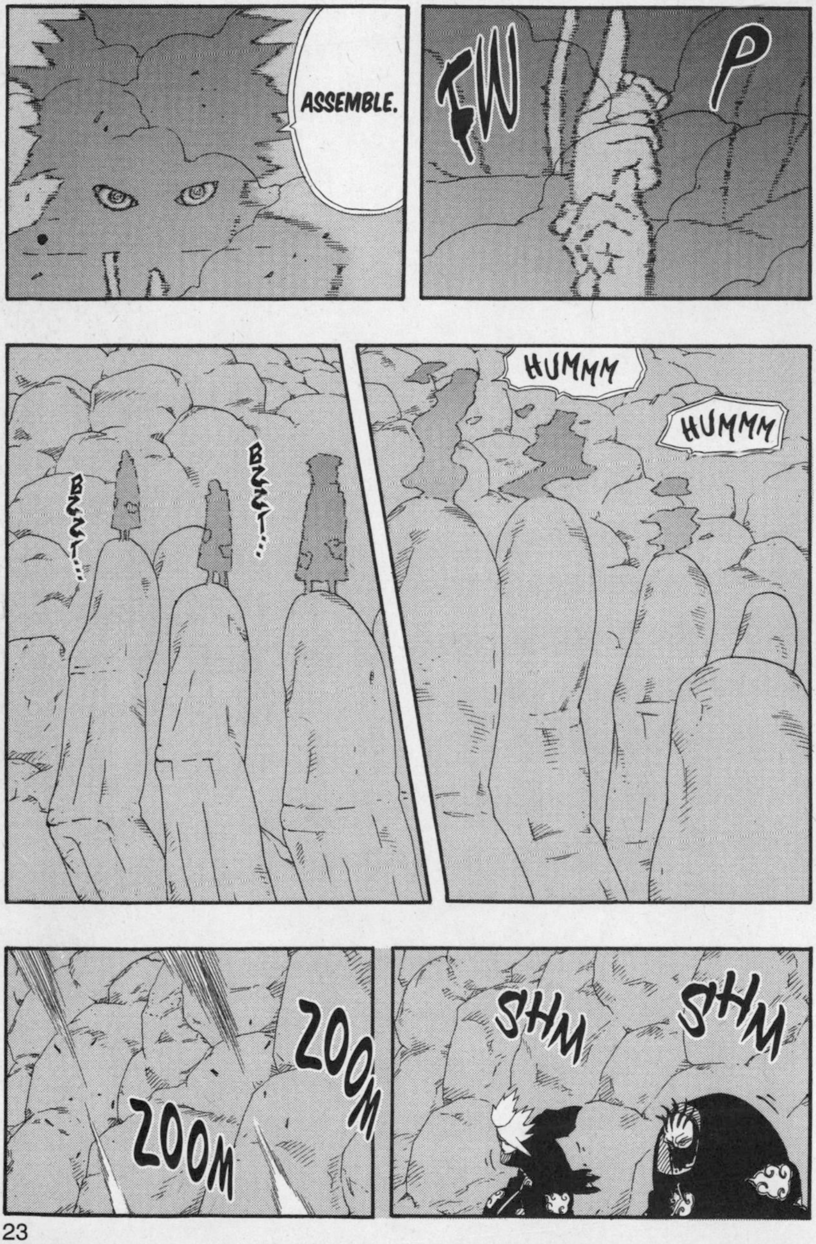
FWP
ASSEMBLE.
HUMMM
HUMMM
BZZT...
BZZT...
BZZT...
SHM
SHM
ZOOM
ZOOM

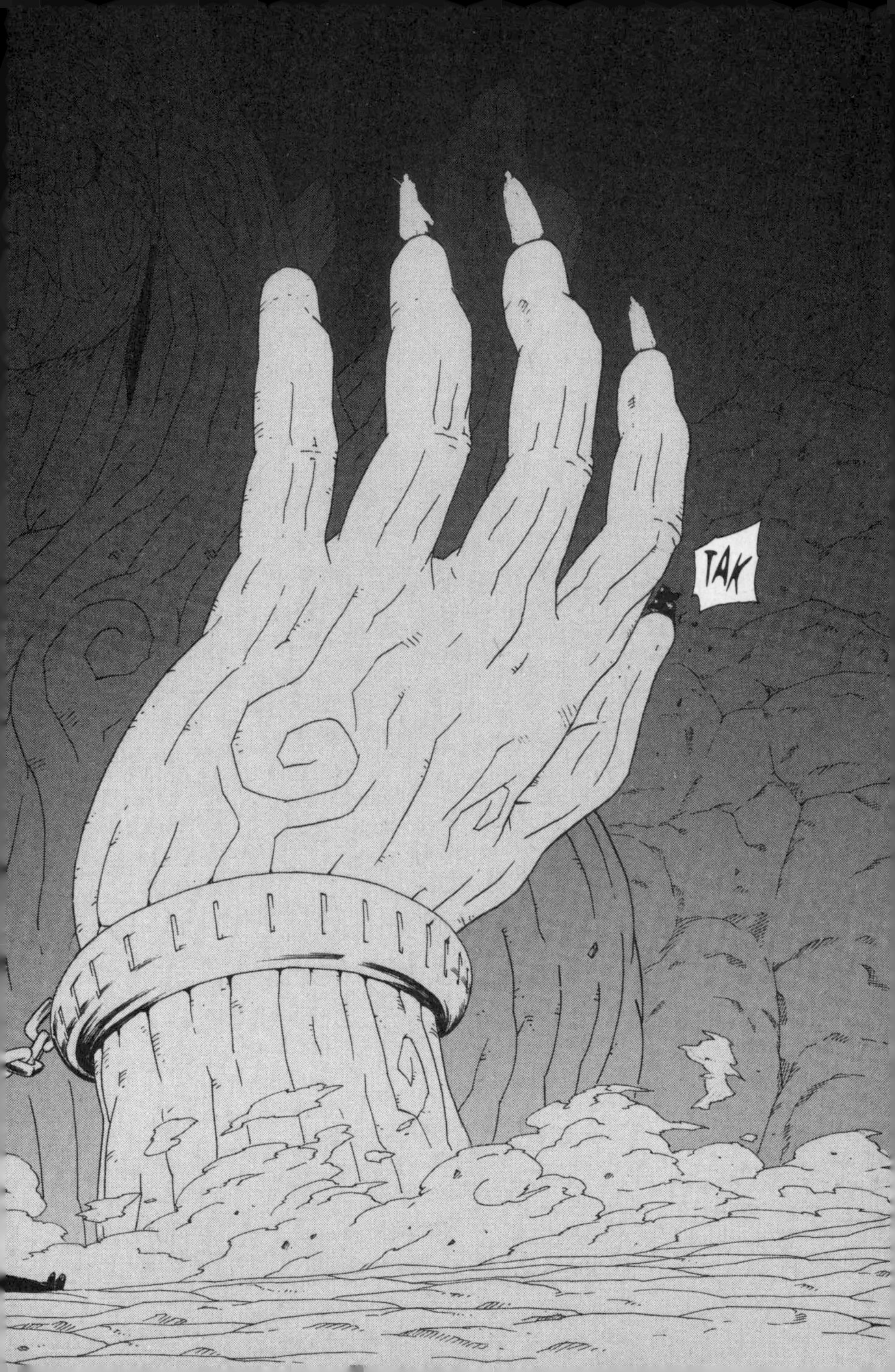
TAK

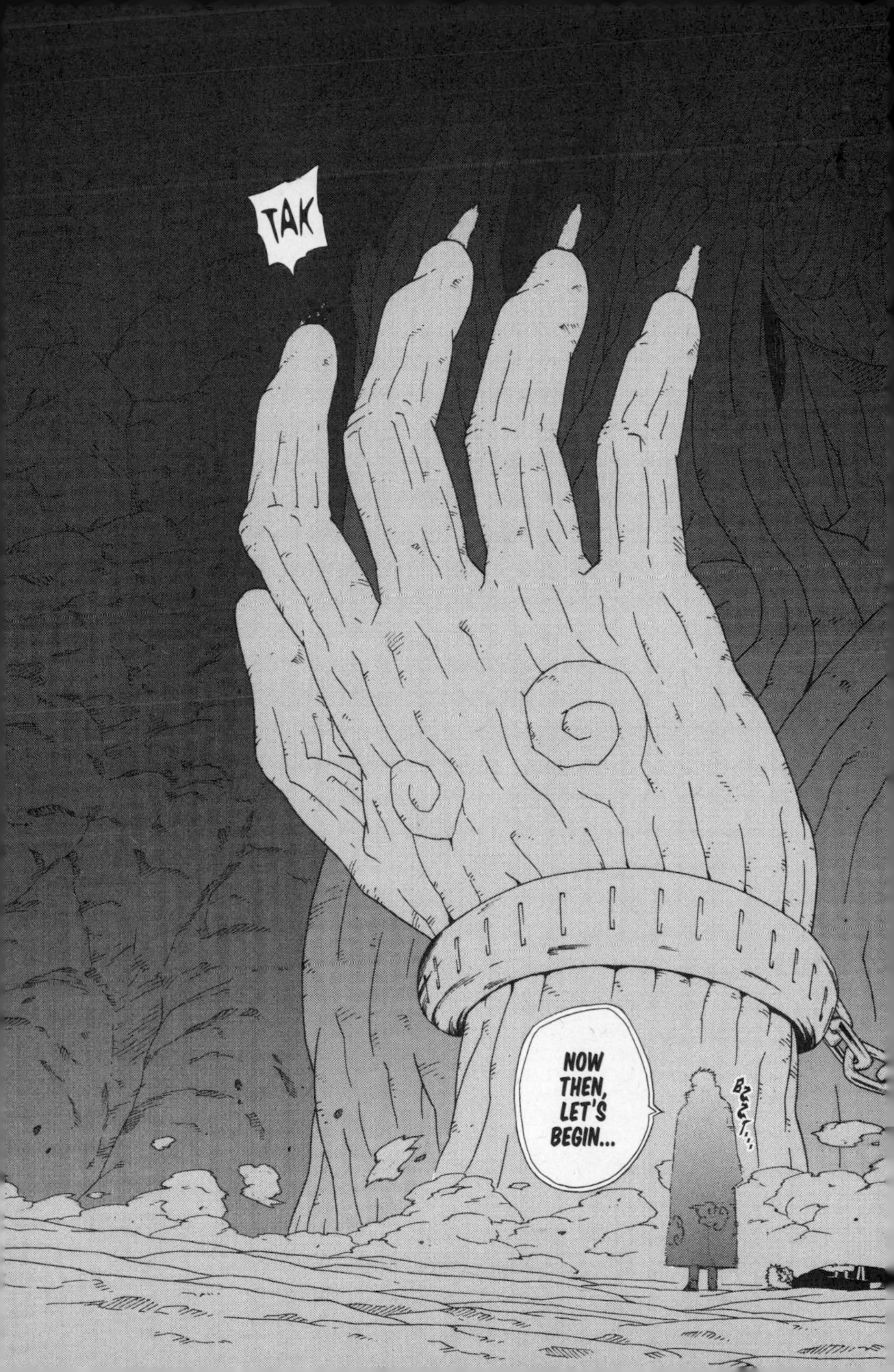
TAK
NOW THEN, LET'S BEGIN...
BZZZT...

THE WORLD OF KISHIMOTO MASASHI
MY PERSONAL HISTORY:
FIGHTING AGAINST CHAOS, PART I

THERE'S ONE THING I HAVE LEARNED FROM MY SIX YEARS' EXPERIENCE CREATING MANGA. WHAT'S THAT, YOU ASK...?

IT IS THAT IF PEOPLE STAY IN ONE PLACE WITH THE SAME PEOPLE WITHOUT SLEEPING FOR A LONG PERIOD OF TIME, THEY WILL SLOWLY GO INSANE. THESE ARE SYMPTOMS THAT APPEAR AMONG MY ASSISTANTS: CRACKING UP OVER AN EXTREMELY LAME JOKE, SPENDING A HALF HOUR TAPE RECORDING FARTS, CONVERSING IN MOANING VOICES, AND SO ON. IN THESE WAYS AND COUNTLESS OTHERS, THINGS START GOING LOOPY.

IN A SENSE, MY ASSISTANTS COME TO BE CONTROLLED BY A KIND OF CHAOS. HOWEVER, THEY AREN'T AWARE OF IT, AND A STATE OF CHAOS BECOMES NORMAL... WHENEVER A NEW PERSON JOINS THE TEAM, THE GAP MY ASSISTANTS FEEL BETWEEN THEMSELVES AND THE NEW GUY MAKES THEM REALIZE JUST HOW WEIRD THEY'VE BECOME. THEN THEY REGRET THE SILLINESS THEY'D BEEN UP TO A LITTLE BIT. BUT... TIME IS A DREADFUL THING, BECAUSE BEFORE YOU KNOW IT THEY'VE ABSORBED THE NEW ASSISTANT AND RETURNED TO THEIR STATE OF CHAOS.

ONE DAY, THE FOLLOWING INCIDENT TOOK PLACE: I GOT STUCK WRITING A MANGA JUST BEFORE THE DEADLINE, SO I LAY DOWN BEHIND MY DESK TO TAKE A SHORT NAP. WHEN I WAS LOOKING FOR SOMETHING TO USE AS A PILLOW, I FOUND A BIG FROG-SHAPED *GAMAGUCHI* CUSHION. (THIS IS A CUSHION MODELED ON THE FROGGIE WALLET THAT NARUTO USES IN THE SERIES. IT WAS MADE AS A PRESENT FOR READERS.)

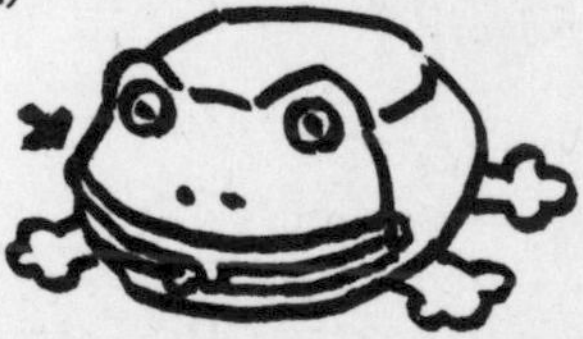

THE CUSHION WAS JUST THE RIGHT SIZE TO LAY MY HEAD ON. THINKING I HAD MADE A GREAT DISCOVERY, I WAS GOING TO TAKE A NAP USING IT AS A PILLOW. ...BUT... THIS COIN PURSE-TYPE CUSHION CAN BE OPENED JUST LIKE A REGULAR COIN PURSE. WHILE GAZING AT IT IN A STUPOR, AN IDEA CROSSED MY MIND. IF IT'S BIG ENOUGH TO LAY MY HEAD ON, WOULDN'T IT BE POSSIBLE TO STICK MY HEAD INSIDE IT? THIS RATHER POINTLESS SUSPICION ENTERED MY HEAD. I SHOULD'VE JUST TAKEN THE NAP IMMEDIATELY; I WAS TIRED, AFTER ALL. BUT FOR SOME REASON, I COULDN'T HELP CONFIRMING MY SUSPICION. SO I PUT MY HEAD IN THE COIN PURSE CUSHION AND FOUND THAT MY HEAD AND NECK JUST BARELY FIT INSIDE IT.

TO THIS DAY, I HAVE NO IDEA WHY I DID THIS. I'M CONVINCED THAT I HAD FALLEN VICTIM TO THE CHAOS. AT THE TIME, I HAD NO IDEA THE DISASTER THAT THIS WOULD LEAD TO. (TO BE CONTINUED...)

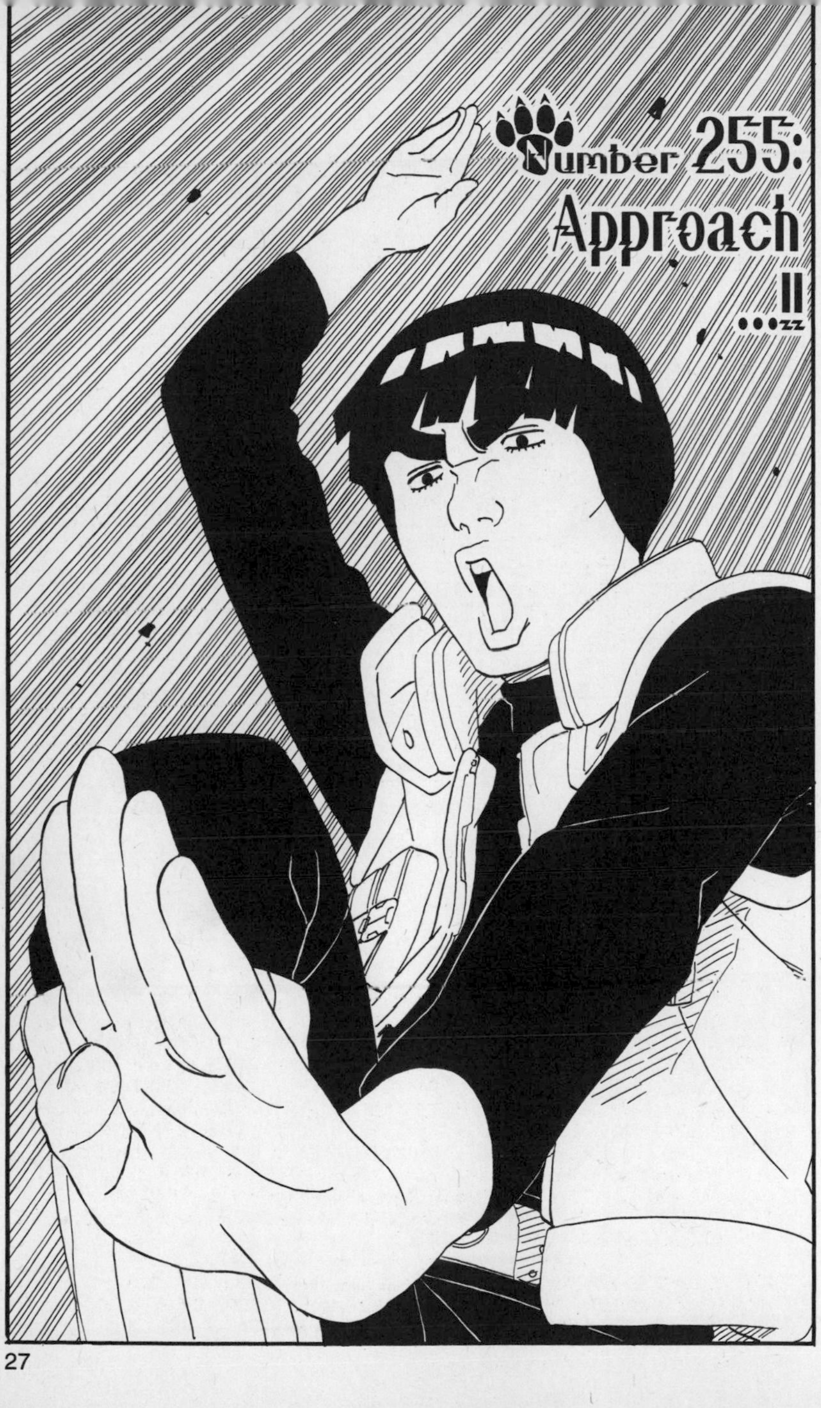
Number 255:
Approach...!!

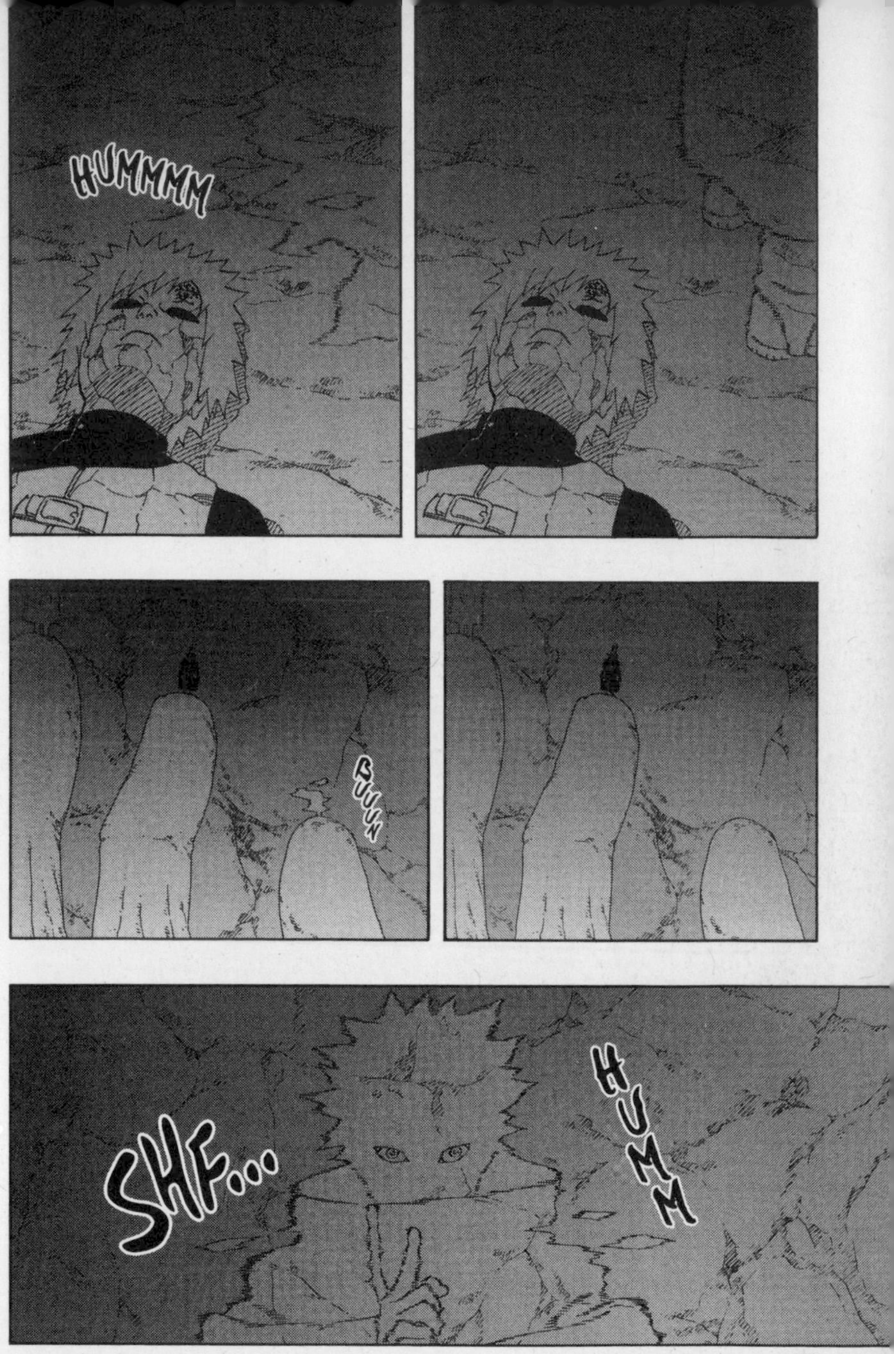
HUMMMM
BUUUN
HUMM
SHF...

READ THIS WAY

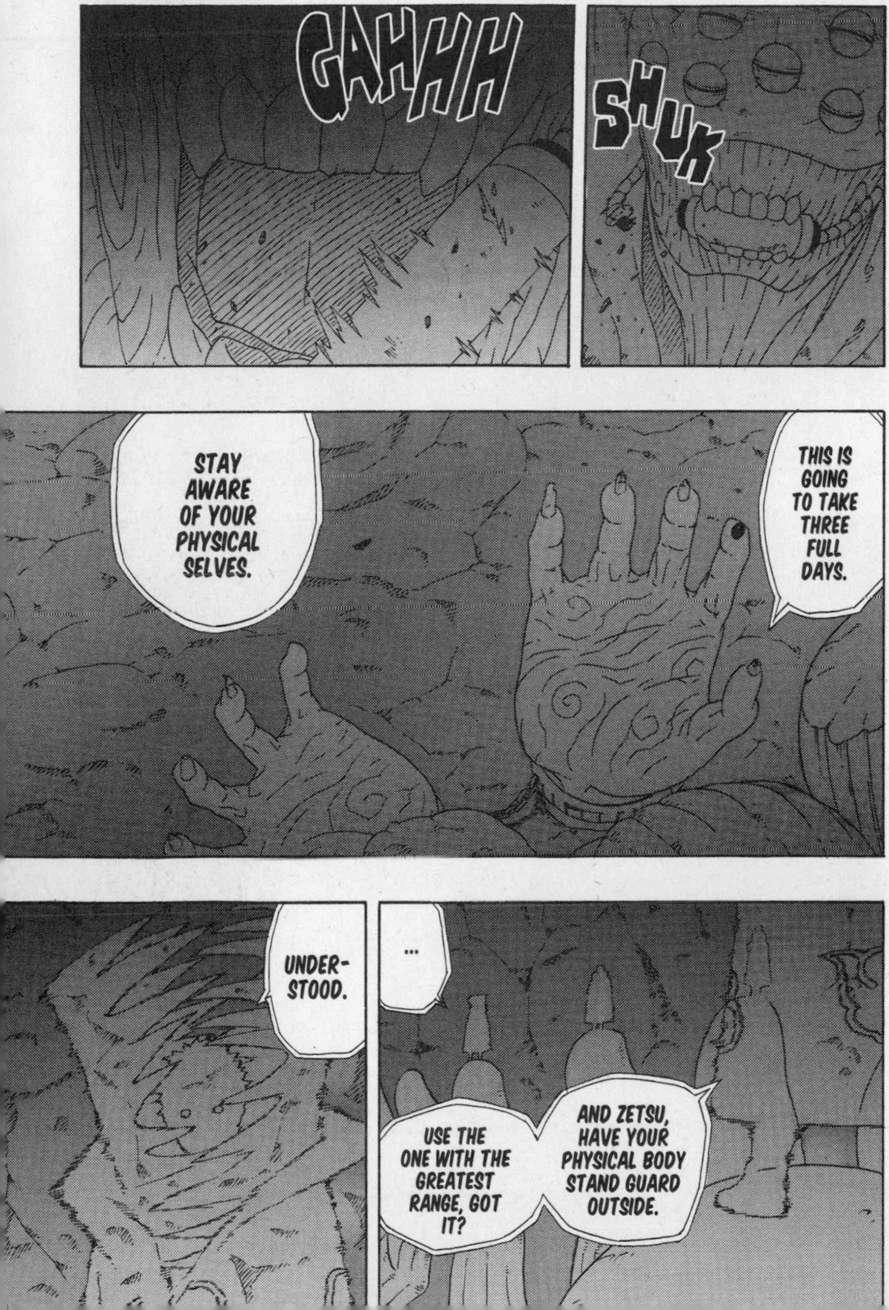
SHUK
GAHHH
THIS IS GOING TO TAKE THREE FULL DAYS.
STAY AWARE OF YOUR PHYSICAL SELVES.
AND ZETSU, HAVE YOUR PHYSICAL BODY STAND GUARD OUTSIDE.
USE THE ONE WITH THE GREATEST RANGE, GOT IT?
...
UNDER-STOOD.

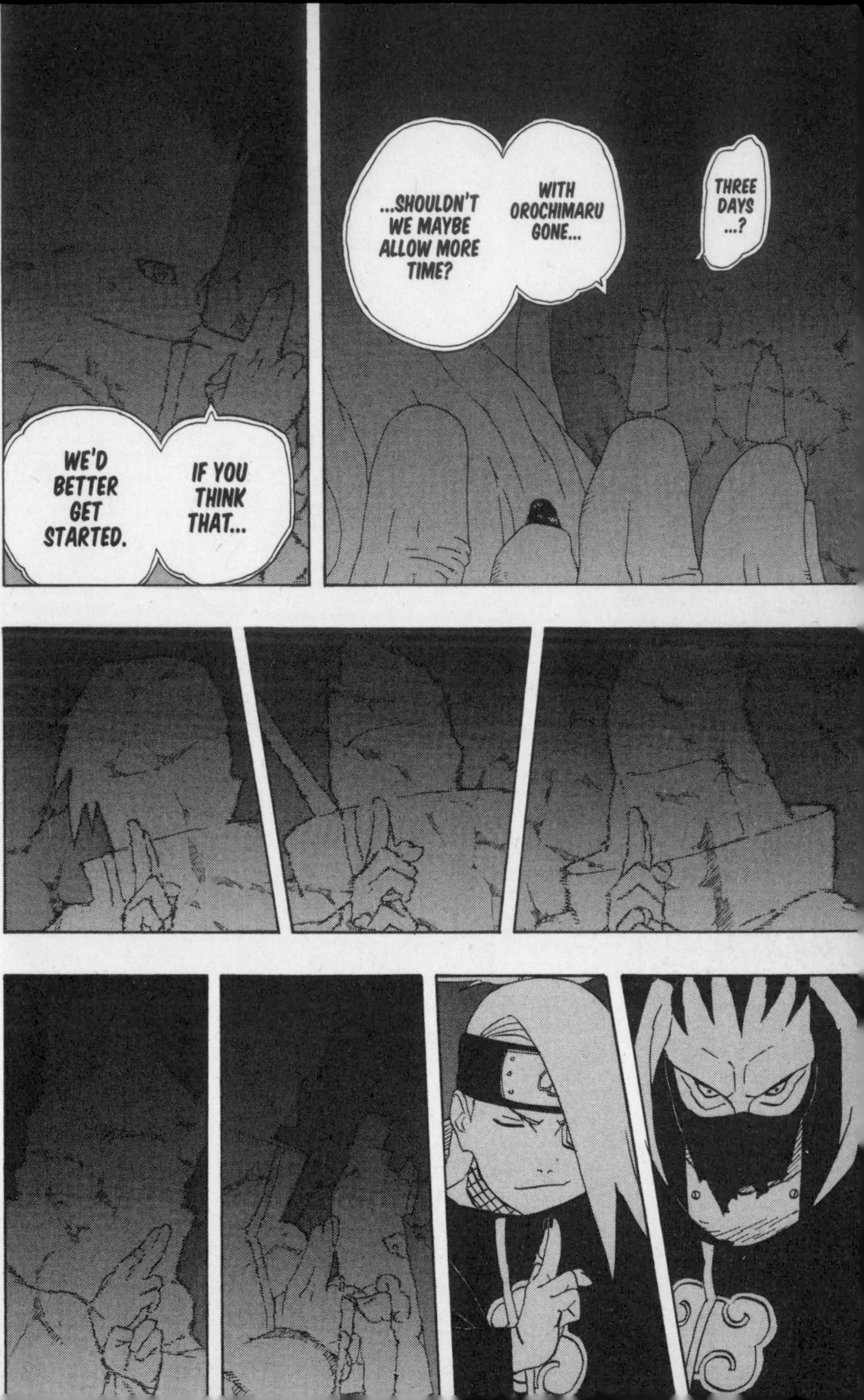
THREE DAYS ...?
WITH OROCHIMARU GONE...
...SHOULDN'T WE MAYBE ALLOW MORE TIME?
IF YOU THINK THAT...
WE'D BETTER GET STARTED.

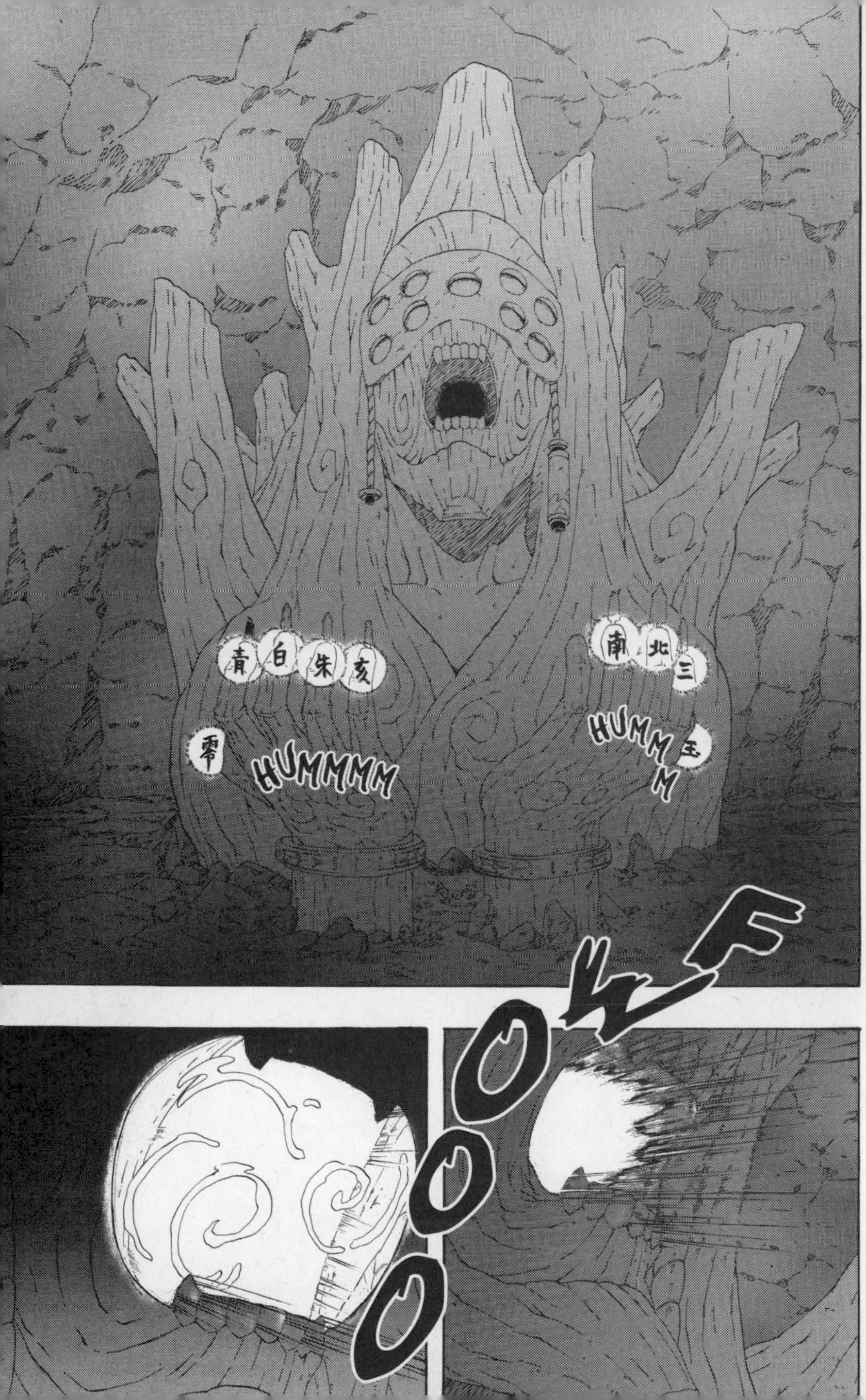
HUMMMM
HUMMMM
OOOOWF

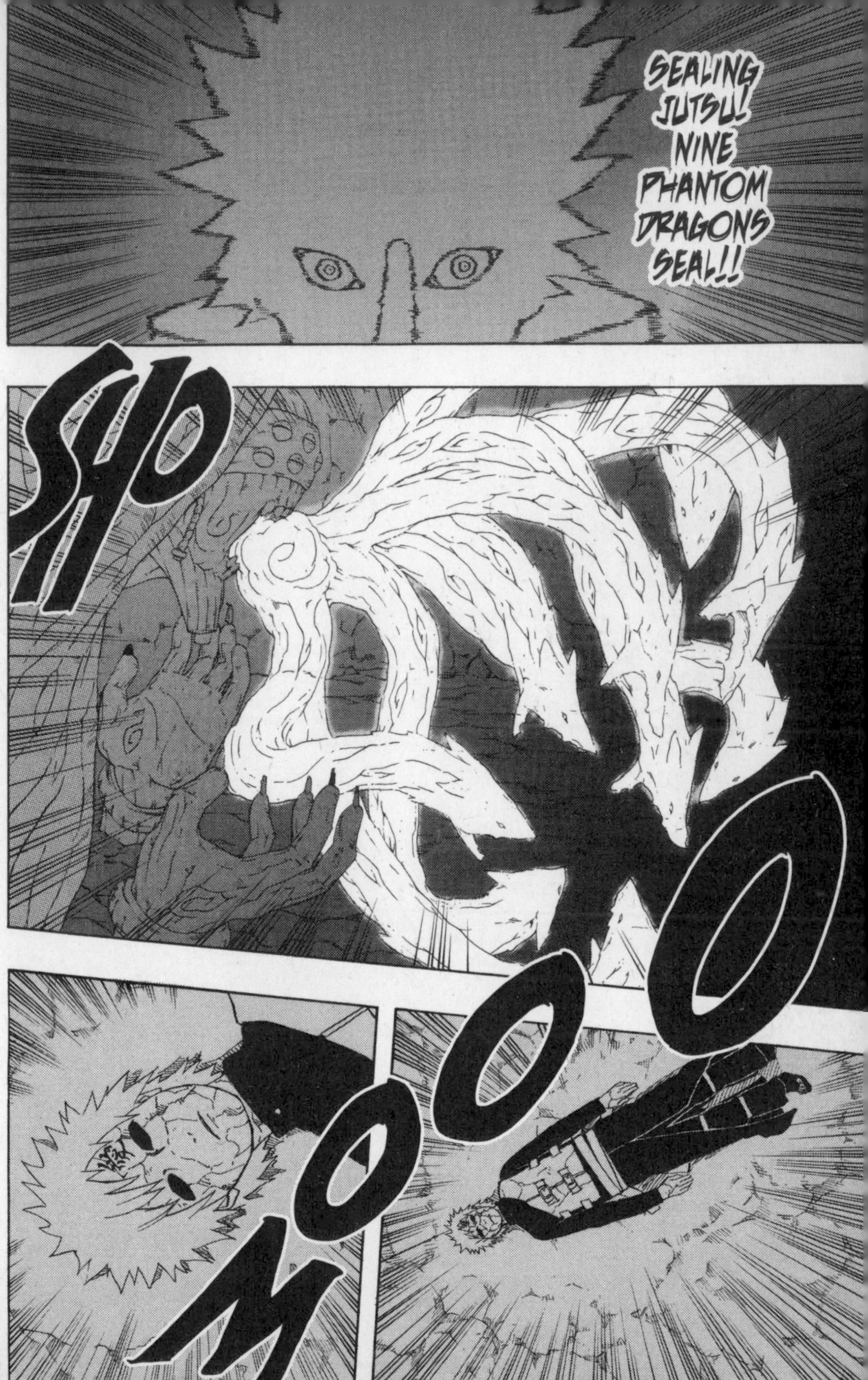
SEALING JUTSU! NINE PHANTOM DRAGONS SEAL!!

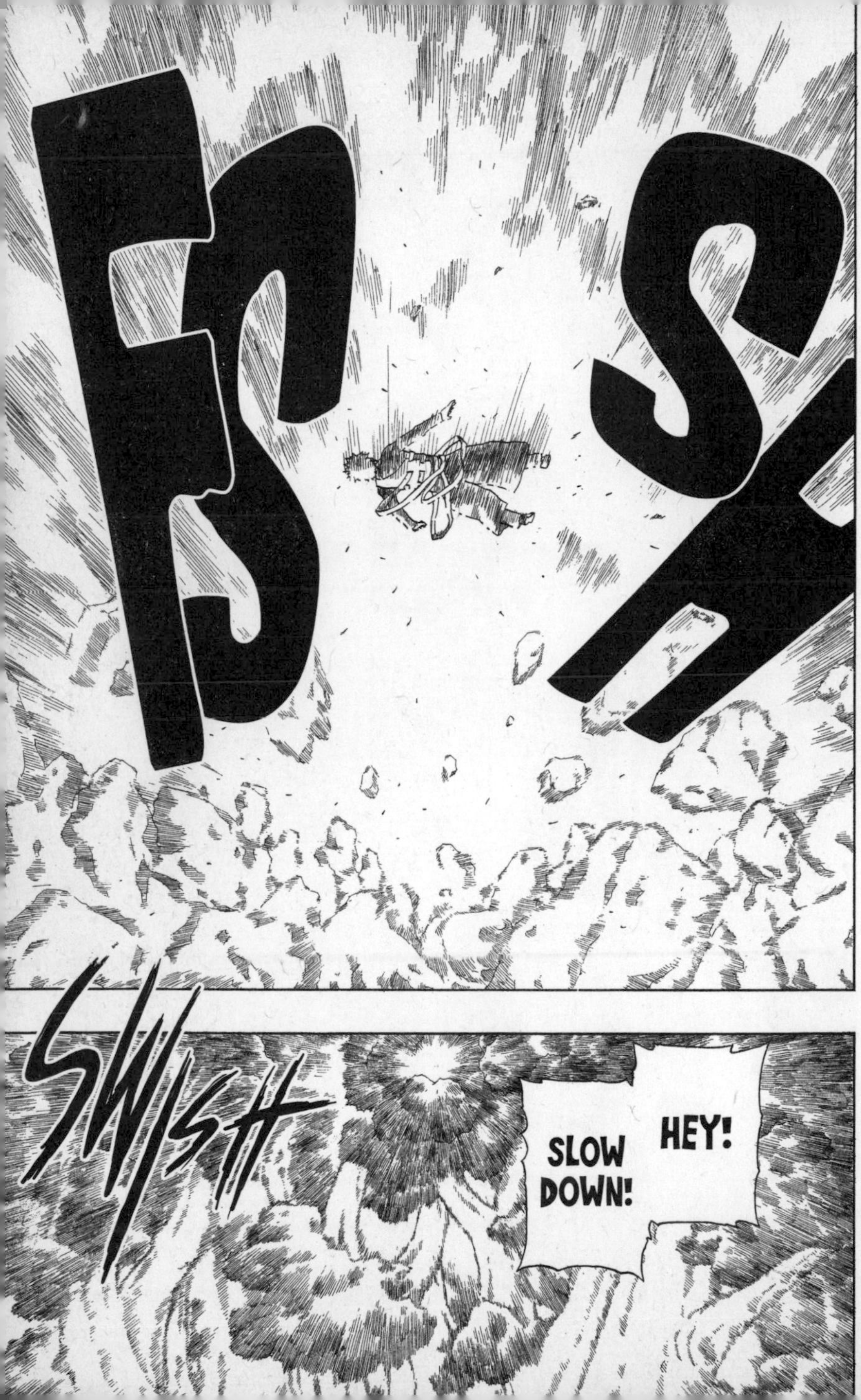
FSSH
SWISH
HEY! SLOW DOWN!

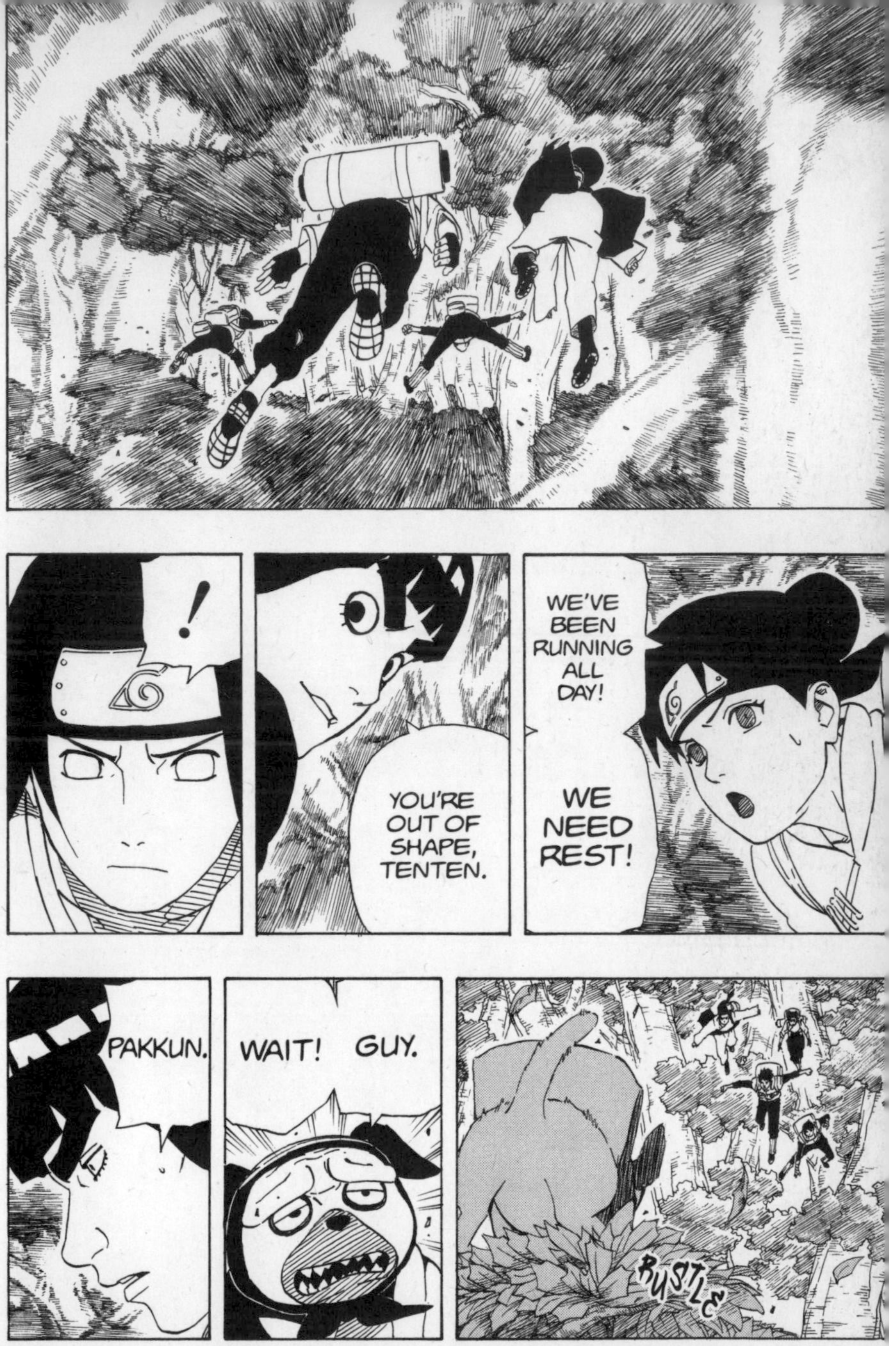
WE'VE BEEN RUNNING ALL DAY!
WE NEED REST!
YOU'RE OUT OF SHAPE, TENTEN.
!
RUSTLE
GUY.
WAIT!
PAKKUN.

READ THIS WAY

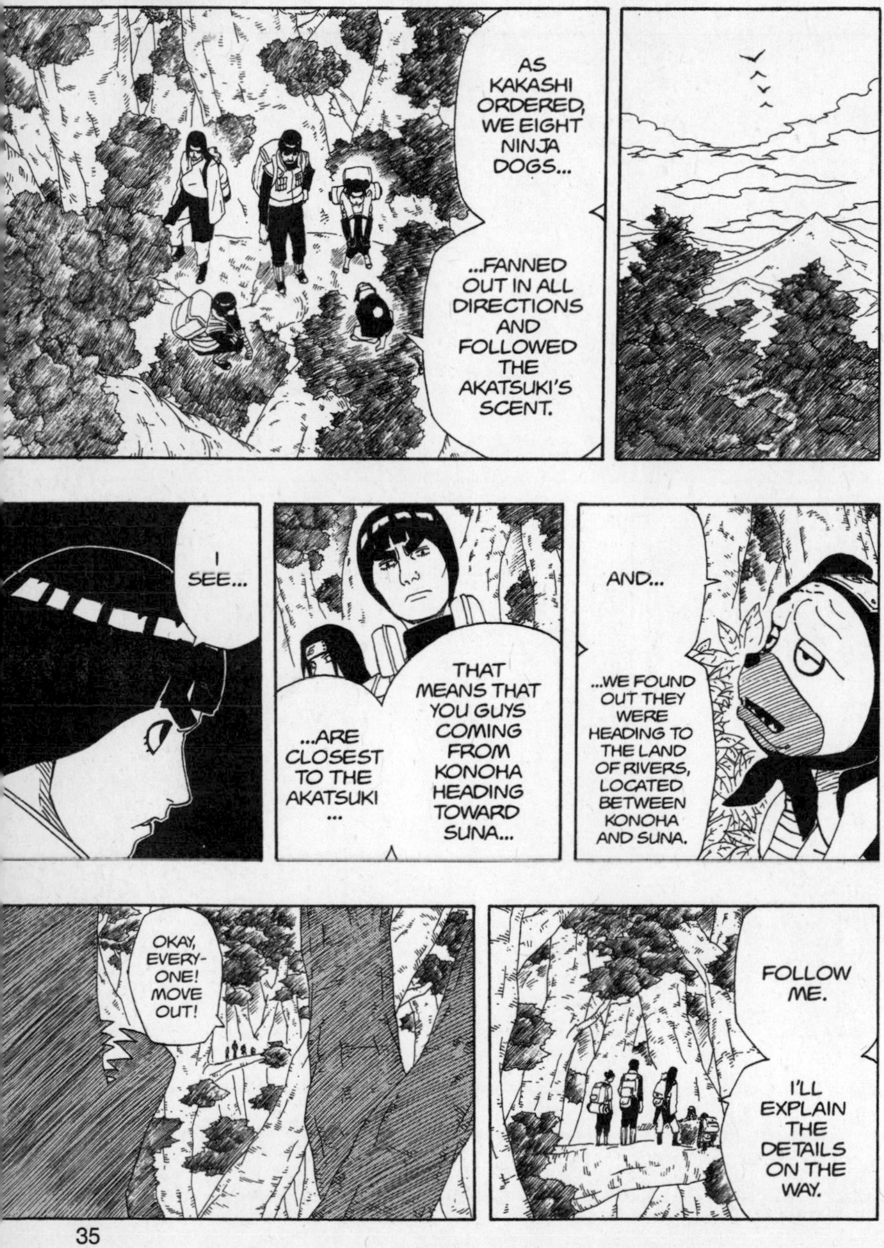
AS KAKASHI ORDERED, WE EIGHT NINJA DOGS...
...FANNED OUT IN ALL DIRECTIONS AND FOLLOWED THE AKATSUKI'S SCENT.
AND...
...WE FOUND OUT THEY WERE HEADING TO THE LAND OF RIVERS, LOCATED BETWEEN KONOHA AND SUNA.
THAT MEANS THAT YOU GUYS COMING FROM KONOHA HEADING TOWARD SUNA...
...ARE CLOSEST TO THE AKATSUKI ...
I SEE...
FOLLOW ME.
I'LL EXPLAIN THE DETAILS ON THE WAY.
OKAY, EVERYONE! MOVE OUT!

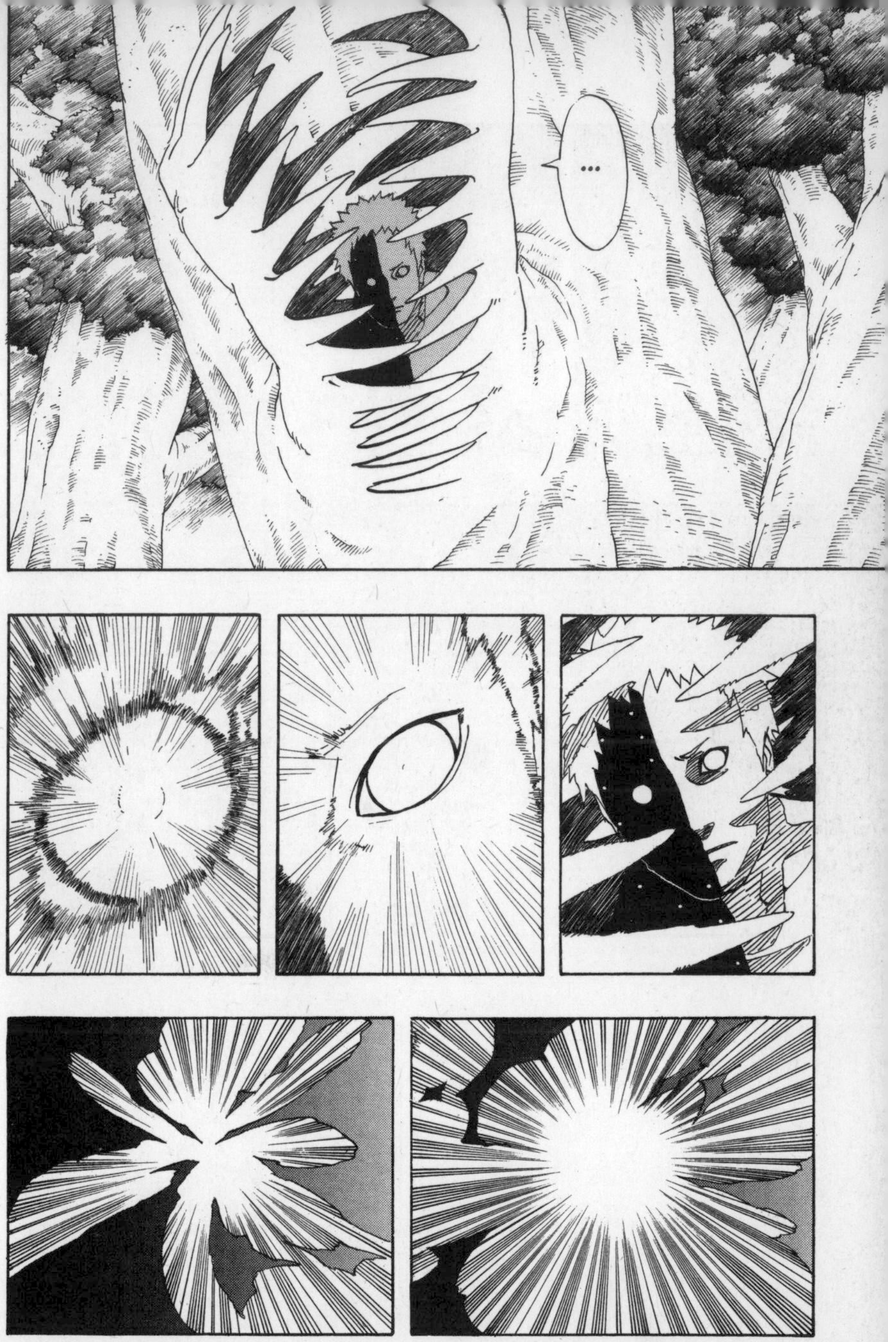
...

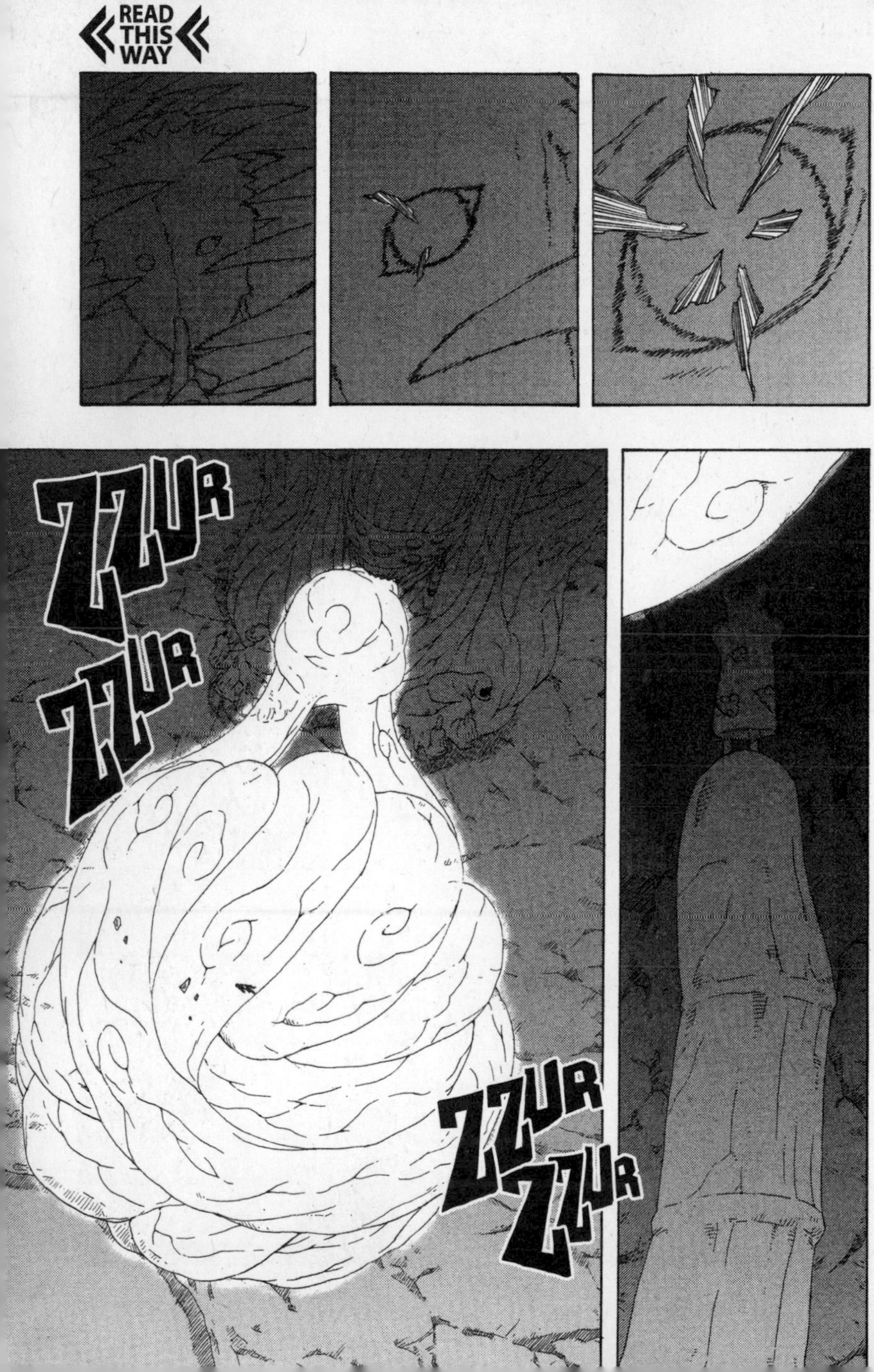
READ THIS WAY
ZZUR
ZZUR
ZZUR
ZZUR

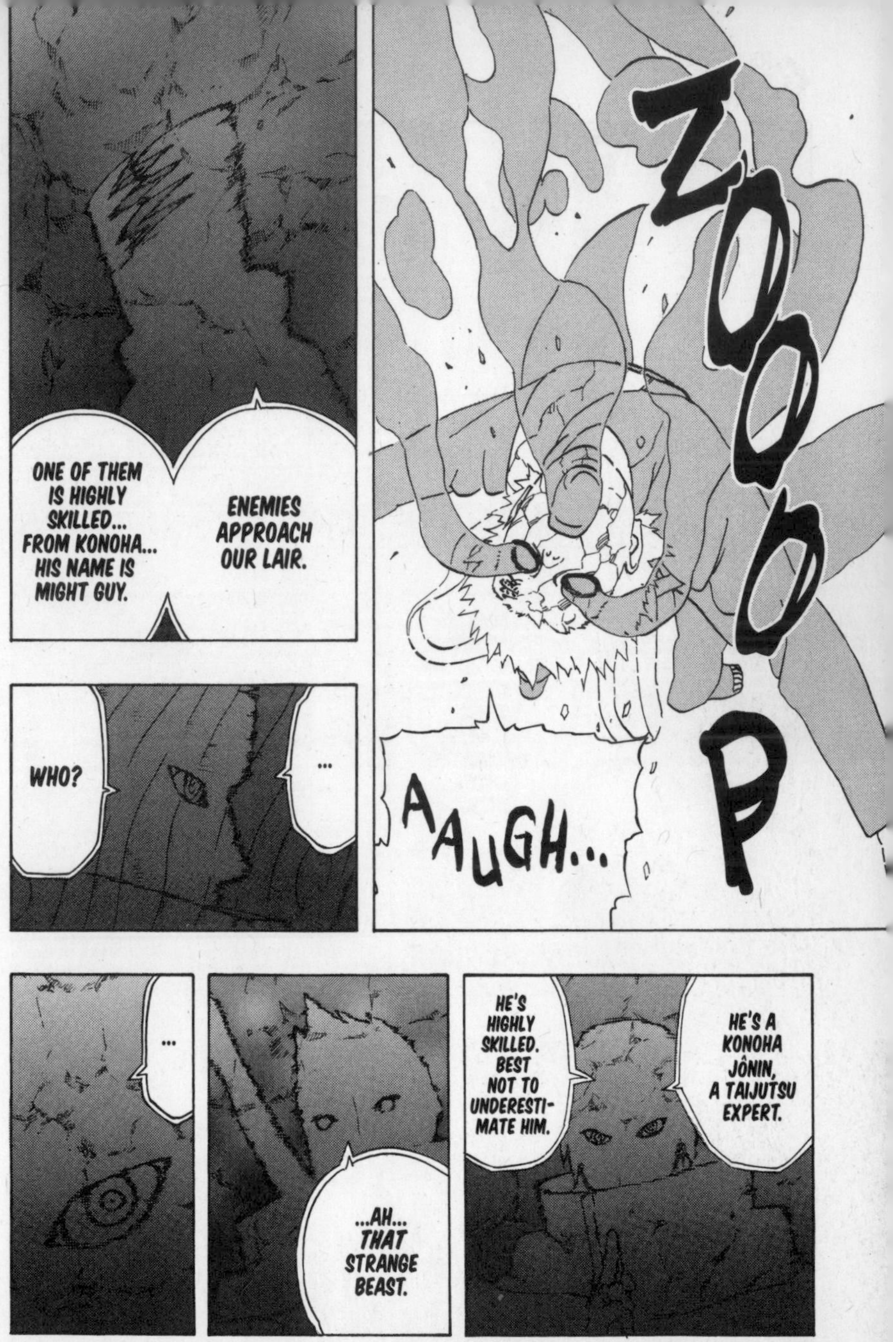
ZOOOOOP
AAUGH...
ENEMIES APPROACH OUR LAIR.
ONE OF THEM IS HIGHLY SKILLED... FROM KONOHA... HIS NAME IS MIGHT GUY.
...
WHO?
HE'S A KONOHA JÔNIN, A TAIJUTSU EXPERT.
HE'S HIGHLY SKILLED. BEST NOT TO UNDERESTI-MATE HIM.
...AH... THAT STRANGE BEAST.
...

READ THIS WAY

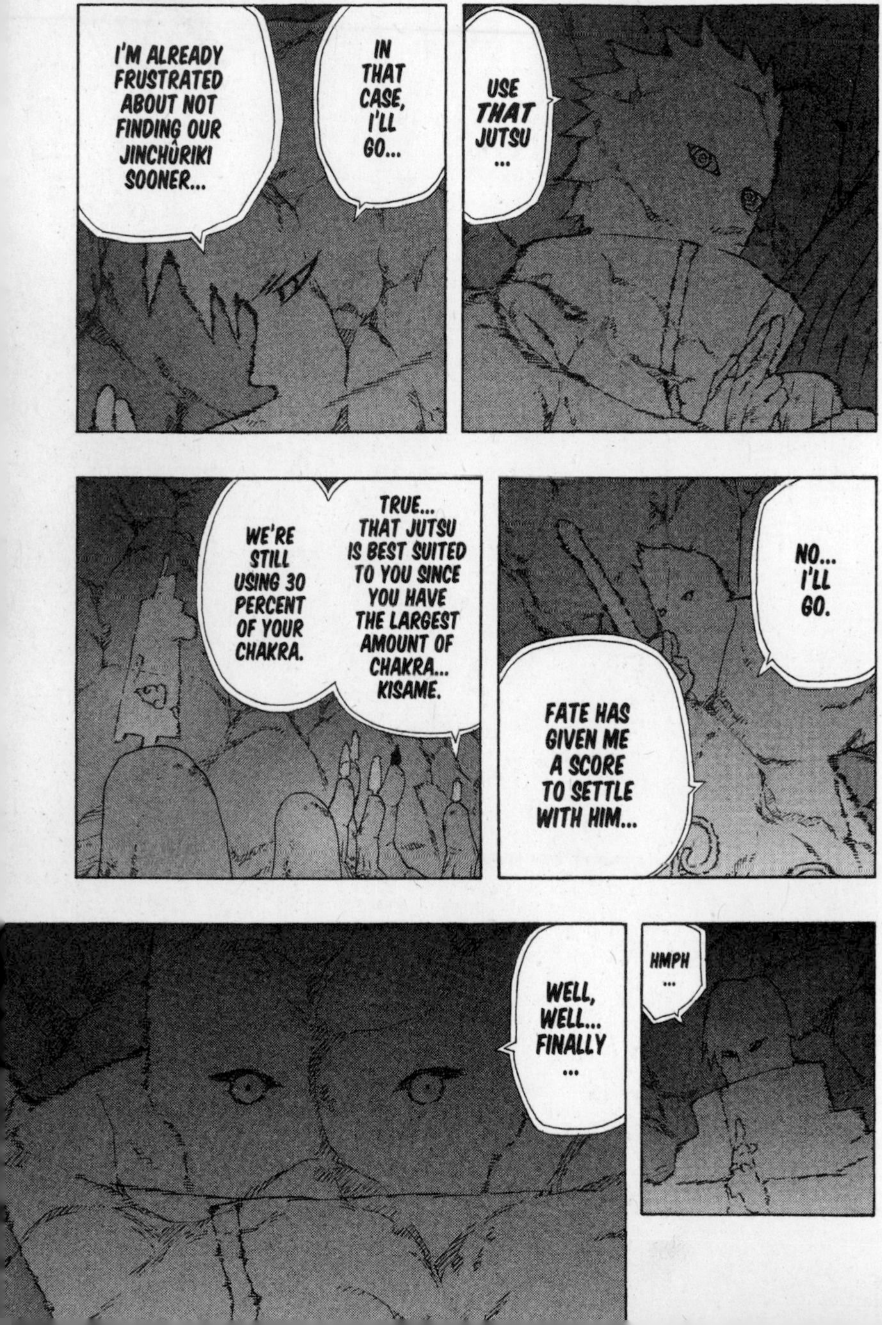
USE *THAT* JUTSU...
IN THAT CASE, I'LL GO...
I'M ALREADY FRUSTRATED ABOUT NOT FINDING OUR JINCHÛRIKI SOONER...
NO... I'LL GO.
FATE HAS GIVEN ME A SCORE TO SETTLE WITH HIM...
TRUE... THAT JUTSU IS BEST SUITED TO YOU SINCE YOU HAVE THE LARGEST AMOUNT OF CHAKRA... KISAME.
WE'RE STILL USING 30 PERCENT OF YOUR CHAKRA.
HMPH...
WELL, WELL... FINALLY...

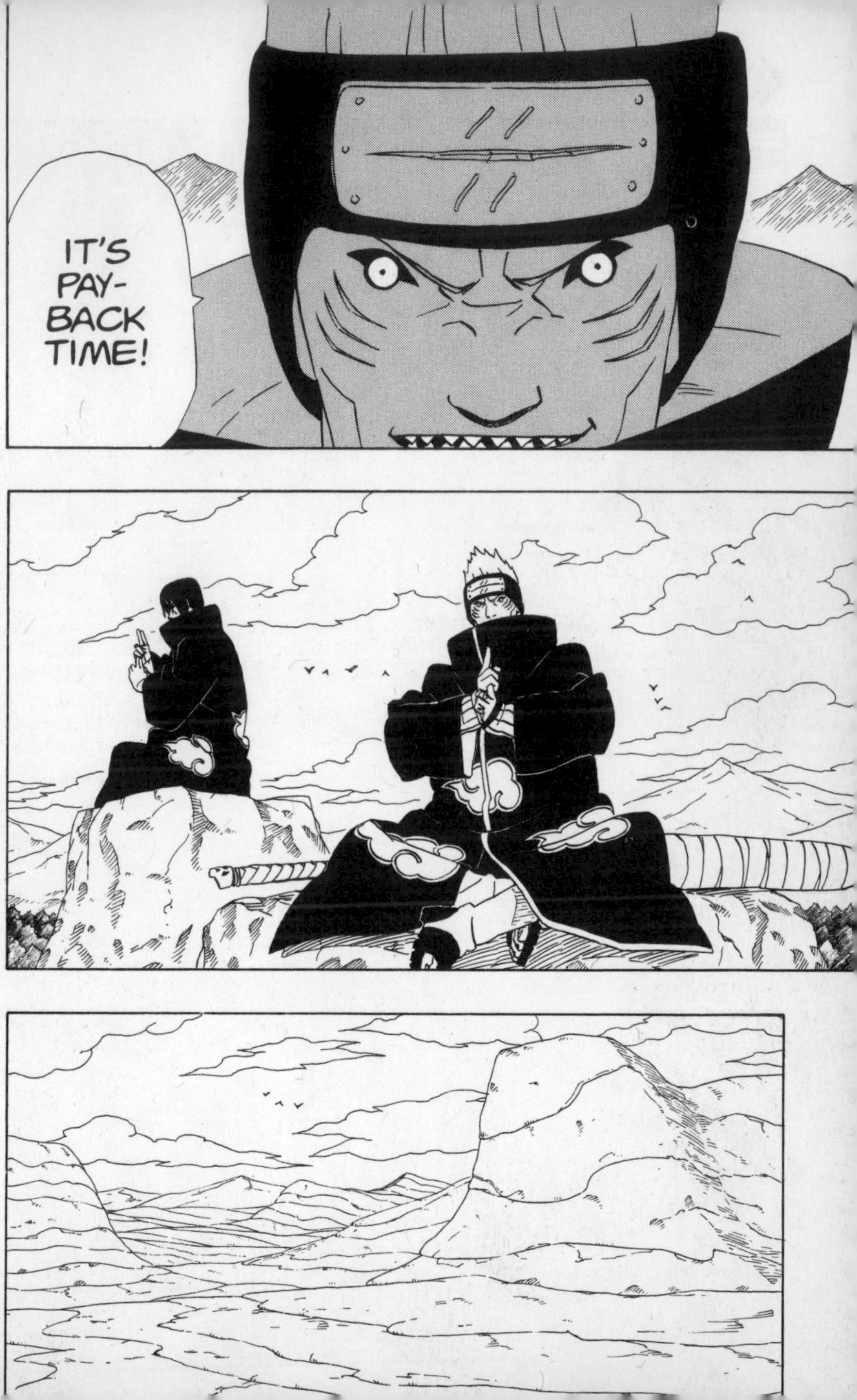
IT'S PAY-BACK TIME!

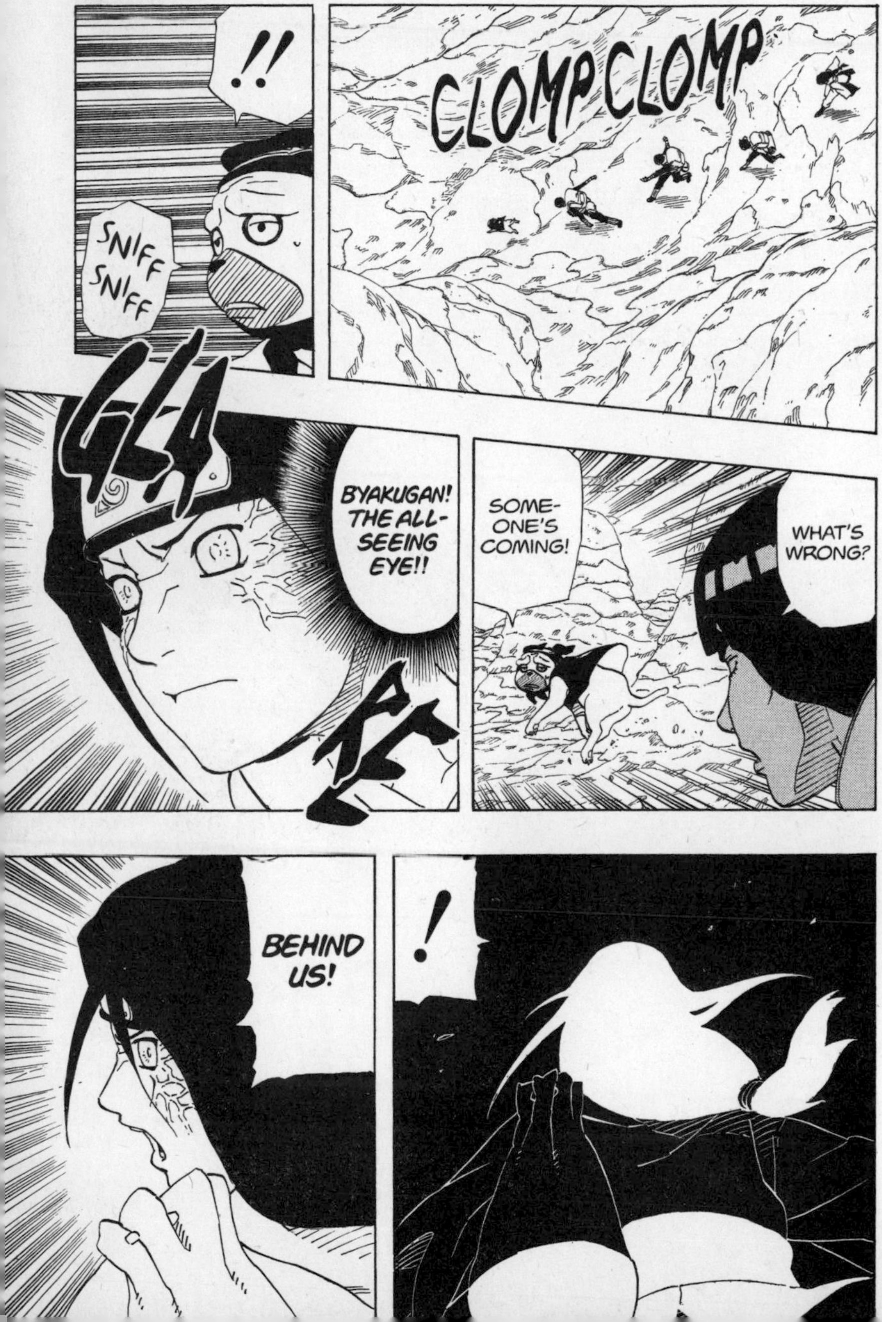
CLOMP CLOMP
!!
SNIFF SNIFF
WHAT'S WRONG?
SOME-ONE'S COMING!
BYAKUGAN! THE ALL-SEEING EYE!!
!
BEHIND US!

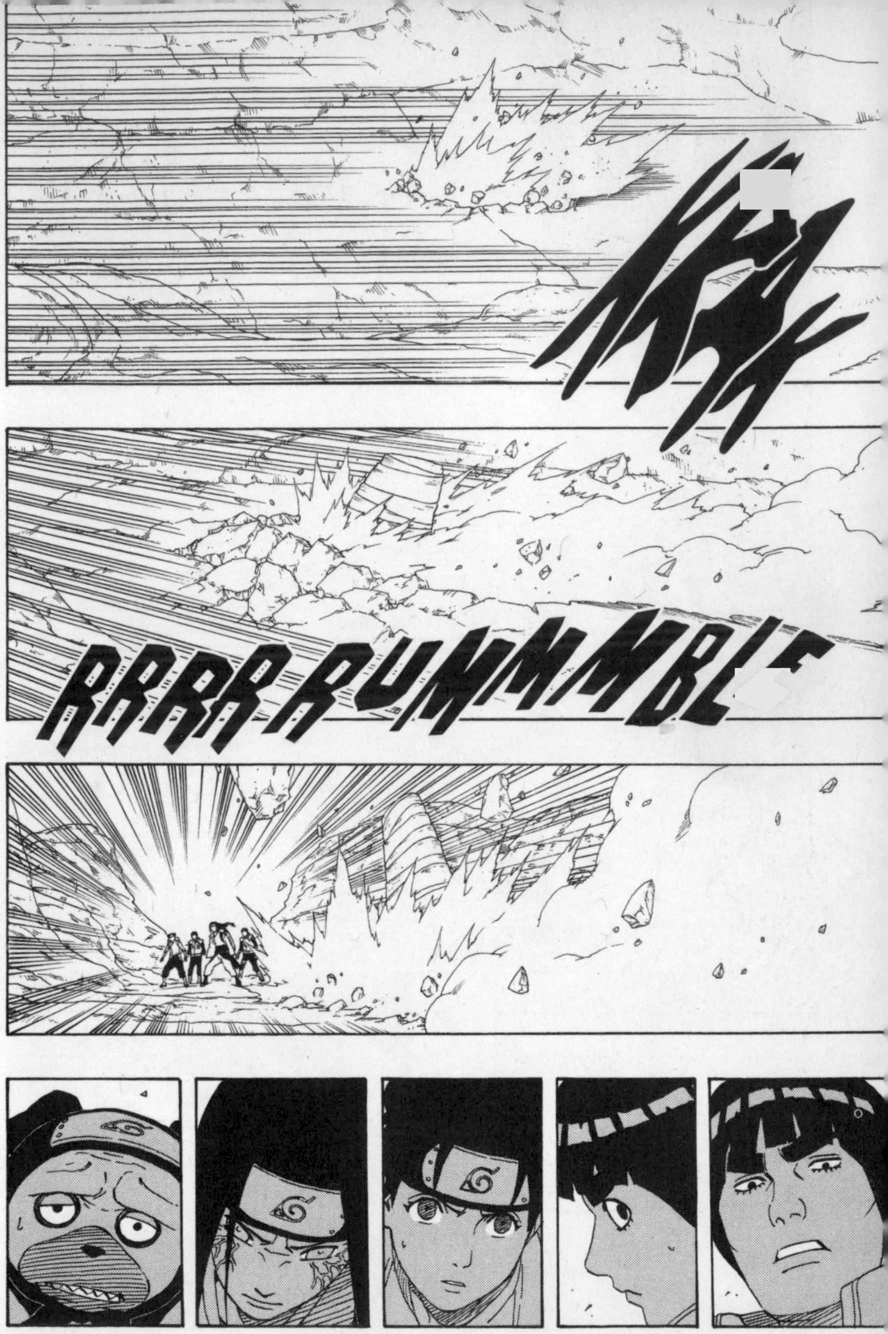
RRRR-RUMMMBLE

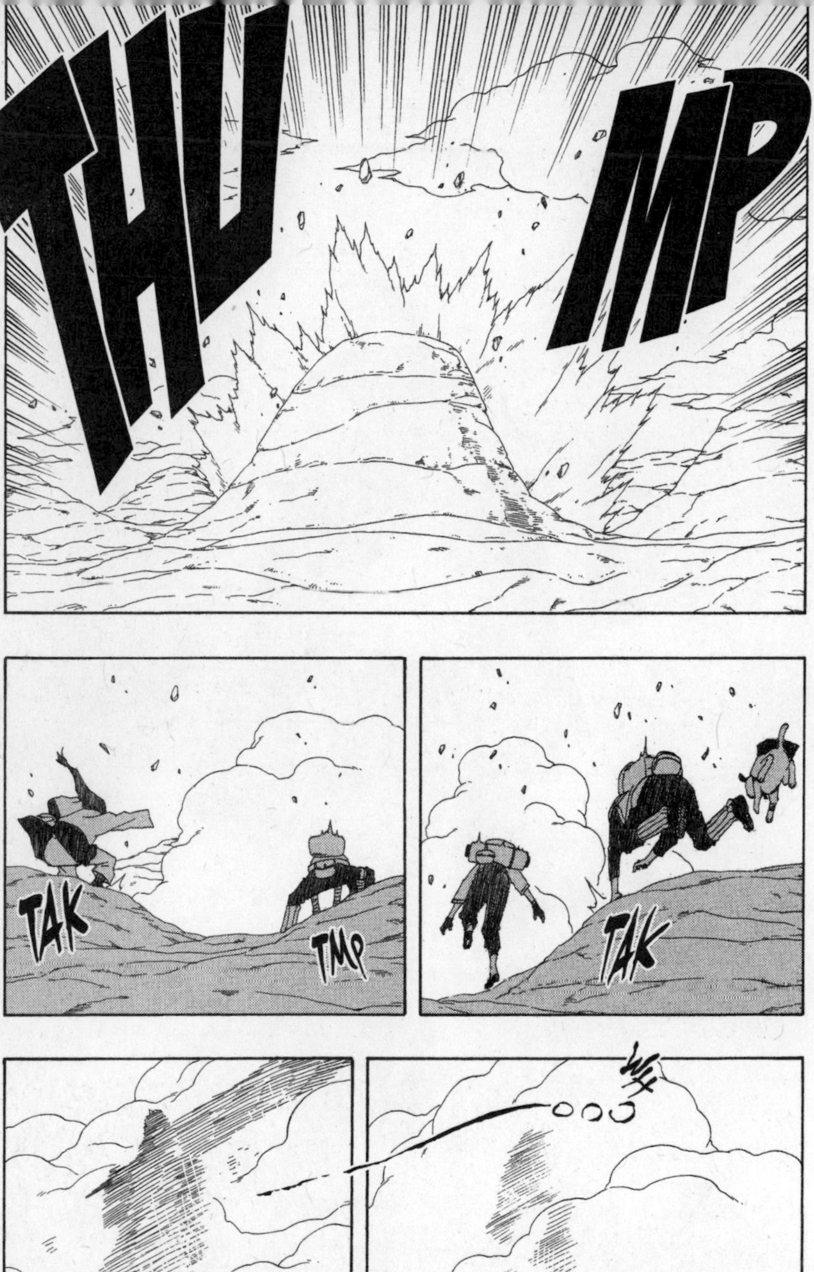
THUMP
TAK
TMP
TAK

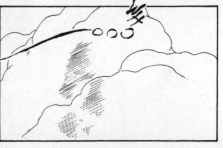

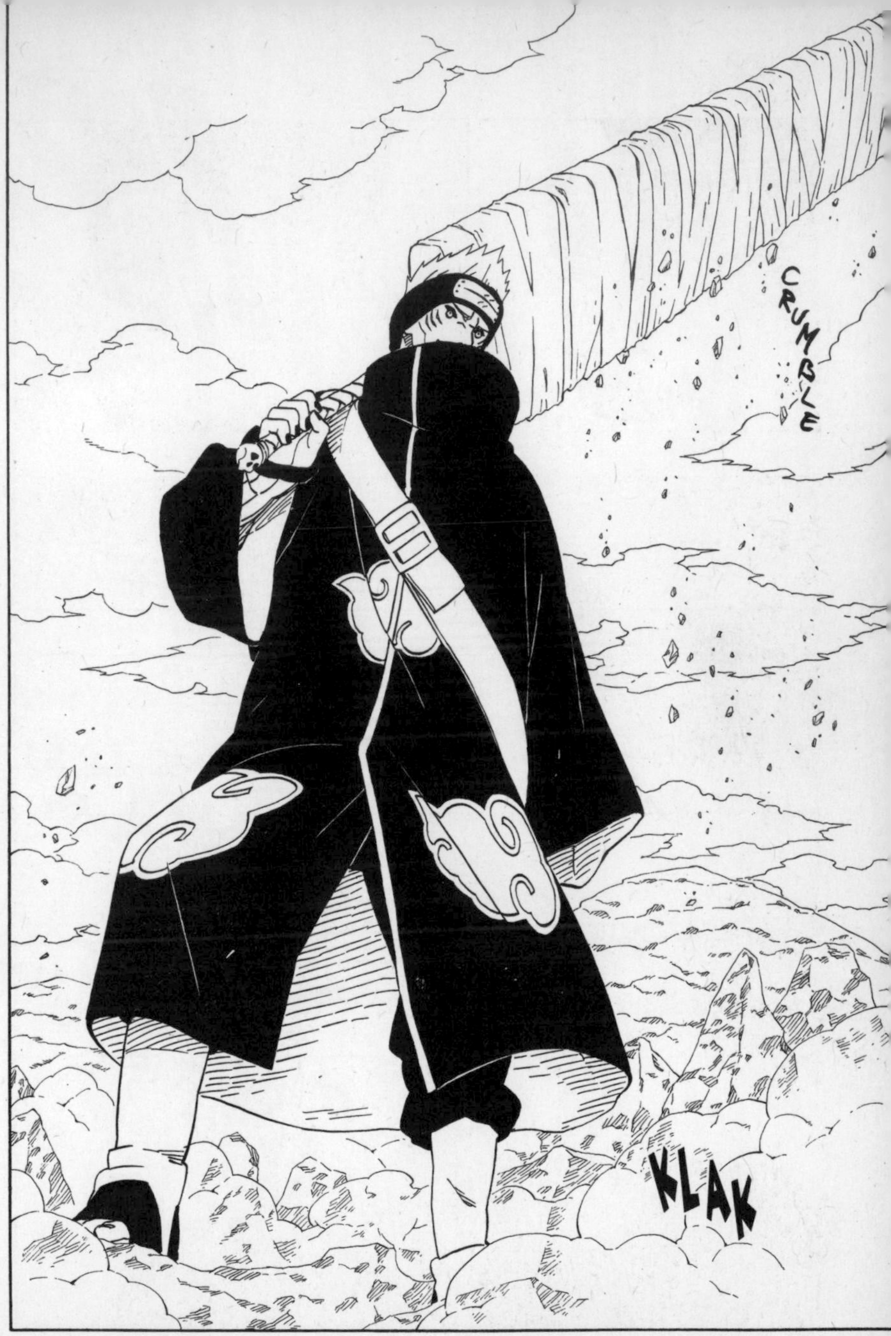
CRUMBLE
KLAK

READ THIS WAY

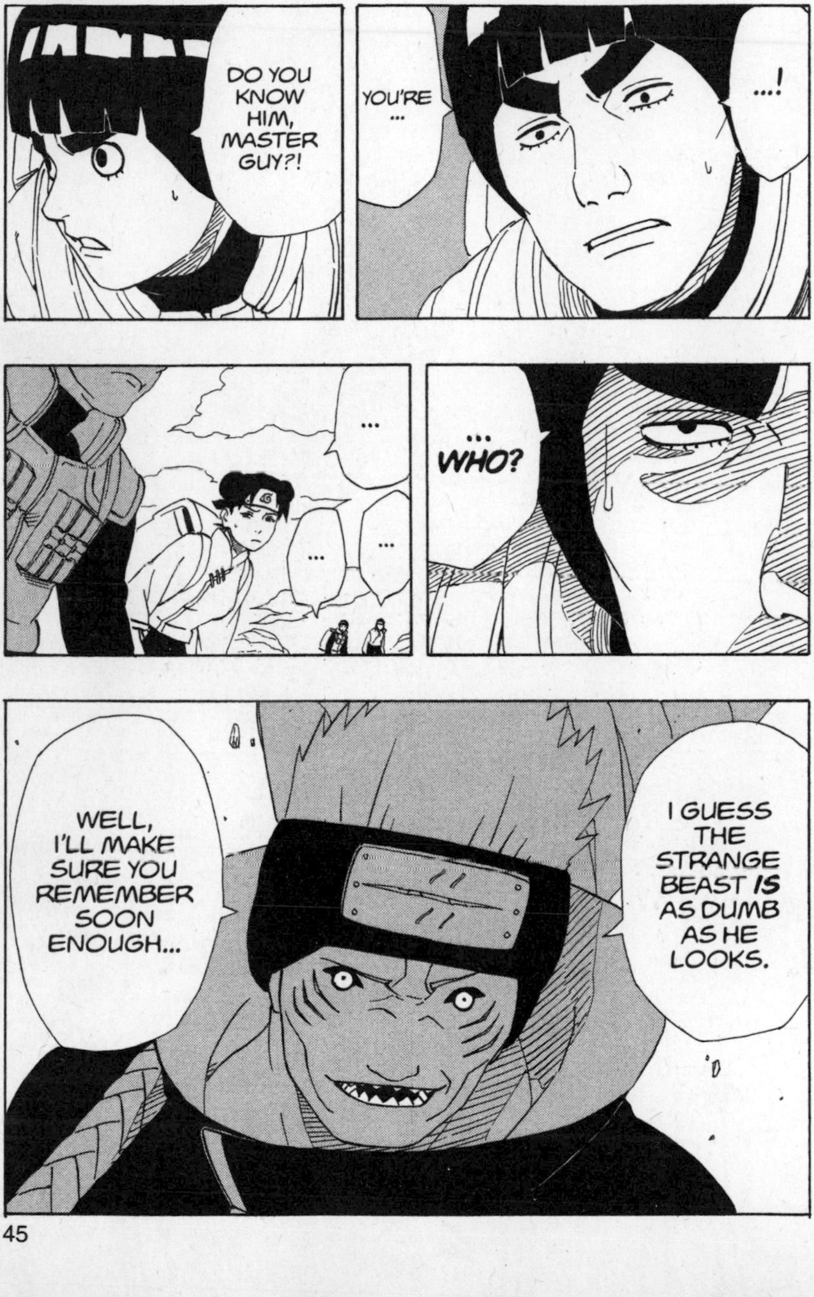
...!
YOU'RE ...
DO YOU KNOW HIM, MASTER GUY?!
... WHO?
...
...
...
I GUESS THE STRANGE BEAST IS AS DUMB AS HE LOOKS.
WELL, I'LL MAKE SURE YOU REMEMBER SOON ENOUGH...

THE WORLD OF KISHIMOTO MASASHI
MY PERSONAL HISTORY:
FIGHTING AGAINST CHAOS, PART 2

WHEN I PUT MY HEAD INTO THE COIN PURSE CUSHION, I WAS SATISFIED TO CONFIRM THAT, JUST AS I SUSPECTED, MY HEAD FIT INSIDE. THEN I TRIED TO PULL MY HEAD OUT OF THE COIN PURSE CUSHION. ...BUT, WHEN I ACTUALLY TRIED TO PULL IT OFF, I COULDN'T! MY EARS WERE COMPLETELY STUCK! THE INSIDE OF THE CUSHION WAS ALMOST ENTIRELY STUFFED WITH COTTON OR SOMETHING AND, AS I HURRIEDLY TRIED TO PULL MY HEAD OUT, THE CUSHION'S INNER SURFACE STUCK TO MY NOSE, AND I COULDN'T BREATHE! "THIS COULD BE VERY BAD!" I THOUGHT AND STARTED TO GET REALLY NERVOUS. I FLOUNDERED AROUND, TRYING TO OPEN THE COIN PURSE CUSHION WITH BOTH ARMS AS HARD AS I COULD.

THEN MY ASSISTANTS NOTICED AND ASKED, "WHAT ARE YOU DOING, MR. KISHIMOTO?" I THOUGHT, "YES!! MY ASSISTANTS WILL RESCUE ME!" AND I TRIED TO ASK THEM FOR HELP. ...JUST THEN I HEARD SOMETHING LIKE THE SOUND OF A CAMERA SHUTTER. I WASN'T SURE FROM INSIDE THE CUSHION BECAUSE I COULDN'T SEE, BUT I COULD IMAGINE WHAT WAS GOING ON. ALL OF MY ASSISTANTS WERE LAUGHING OUT LOUD AND TAKING PICTURES WITH THEIR CELL PHONE CAMERAS! OF ALL THINGS, THEY WERE TAKING PICTURES! THEY WEREN'T RESCUING ME; THEY WERE LAUGHING AND TAKING PICTURES! "NO! THEY'RE NOT TAKING THIS SERIOUSLY!!" I THOUGHT, AND MADE UP MY MIND THAT I HAD TO GET THE CUSHION OFF BY MYSELF. I PULLED HARD AND IT HURT SO MUCH THAT I THOUGHT MY EARS WERE GOING TO TEAR OFF. THEN, FINALLY, I WAS ABLE TO FREE MYSELF. NEEDLESS TO SAY, MY NAP TIME WAS COMPLETELY RUINED BY THAT CRAZY INCIDENT. I EXPECTED THERE WOULD BE AT LEAST ONE SANE PERSON WHO WOULD SAY, "ARE YOU OKAY, MR. KISHIMOTO?!" ...BUT THERE WASN'T. IT'S TRUE THAT THE ASSISTANTS HAD VERY LITTLE SLEEP AND WENT A BIT NUTTY. ALL OF THEM WERE UNDER THE SPELL OF THE USUAL CHAOS. IT WAS THEN THAT I PLEDGED... I WILL FIGHT AGAINST THIS CHAOS!

WARNING: DON'T TRY THIS AT HOME!

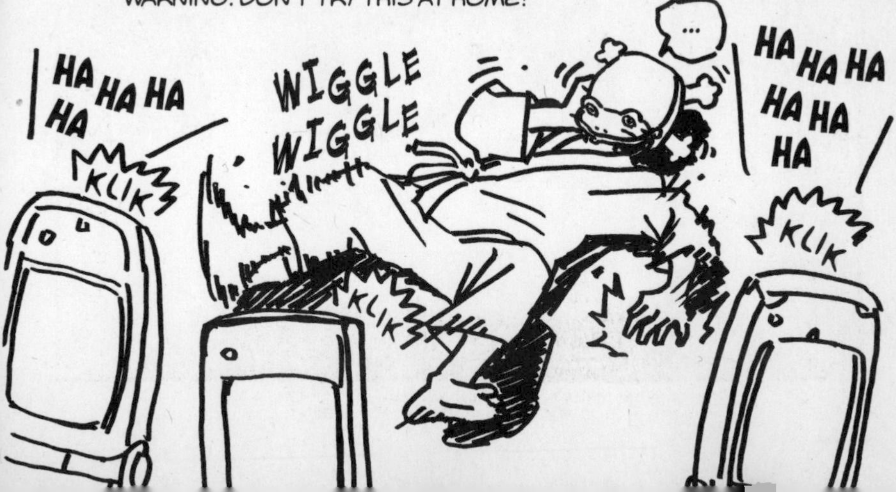
HA HA HA HA HA HA
...
HA HA HA HA HA HA
WIGGLE WIGGLE
KLIK
KLIK
KLIK

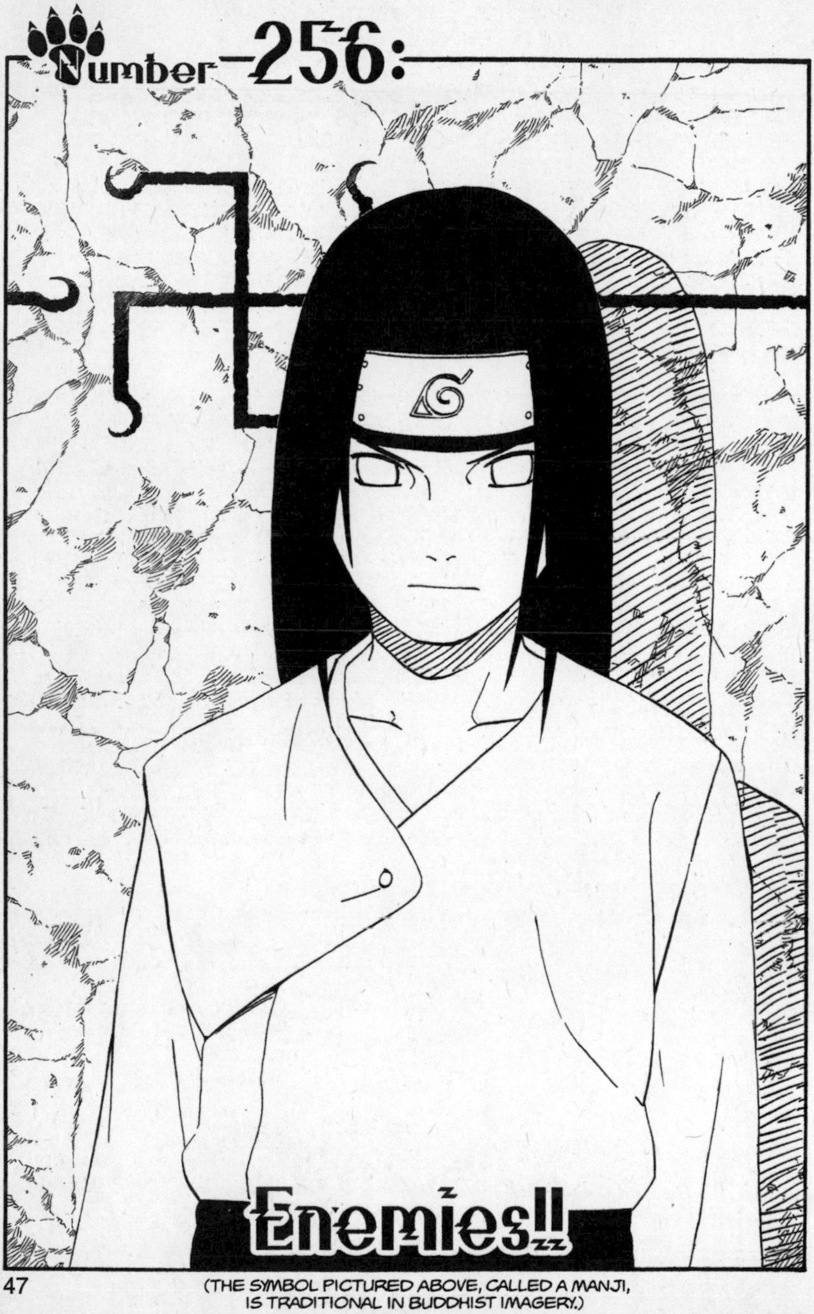
Number 256:
Enemies!!

(THE SYMBOL PICTURED ABOVE, CALLED A MANJI, IS TRADITIONAL IN BUDDHIST IMAGERY.)

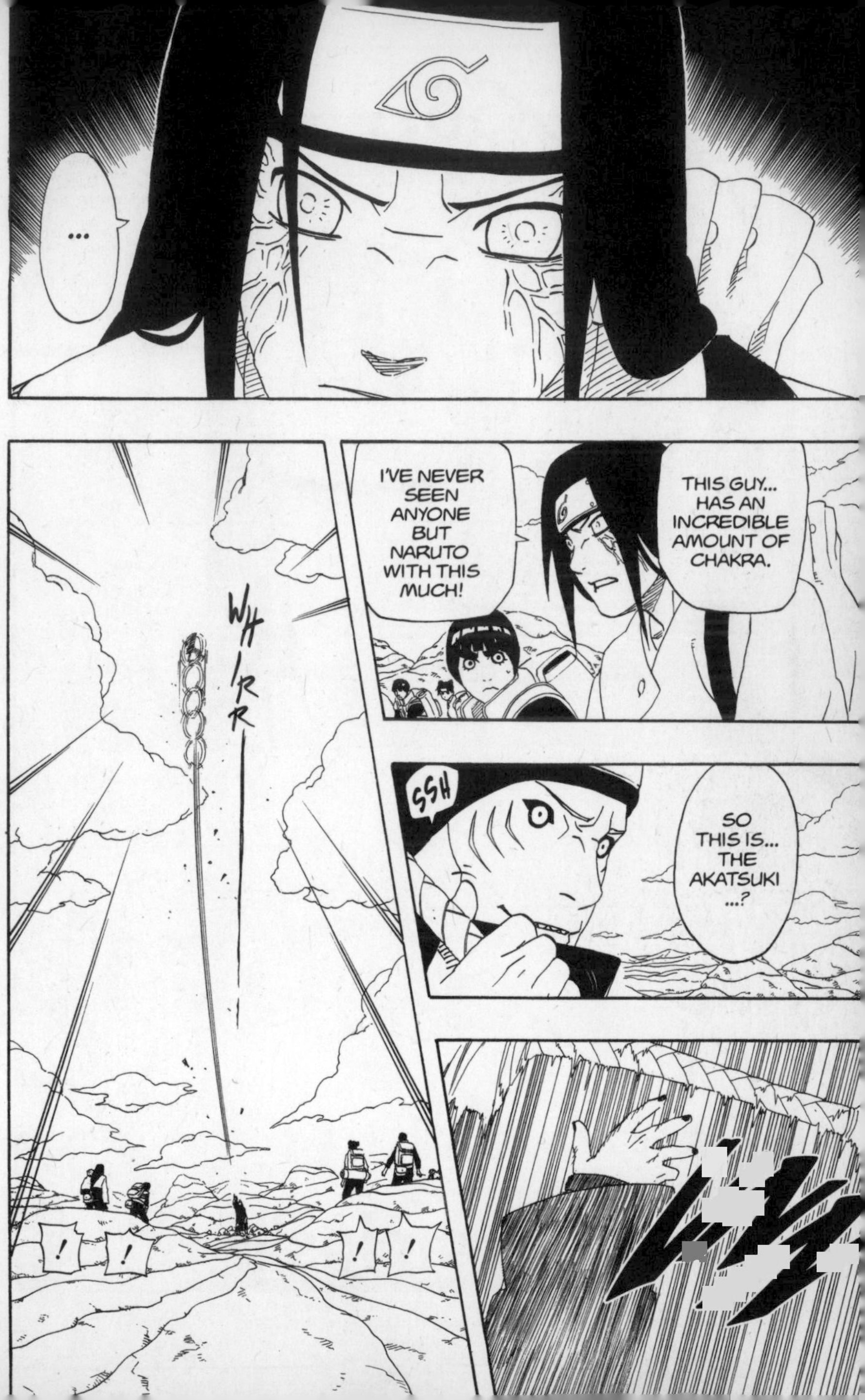
...
THIS GUY... HAS AN INCREDIBLE AMOUNT OF CHAKRA.
I'VE NEVER SEEN ANYONE BUT NARUTO WITH THIS MUCH!
SO THIS IS... THE AKATSUKI ...?
SSH
WHIRR
!
!
!
!

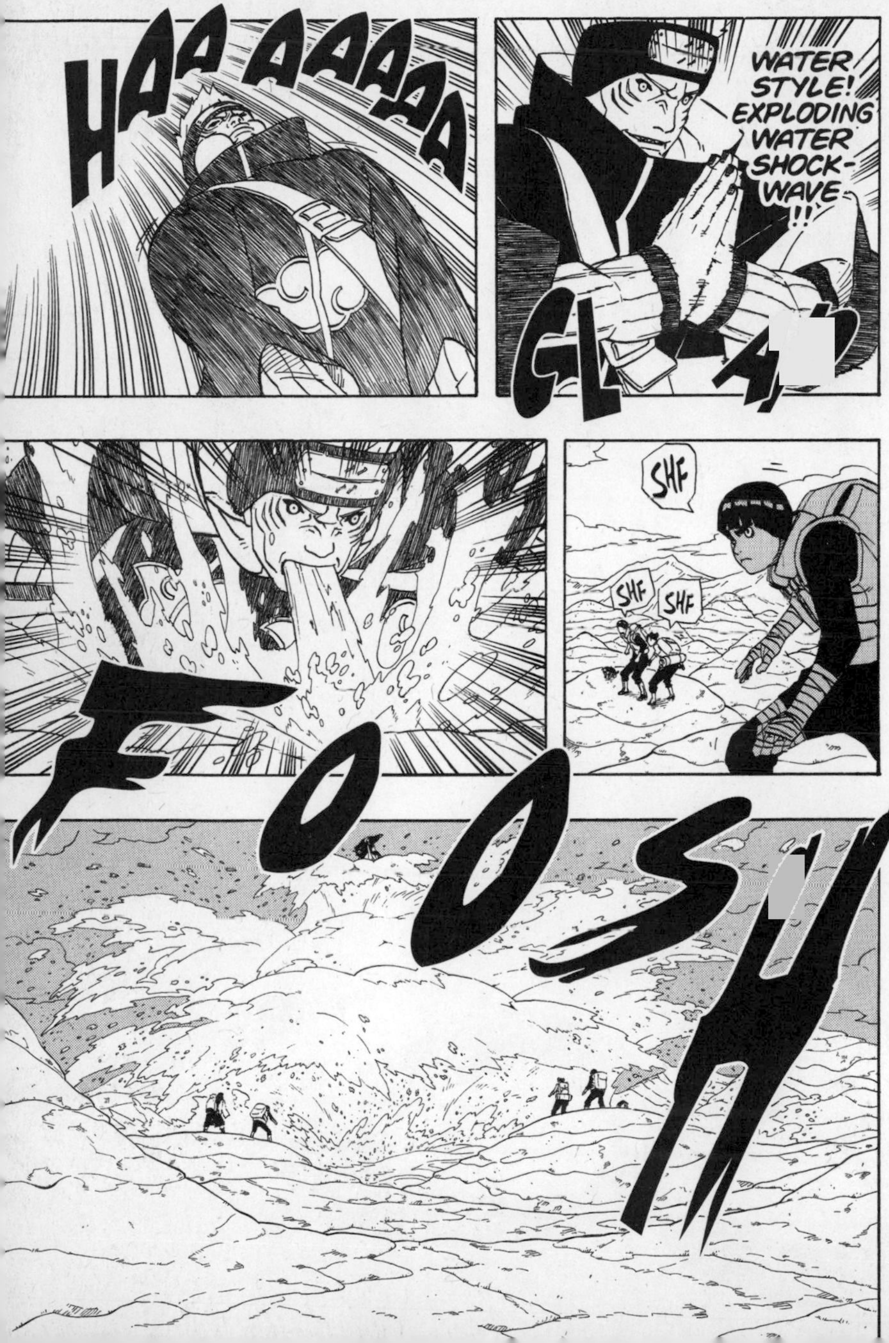
WATER STYLE! EXPLODING WATER SHOCK-WAVE!!
HAAAAAAA
SHF
SHF
SHF
FOOSH

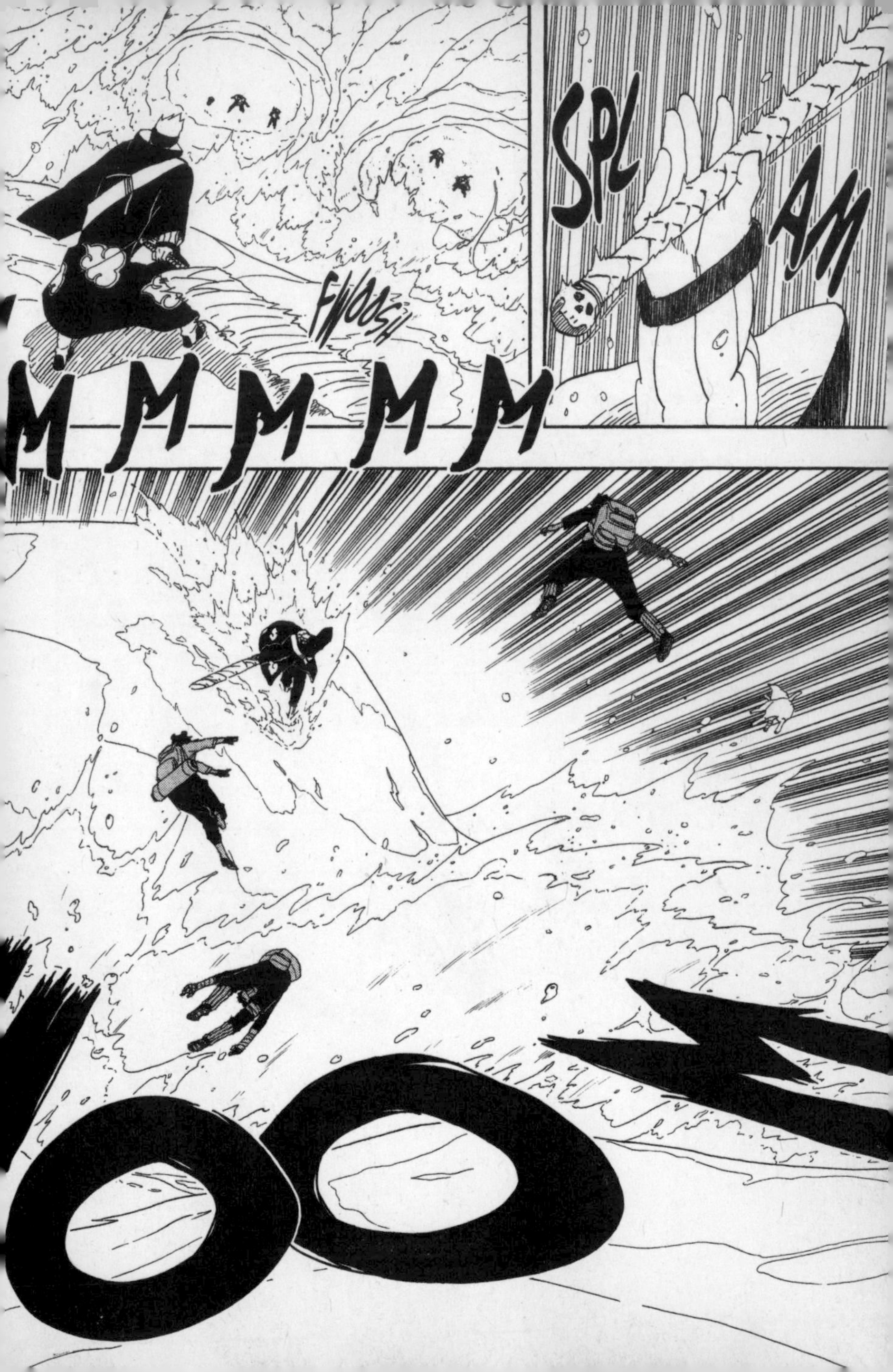
SPLAM
FWOOSH
MMMMMM
OOM

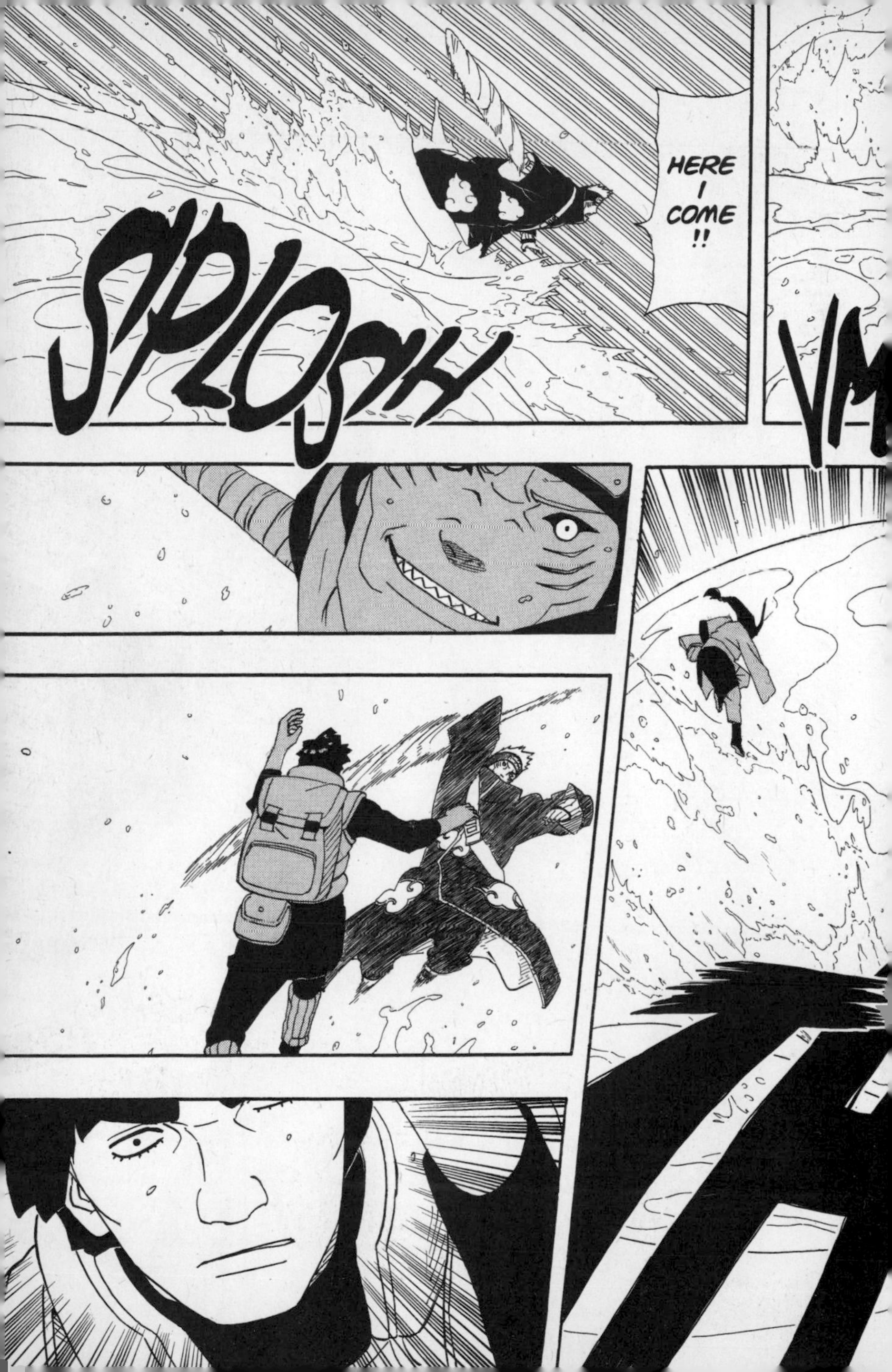
VM
HERE I COME!!
SPLOSH

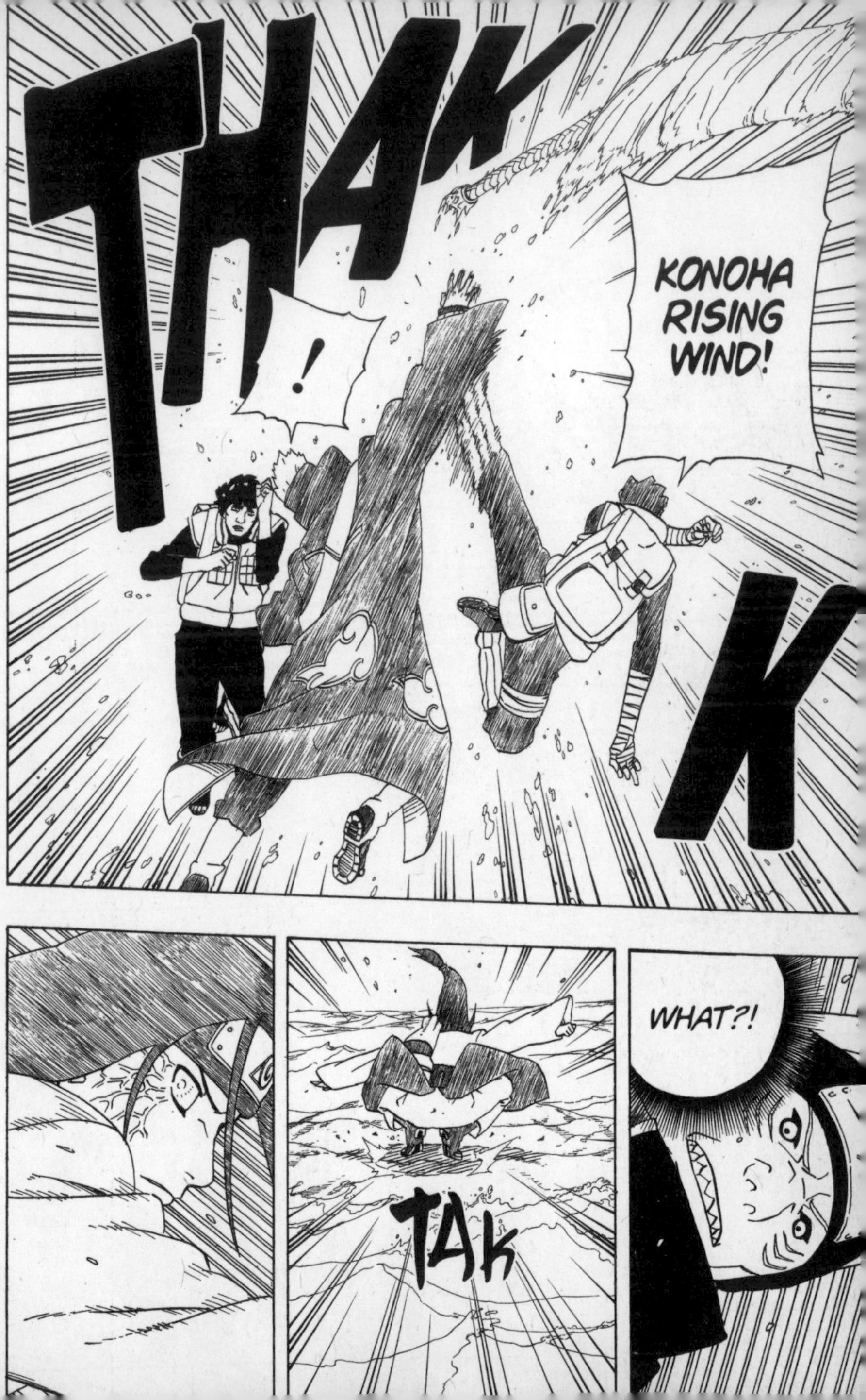
KONOHA RISING WIND!
!
THAK
K
WHAT?!
TAK

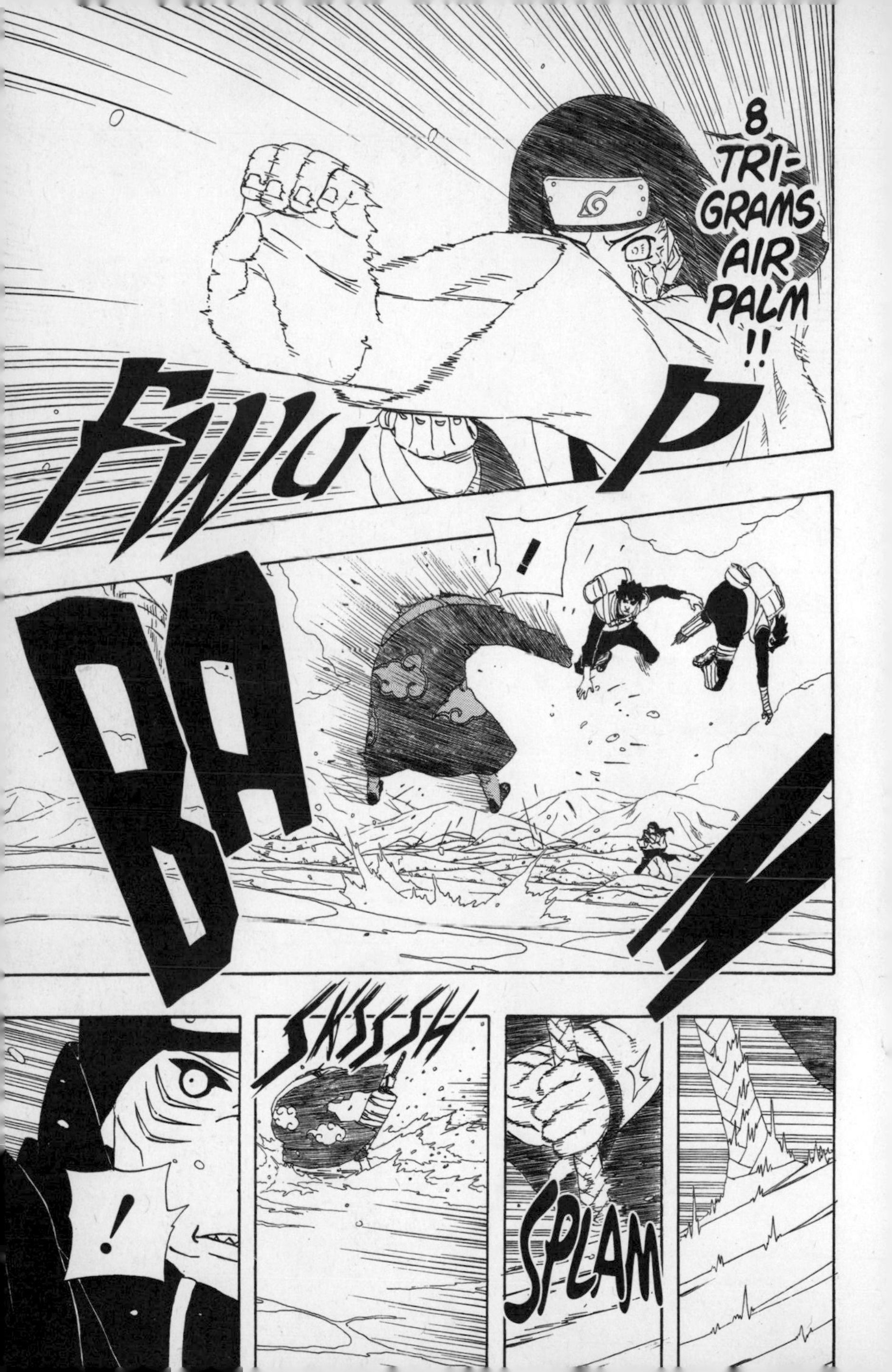
8 TRI-GRAMS AIR PALM!!
FWUP
!
BAM
SPLAM
SKSSSH
!

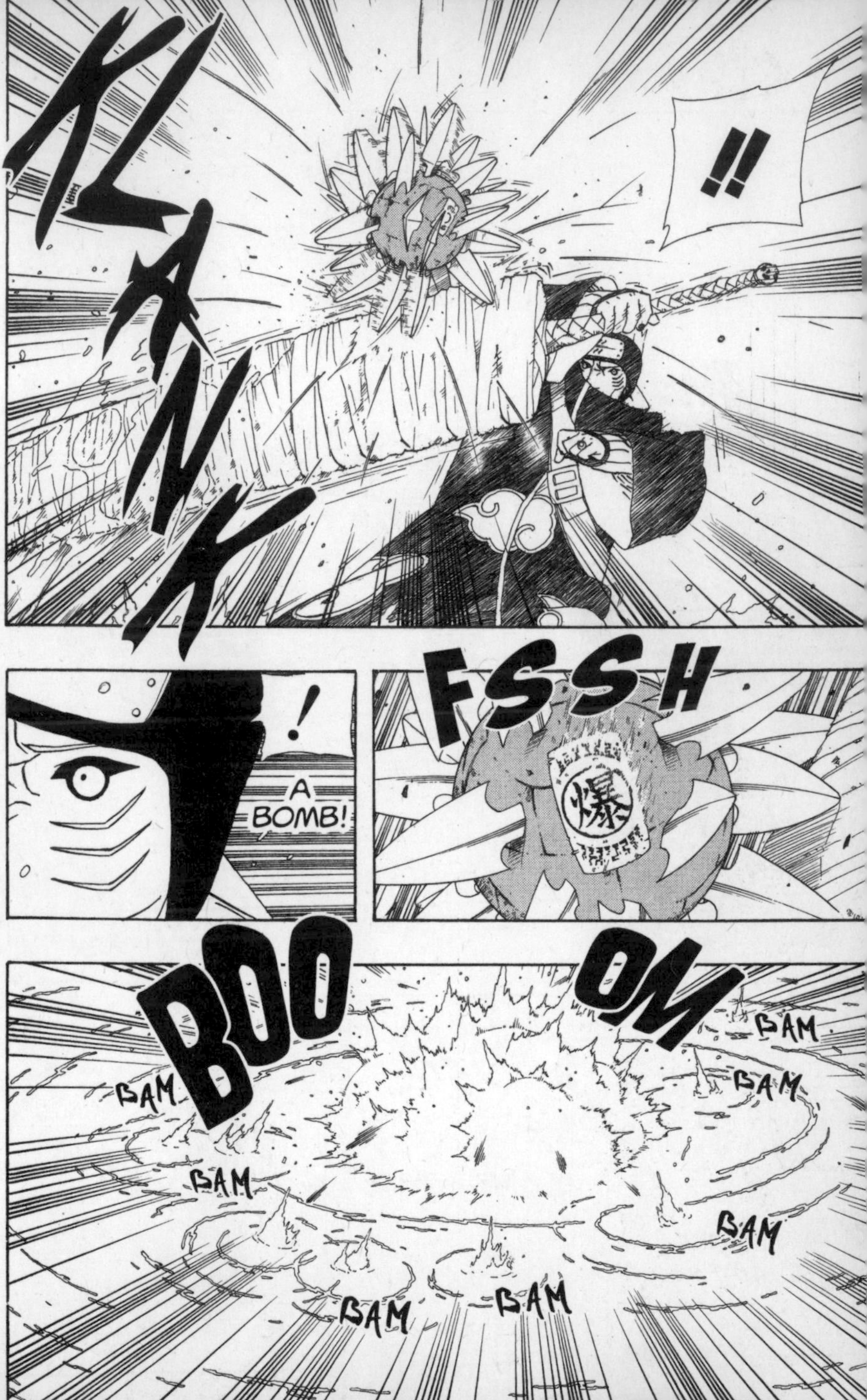
!!
KLANK
FSSH
!
A BOMB!
BOOOM
BAM
BAM
BAM
BAM
BAM
BAM
BAM

READ THIS WAY

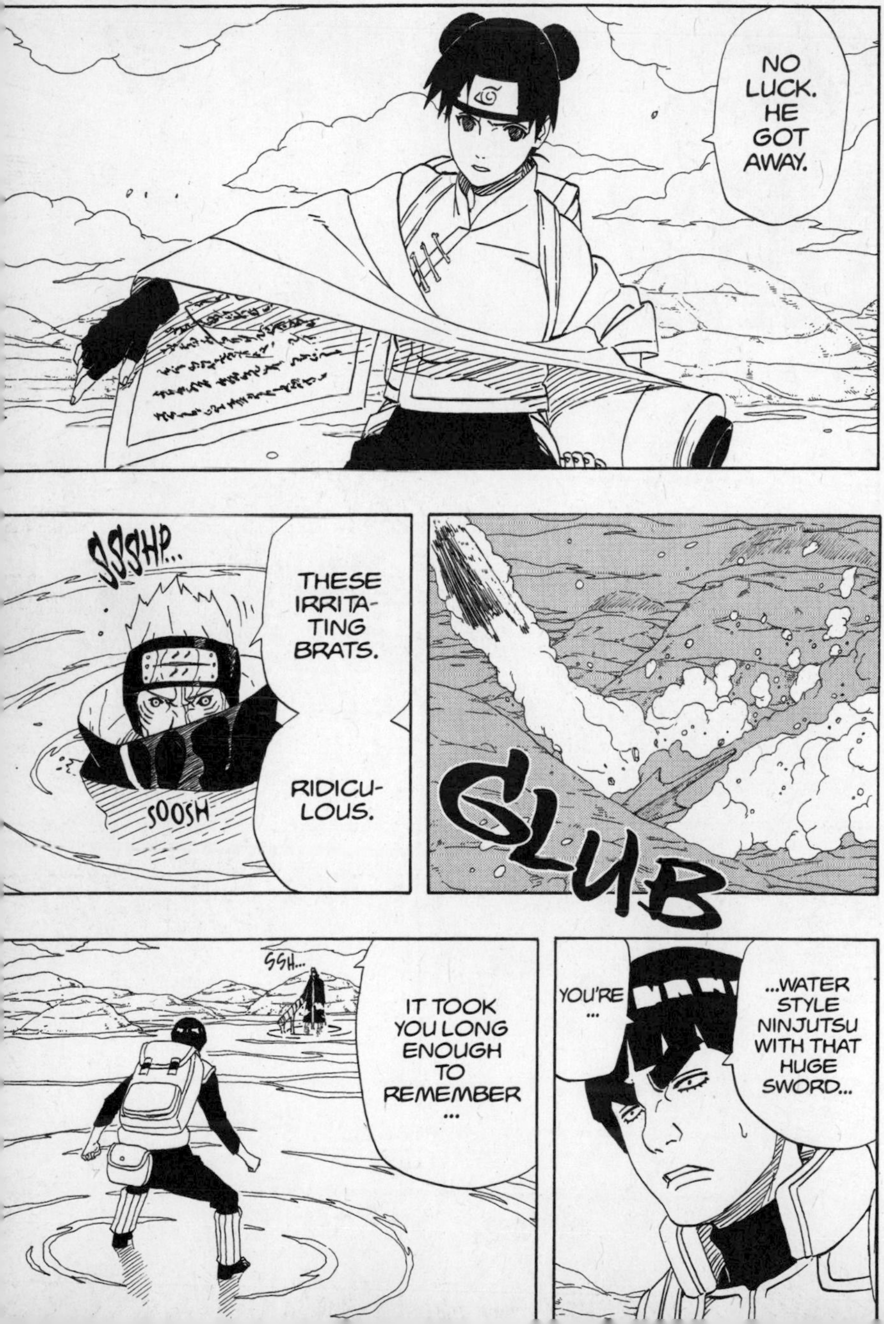
NO LUCK. HE GOT AWAY.
CLUB
THESE IRRITATING BRATS.
RIDICULOUS.
SSSHP...
SOOSH
YOU'RE ...
...WATER STYLE NINJUTSU WITH THAT HUGE SWORD...
IT TOOK YOU LONG ENOUGH TO REMEMBER ...
SSH...

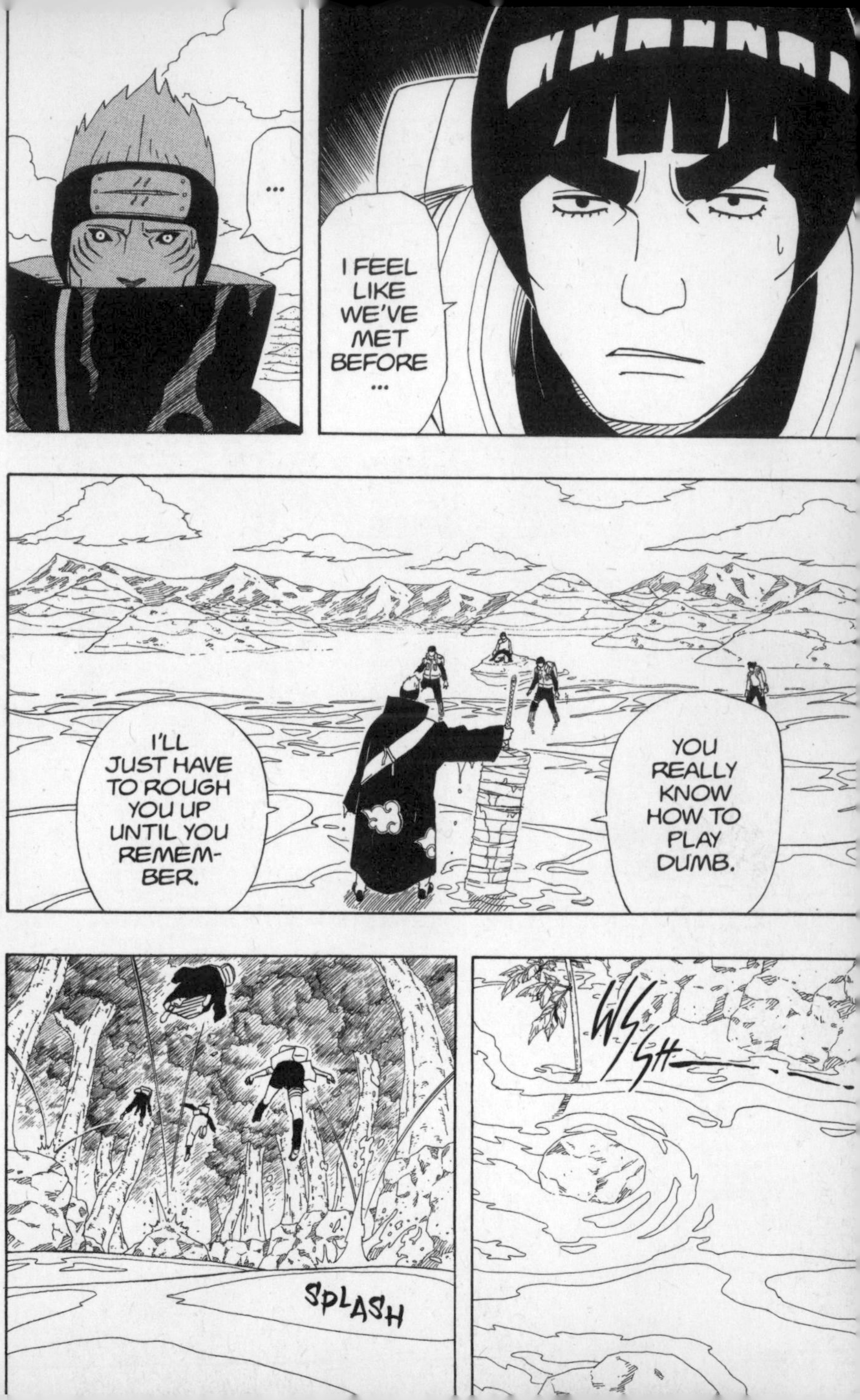
I FEEL LIKE WE'VE MET BEFORE ...
...
YOU REALLY KNOW HOW TO PLAY DUMB.
I'LL JUST HAVE TO ROUGH YOU UP UNTIL YOU REMEM-BER.
WSSH
SPLASH

READ THIS WAY

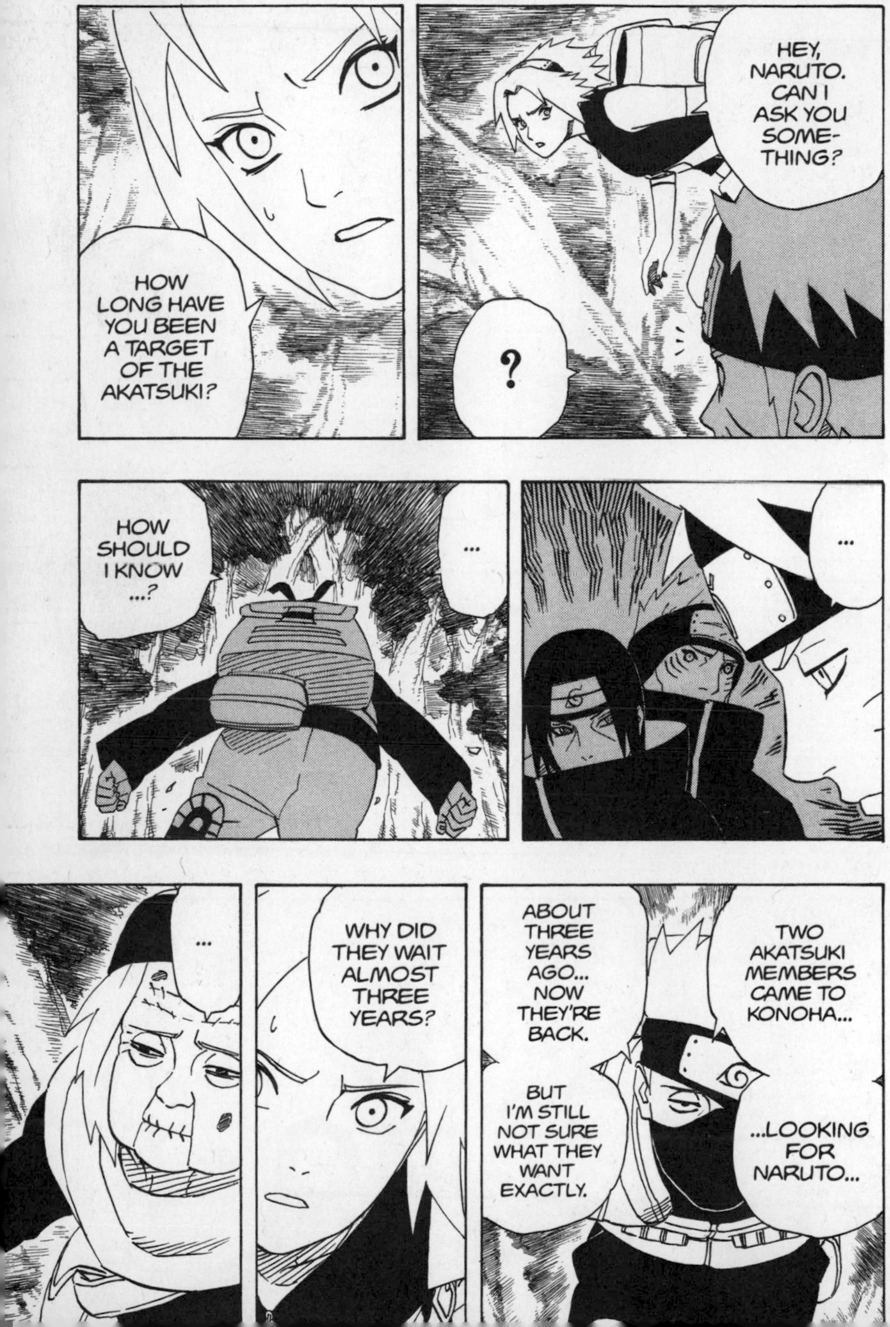
HEY, NARUTO. CAN I ASK YOU SOME-THING?
?
HOW LONG HAVE YOU BEEN A TARGET OF THE AKATSUKI?
...
...
HOW SHOULD I KNOW ...?
TWO AKATSUKI MEMBERS CAME TO KONOHA...
...LOOKING FOR NARUTO...
ABOUT THREE YEARS AGO... NOW THEY'RE BACK.
BUT I'M STILL NOT SURE WHAT THEY WANT EXACTLY.
WHY DID THEY WAIT ALMOST THREE YEARS?
...

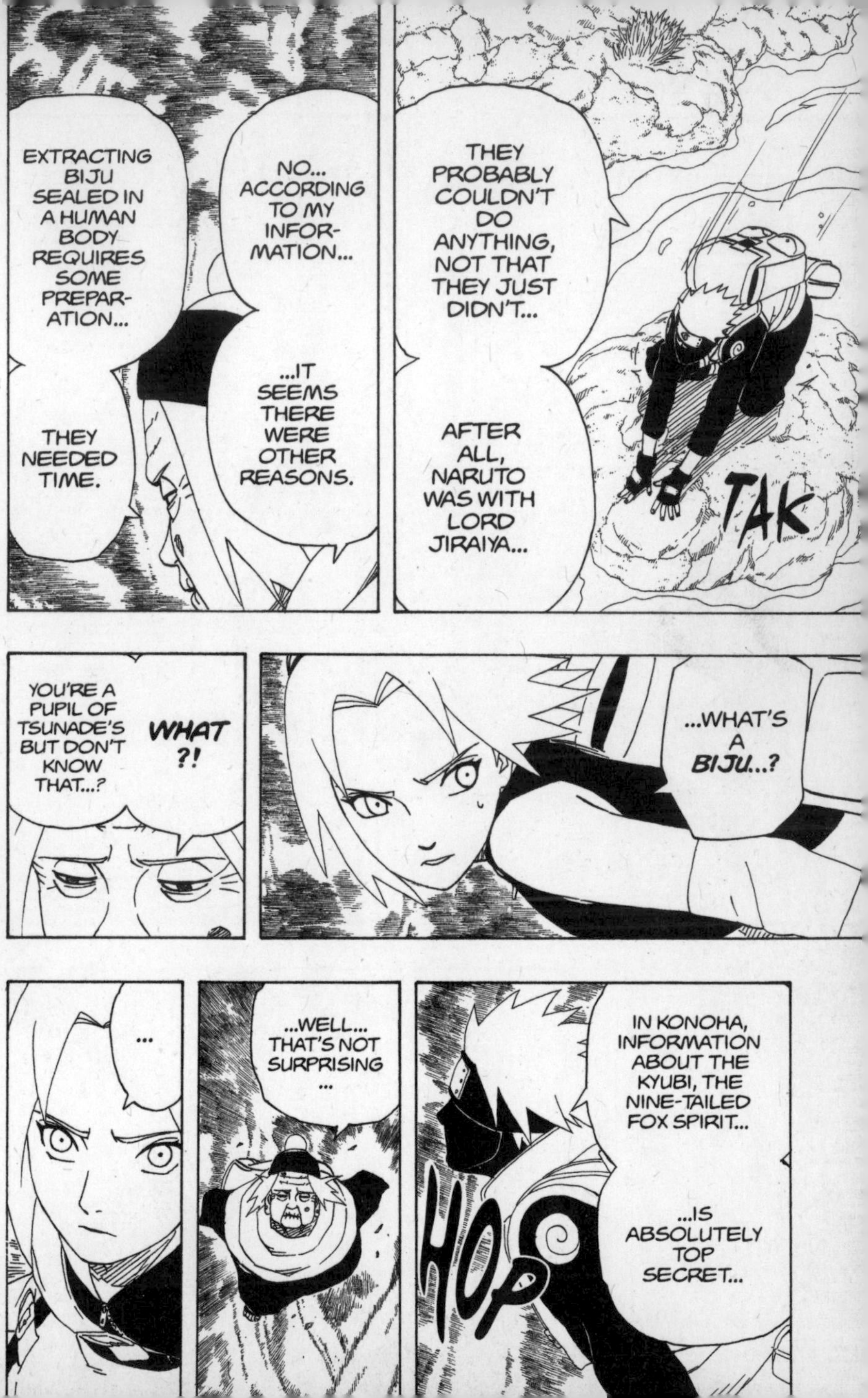
TAK
THEY PROBABLY COULDN'T DO ANYTHING, NOT THAT THEY JUST DIDN'T...
AFTER ALL, NARUTO WAS WITH LORD JIRAIYA...
NO... ACCORDING TO MY INFORMATION...
...IT SEEMS THERE WERE OTHER REASONS.
EXTRACTING BIJU SEALED IN A HUMAN BODY REQUIRES SOME PREPARATION...
THEY NEEDED TIME.
...WHAT'S A BIJU...?
WHAT ?!
YOU'RE A PUPIL OF TSUNADE'S BUT DON'T KNOW THAT...?
IN KONOHA, INFORMATION ABOUT THE KYUBI, THE NINE-TAILED FOX SPIRIT...
...IS ABSOLUTELY TOP SECRET...
HOP
...WELL... THAT'S NOT SURPRISING ...
...

READ THIS WAY

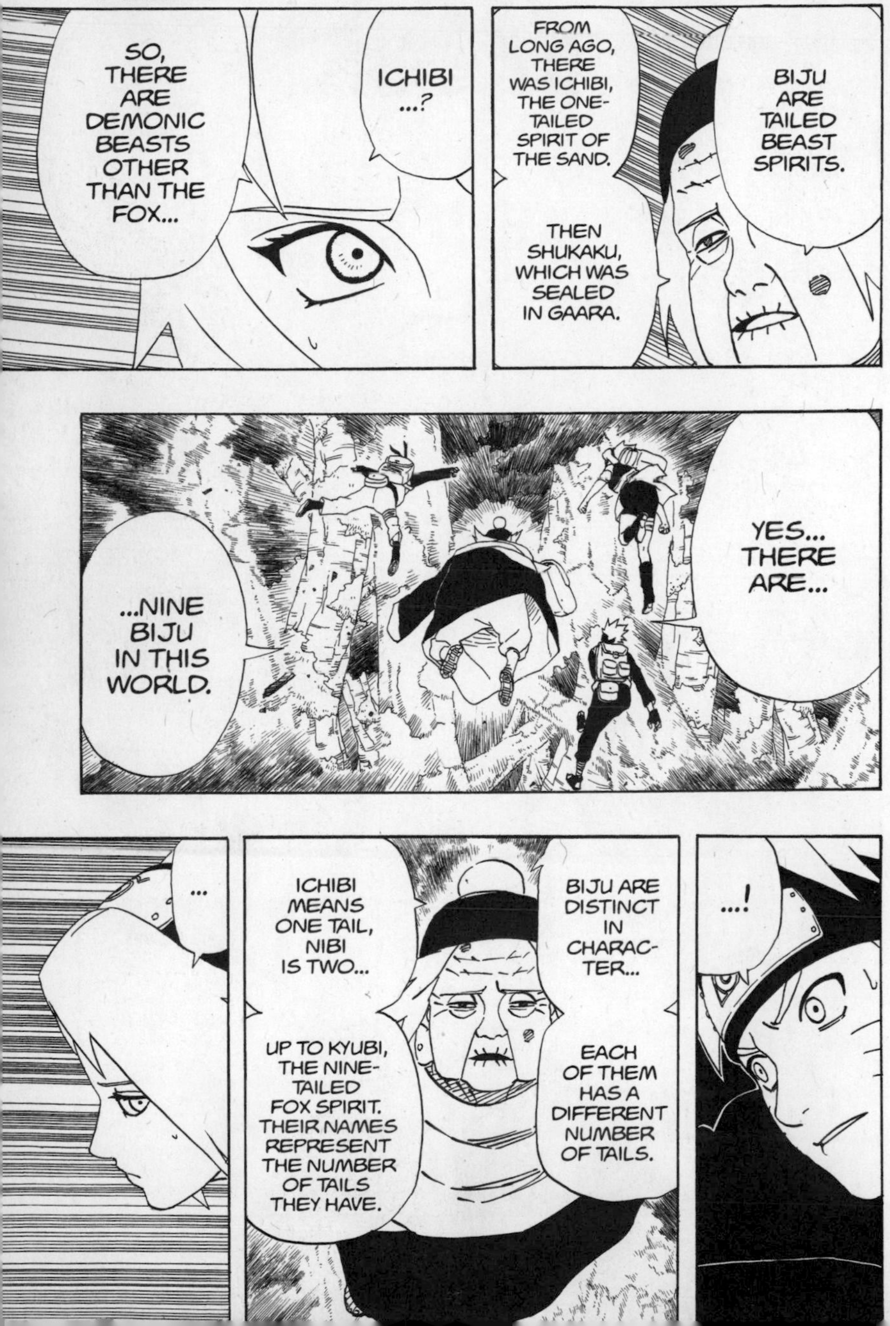
BIJU ARE TAILED BEAST SPIRITS.
FROM LONG AGO, THERE WAS ICHIBI, THE ONE-TAILED SPIRIT OF THE SAND.
THEN SHUKAKU, WHICH WAS SEALED IN GAARA.
ICHIBI ...?
SO, THERE ARE DEMONIC BEASTS OTHER THAN THE FOX...
YES... THERE ARE...
...NINE BIJU IN THIS WORLD.
...!
BIJU ARE DISTINCT IN CHARACTER...
EACH OF THEM HAS A DIFFERENT NUMBER OF TAILS.
ICHIBI MEANS ONE TAIL, NIBI IS TWO...
UP TO KYUBI, THE NINE-TAILED FOX SPIRIT. THEIR NAMES REPRESENT THE NUMBER OF TAILS THEY HAVE.
...

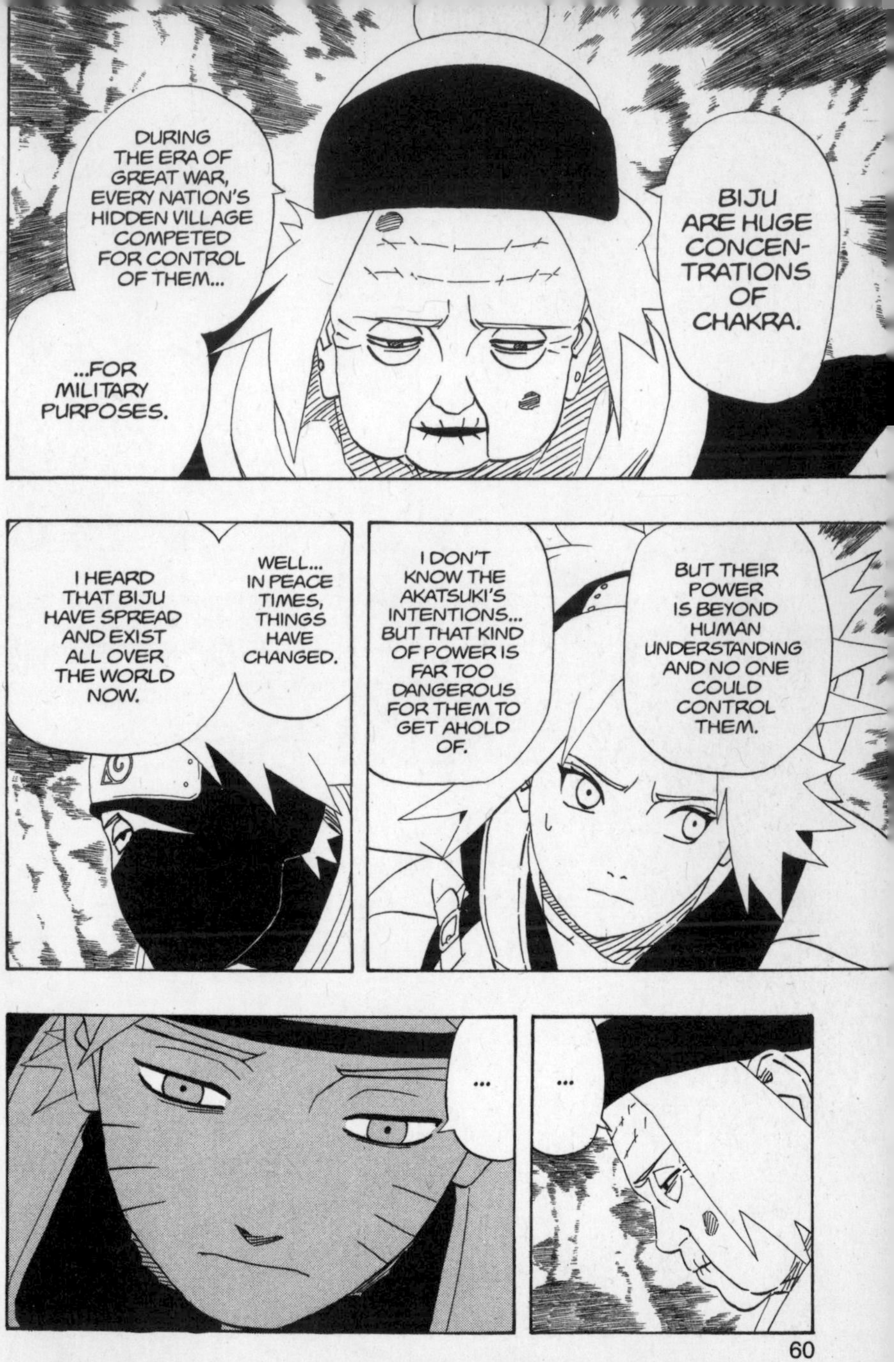
BIJU ARE HUGE CONCEN-TRATIONS OF CHAKRA.
DURING THE ERA OF GREAT WAR, EVERY NATION'S HIDDEN VILLAGE COMPETED FOR CONTROL OF THEM...
...FOR MILITARY PURPOSES.
BUT THEIR POWER IS BEYOND HUMAN UNDERSTANDING AND NO ONE COULD CONTROL THEM.
I DON'T KNOW THE AKATSUKI'S INTENTIONS... BUT THAT KIND OF POWER IS FAR TOO DANGEROUS FOR THEM TO GET AHOLD OF.
WELL... IN PEACE TIMES, THINGS HAVE CHANGED.
I HEARD THAT BIJU HAVE SPREAD AND EXIST ALL OVER THE WORLD NOW.
...
...

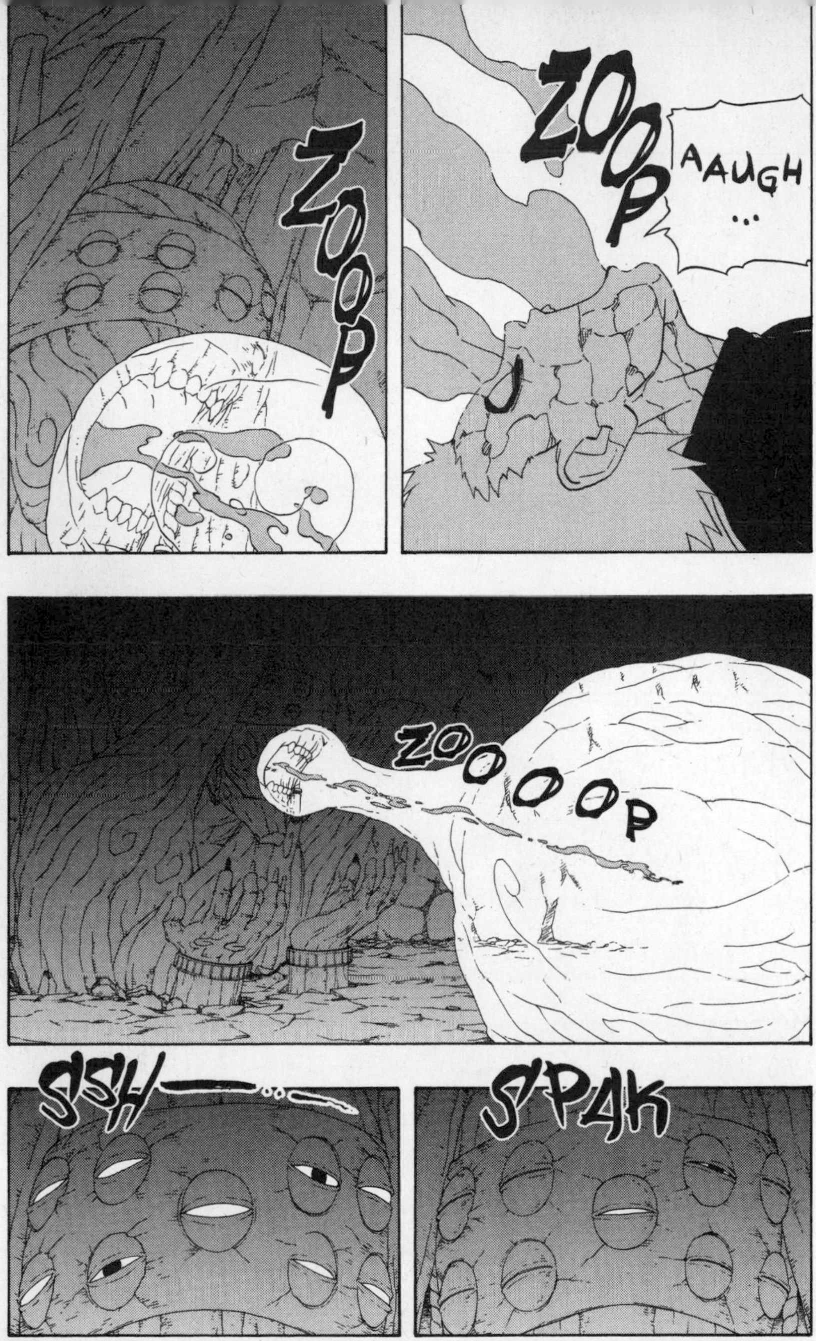
ZOOP
AAUGH ...
ZOOP
ZOOOOOP
SPAK
SSH—

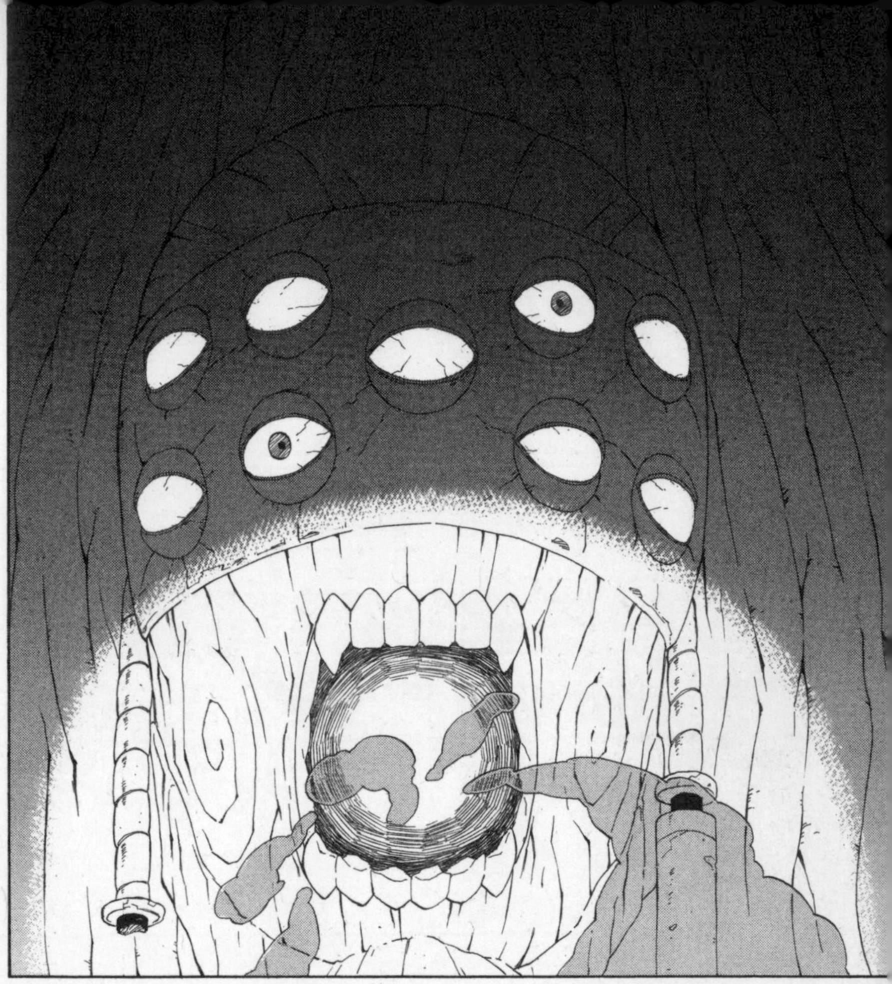
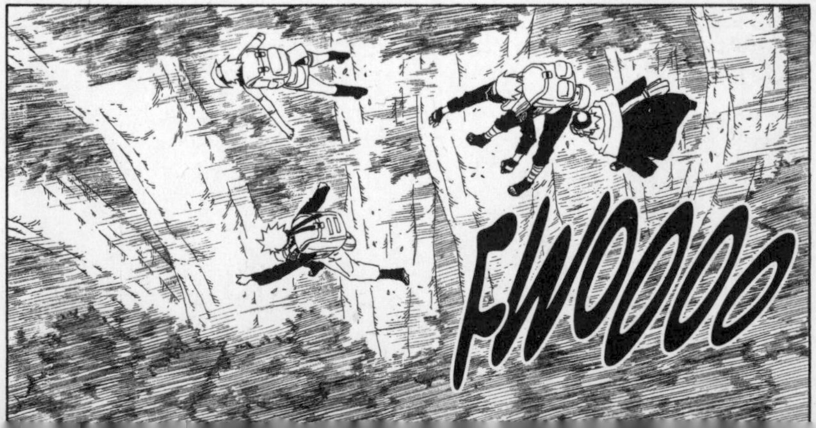
FWOOOO

READ THIS WAY

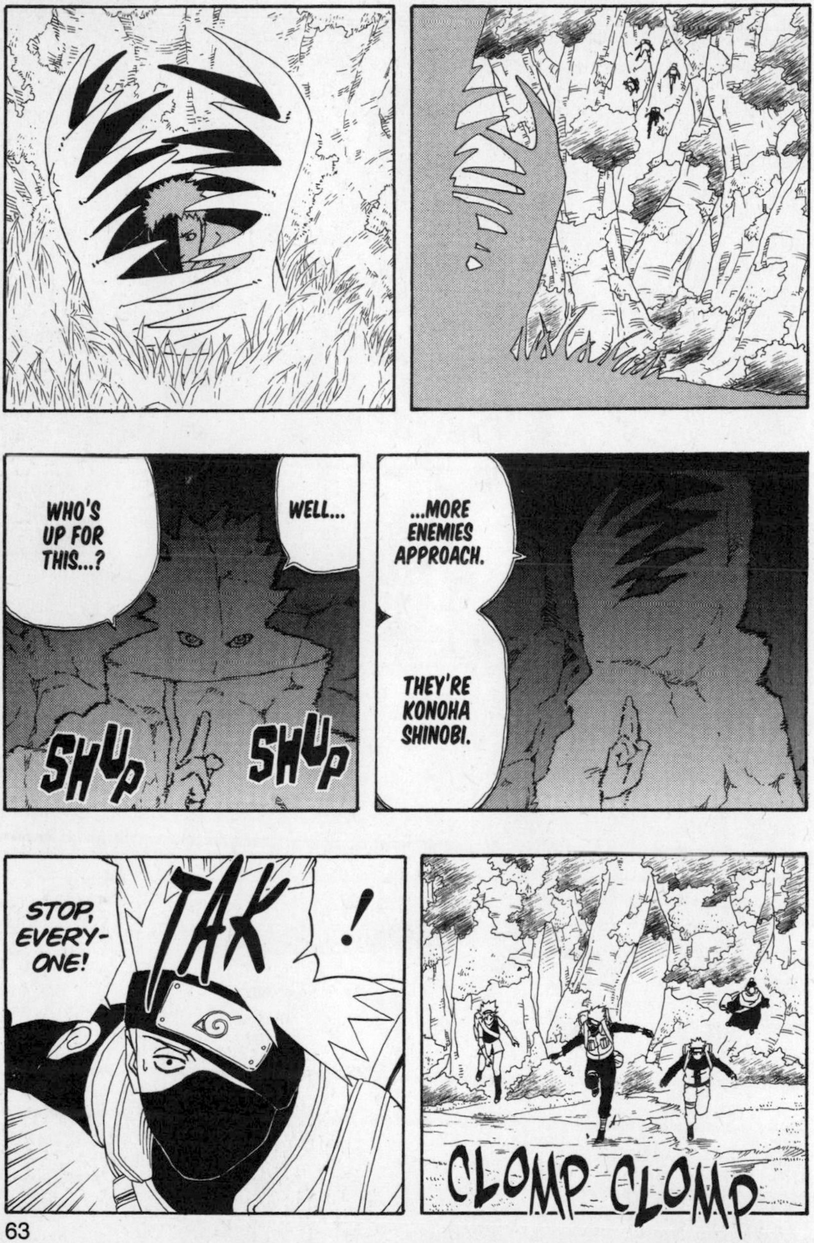

...MORE ENEMIES APPROACH.
THEY'RE KONOHA SHINOBI.
WELL...
WHO'S UP FOR THIS...?
SHUP SHUP
CLOMP CLOMP
TAK !
STOP, EVERY-ONE!

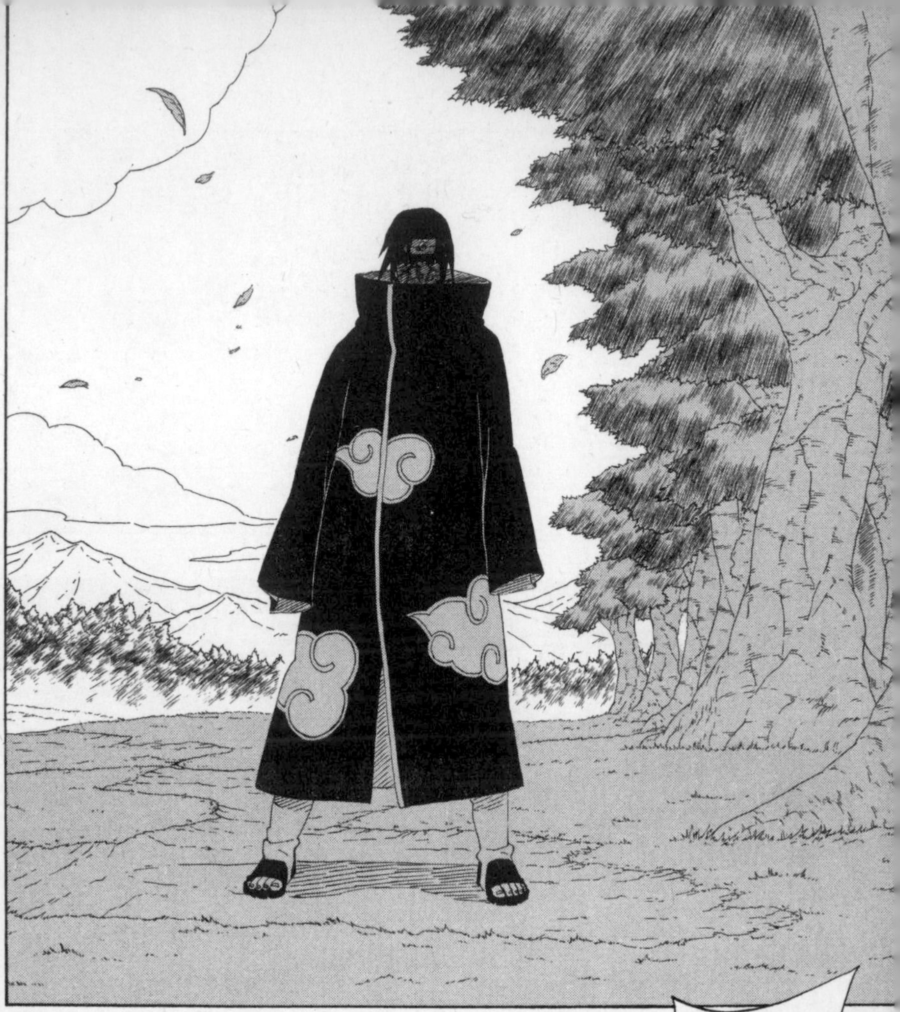

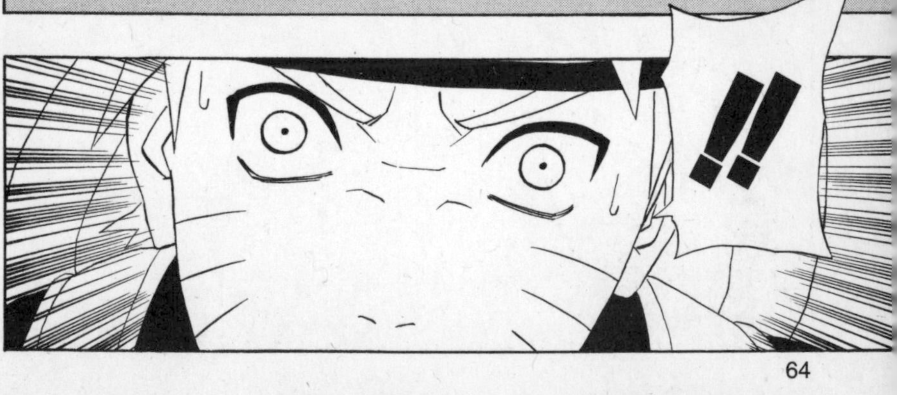
!!

READ THIS WAY

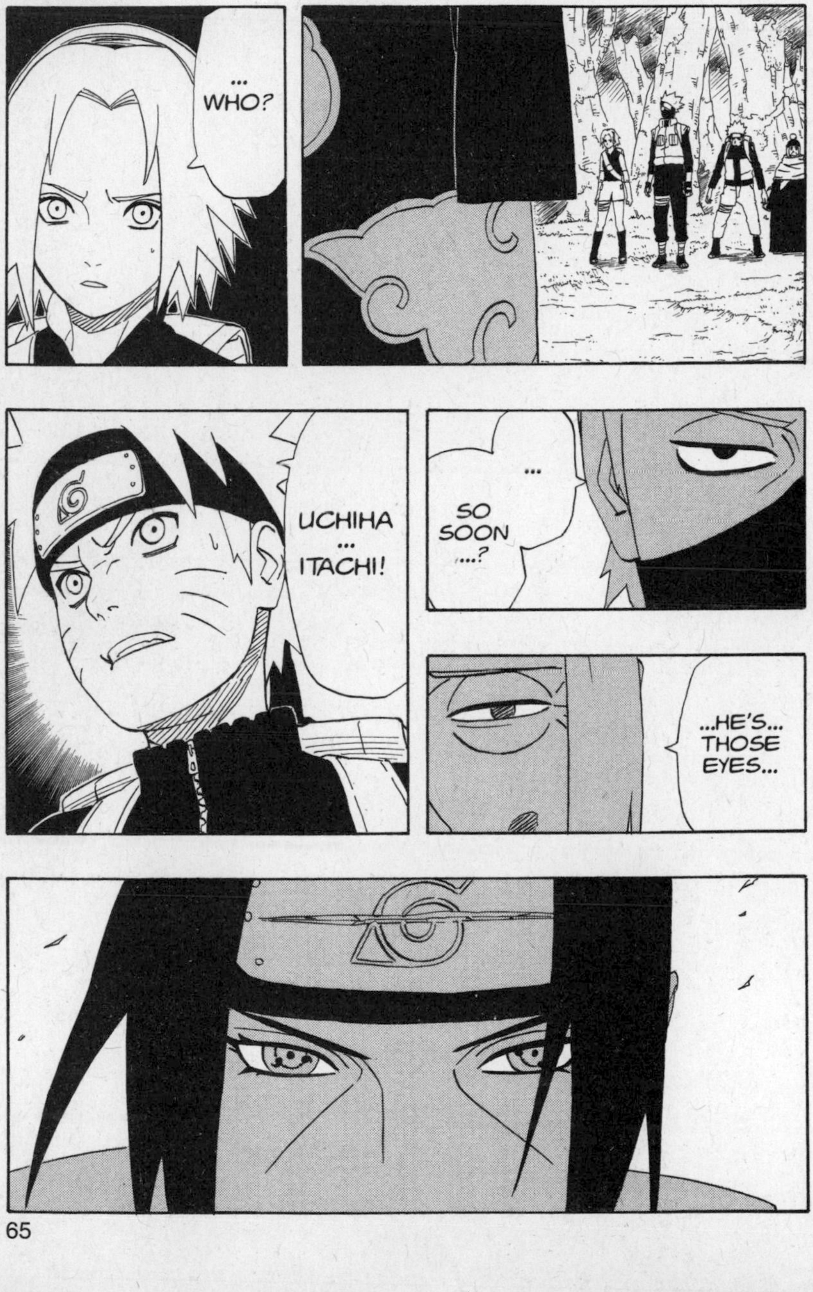
... WHO?
... SO SOON ....?
...HE'S... THOSE EYES...
UCHIHA ... ITACHI!

NARUTO

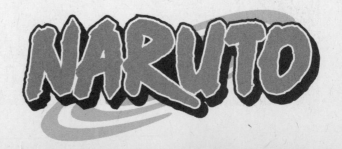

Number 257: Kakashi Comes Through

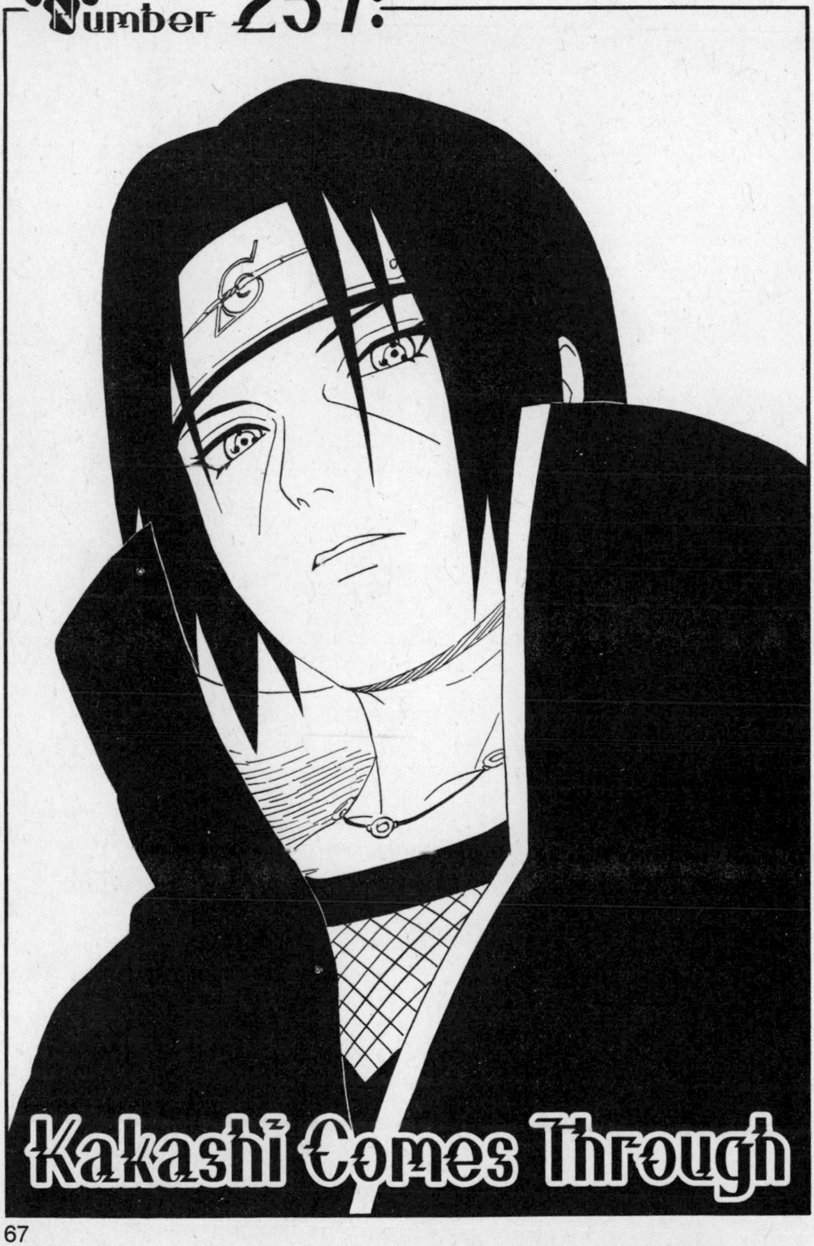

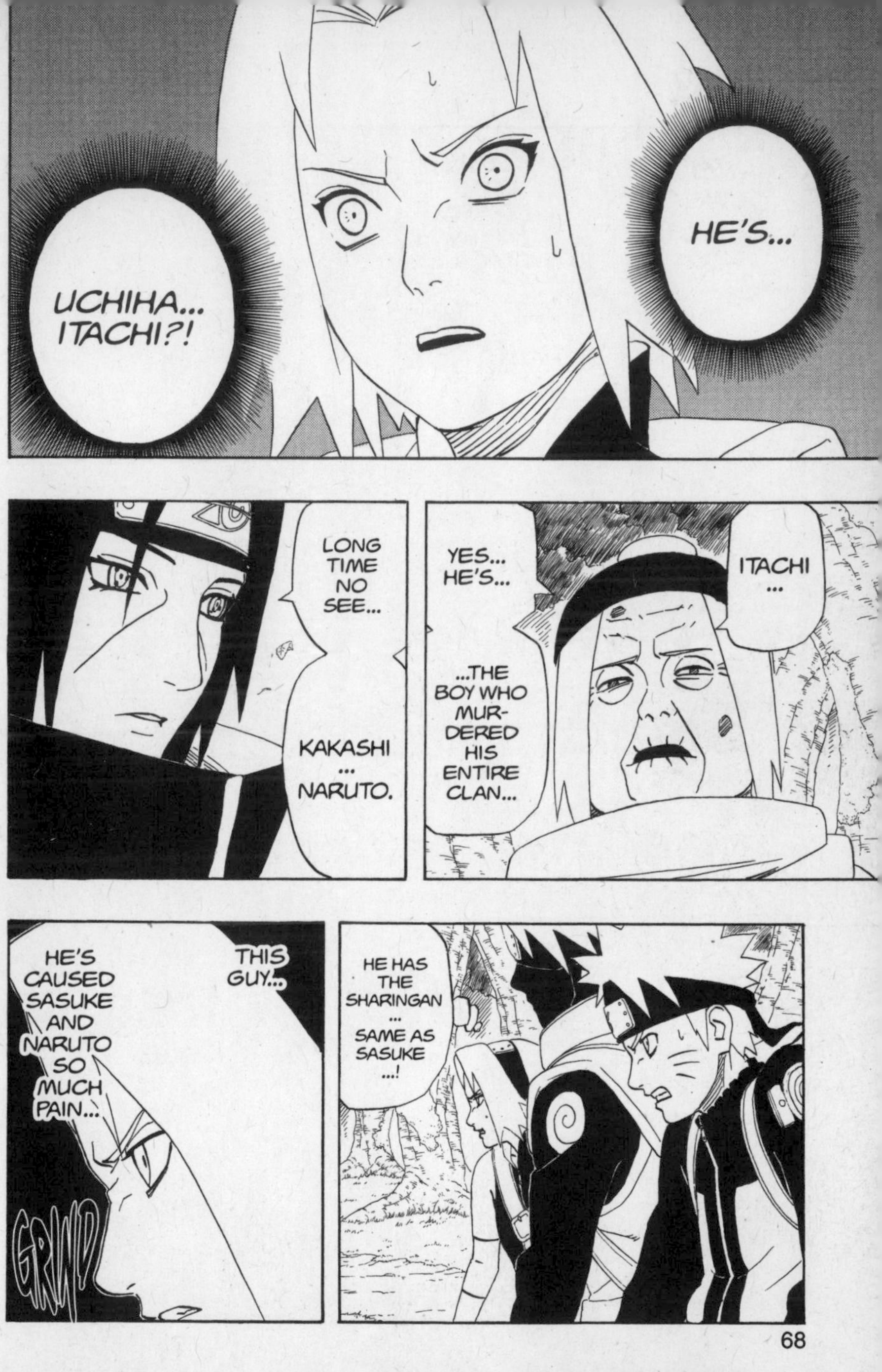
HE'S...
UCHIHA... ITACHI?!
ITACHI ...
YES... HE'S...
...THE BOY WHO MUR- DERED HIS ENTIRE CLAN...
LONG TIME NO SEE...
KAKASHI ... NARUTO.
HE HAS THE SHARINGAN ... SAME AS SASUKE ...!
THIS GUY...
HE'S CAUSED SASUKE AND NARUTO SO MUCH PAIN...
GRIND

READ THIS WAY

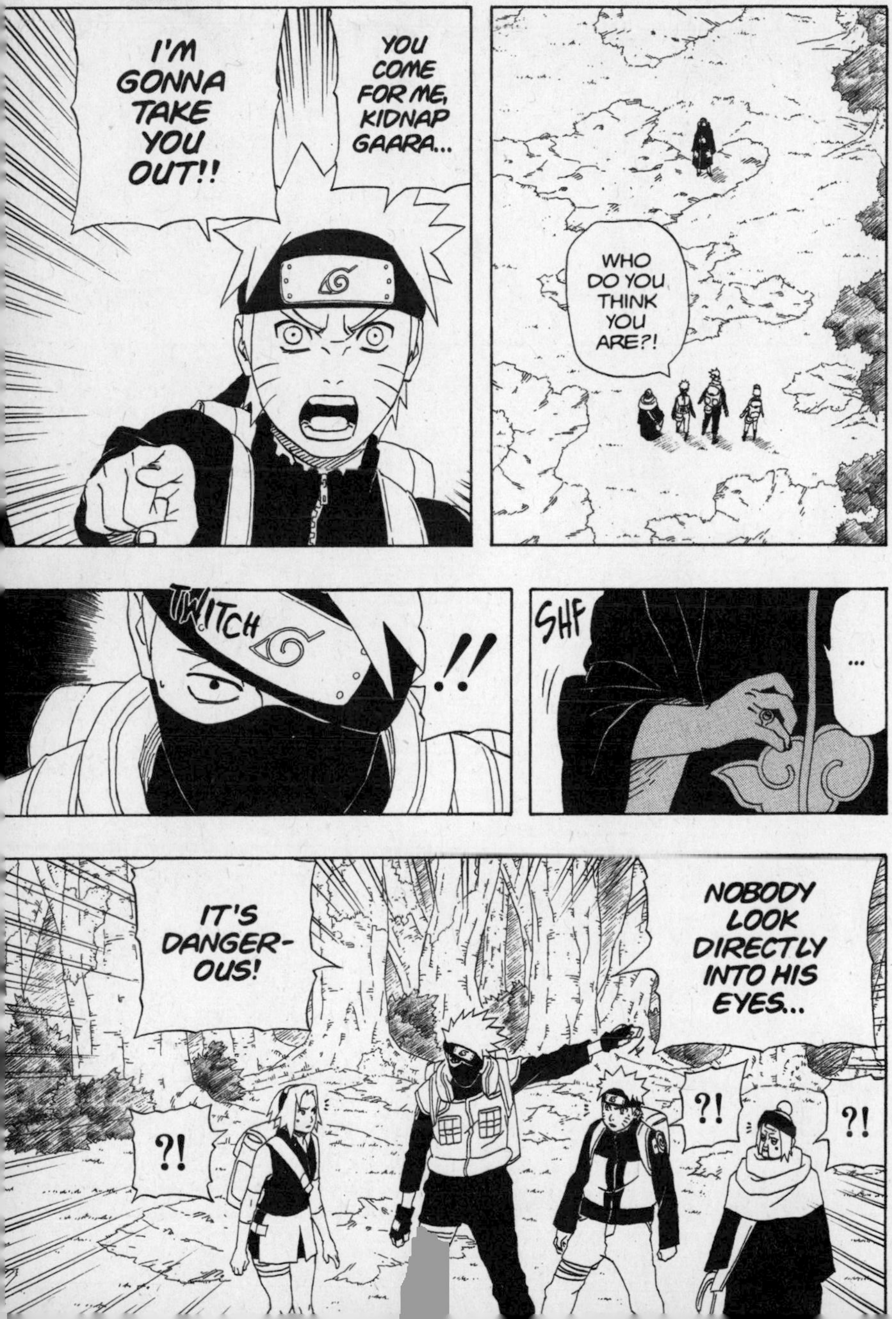

WHO DO YOU THINK YOU ARE?!
YOU COME FOR ME, KIDNAP GAARA...
I'M GONNA TAKE YOU OUT!!
SHF
...
TWITCH
!!
NOBODY LOOK DIRECTLY INTO HIS EYES...
IT'S DANGER-OUS!
?!
?!
?!

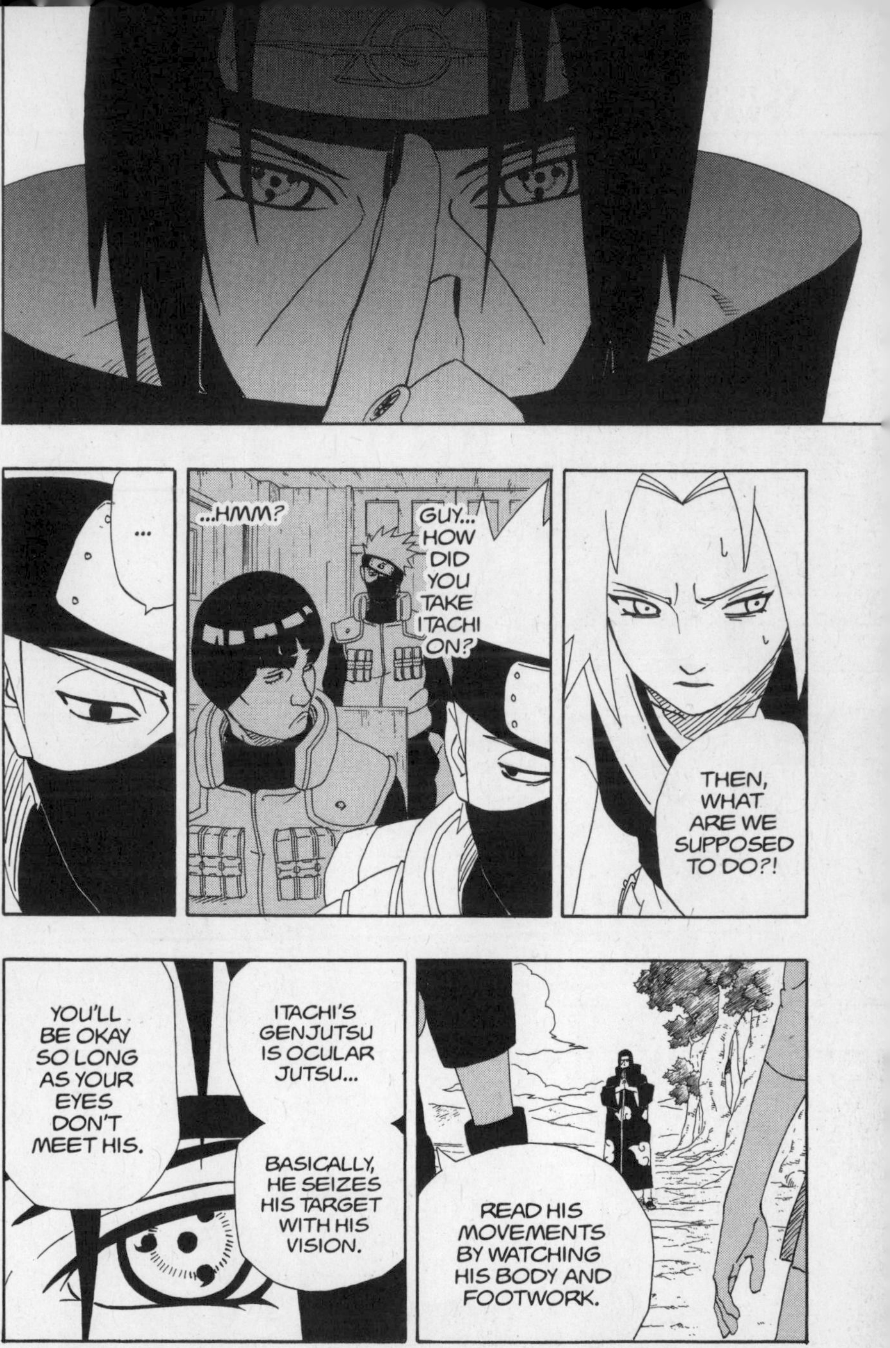
THEN, WHAT ARE WE SUPPOSED TO DO?!
GUY... HOW DID YOU TAKE ITACHI ON?
...HMM?
...
READ HIS MOVEMENTS BY WATCHING HIS BODY AND FOOTWORK.
ITACHI'S GENJUTSU IS OCULAR JUTSU...
BASICALLY, HE SEIZES HIS TARGET WITH HIS VISION.
YOU'LL BE OKAY SO LONG AS YOUR EYES DON'T MEET HIS.

READ THIS WAY

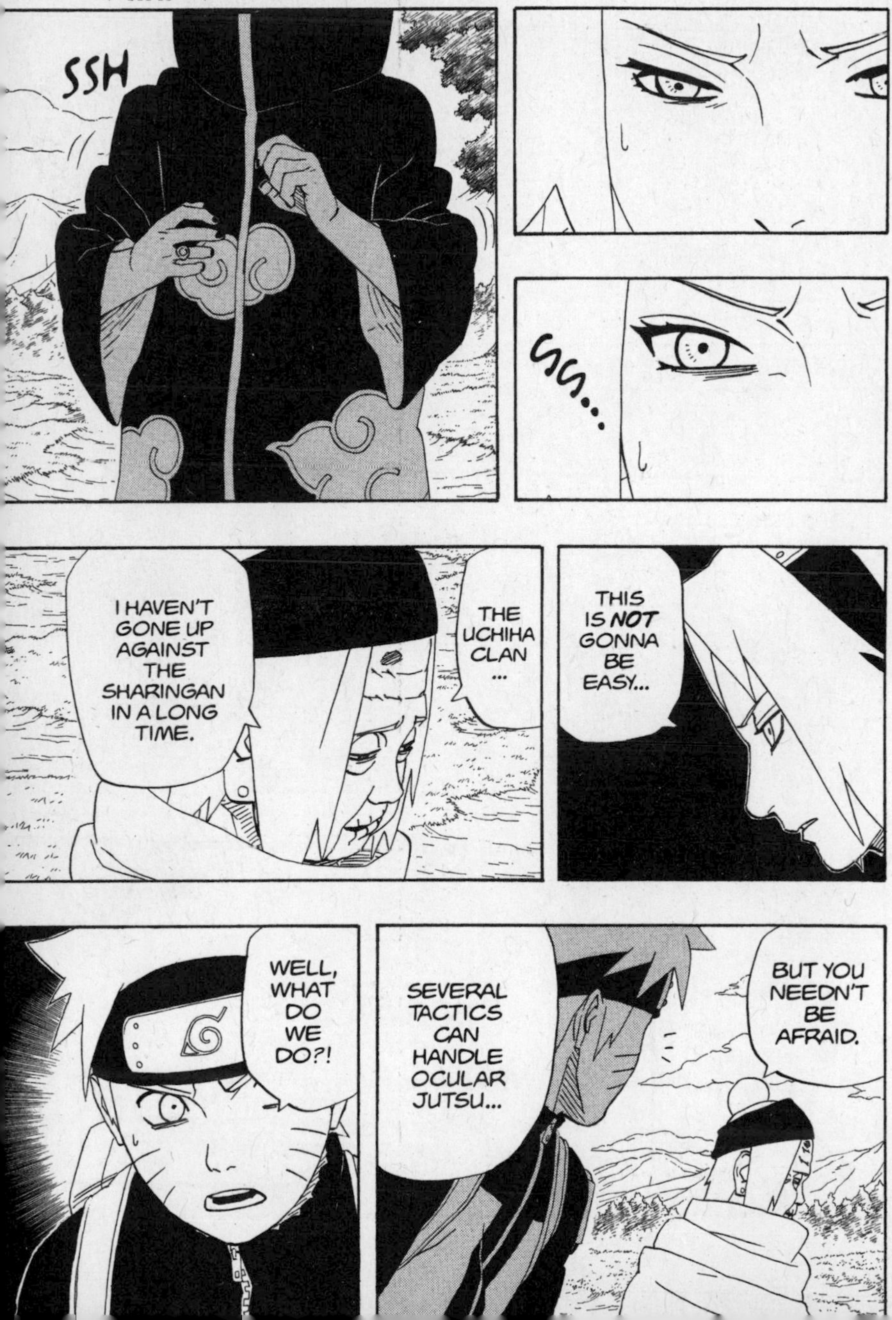
SS...
SSH
THIS IS NOT GONNA BE EASY...
THE UCHIHA CLAN ...
I HAVEN'T GONE UP AGAINST THE SHARINGAN IN A LONG TIME.
BUT YOU NEEDN'T BE AFRAID.
SEVERAL TACTICS CAN HANDLE OCULAR JUTSU...
WELL, WHAT DO WE DO?!

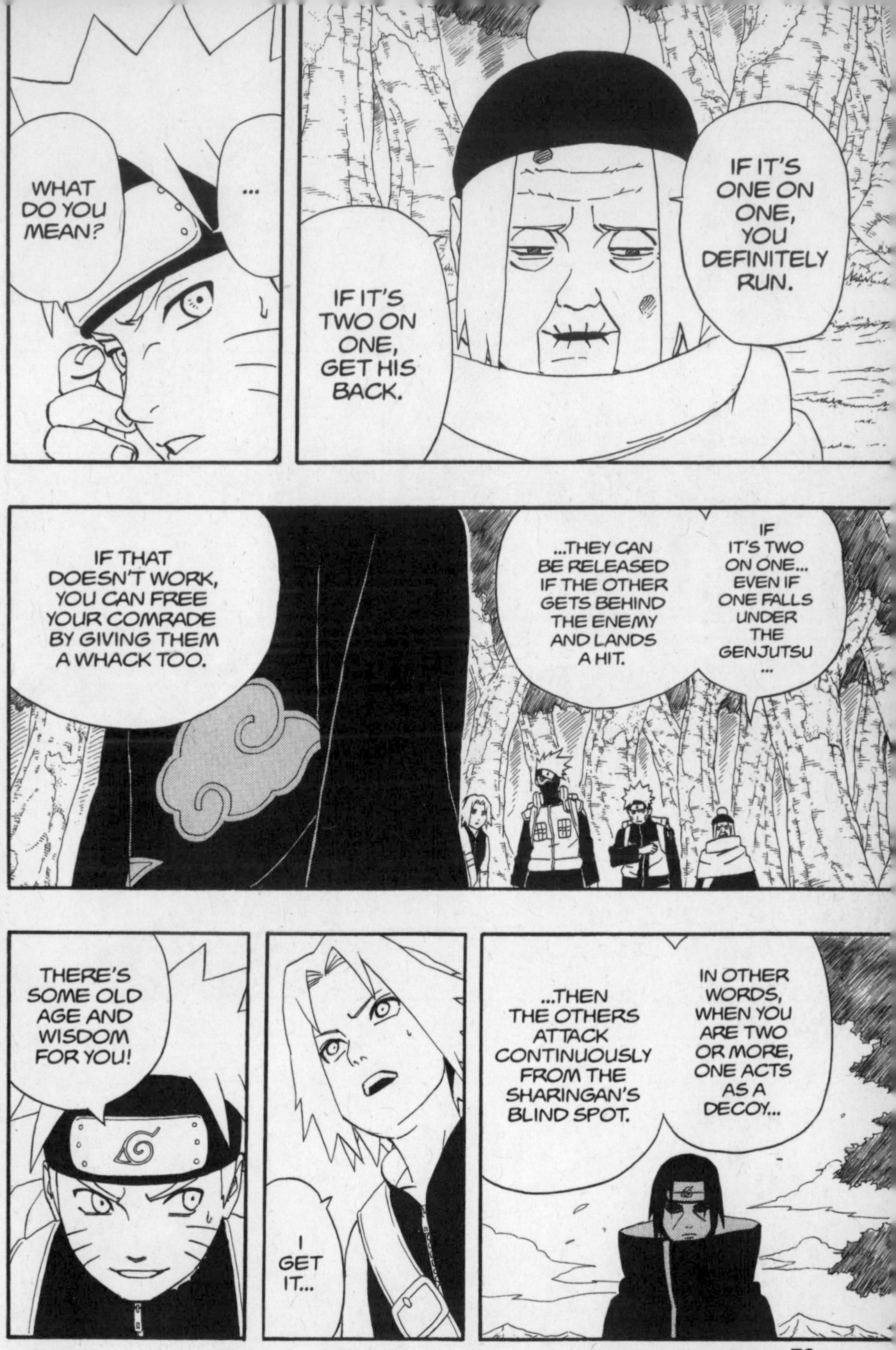
IF IT'S ONE ON ONE, YOU DEFINITELY RUN.
IF IT'S TWO ON ONE, GET HIS BACK.
...
WHAT DO YOU MEAN?
IF IT'S TWO ON ONE... EVEN IF ONE FALLS UNDER THE GENJUTSU ...
...THEY CAN BE RELEASED IF THE OTHER GETS BEHIND THE ENEMY AND LANDS A HIT.
IF THAT DOESN'T WORK, YOU CAN FREE YOUR COMRADE BY GIVING THEM A WHACK TOO.
IN OTHER WORDS, WHEN YOU ARE TWO OR MORE, ONE ACTS AS A DECOY...
...THEN THE OTHERS ATTACK CONTINUOUSLY FROM THE SHARINGAN'S BLIND SPOT.
I GET IT...
THERE'S SOME OLD AGE AND WISDOM FOR YOU!

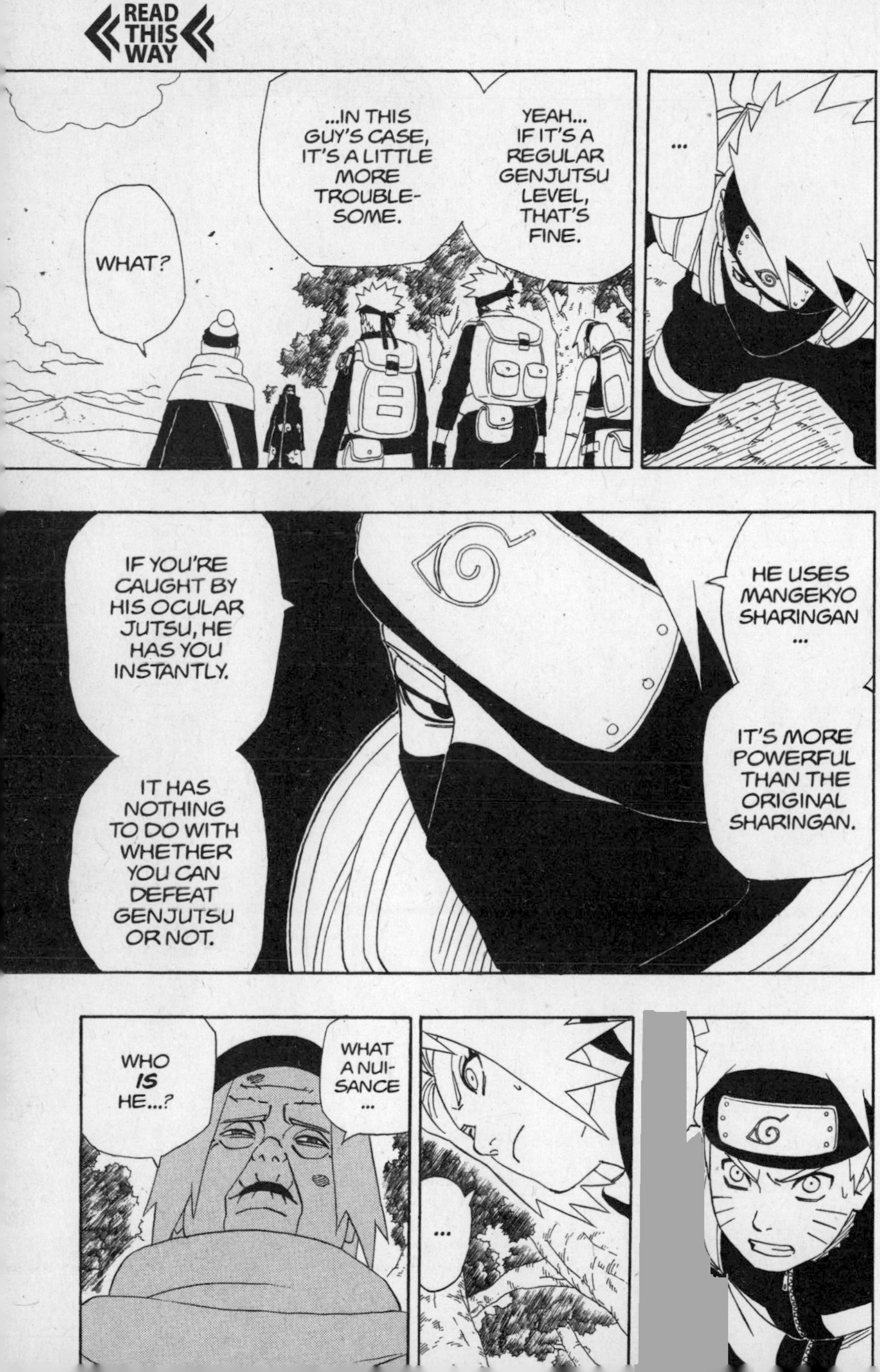
READ THIS WAY
...
YEAH... IF IT'S A REGULAR GENJUTSU LEVEL, THAT'S FINE.
...IN THIS GUY'S CASE, IT'S A LITTLE MORE TROUBLE-SOME.
WHAT?
HE USES MANGEKYO SHARINGAN ...
IT'S MORE POWERFUL THAN THE ORIGINAL SHARINGAN.
IF YOU'RE CAUGHT BY HIS OCULAR JUTSU, HE HAS YOU INSTANTLY.
IT HAS NOTHING TO DO WITH WHETHER YOU CAN DEFEAT GENJUTSU OR NOT.
...
WHAT A NUI-SANCE ...
WHO *IS* HE...?

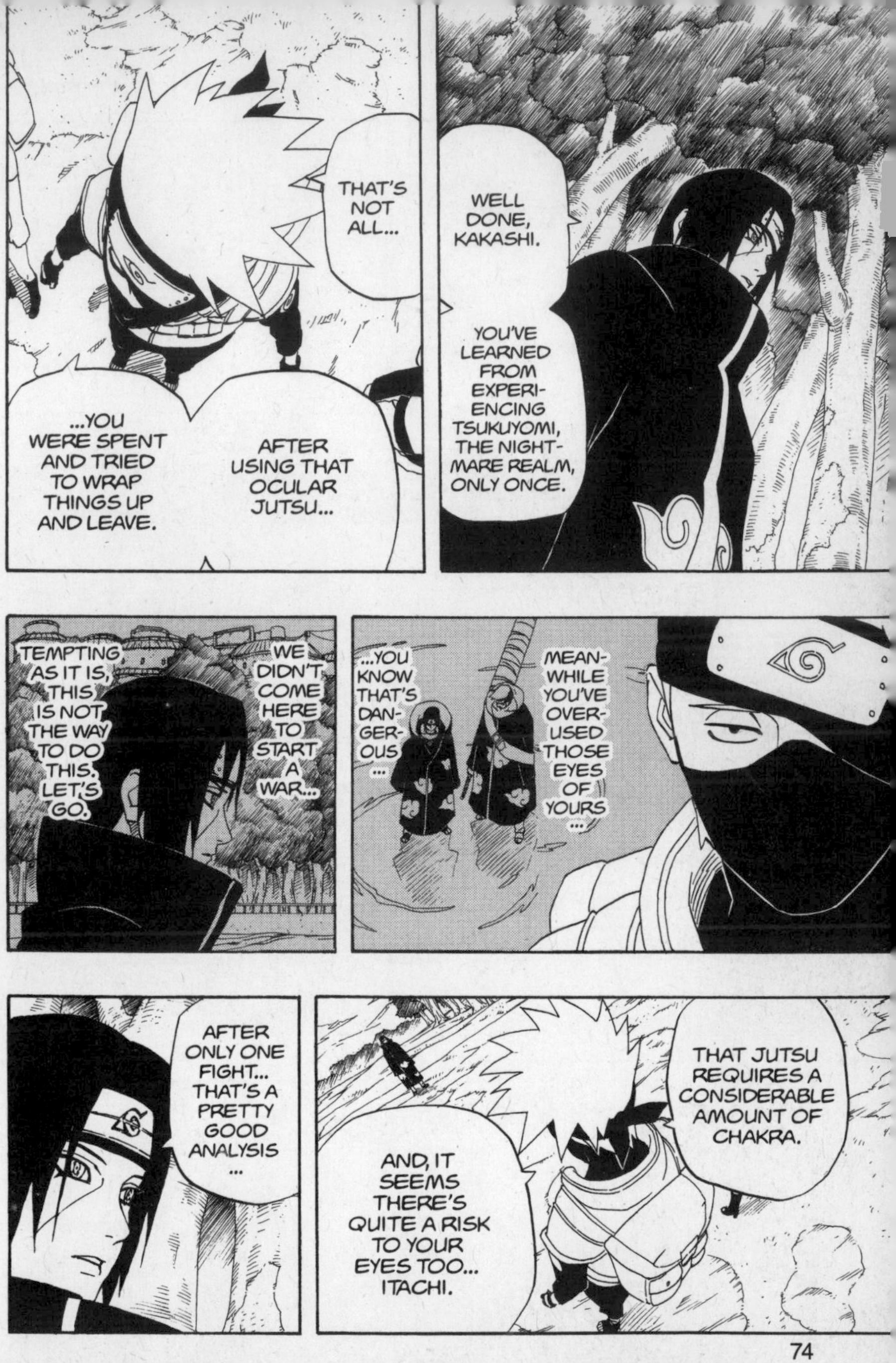
WELL DONE, KAKASHI.
YOU'VE LEARNED FROM EXPERIENCING TSUKUYOMI, THE NIGHTMARE REALM, ONLY ONCE.
THAT'S NOT ALL...
AFTER USING THAT OCULAR JUTSU...
...YOU WERE SPENT AND TRIED TO WRAP THINGS UP AND LEAVE.
MEANWHILE YOU'VE OVERUSED THOSE EYES OF YOURS...
...YOU KNOW THAT'S DANGEROUS...
WE DIDN'T COME HERE TO START A WAR...
TEMPTING AS IT IS, THIS IS NOT THE WAY TO DO THIS. LET'S GO.
THAT JUTSU REQUIRES A CONSIDERABLE AMOUNT OF CHAKRA.
AND, IT SEEMS THERE'S QUITE A RISK TO YOUR EYES TOO... ITACHI.
AFTER ONLY ONE FIGHT... THAT'S A PRETTY GOOD ANALYSIS...

...OF YOUR EYESIGHT HAVE YOU LOST?

FWIP

HOW MUCH...

ITACHI!!

SH—

...

...

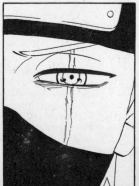

...

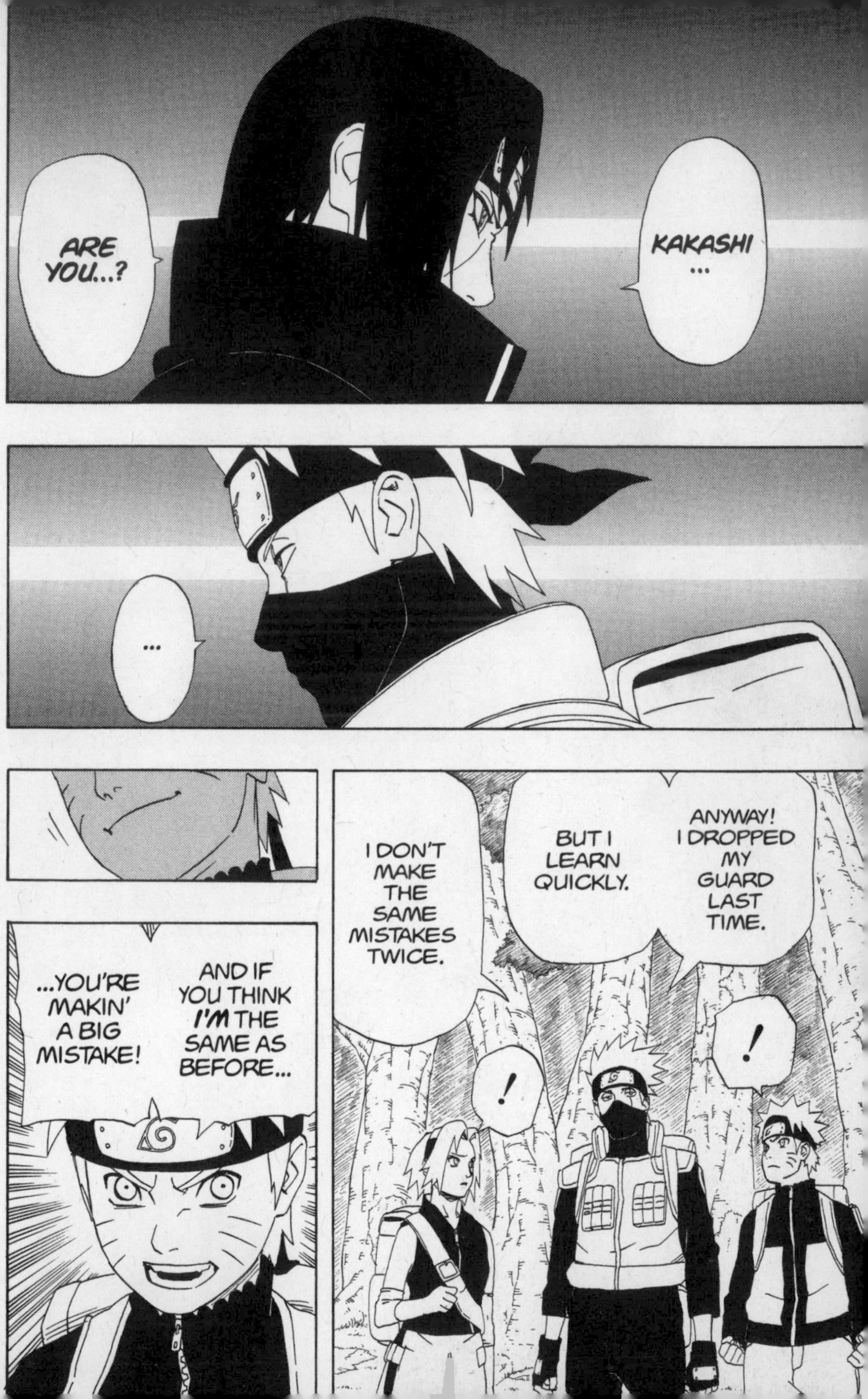
KAKASHI ...
ARE YOU...?
...
ANYWAY! I DROPPED MY GUARD LAST TIME.
BUT I LEARN QUICKLY.
I DON'T MAKE THE SAME MISTAKES TWICE.
!
!
AND IF YOU THINK *I'M* THE SAME AS BEFORE...
...YOU'RE MAKIN' A BIG MISTAKE!

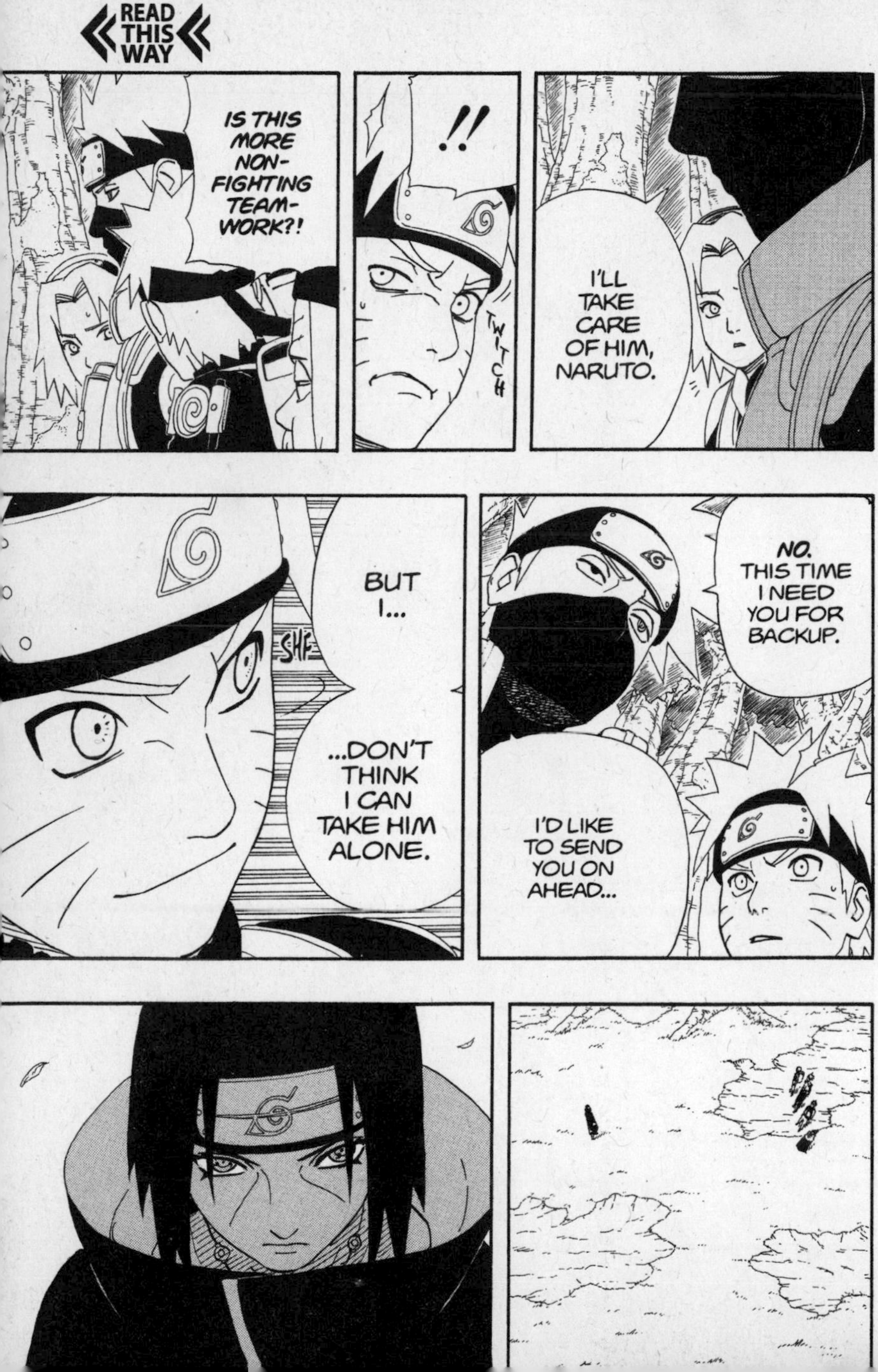
READ THIS WAY
I'LL TAKE CARE OF HIM, NARUTO.
!!
TWITCH
IS THIS MORE NON-FIGHTING TEAM-WORK?!
NO. THIS TIME I NEED YOU FOR BACKUP.
I'D LIKE TO SEND YOU ON AHEAD...
BUT I...
SHF
...DON'T THINK I CAN TAKE HIM ALONE.

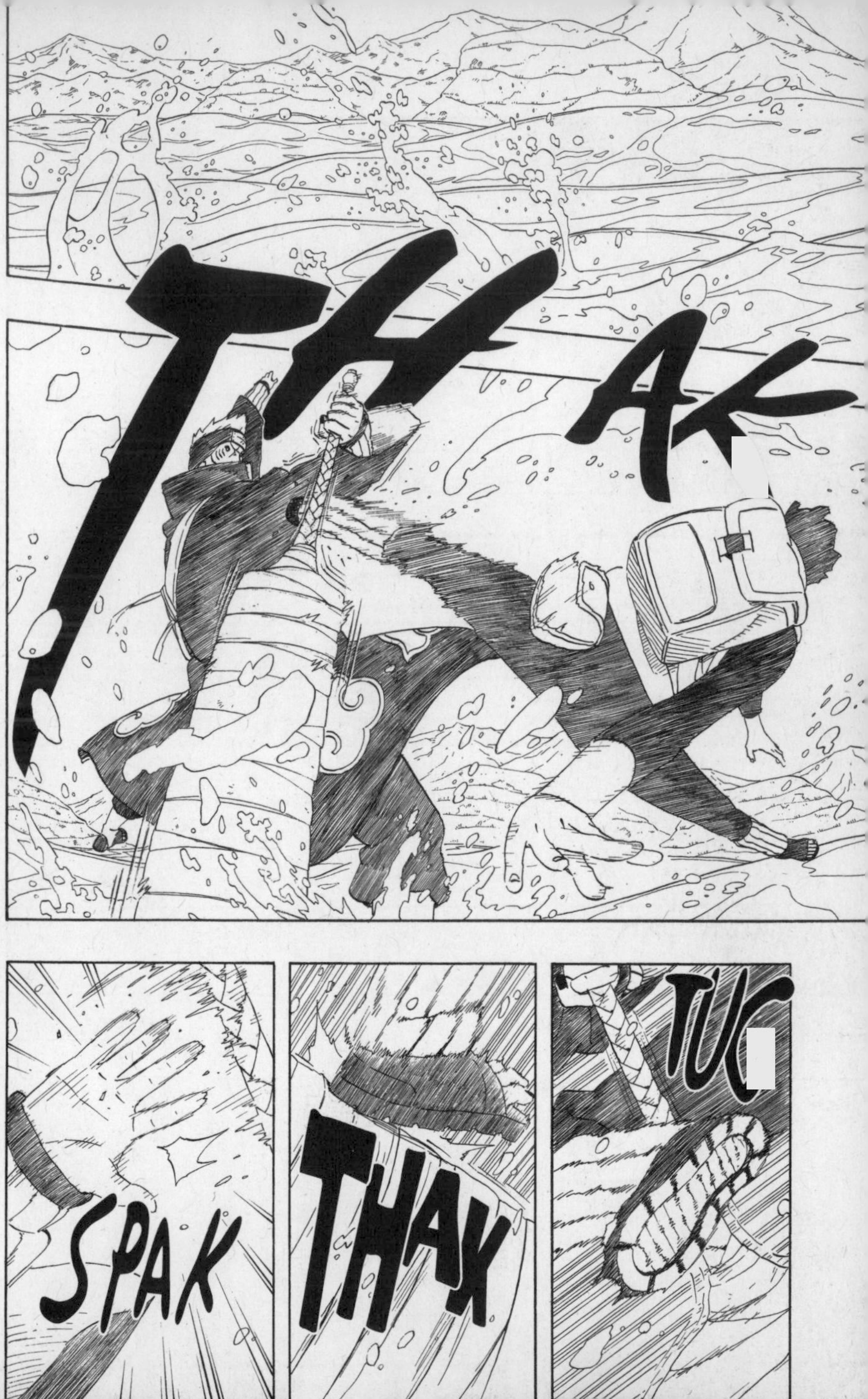
THAK
TUG
THAK
SPAK

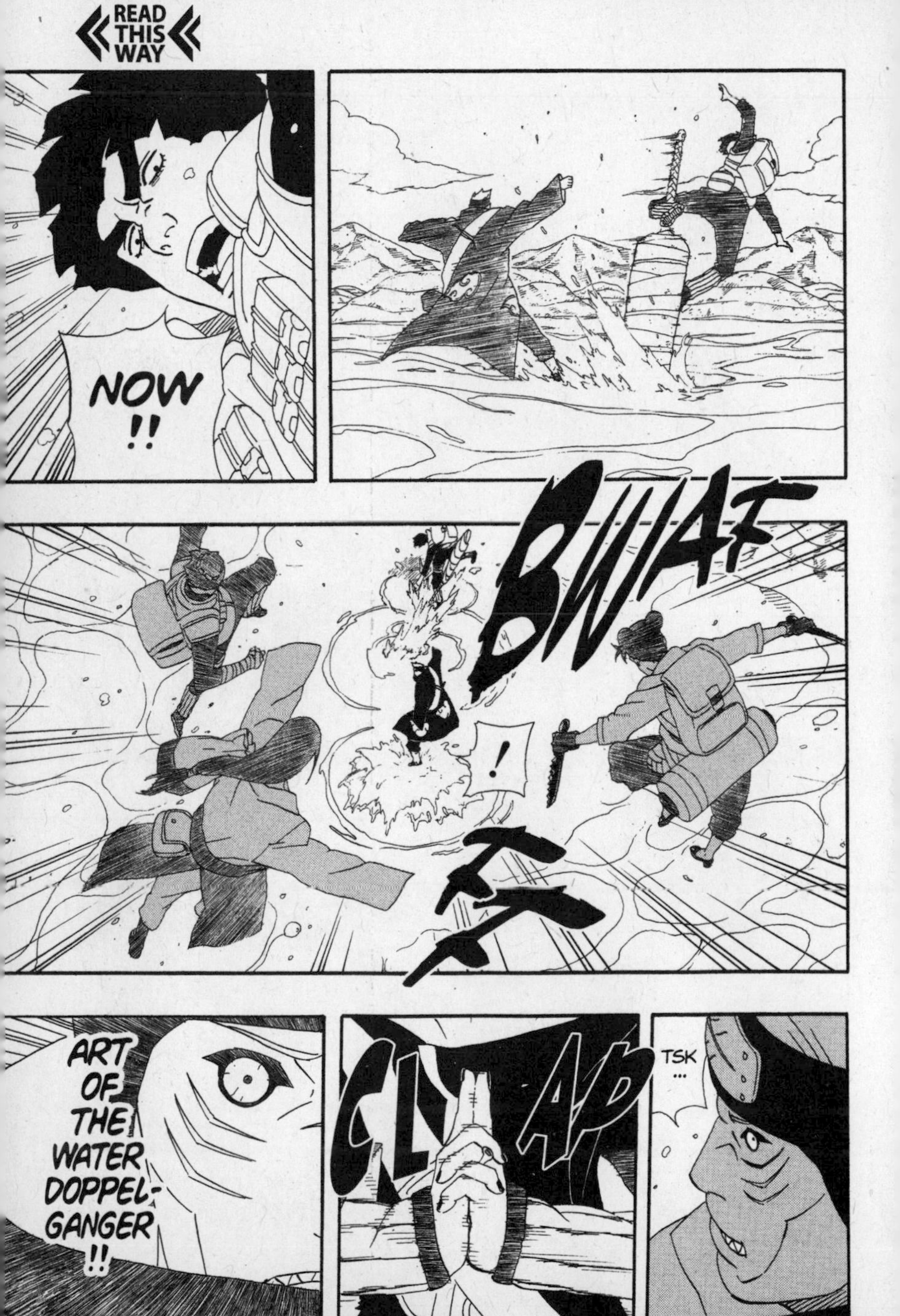
READ THIS WAY
NOW !!
BWAF
!
TSK ...
CLAP
ART OF THE WATER DOPPEL-GANGER !!

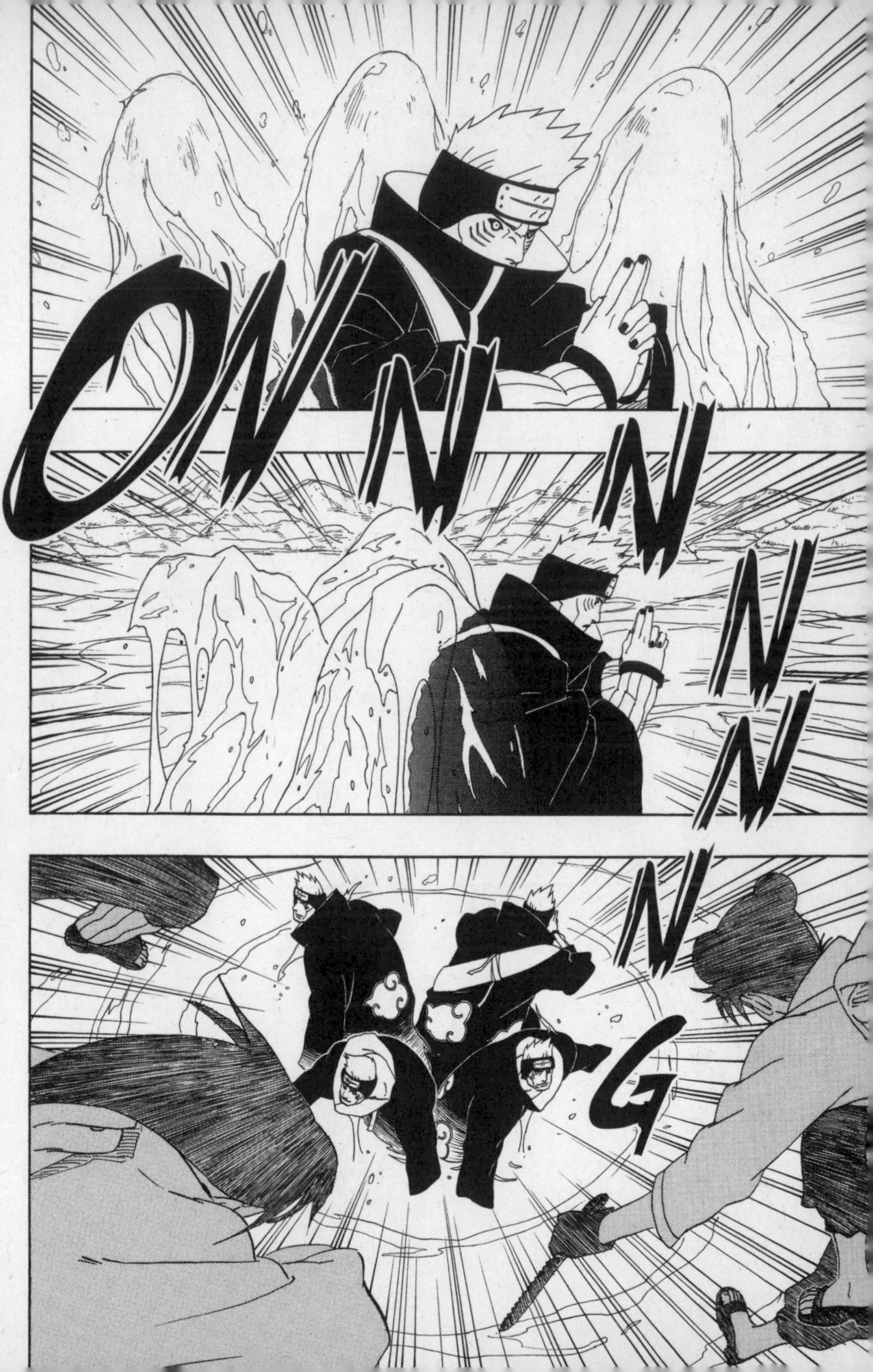
OWNNNNNNNNG

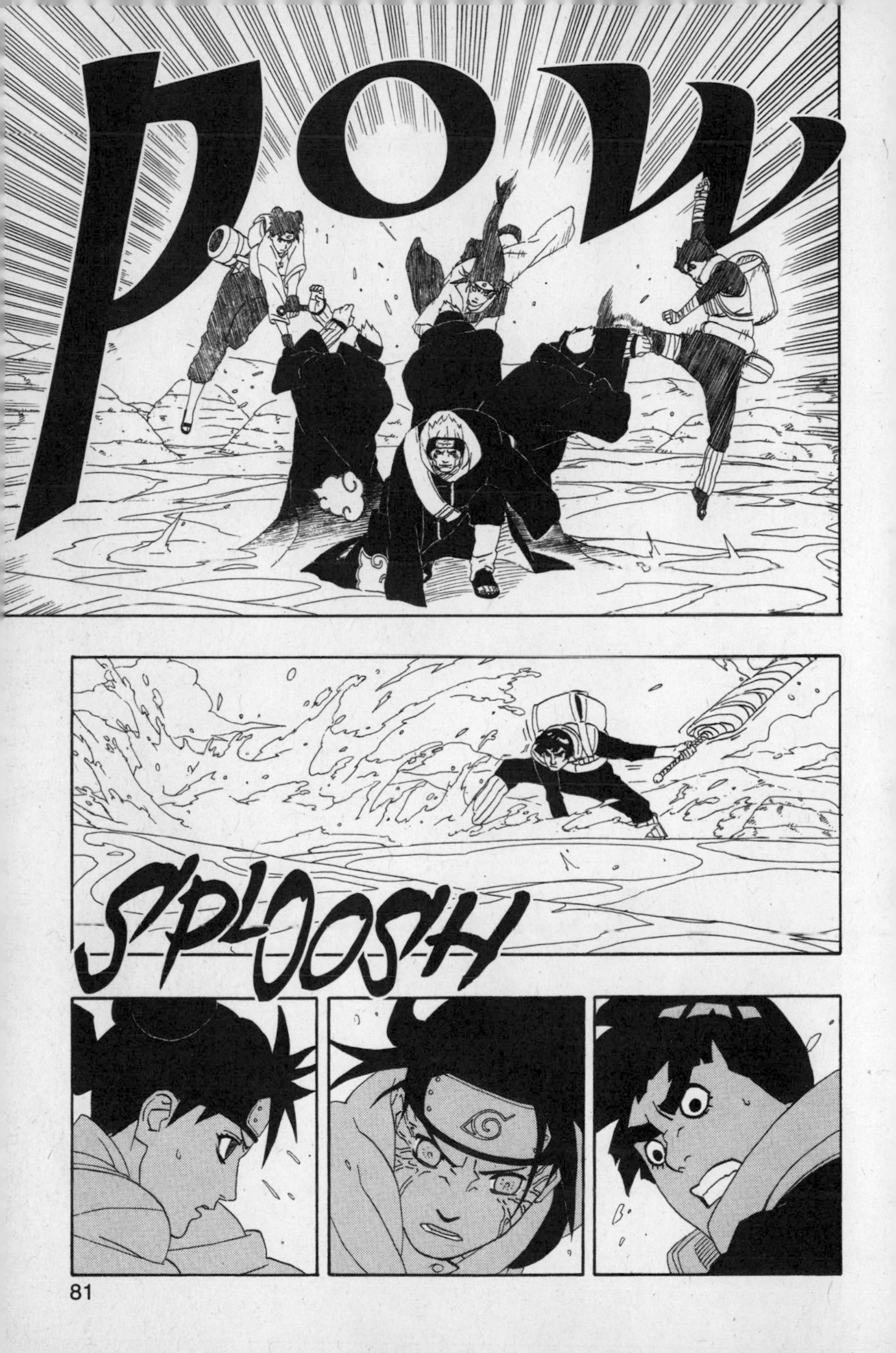
POW
SPLOOSH

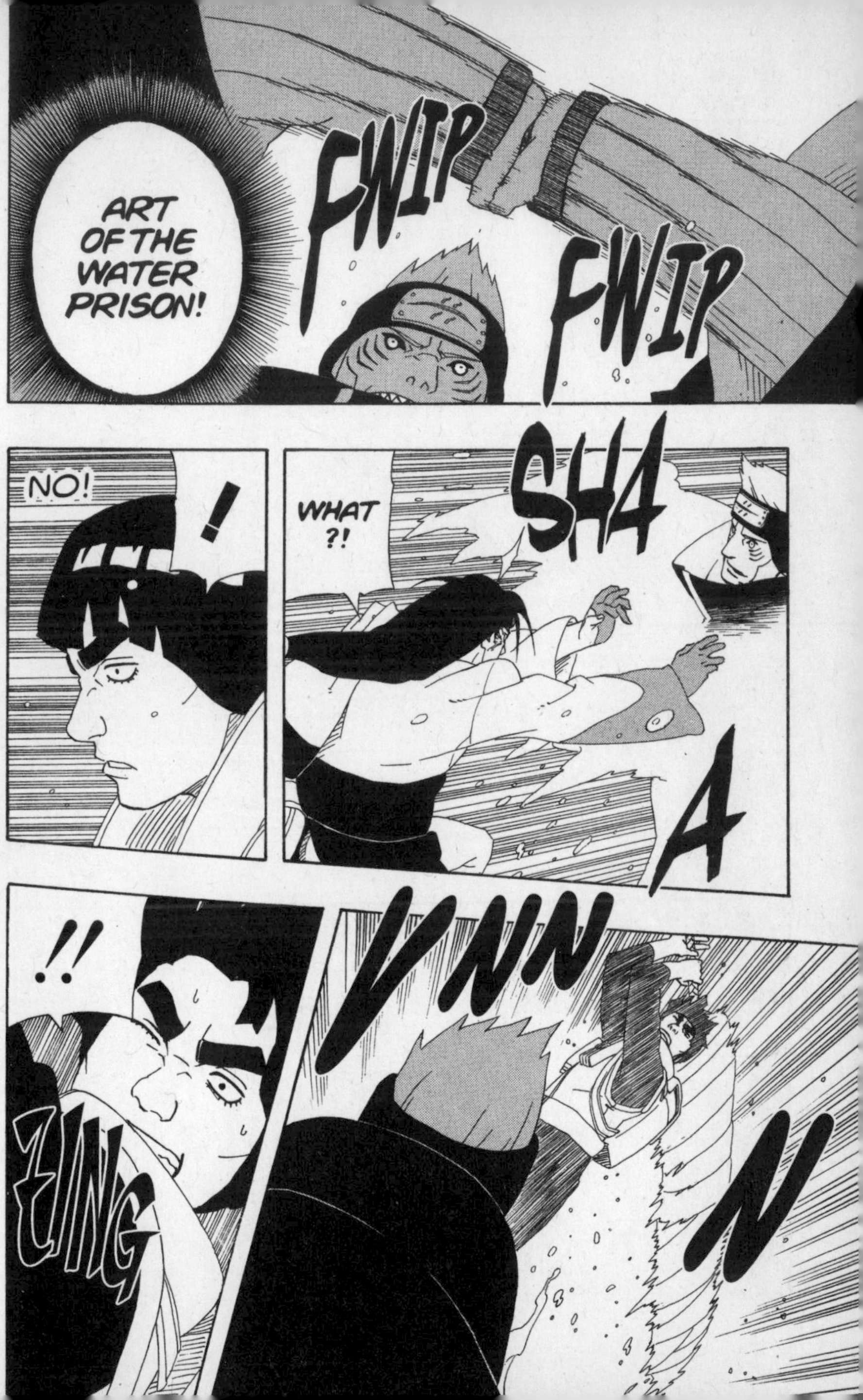
ART OF THE WATER PRISON!
FWIP
FWIP
SHAA
WHAT ?!
!
NO!
VNNN
!!
ZING

READ THIS WAY

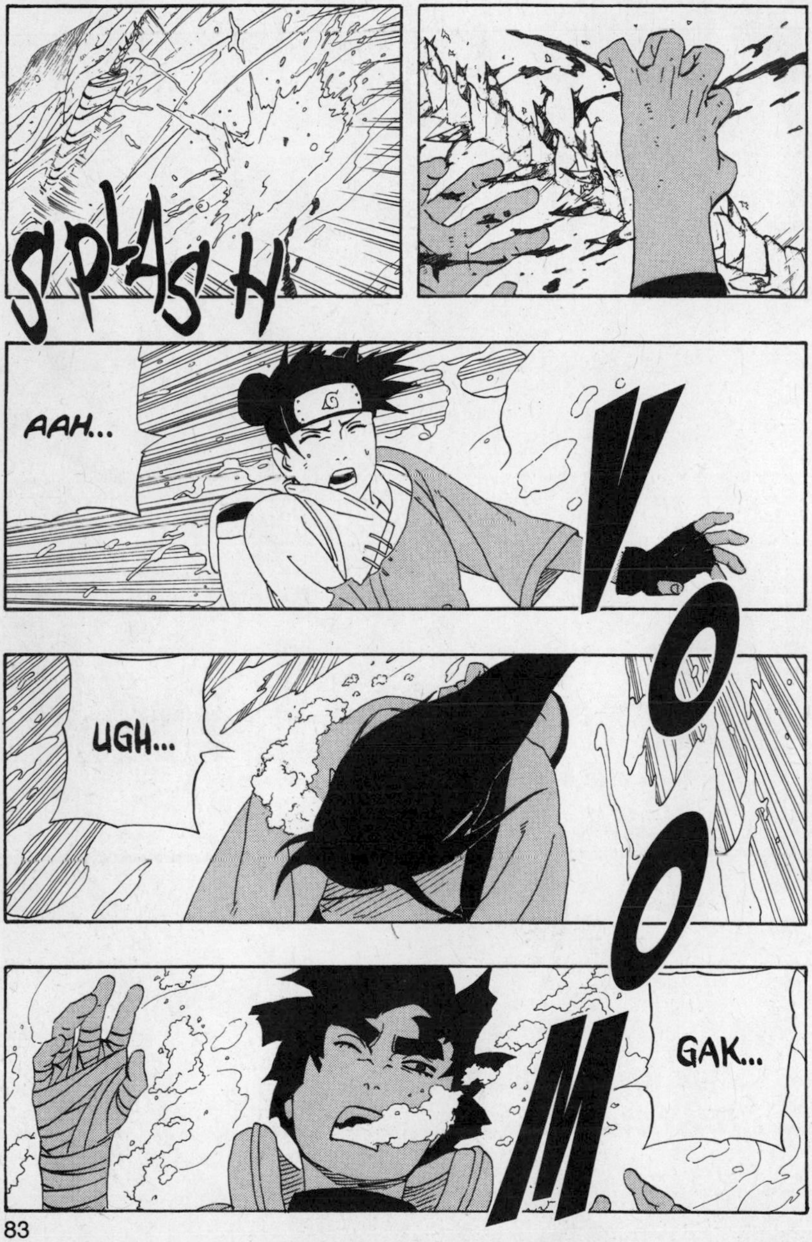
SPLASH
AAH...
VOOOM
UGH...
GAK...

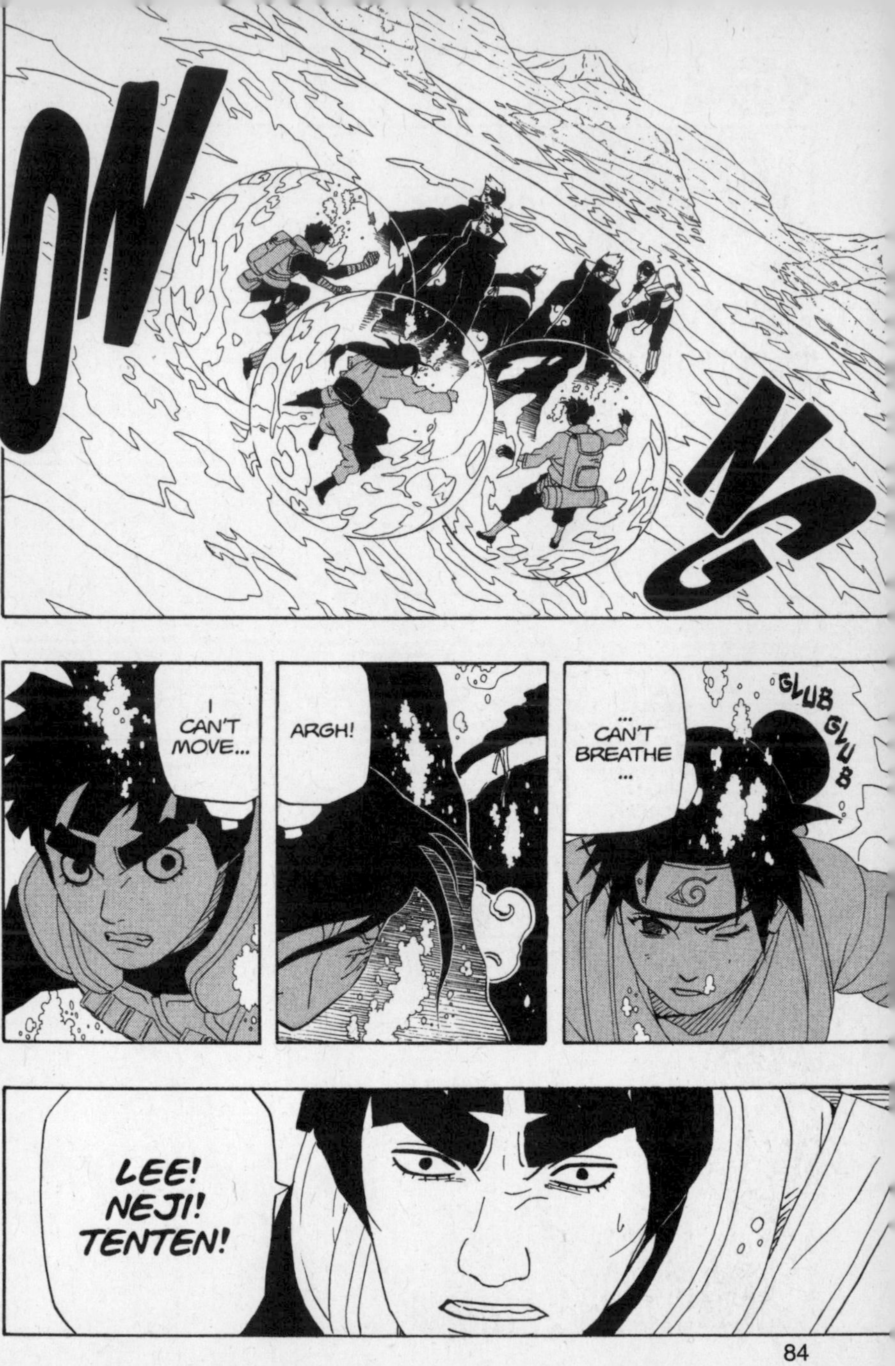
... CAN'T BREATHE ...
GLUB GLUB
ARGH!
I CAN'T MOVE...
LEE! NEJI! TENTEN!

READ THIS WAY

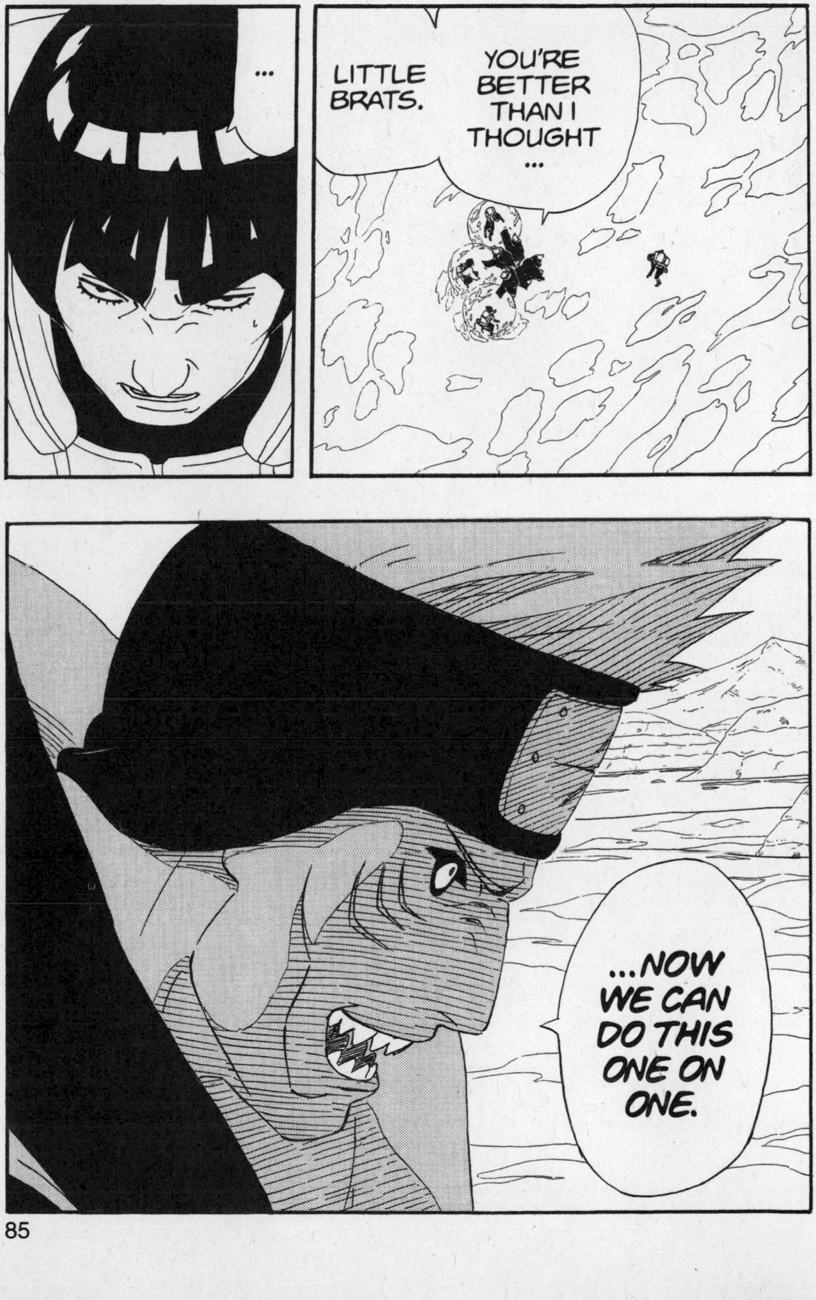
YOU'RE BETTER THAN I THOUGHT ...
LITTLE BRATS.
...
...NOW WE CAN DO THIS ONE ON ONE.

NARUTO

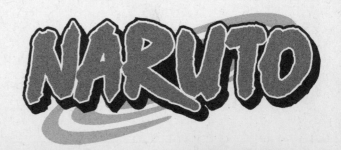

Number 258: Guy vs. Kisame!!

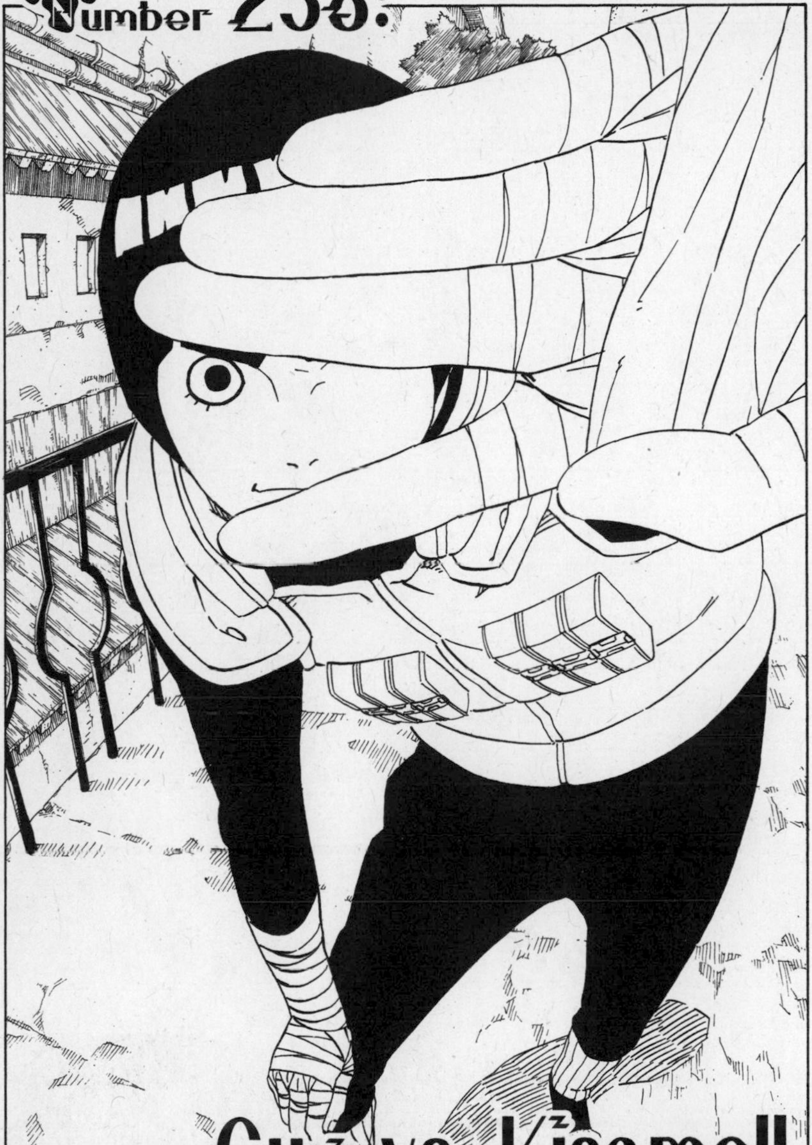

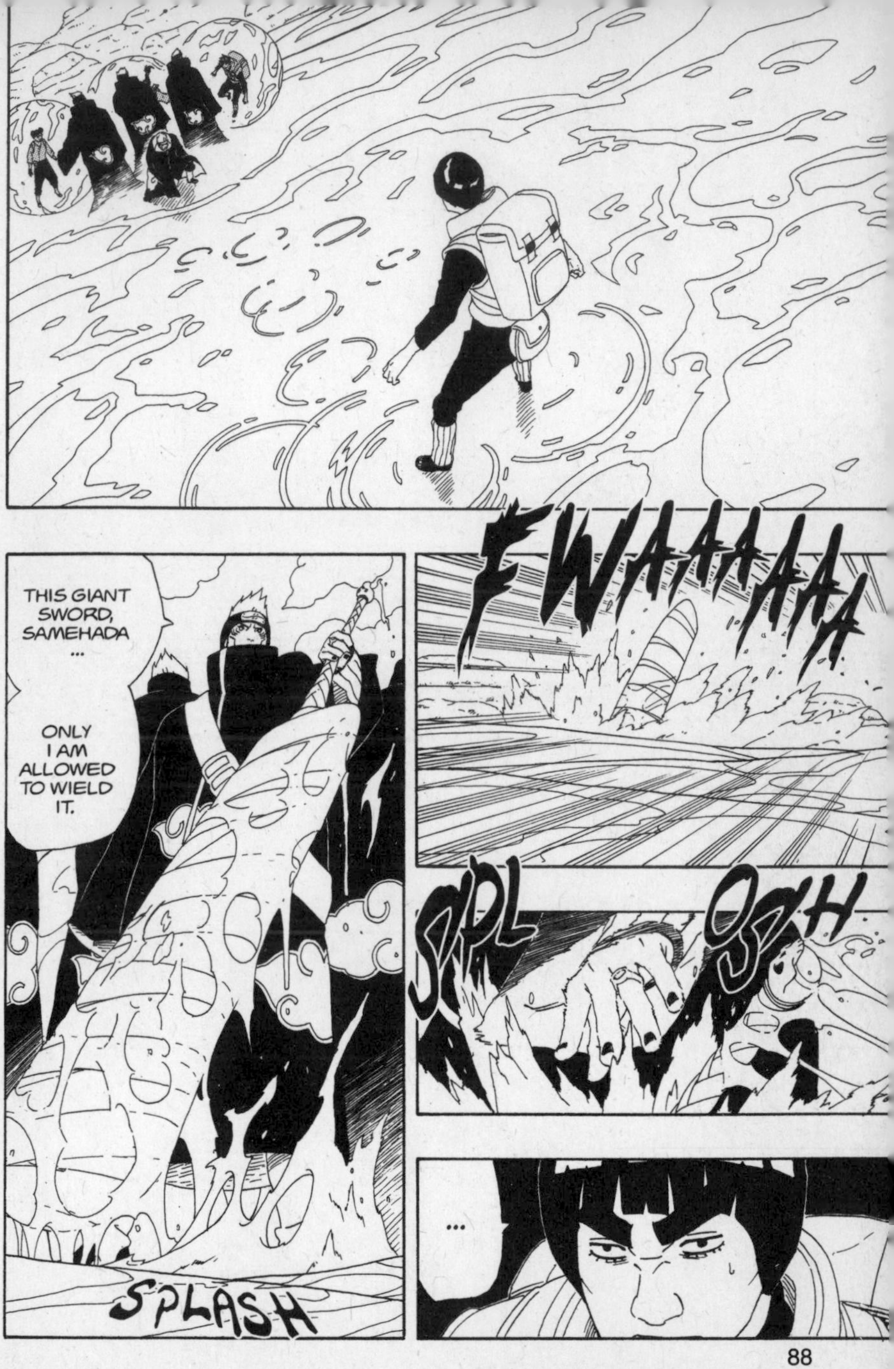
FWAAAAAA
SPLOSH
...
THIS GIANT SWORD, SAMEHADA ...
ONLY I AM ALLOWED TO WIELD IT.
SPLASH

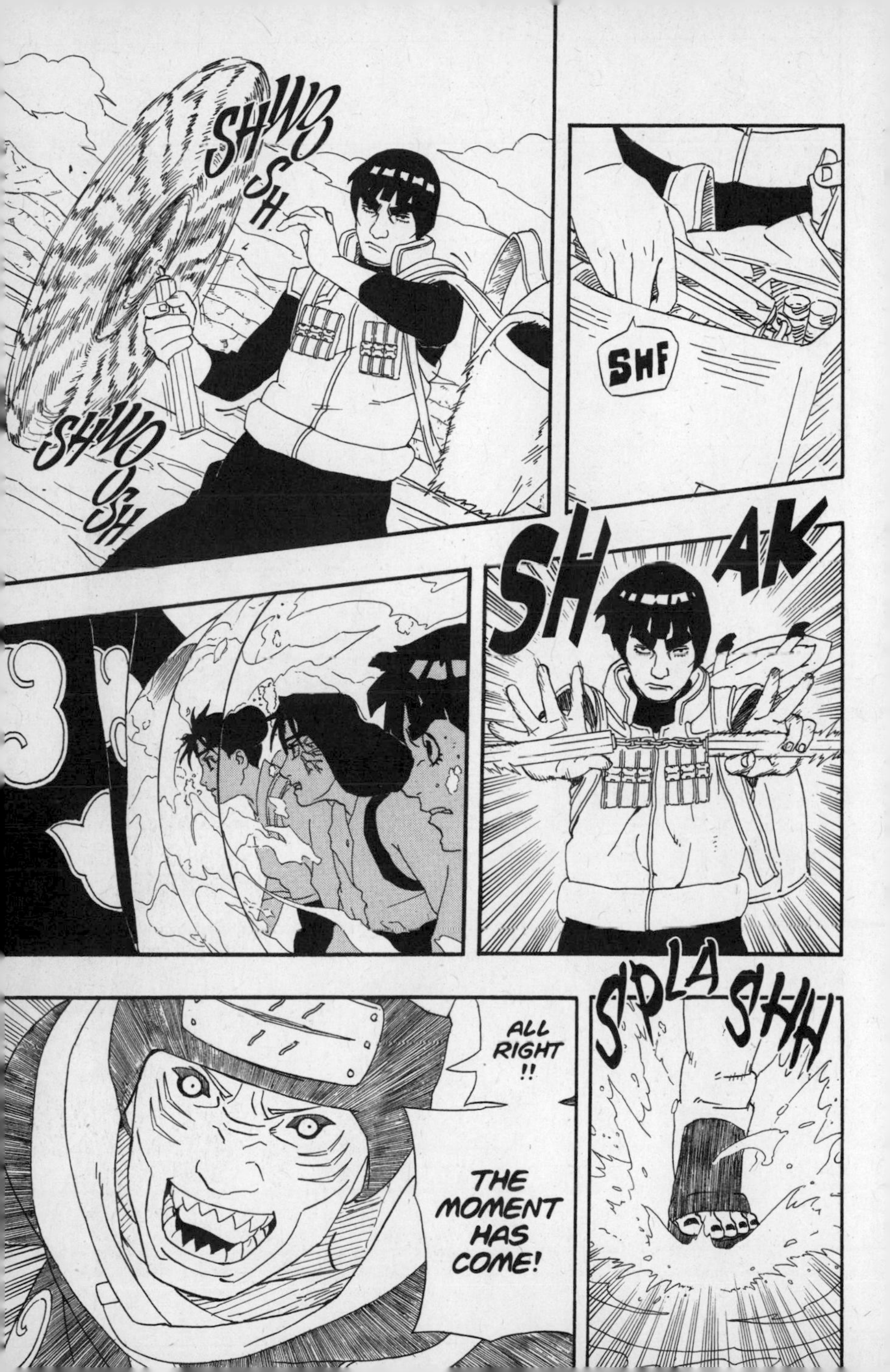
SHF
SHWOOSH
SHWOOSH
SHAK
SPLASHH
ALL RIGHT!!
THE MOMENT HAS COME!

FWP

IT'S ABOUT TIME FOR YOU TO COME WITH ME...

...NARUTO.

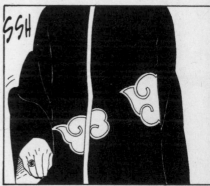

SSH

ZOOM

I'LL GO! YOU STAY BACK!

...

READ THIS WAY

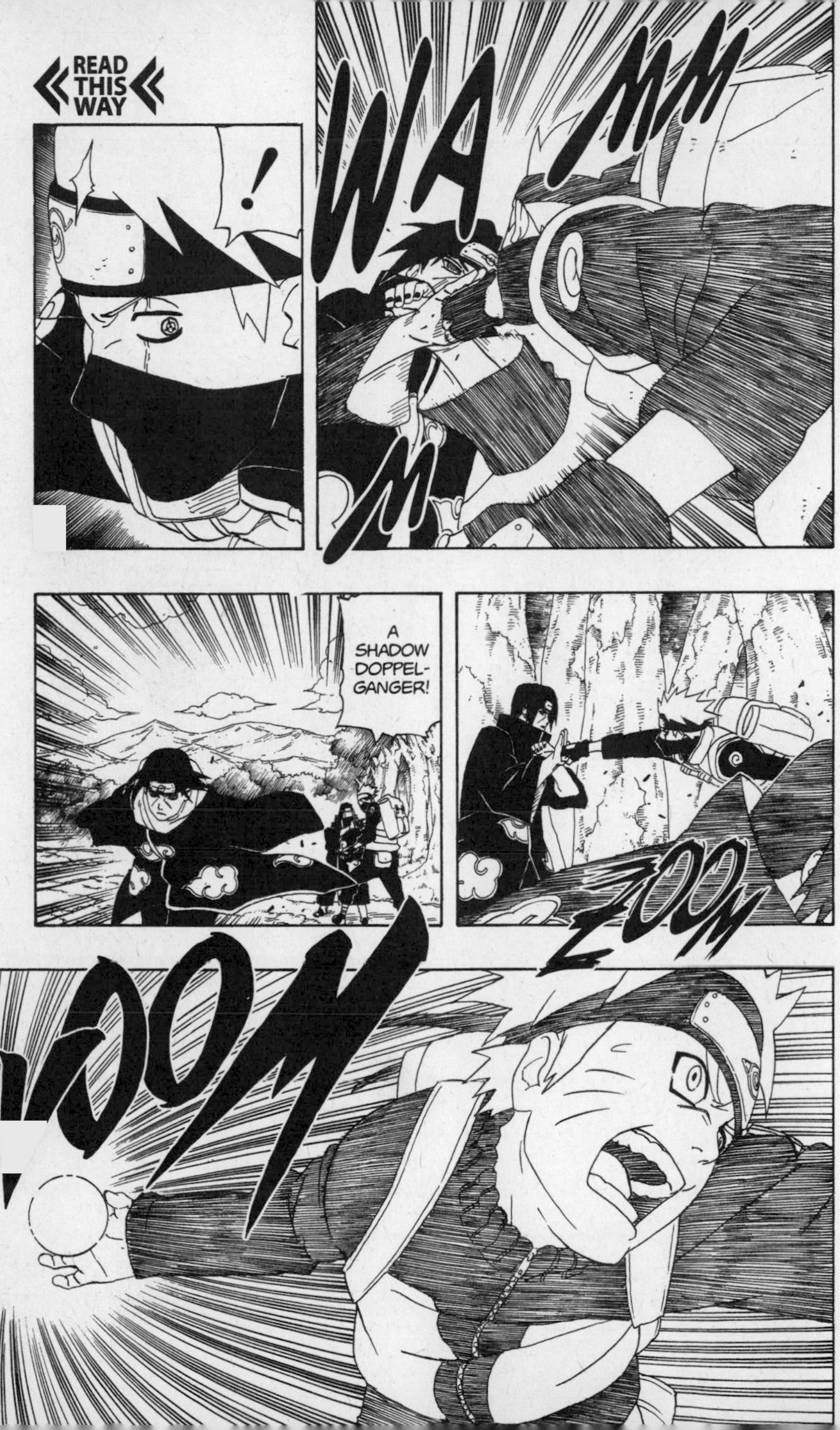
WAMM
!
ZOOM
A SHADOW DOPPEL-GANGER!

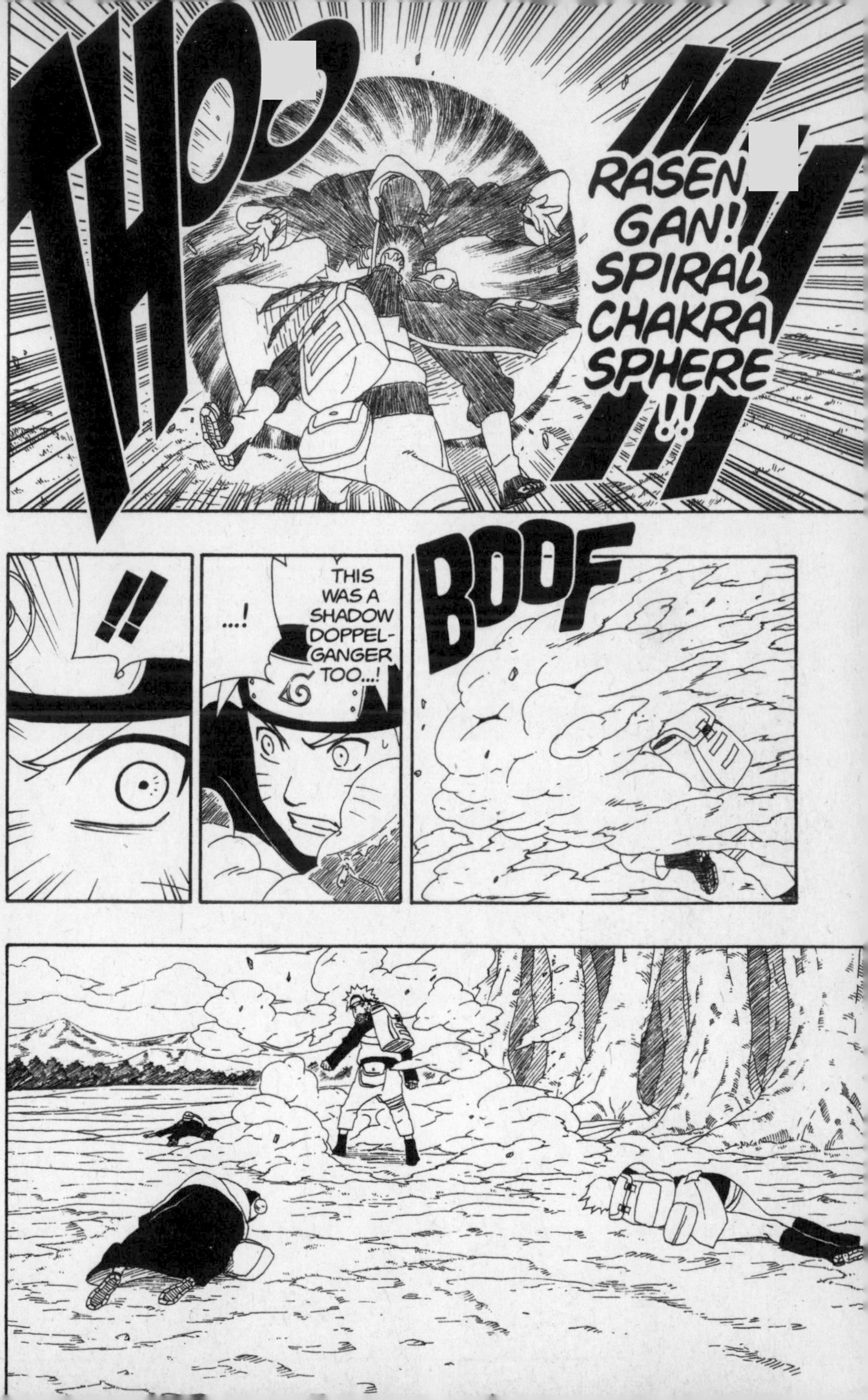
THOOM
RASEN GAN! SPIRAL CHAKRA SPHERE!!
BOOF
...!
THIS WAS A SHADOW DOPPEL-GANGER TOO...!
!!

READ THIS WAY

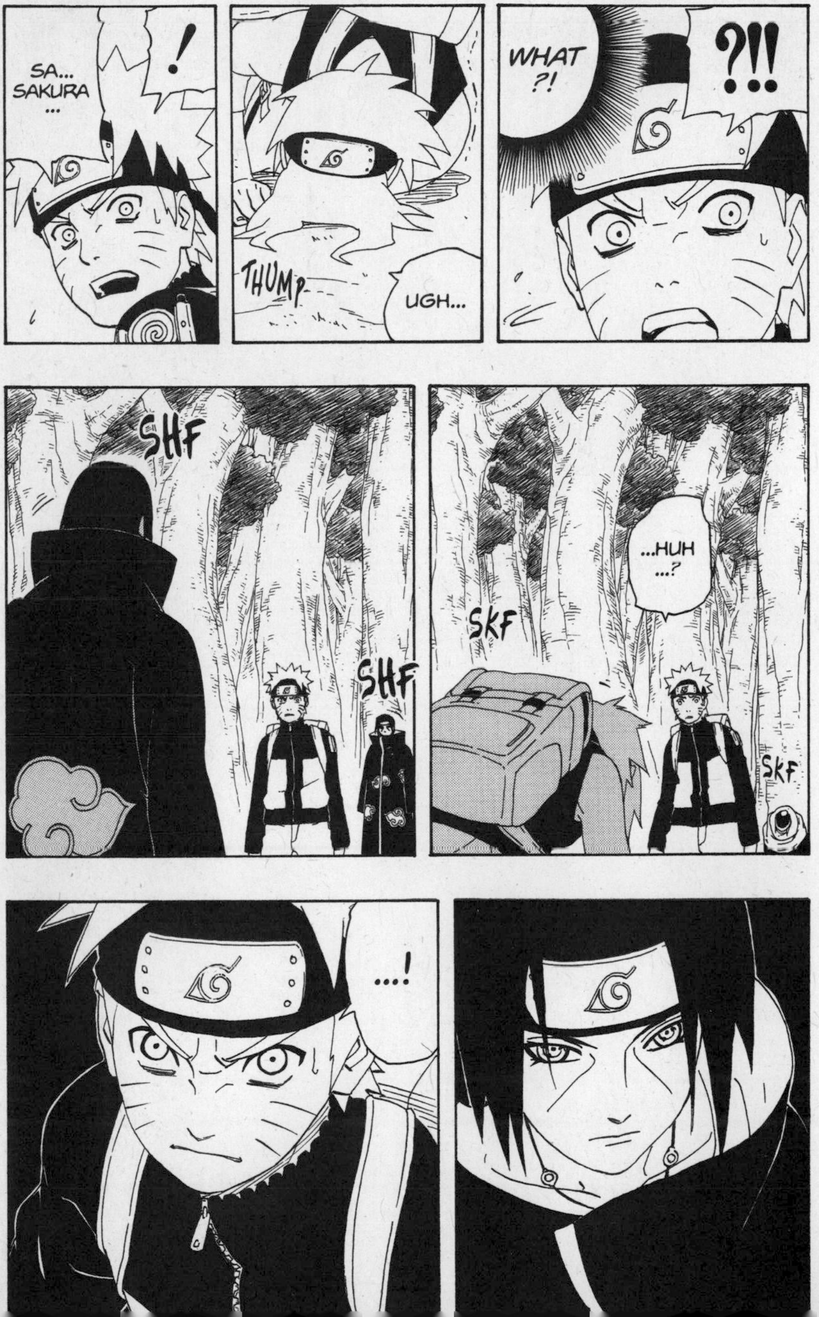

?!!
WHAT ?!
UGH...
THUMP
!
SA... SAKURA ...
...HUH ...?
SKF
SKF
SHF
SHF
...!

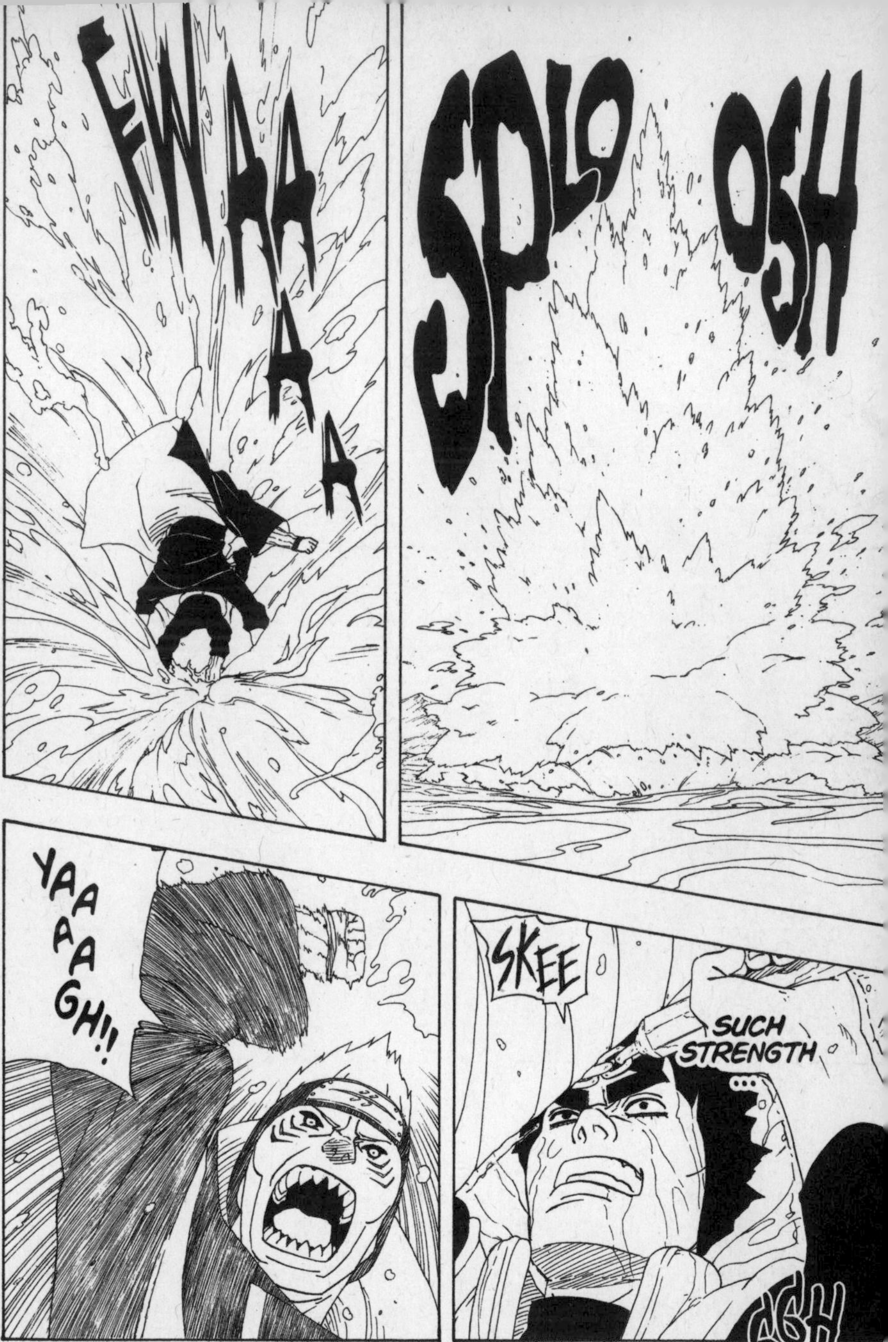
SPLOOSH
FWAAAA
SKEE
SUCH STRENGTH...
GGH
YAAAAGH!!

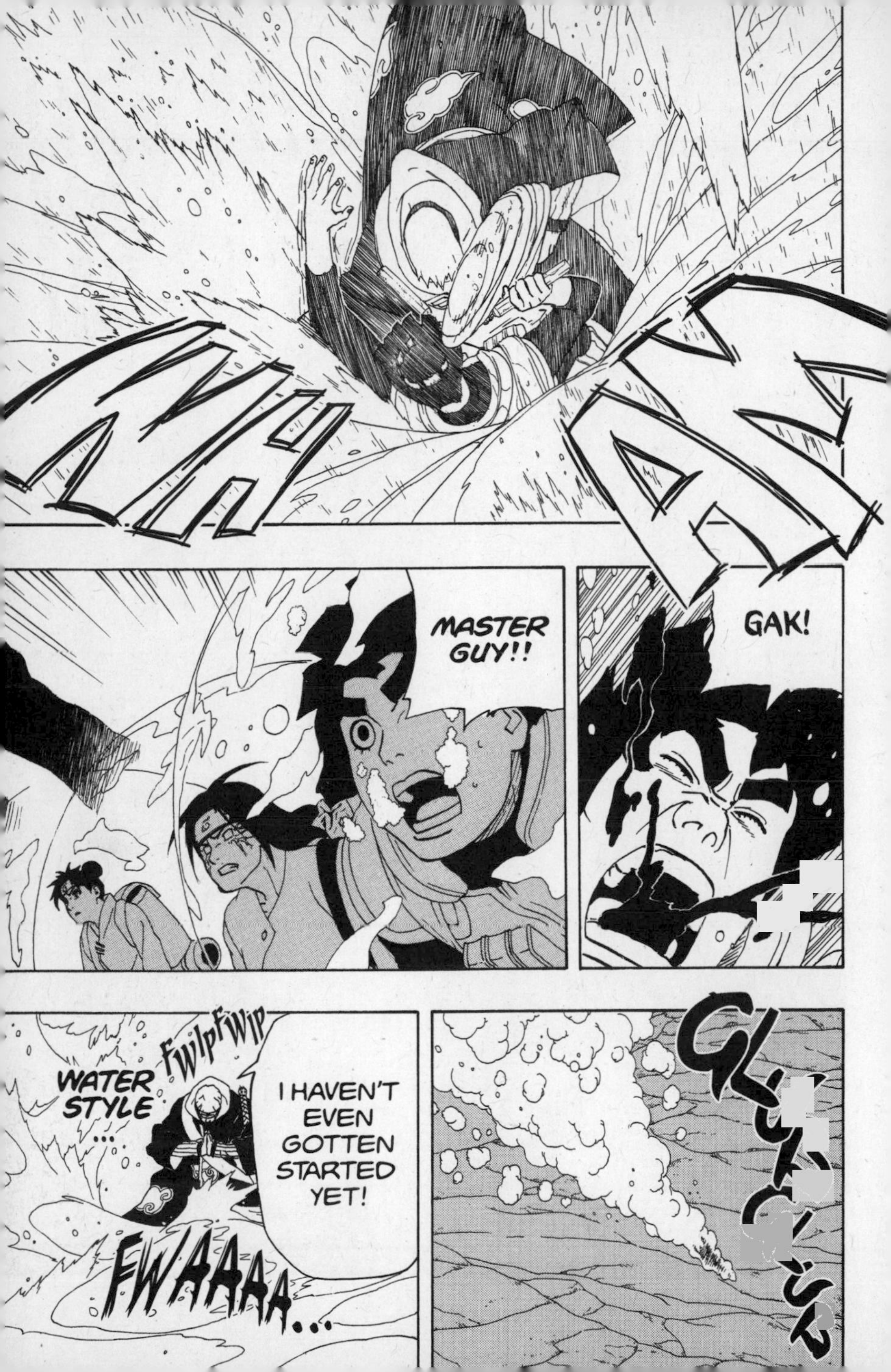
GAK!
MASTER GUY!!
I HAVEN'T EVEN GOTTEN STARTED YET!
FWIPFWIP
WATER STYLE...
FWAAAA...

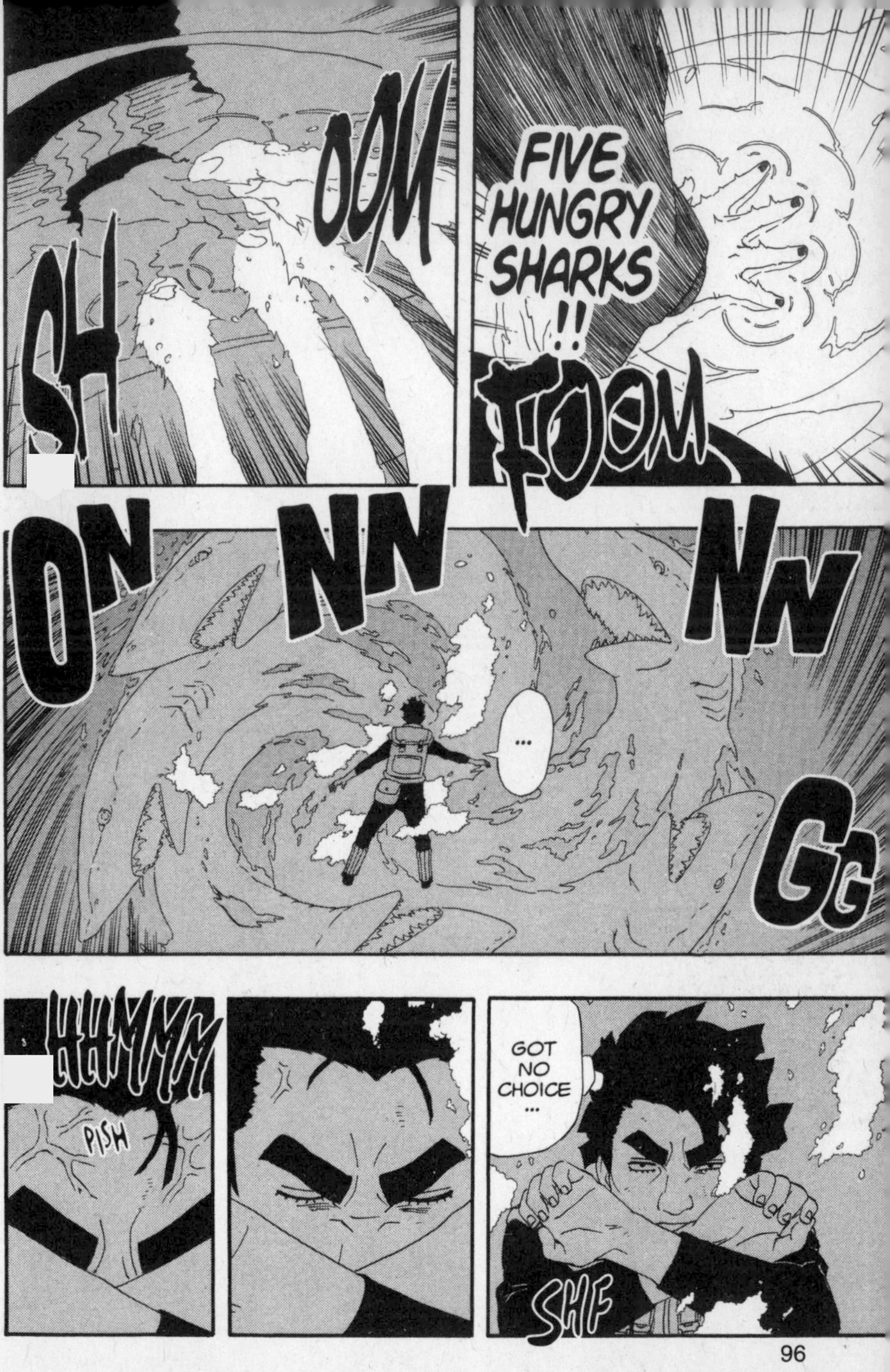
FIVE HUNGRY SHARKS !!
FOOM
SH
OOM
ON
NN
NN
GG
...
GOT NO CHOICE ...
SHF
HHMMM
PISH

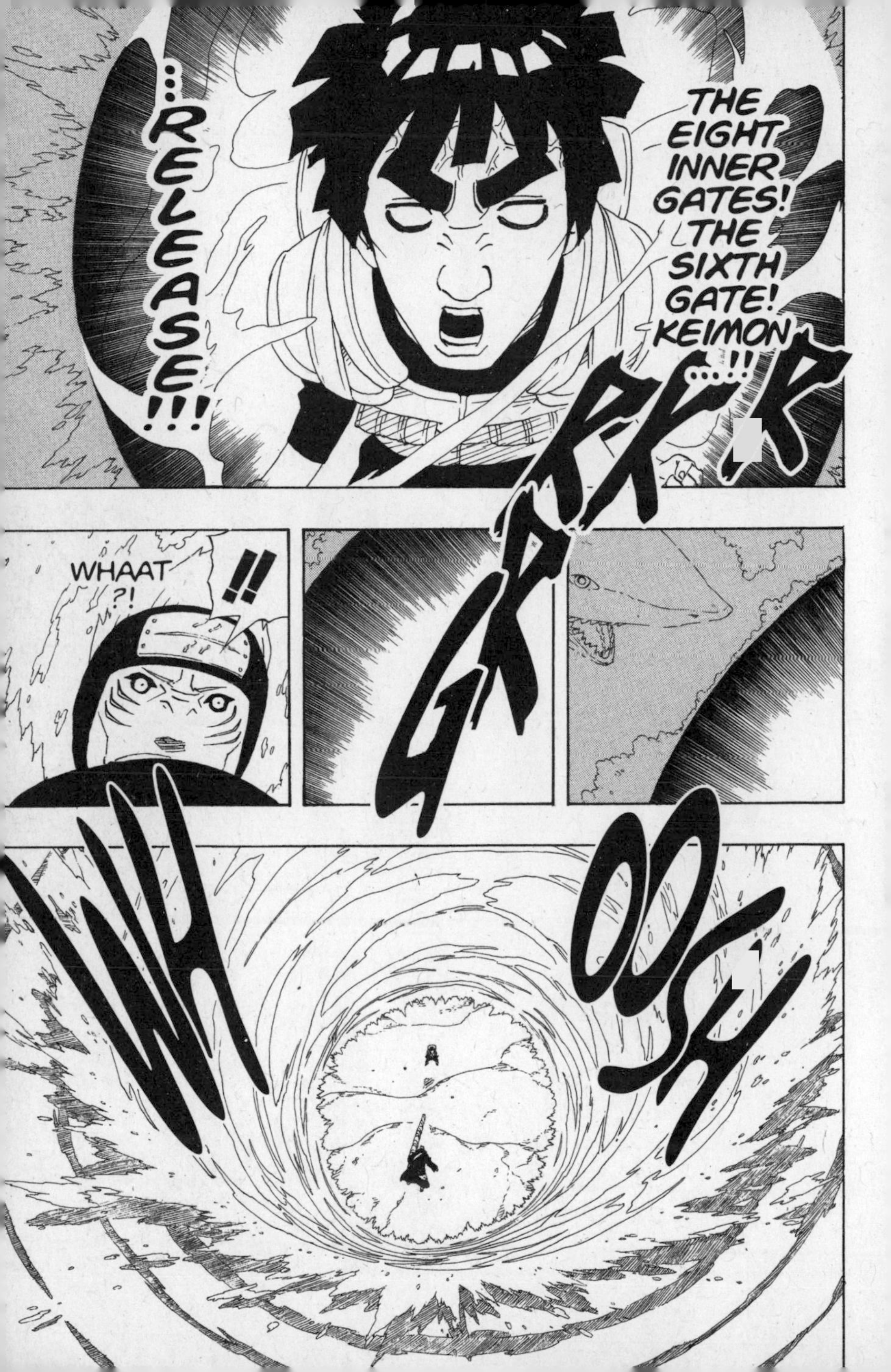
THE EIGHT INNER GATES! THE SIXTH GATE! KEIMON...!!
...RELEASE!!!
GRRRR
WHAAT?!
!!
WHOOSH

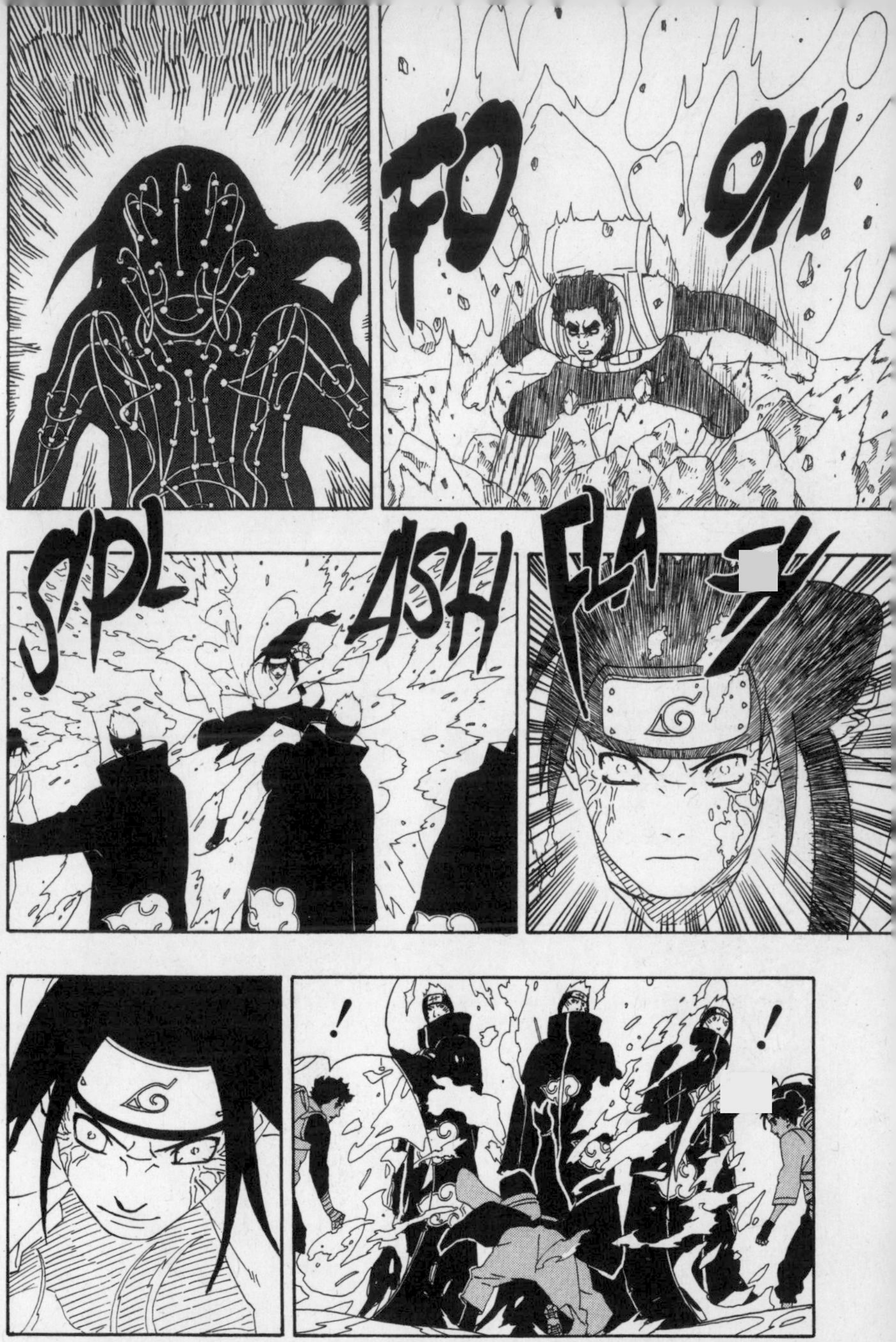
FOOM
FLASH
SPLASH
!
!

READ THIS WAY

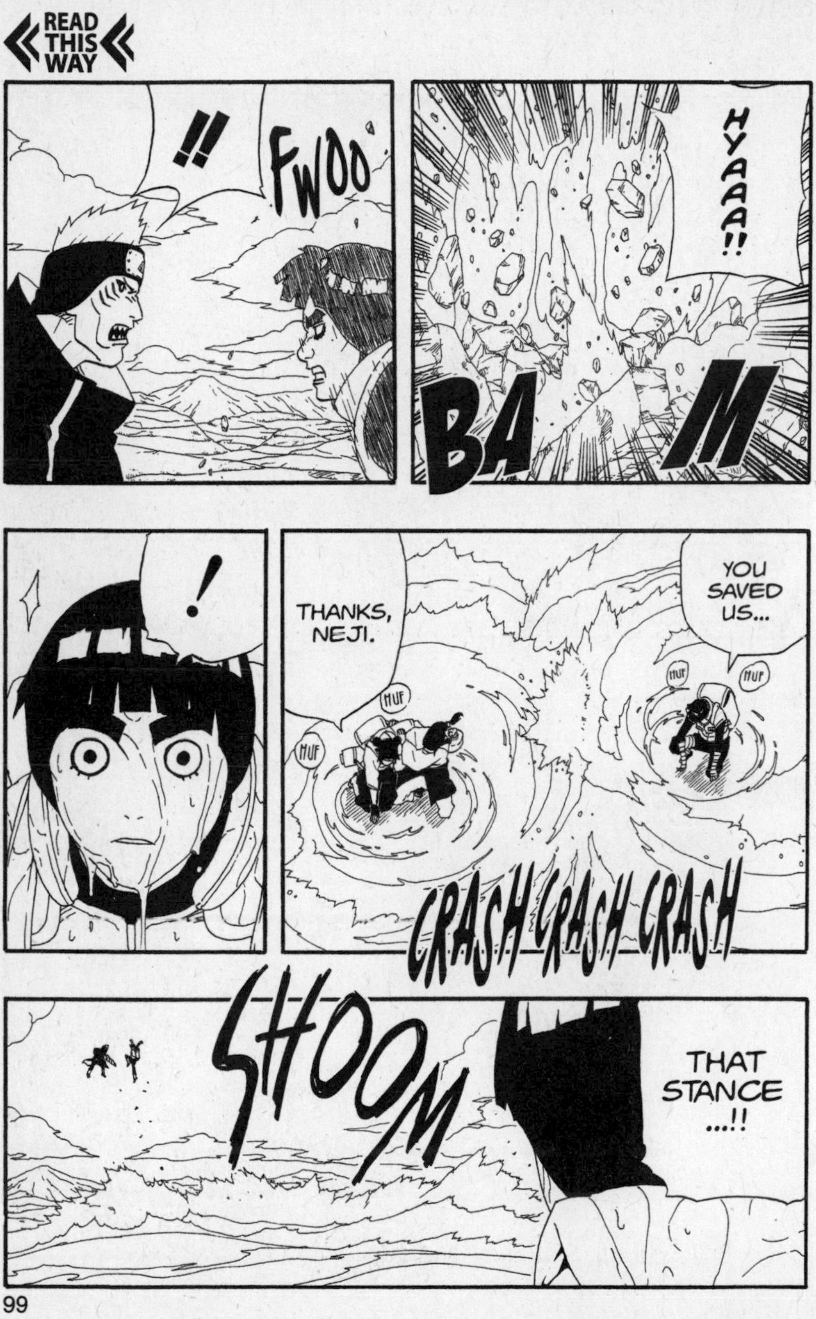
HYAAAA!!
BAM
!!
FWOO
YOU SAVED US...
HUF
HUF
THANKS, NEJI.
HUF
HUF
CRASH CRASH CRASH
!
THAT STANCE ...!!
SHOOM

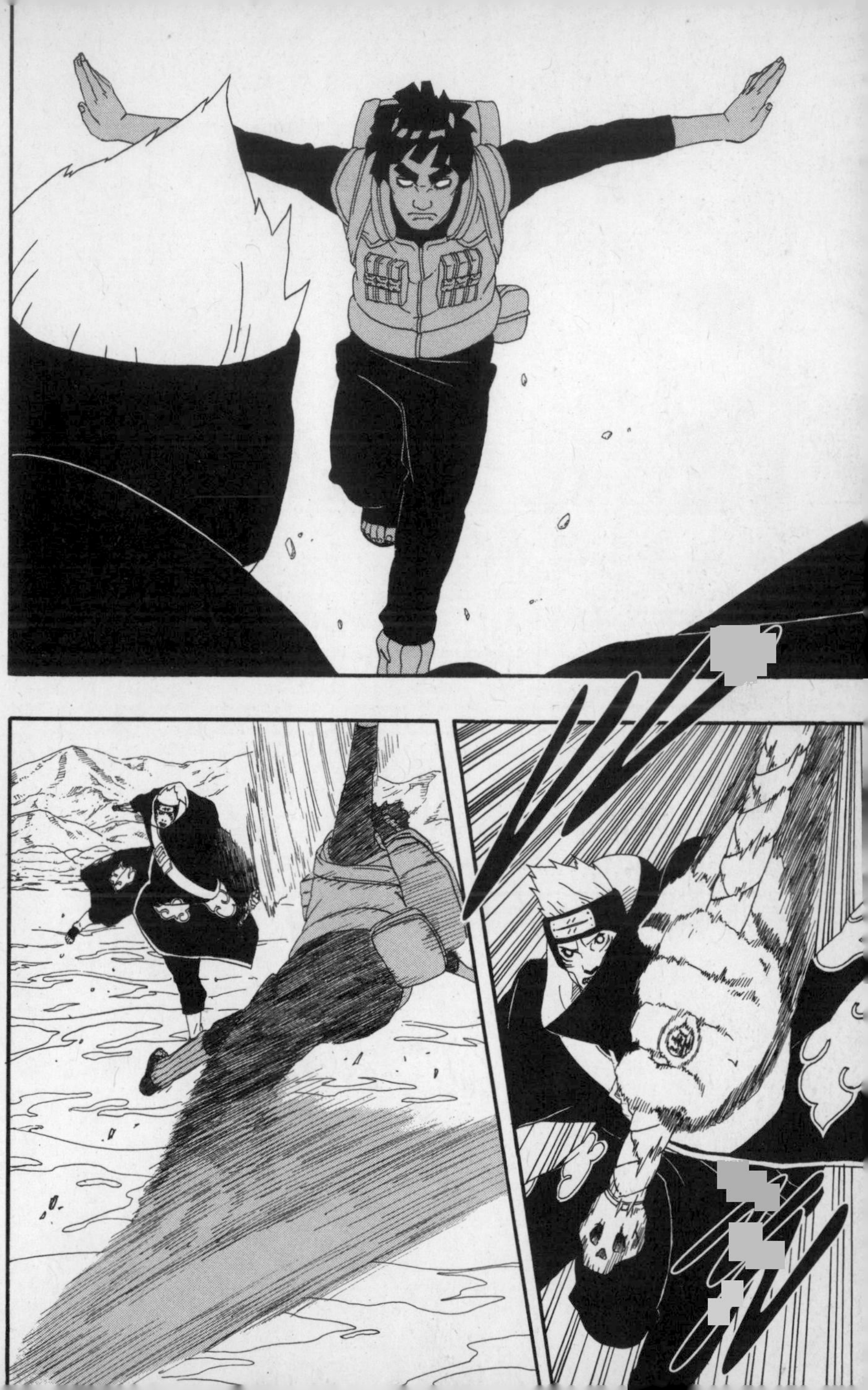

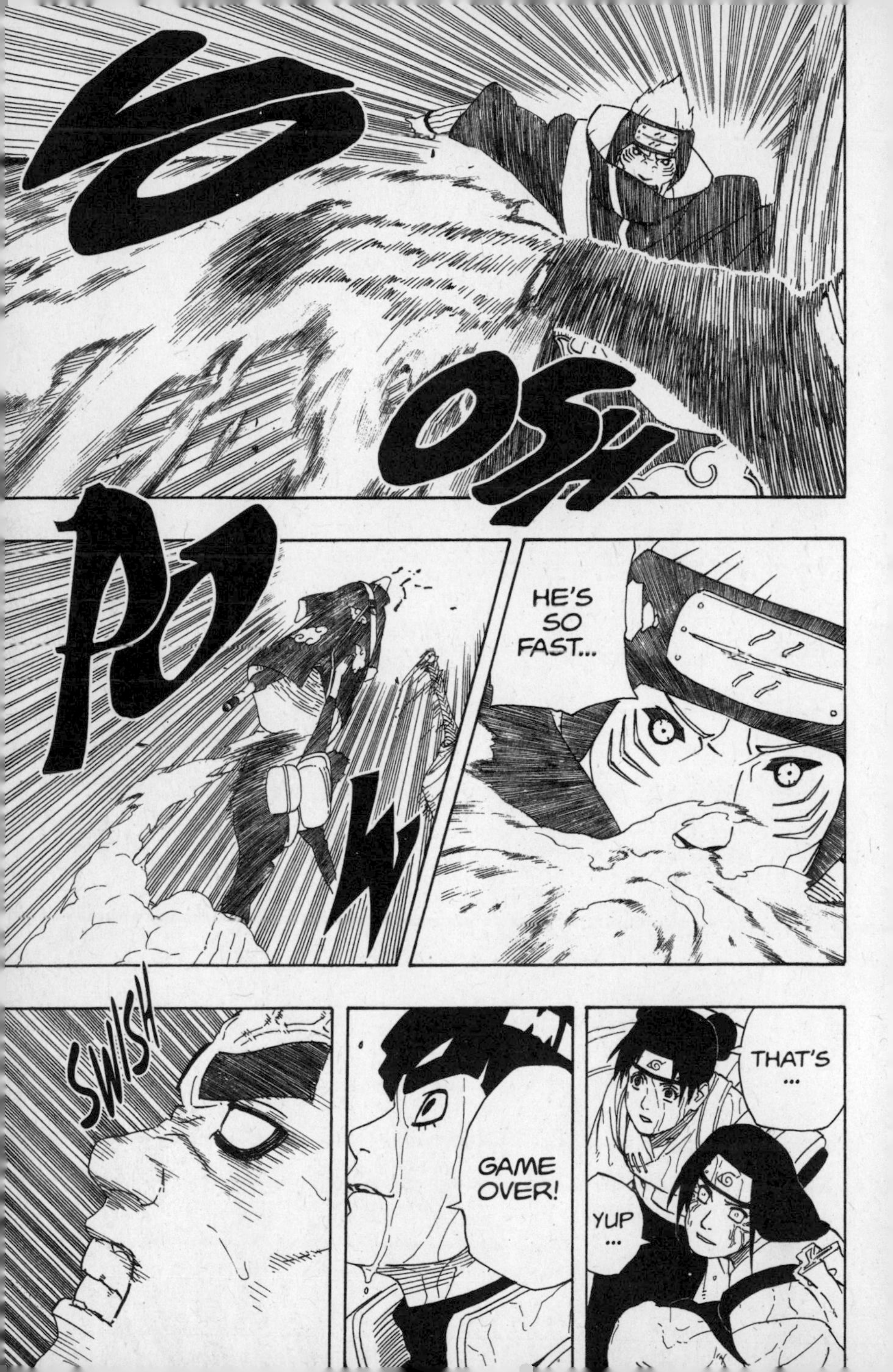
HE'S SO FAST...
POW
THAT'S ...
YUP ...
GAME OVER!
SWISH

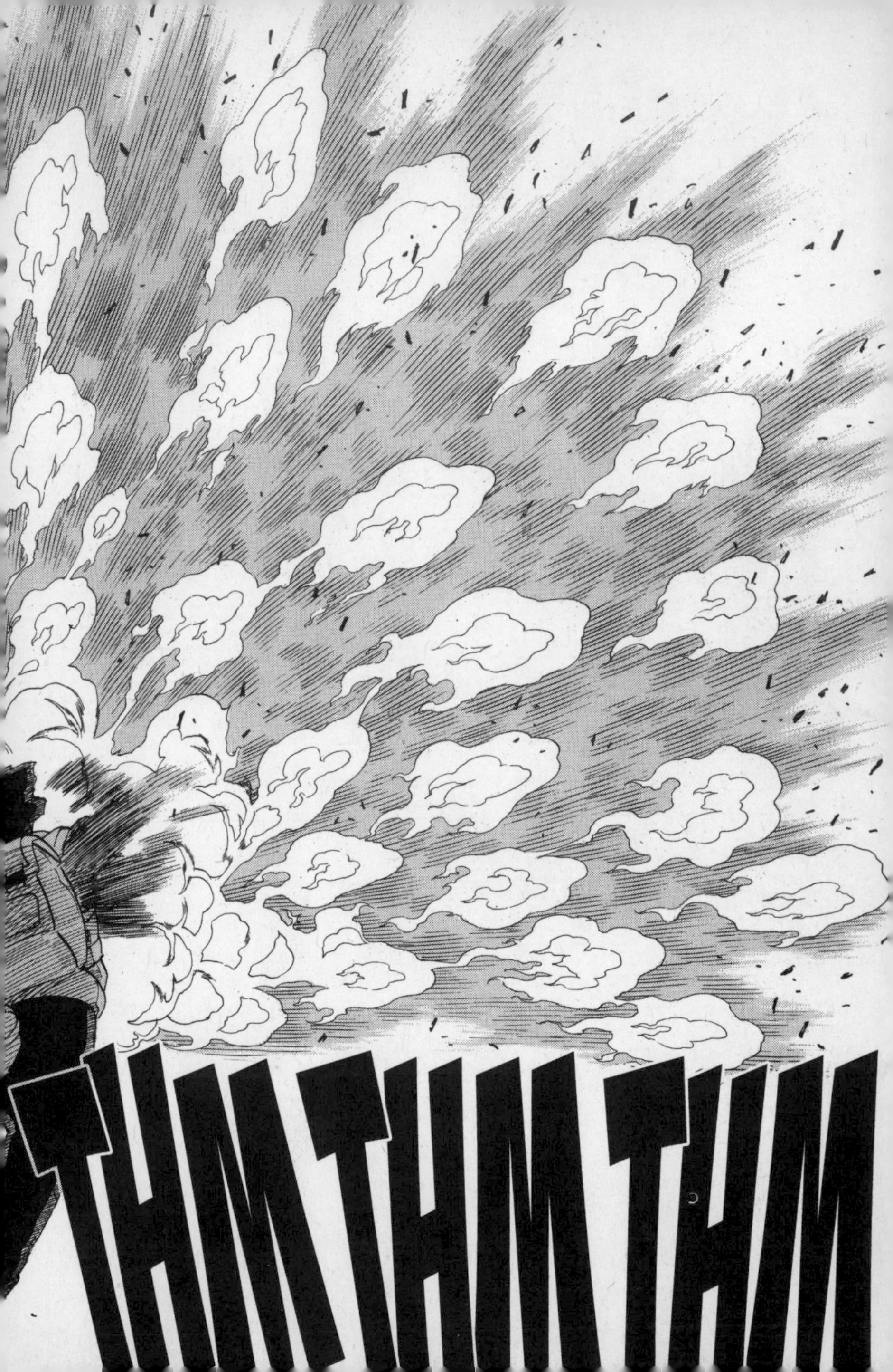
THM THM THM

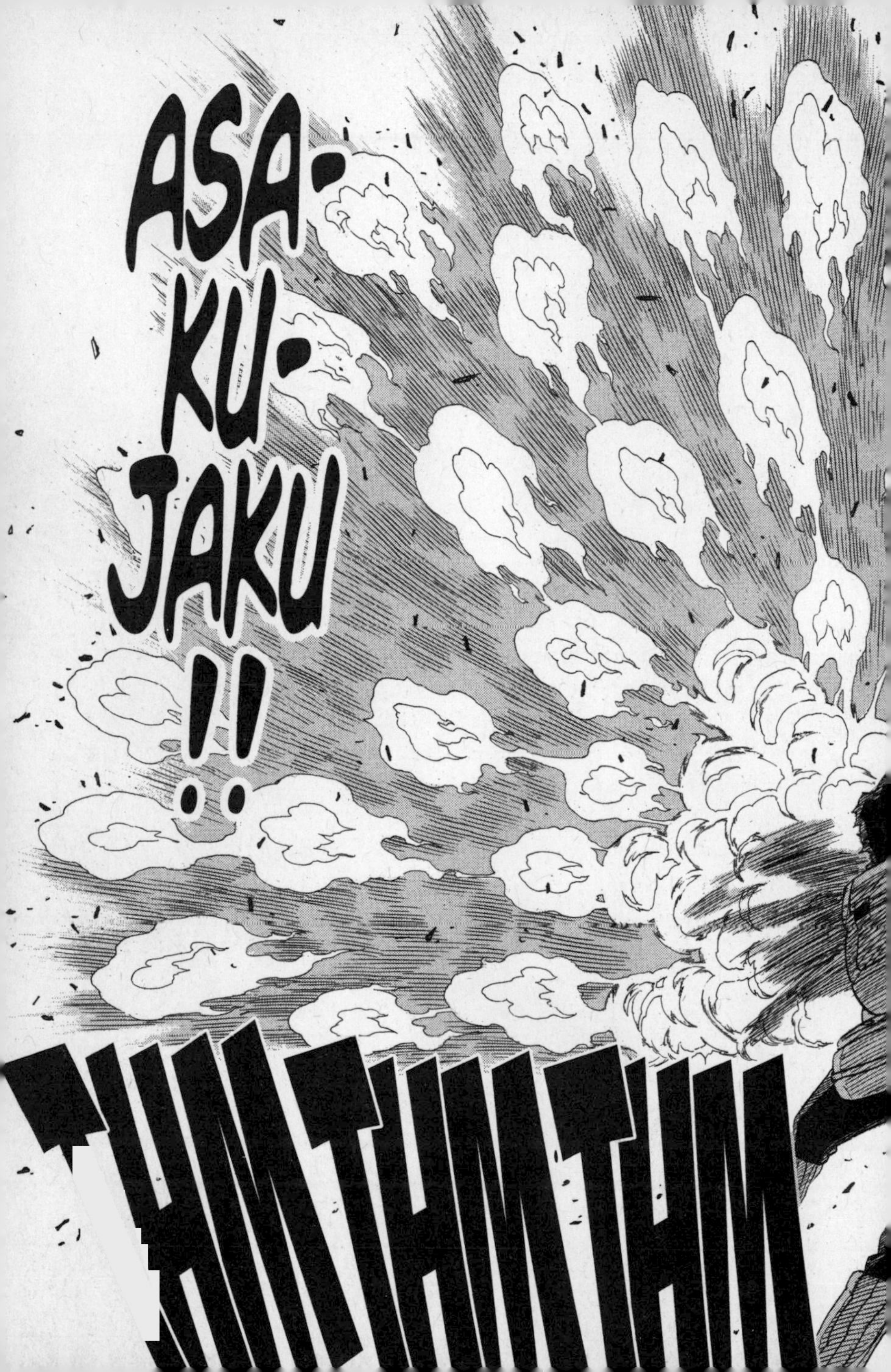
ASA-KU-JAKU!!
THM THM THM

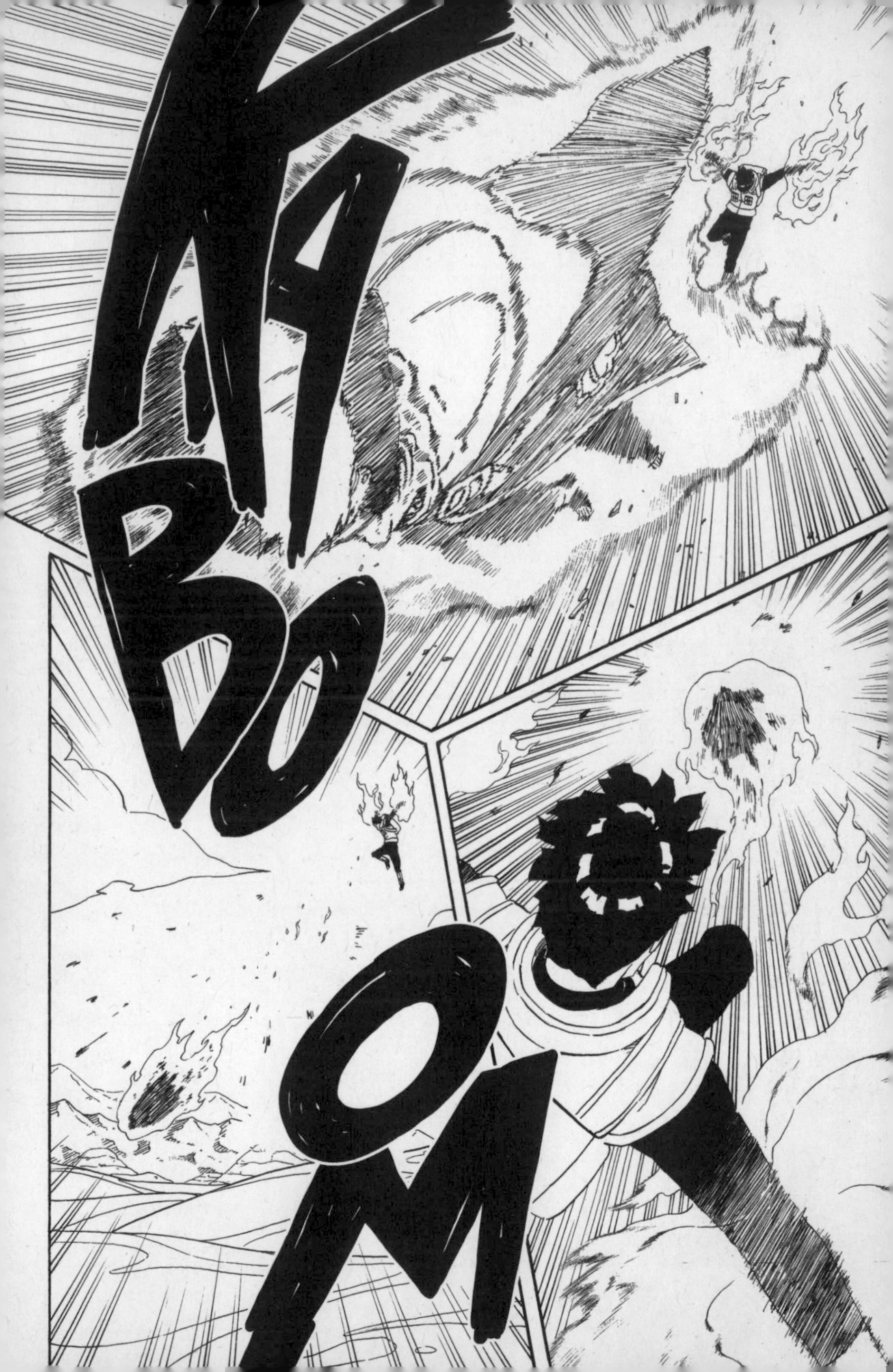
KABOOM

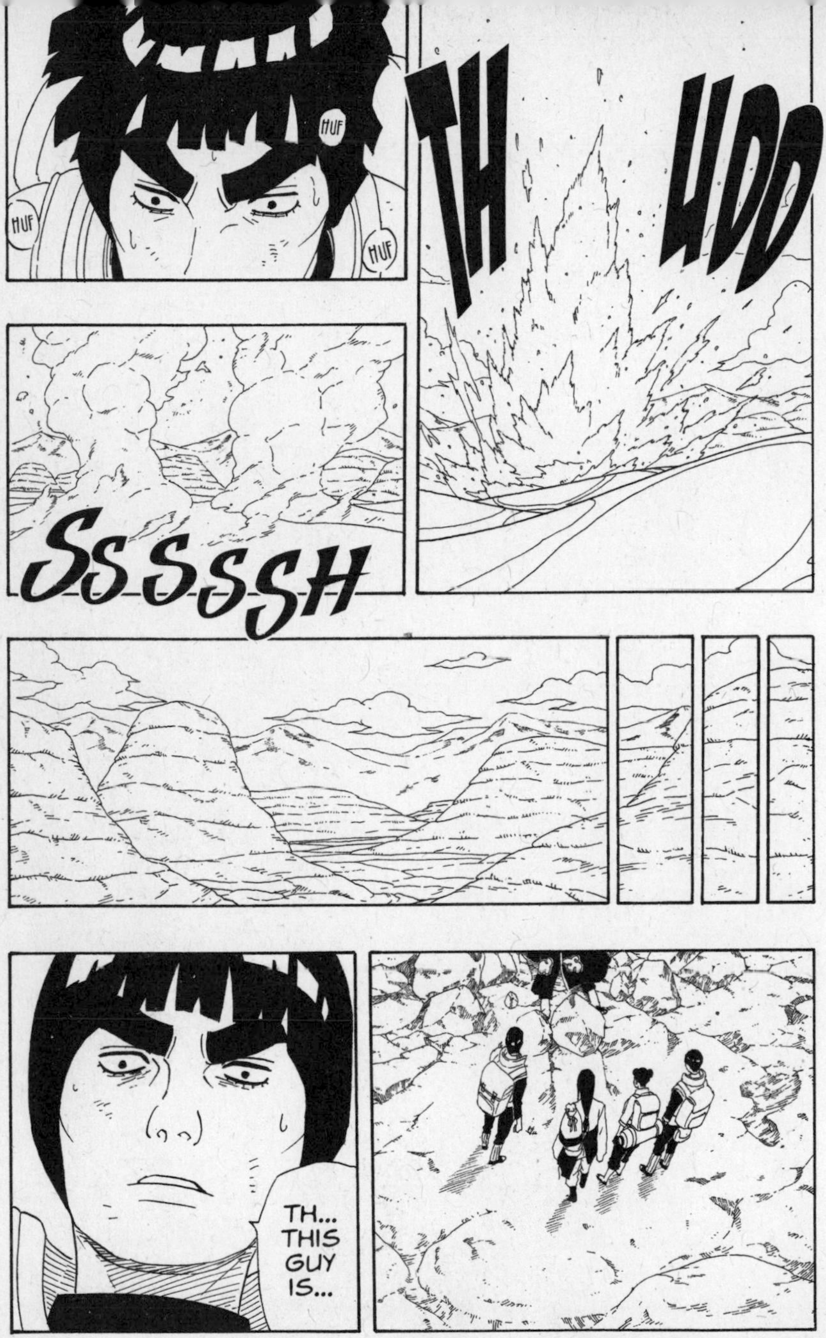
THUDD
HUF
HUF
HUF
SSSSH
TH... THIS GUY IS...

NARUTO

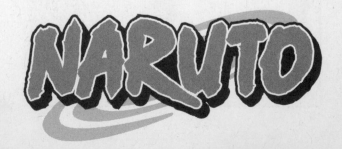

Number 259: The Power of Itachi...!!

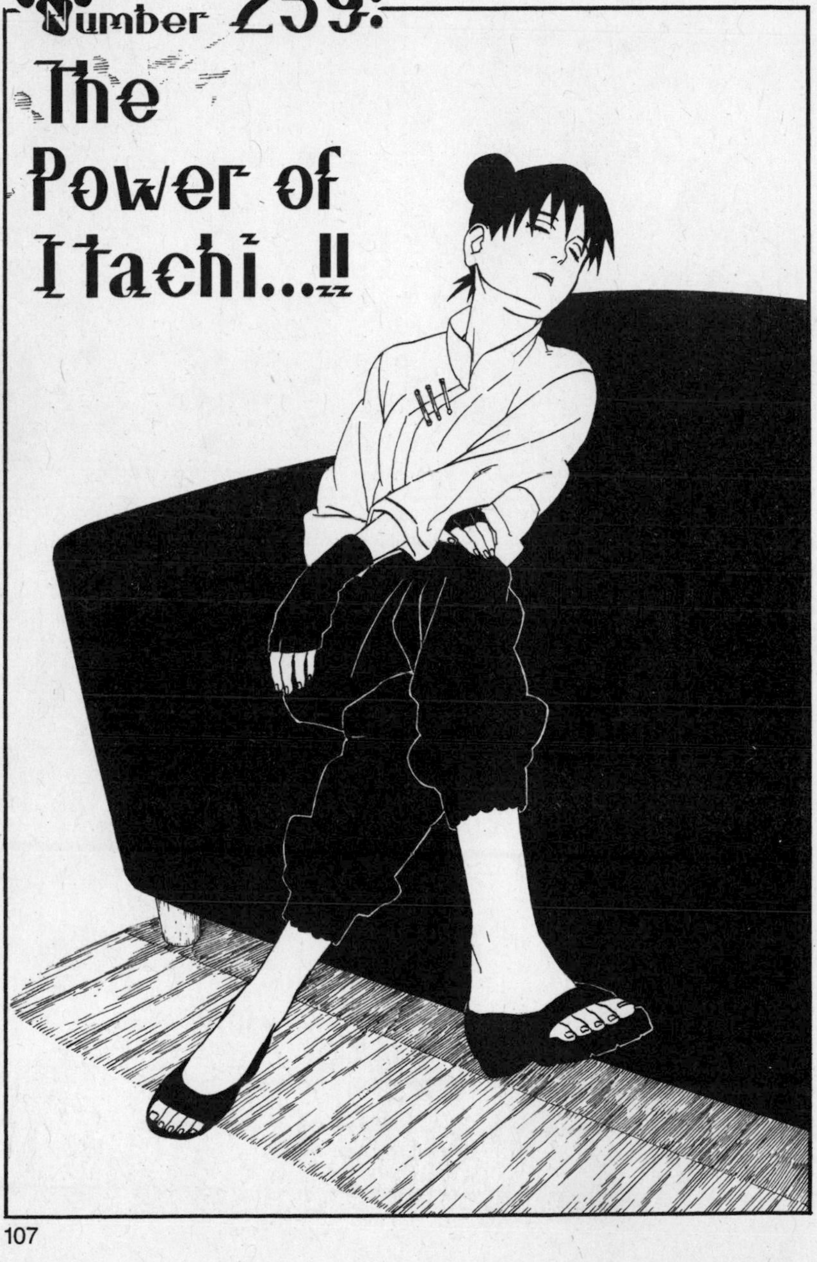

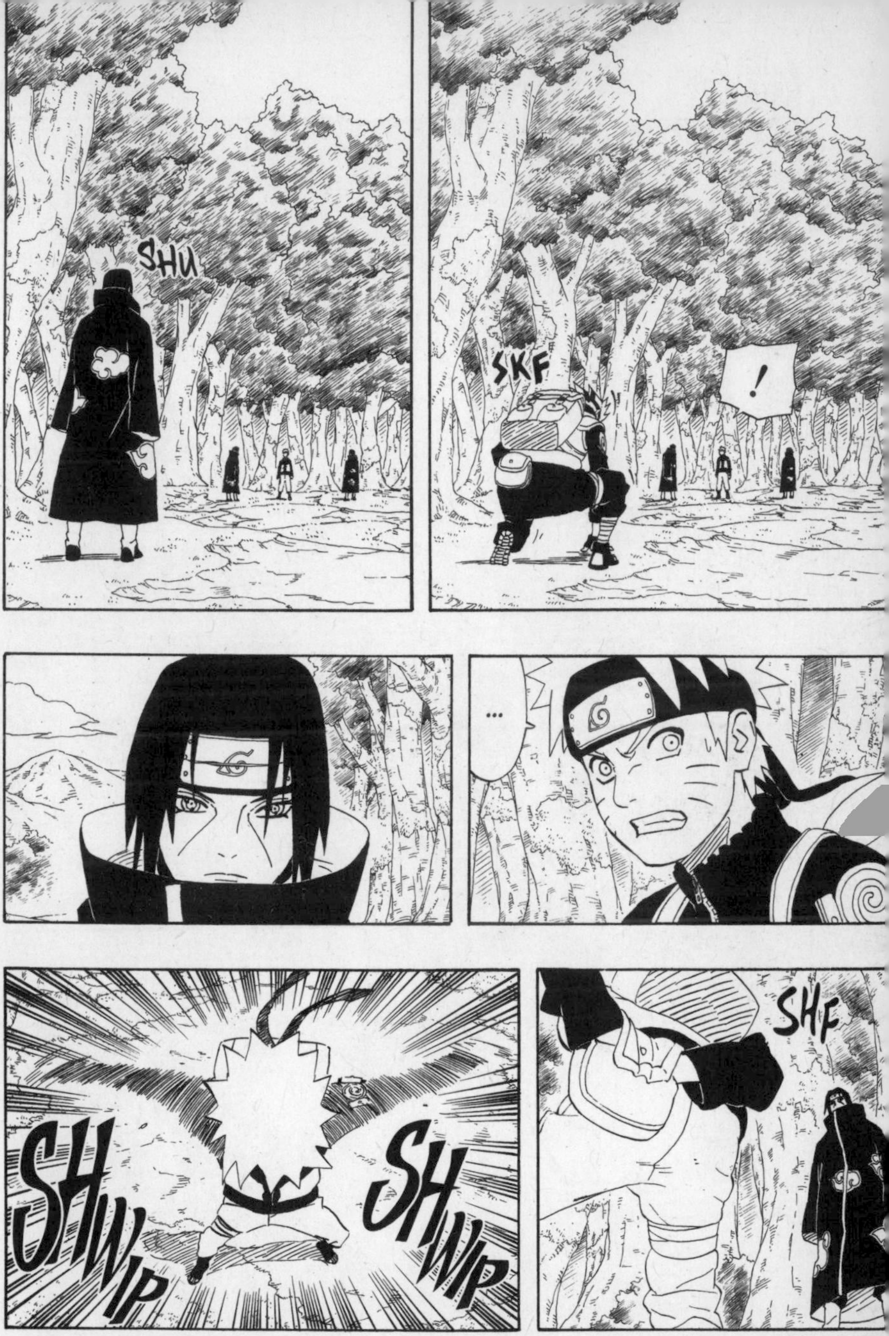
SKF
!
SHU
...
SHF
SHWIP
SHWIP

READ THIS WAY

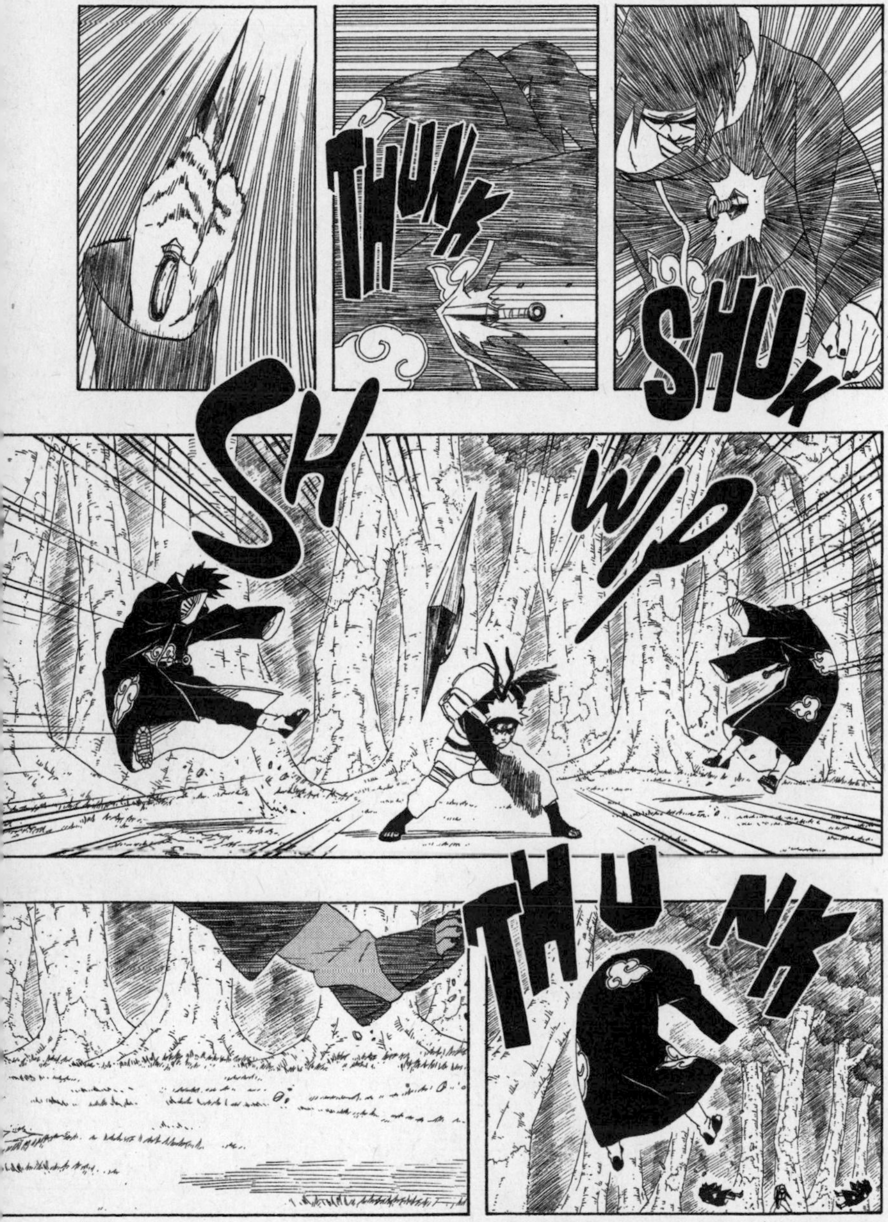
SHUK
THUNK
SHWIP
THUNK

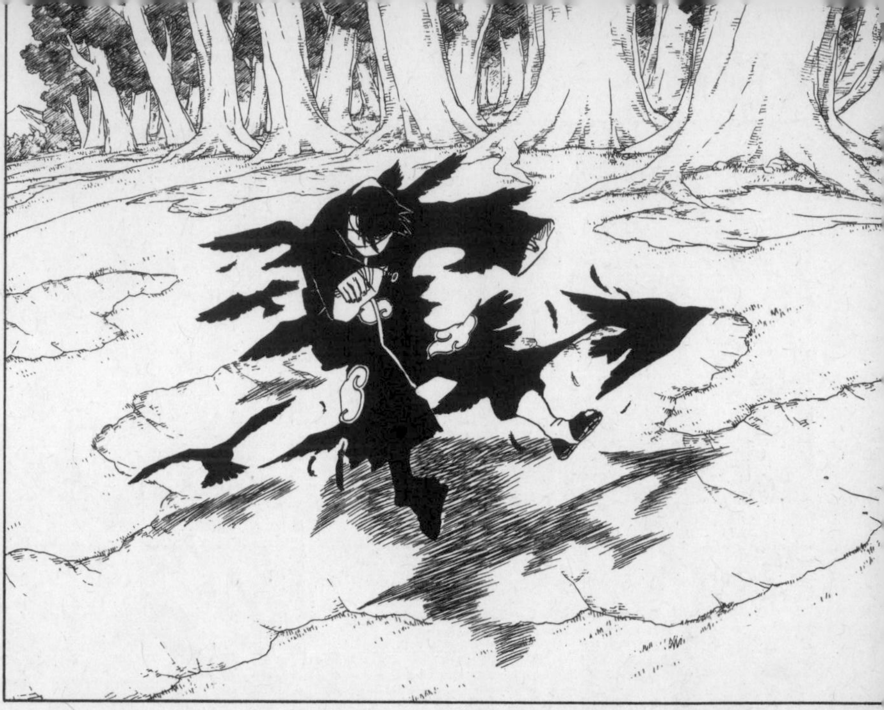

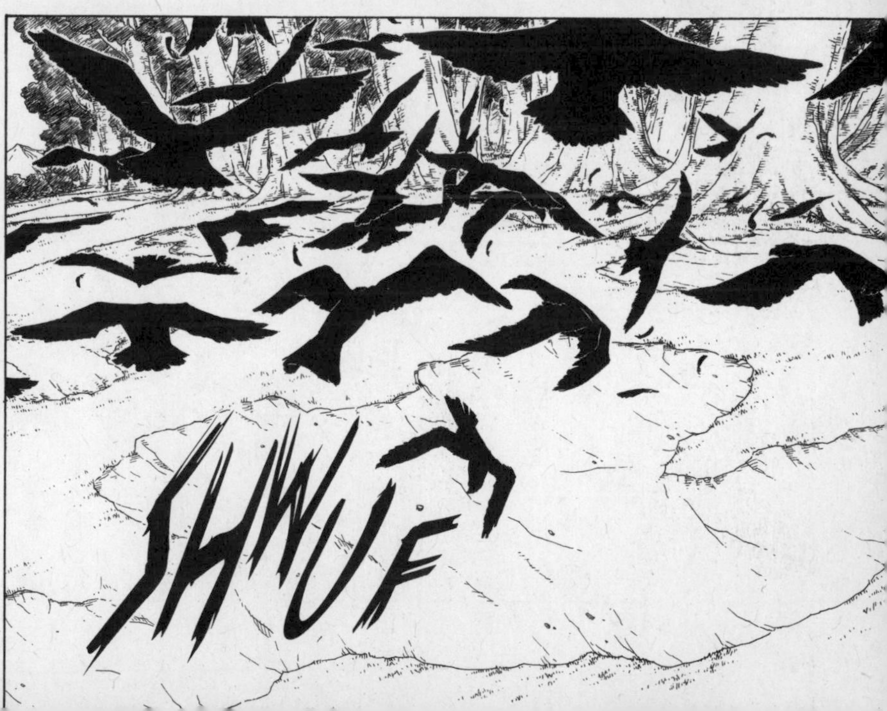
SHWUF

READ THIS WAY

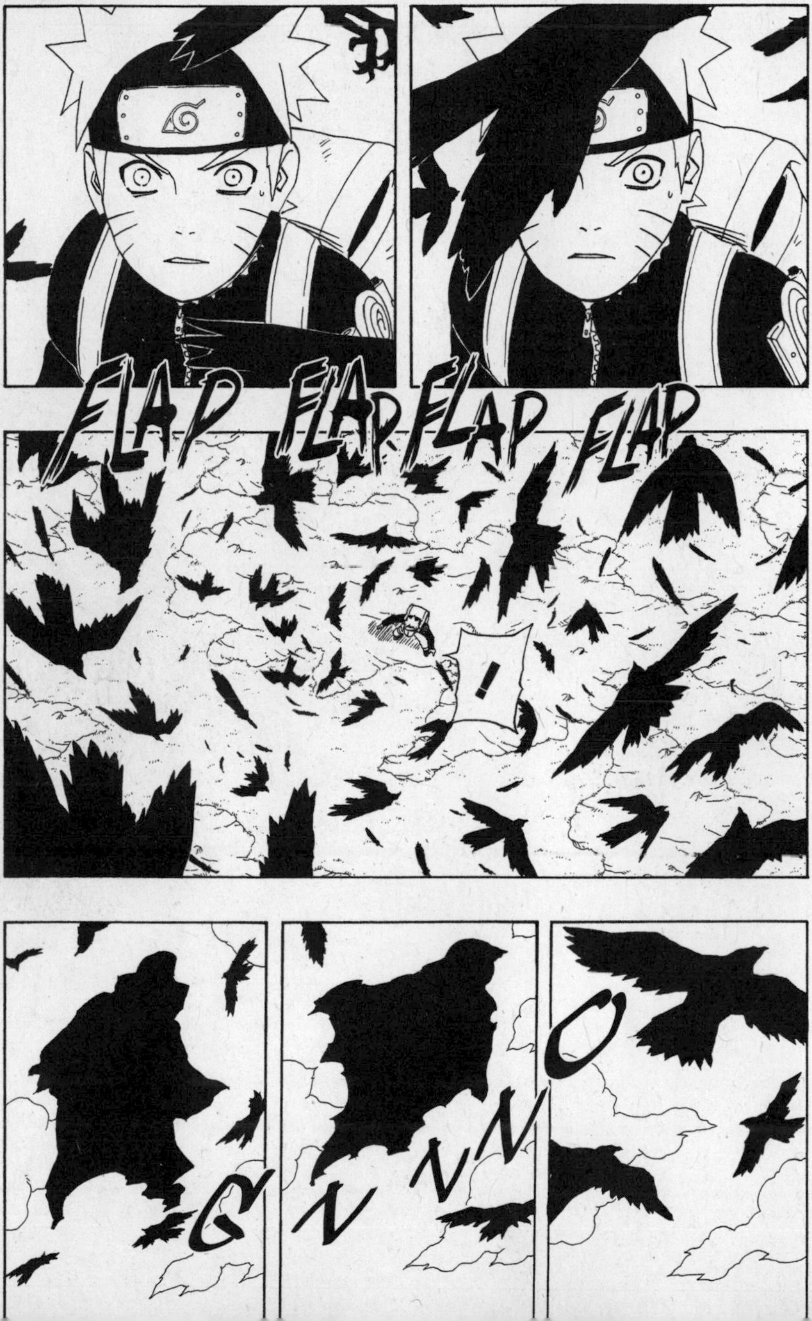
FLAP FLAP FLAP FLAP
!
GNNNO

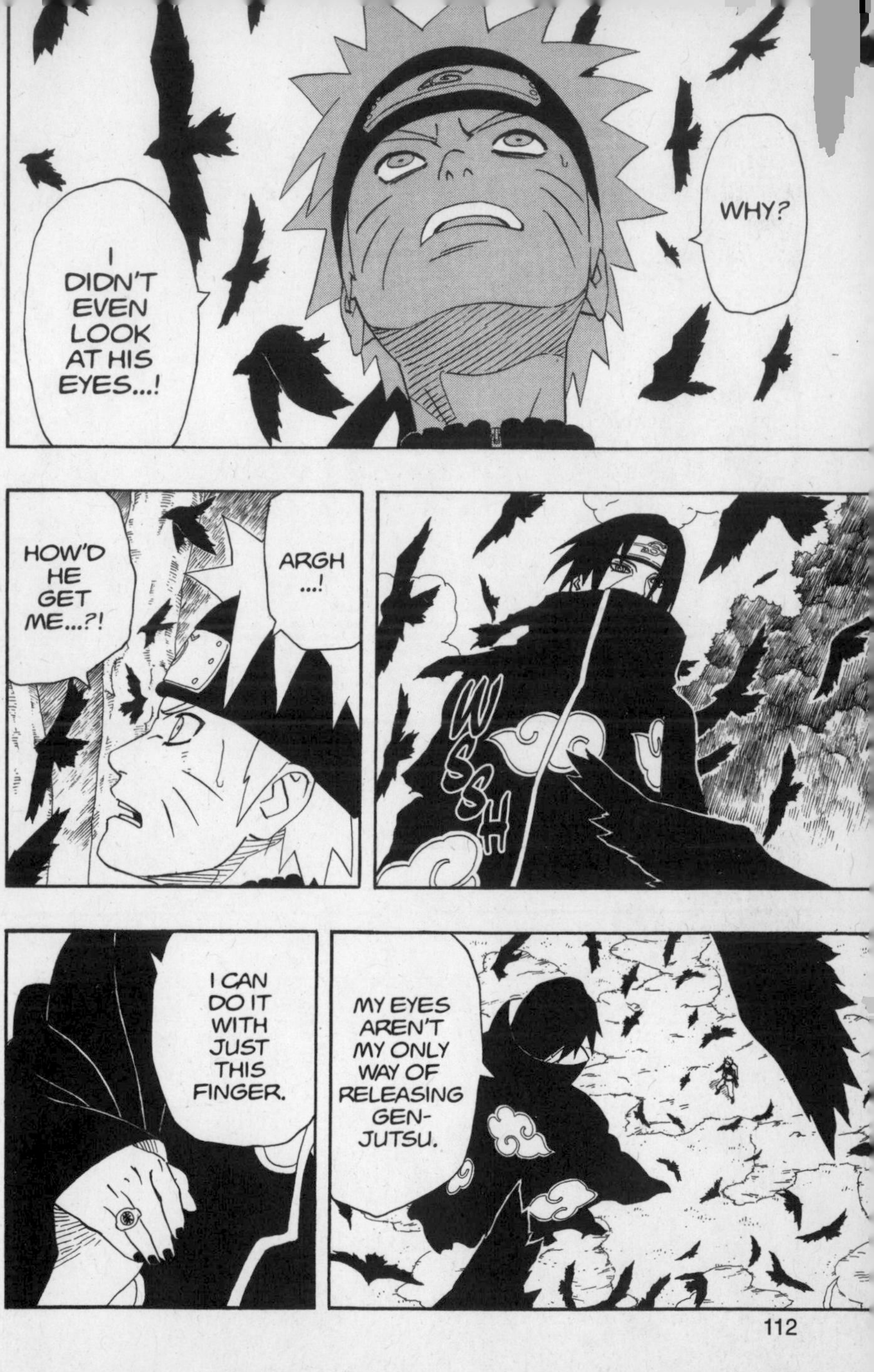
WHY?
I DIDN'T EVEN LOOK AT HIS EYES...!
WSSH
ARGH ...!
HOW'D HE GET ME...?!
MY EYES AREN'T MY ONLY WAY OF RELEASING GEN-JUTSU.
I CAN DO IT WITH JUST THIS FINGER.

READ THIS WAY

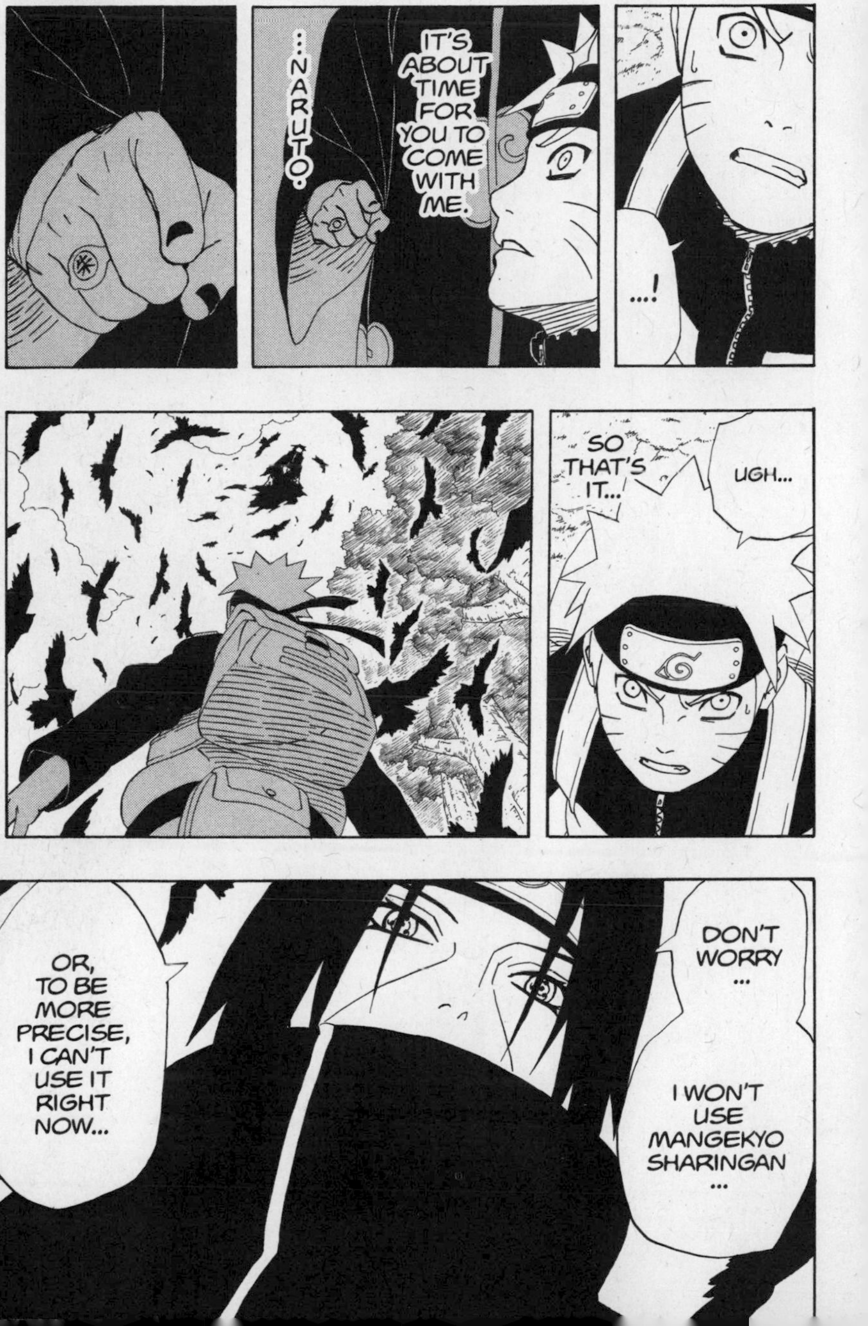
...!
...NARUTO.
IT'S ABOUT TIME FOR YOU TO COME WITH ME.
UGH...
SO THAT'S IT...
DON'T WORRY...
I WON'T USE MANGEKYO SHARINGAN...
OR, TO BE MORE PRECISE, I CAN'T USE IT RIGHT NOW...

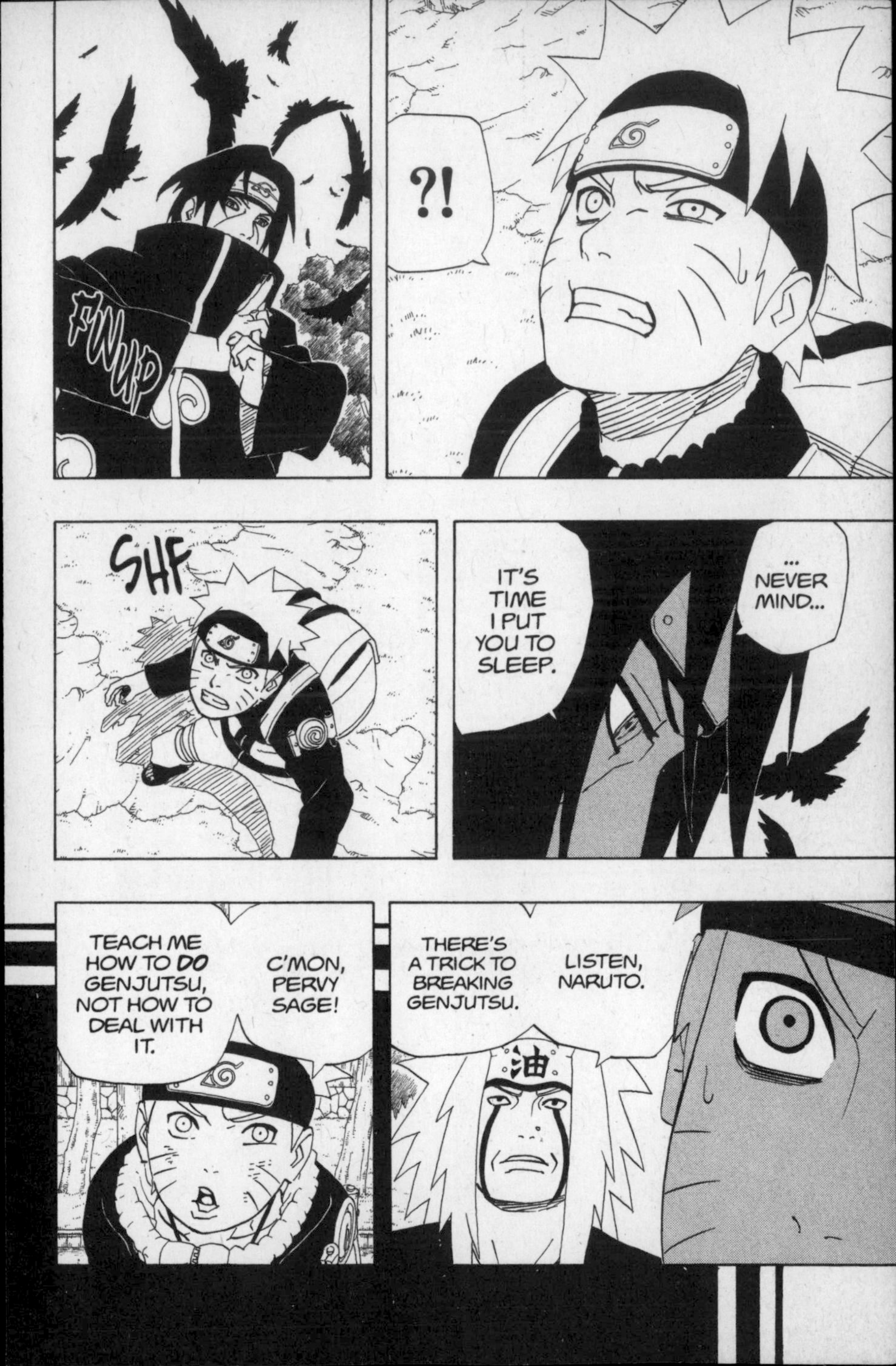
?!
FWUP
... NEVER MIND...
IT'S TIME I PUT YOU TO SLEEP.
SHF
LISTEN, NARUTO.
THERE'S A TRICK TO BREAKING GENJUTSU.
C'MON, PERVY SAGE!
TEACH ME HOW TO **DO** GENJUTSU, NOT HOW TO DEAL WITH IT.

READ THIS WAY

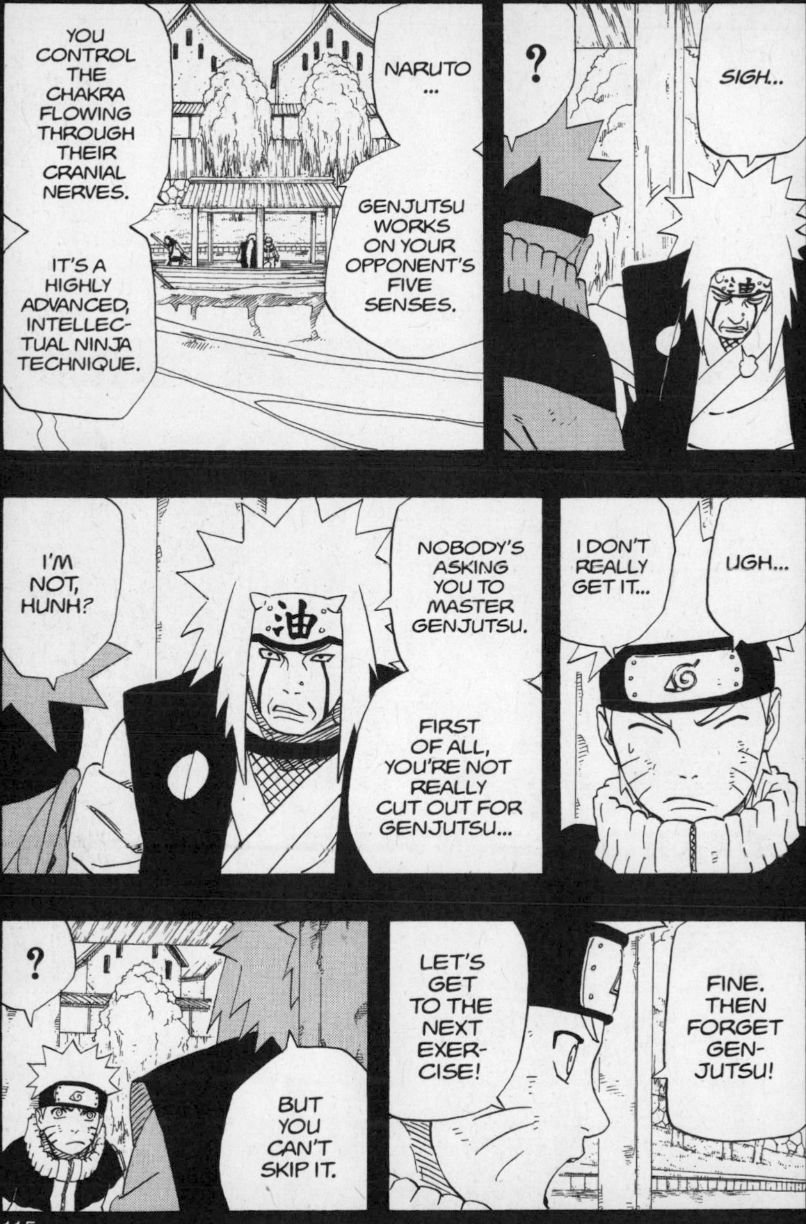

SIGH...
?
NARUTO ...
GENJUTSU WORKS ON YOUR OPPONENT'S FIVE SENSES.
YOU CONTROL THE CHAKRA FLOWING THROUGH THEIR CRANIAL NERVES.
IT'S A HIGHLY ADVANCED, INTELLECTUAL NINJA TECHNIQUE.
UGH...
I DON'T REALLY GET IT...
NOBODY'S ASKING YOU TO MASTER GENJUTSU.
FIRST OF ALL, YOU'RE NOT REALLY CUT OUT FOR GENJUTSU...
I'M NOT, HUNH?
FINE. THEN FORGET GEN-JUTSU!
LET'S GET TO THE NEXT EXER-CISE!
BUT YOU CAN'T SKIP IT.
?

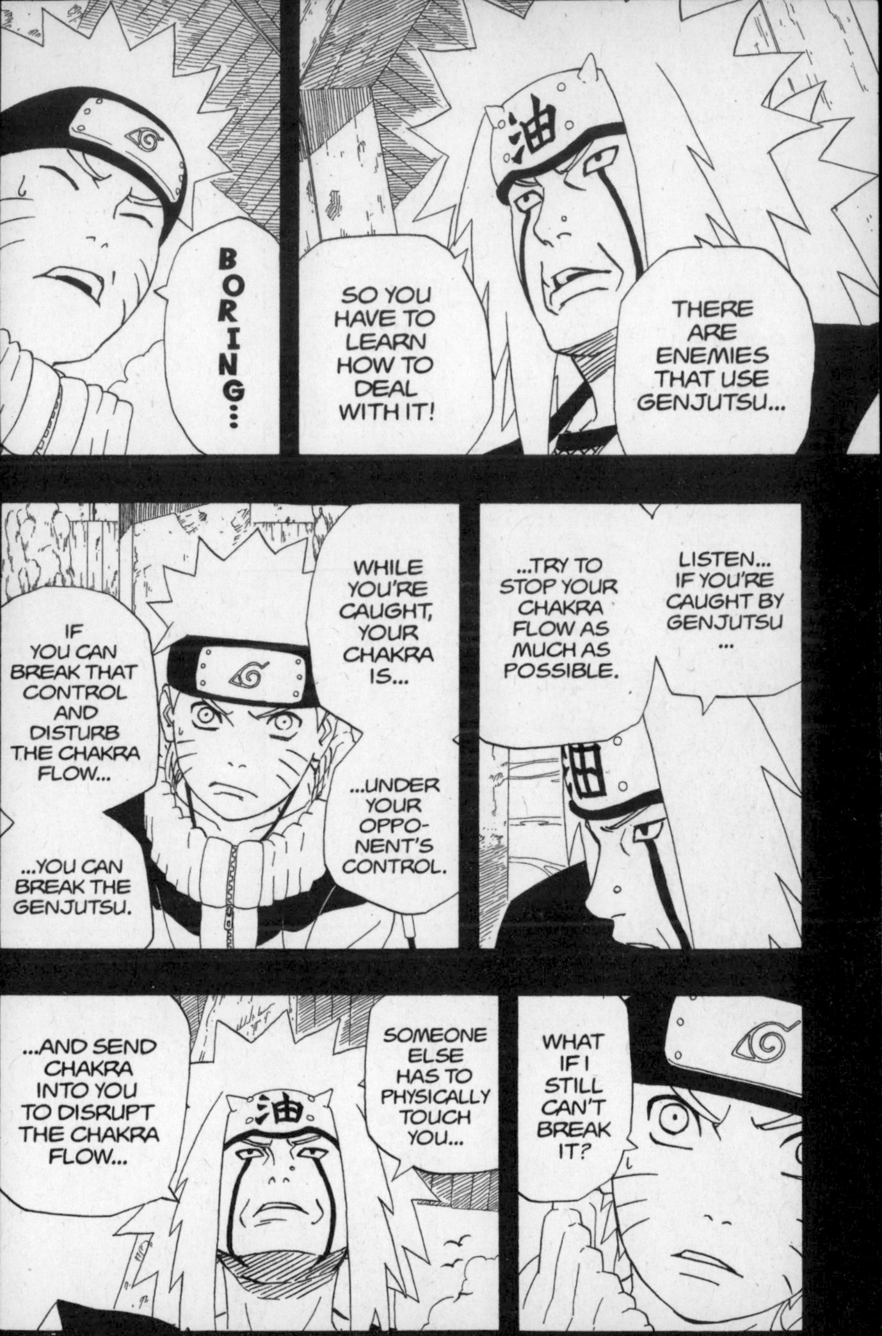
THERE ARE ENEMIES THAT USE GENJUTSU...
SO YOU HAVE TO LEARN HOW TO DEAL WITH IT!
BORING...
LISTEN... IF YOU'RE CAUGHT BY GENJUTSU ...
...TRY TO STOP YOUR CHAKRA FLOW AS MUCH AS POSSIBLE.
WHILE YOU'RE CAUGHT, YOUR CHAKRA IS...
...UNDER YOUR OPPO-NENT'S CONTROL.
IF YOU CAN BREAK THAT CONTROL AND DISTURB THE CHAKRA FLOW...
...YOU CAN BREAK THE GENJUTSU.
WHAT IF I STILL CAN'T BREAK IT?
SOMEONE ELSE HAS TO PHYSICALLY TOUCH YOU...
...AND SEND CHAKRA INTO YOU TO DISRUPT THE CHAKRA FLOW...

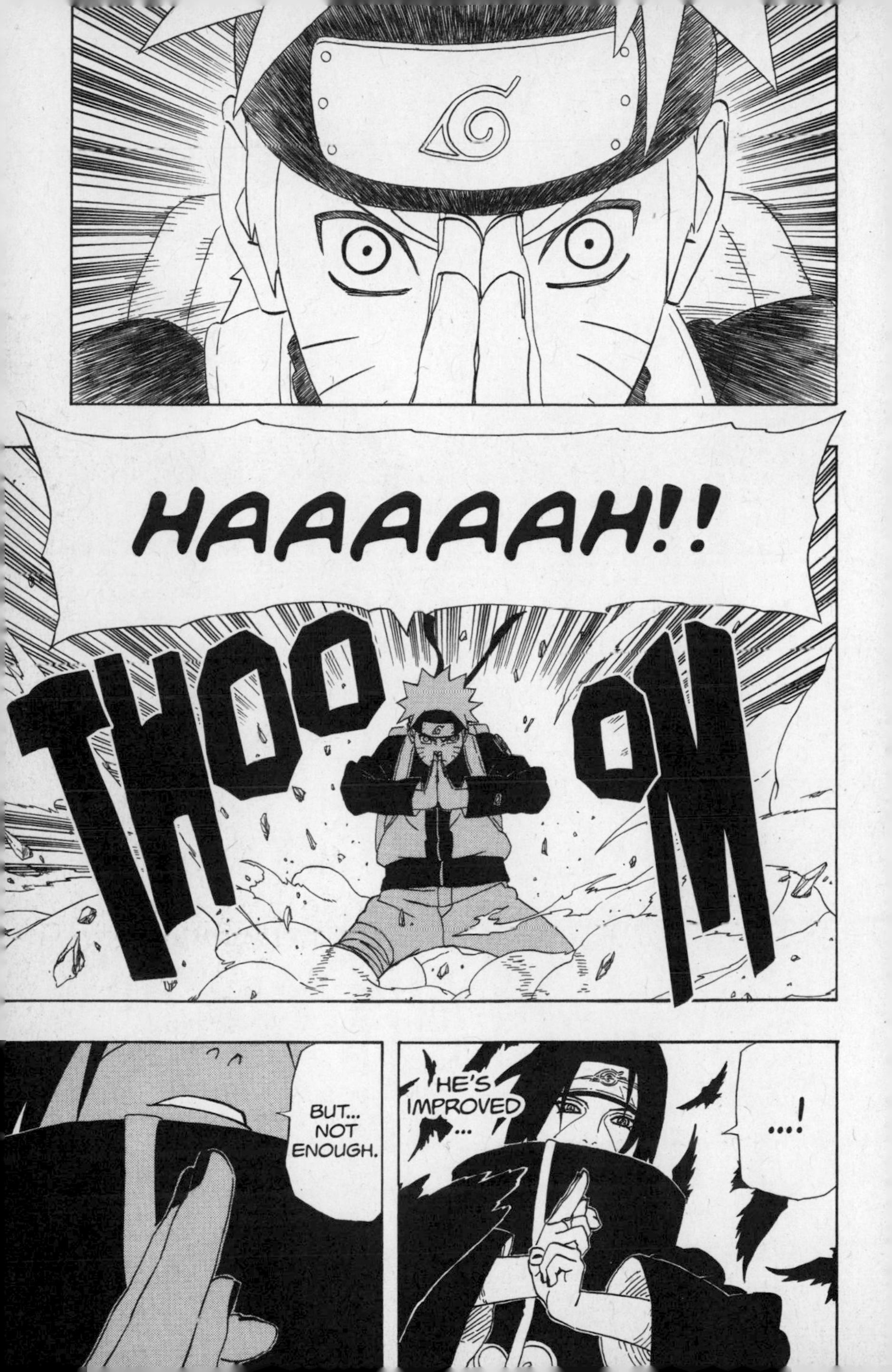
HAAAAAH!!
THOOOOM
...!
HE'S IMPROVED...
BUT... NOT ENOUGH.

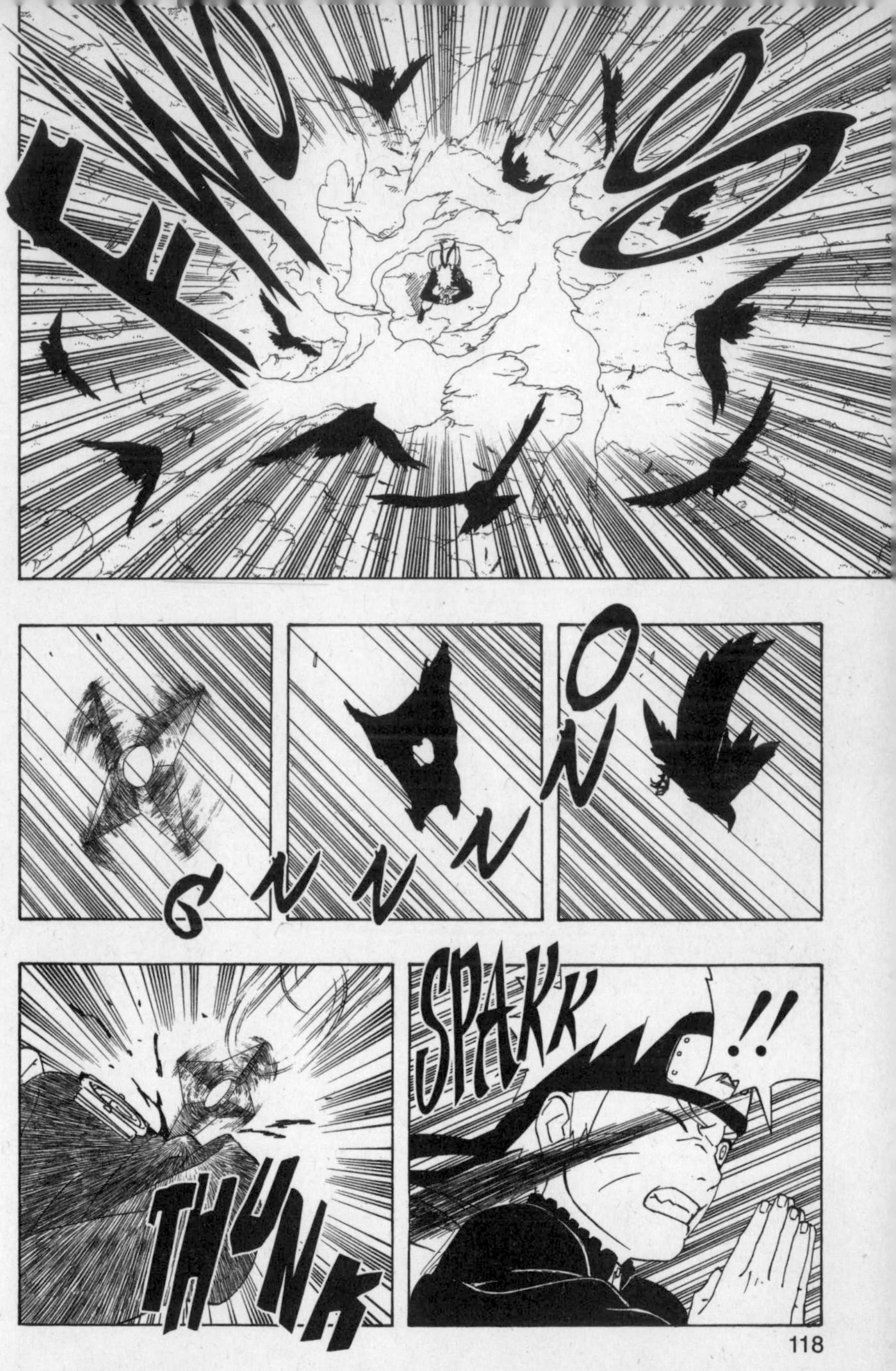
SPAKK
!!
THUNK

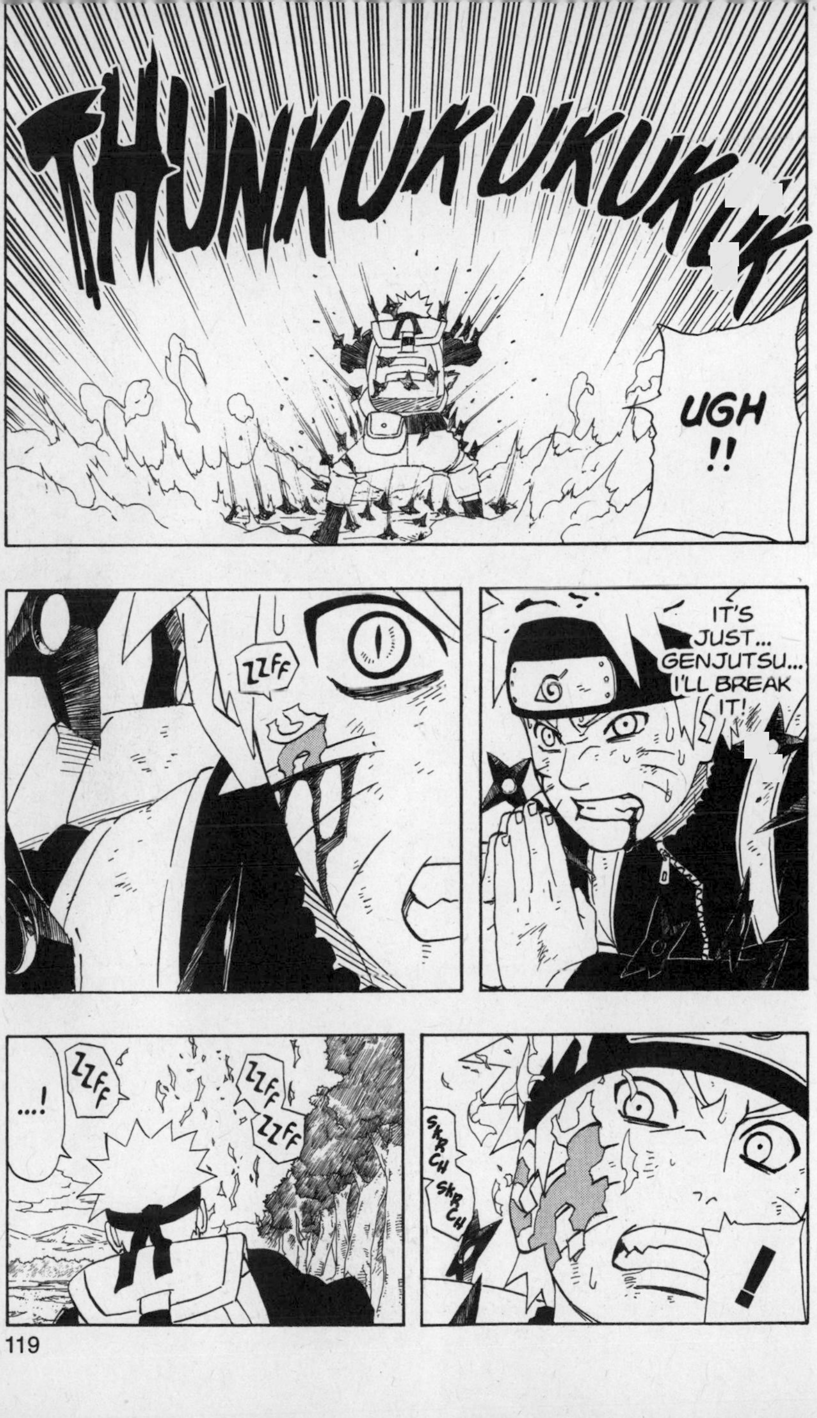
THUNKUKUKUKUK
UGH !!
IT'S JUST... GENJUTSU... I'LL BREAK IT!
ZZFF
SKRCH SKRCH
!
ZZFF
ZZFF
ZZFF
...!

HUMMM

ACK!!

CLOMB

I FAILED TO KILL YOU BEFORE.

CLOMP

!

SHUU

ZZZZIP

CHUP

121

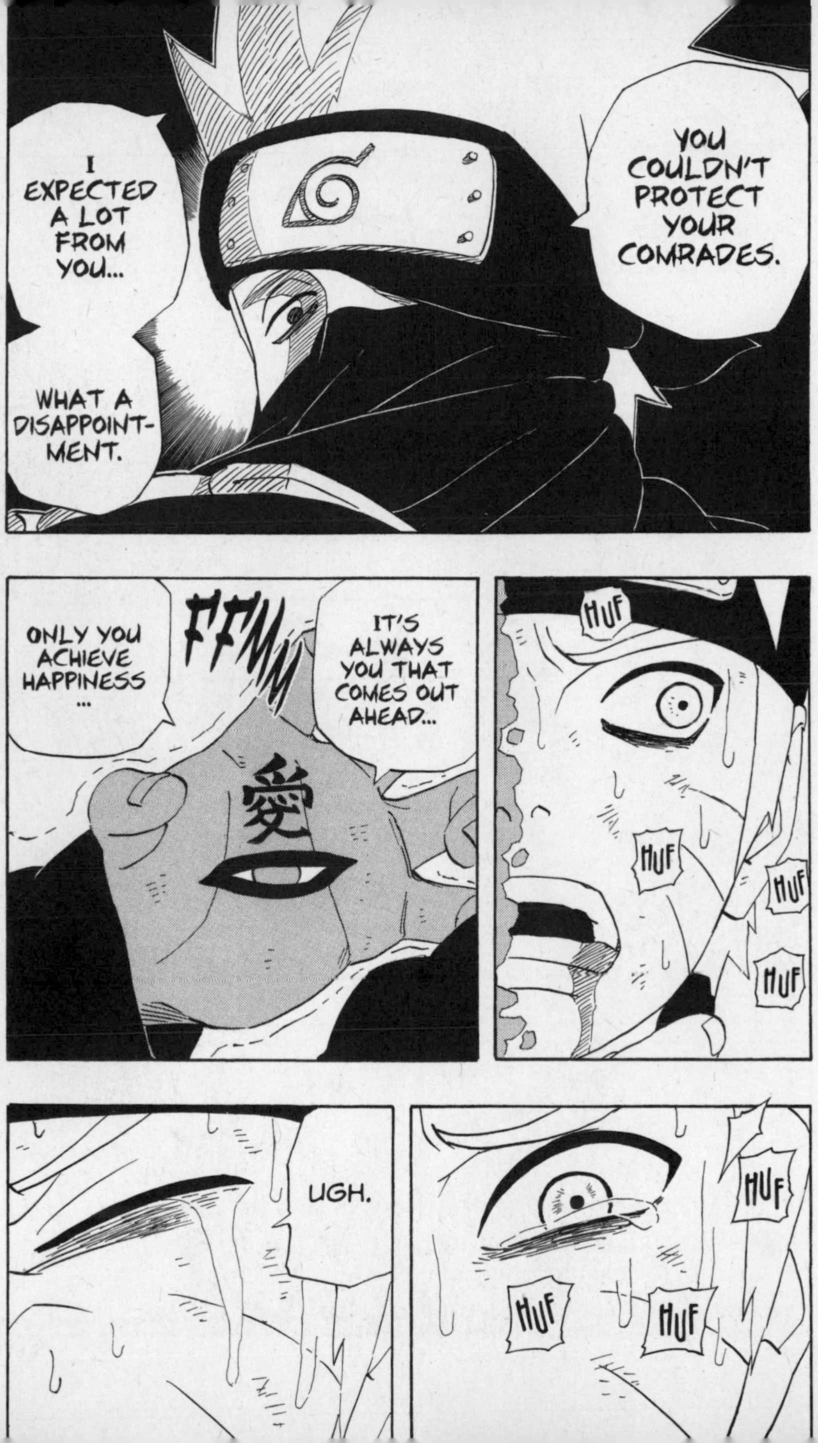
YOU COULDN'T PROTECT YOUR COMRADES.
I EXPECTED A LOT FROM YOU...
WHAT A DISAPPOINTMENT.
HUF
HUF
HUF
HUF
IT'S ALWAYS YOU THAT COMES OUT AHEAD...
FFMM
ONLY YOU ACHIEVE HAPPINESS...
HUF
HUF
HUF
UGH.

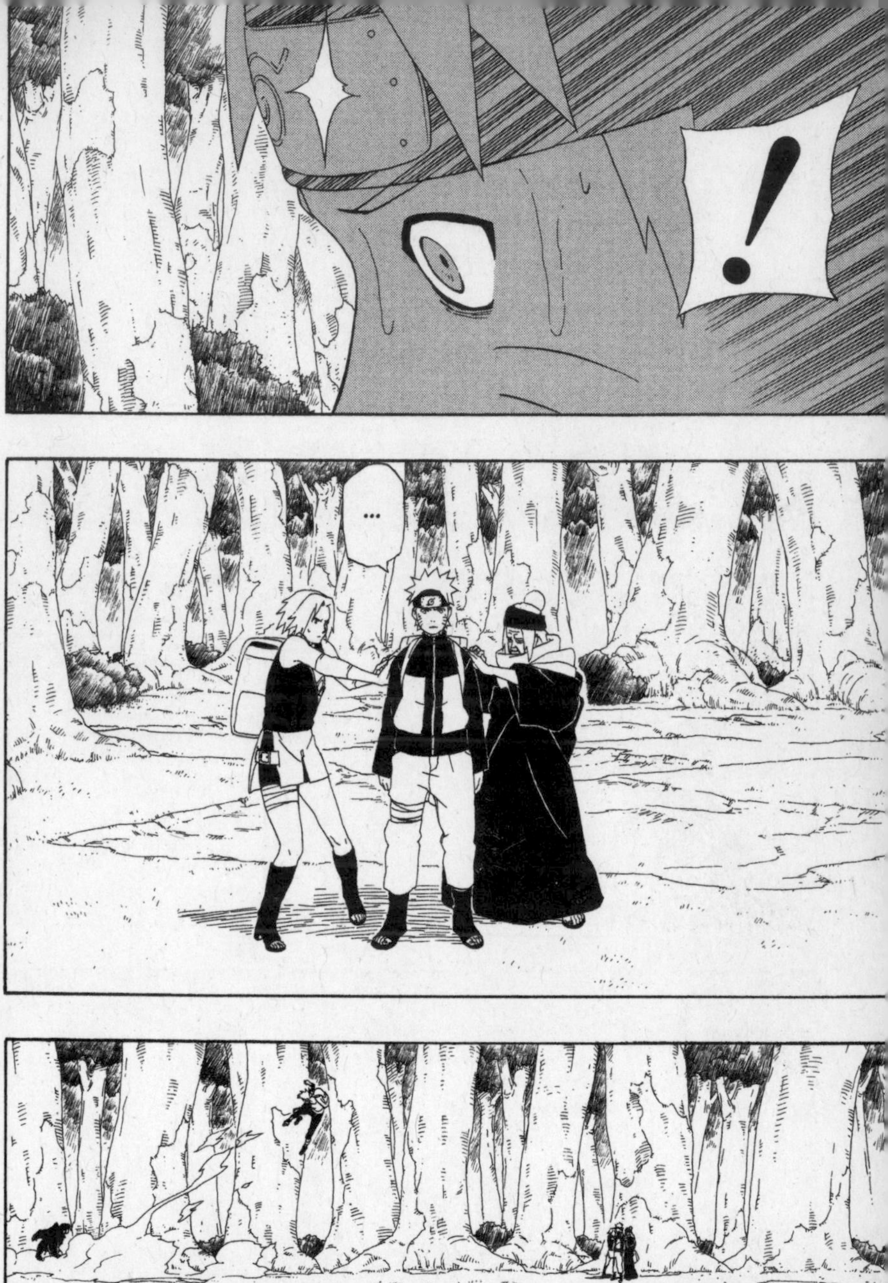
!
...

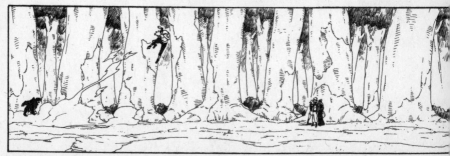

READ THIS WAY

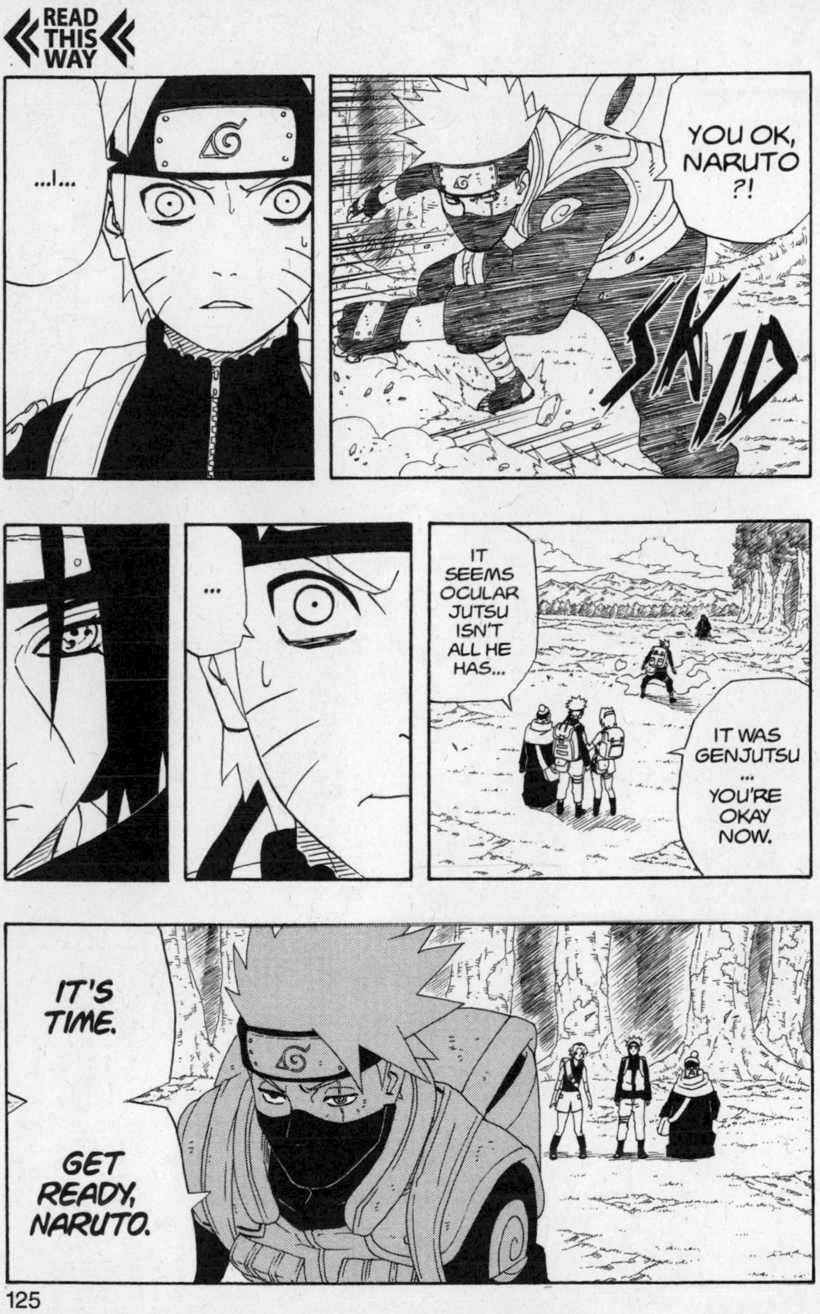
YOU OK, NARUTO ?!
SKID
...I...
IT SEEMS OCULAR JUTSU ISN'T ALL HE HAS...
IT WAS GENJUTSU ... YOU'RE OKAY NOW.
...
IT'S TIME.
GET READY, NARUTO.

NARUTO

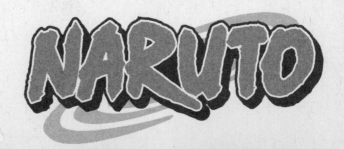

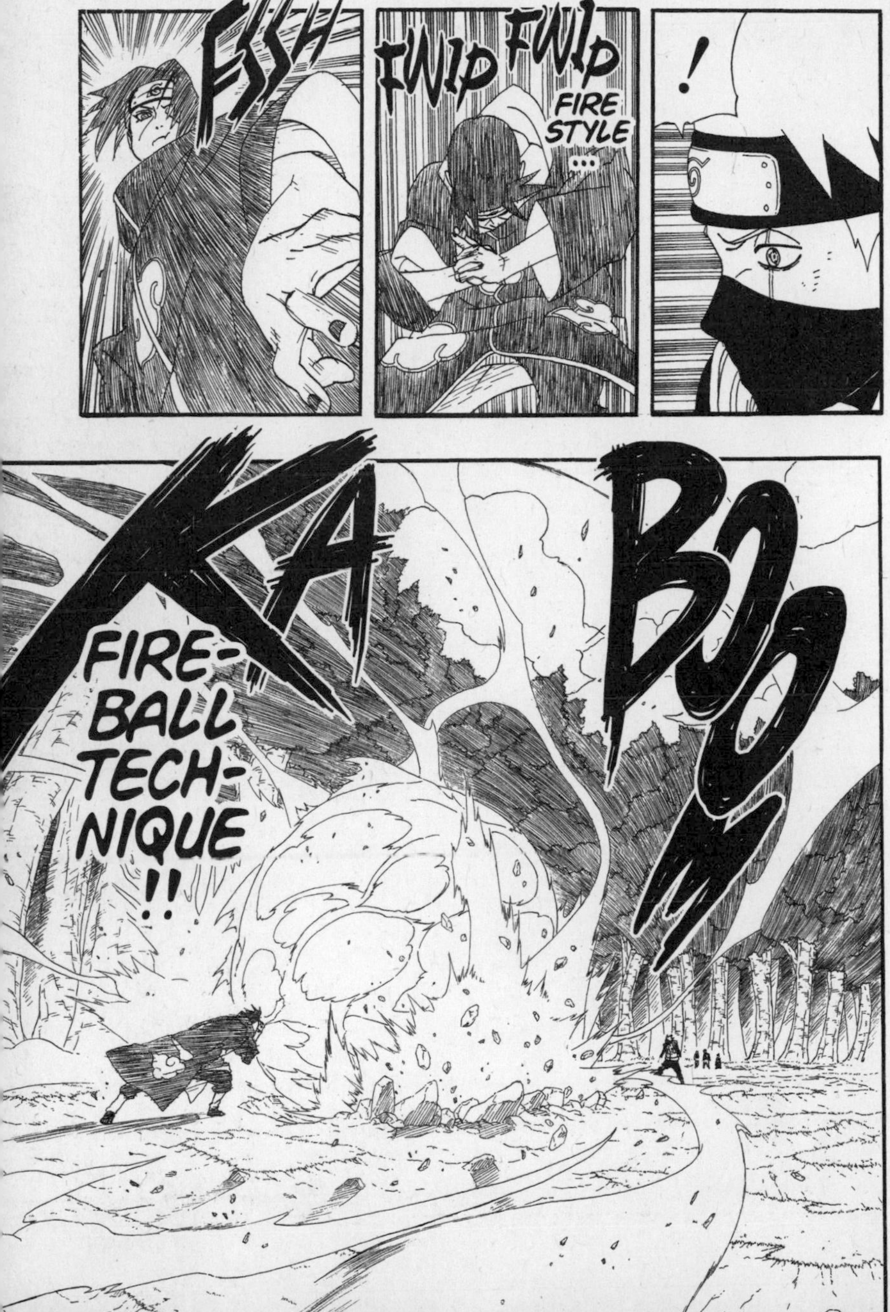
!
FWIP FWIP
FIRE STYLE ...
FSSH
KA BOOM
FIRE-BALL TECH-NIQUE!!

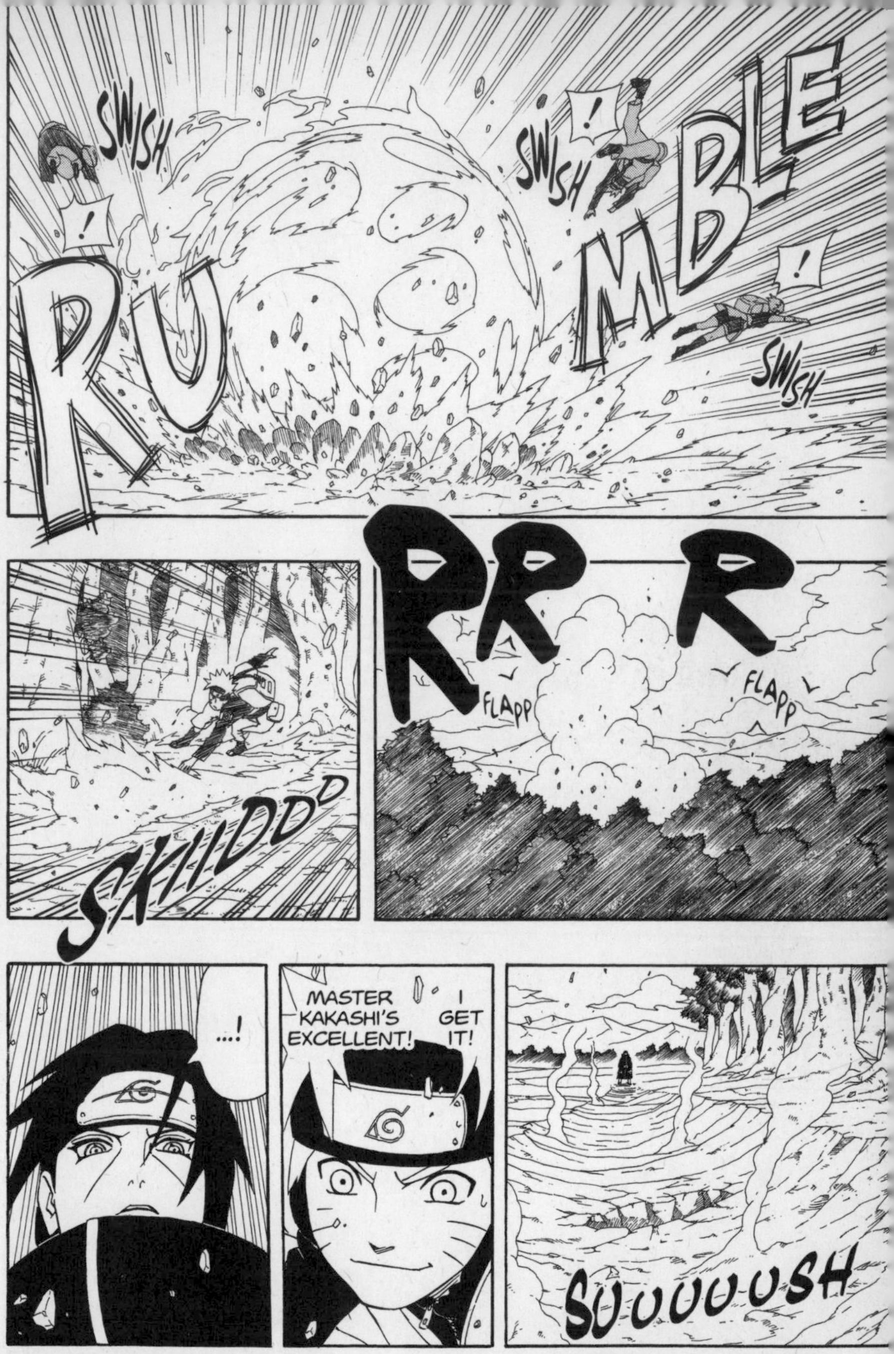

SWISH
!
SWISH
!
RUMBLE
!
SWISH
RRRR
FLAPP
FLAPP
SKIIDDD
SUUUUUSH
MASTER KAKASHI'S EXCELLENT!
I GET IT!
...!

READ THIS WAY

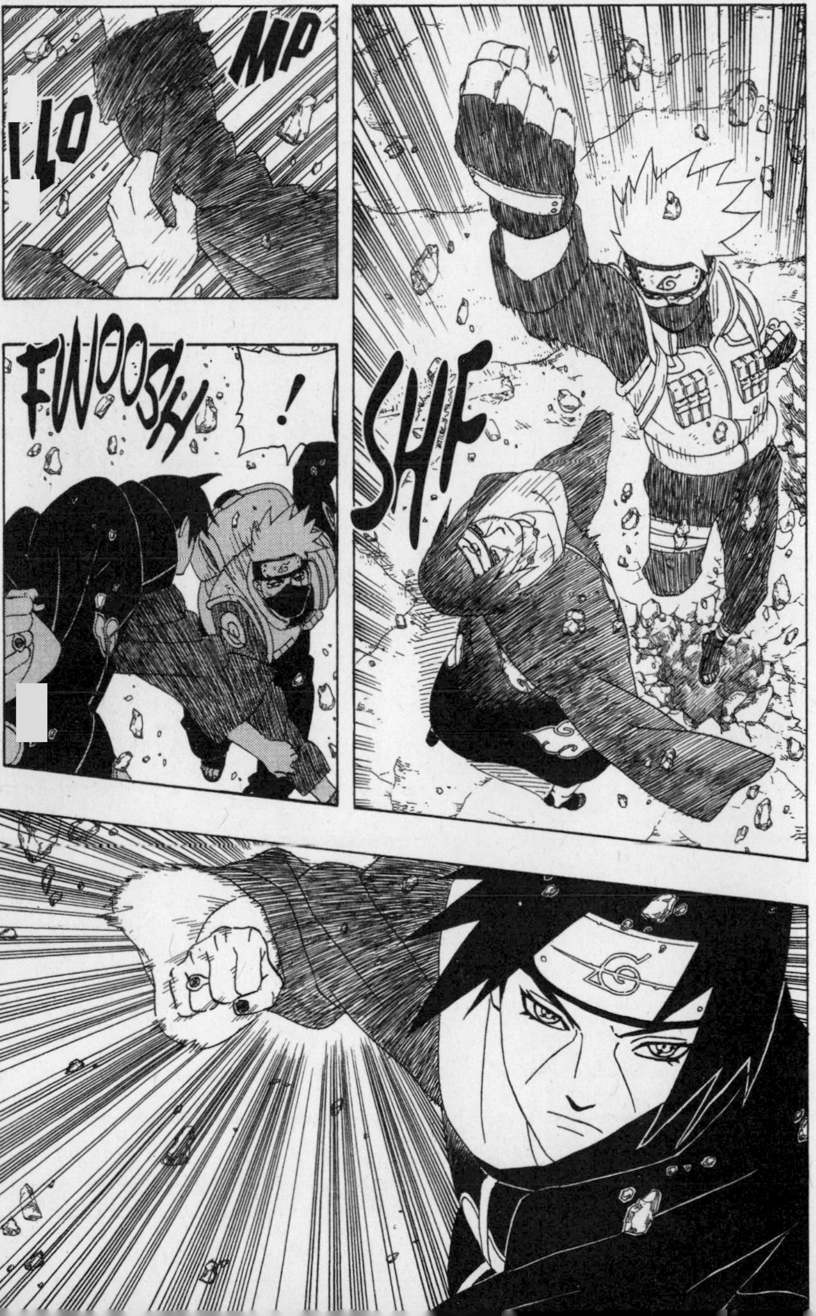
SHF
FWOOSH
!

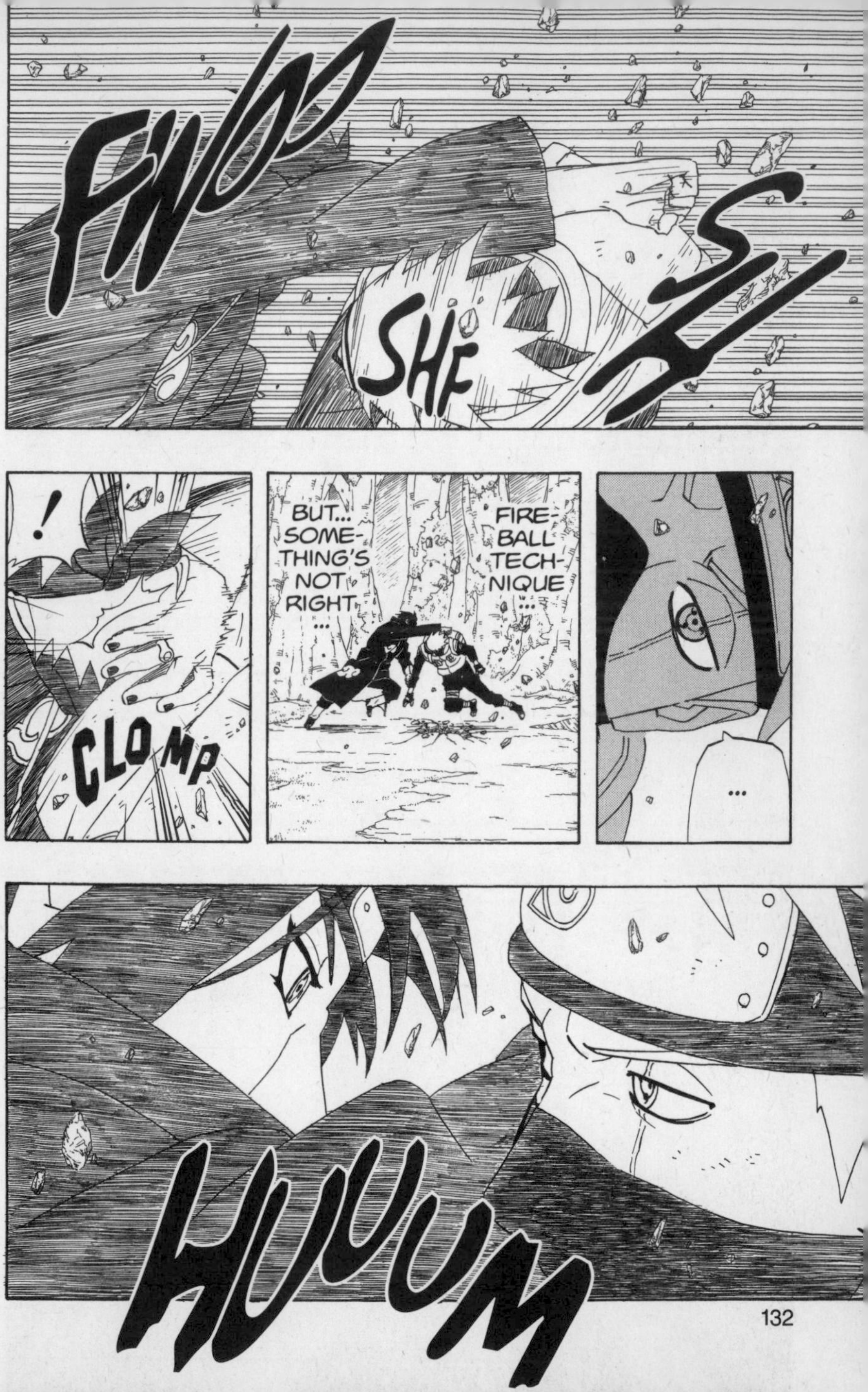
FWOOSH
SHF
...
FIRE-BALL TECHNIQUE...
BUT... SOMETHING'S NOT RIGHT...
!
CLOMP
HWUUUM

READ THIS WAY

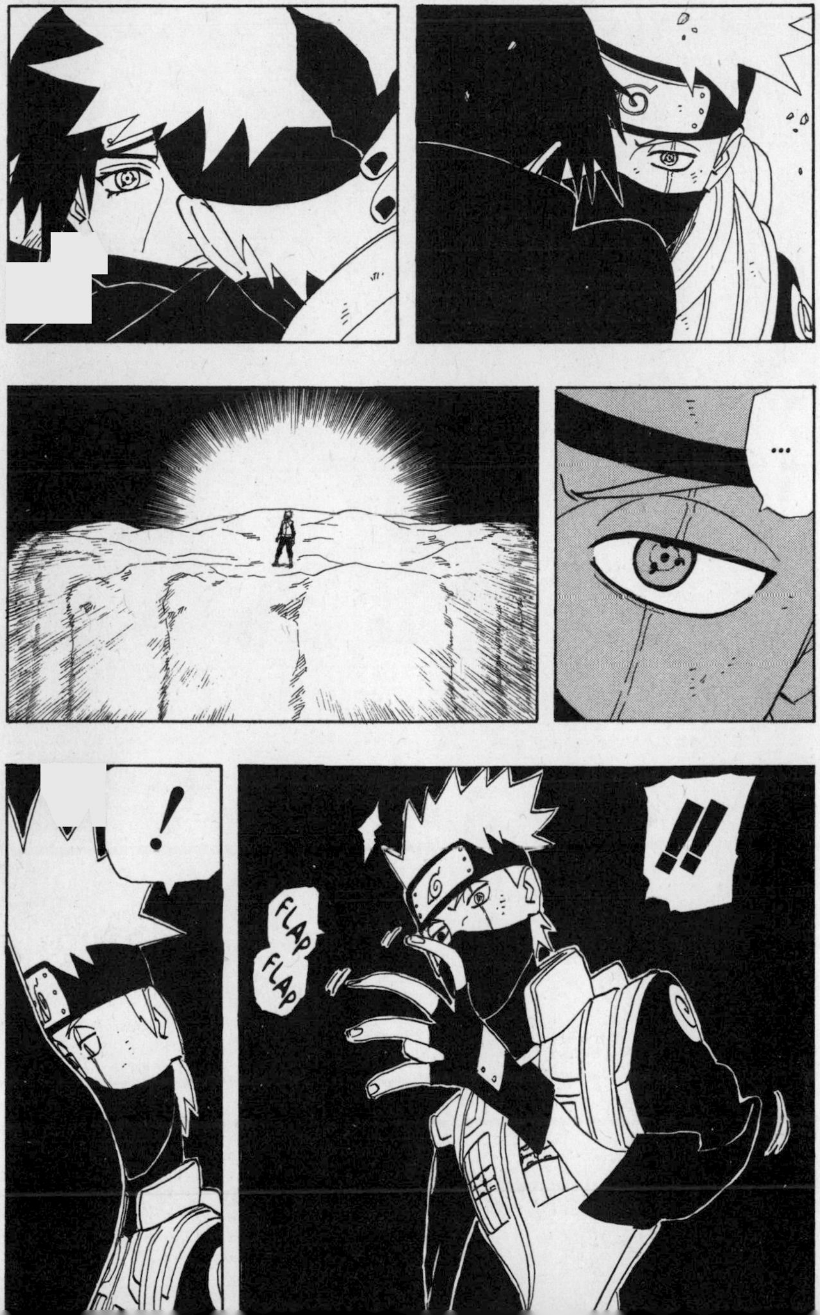
...
!!
FLAP
FLAP
!

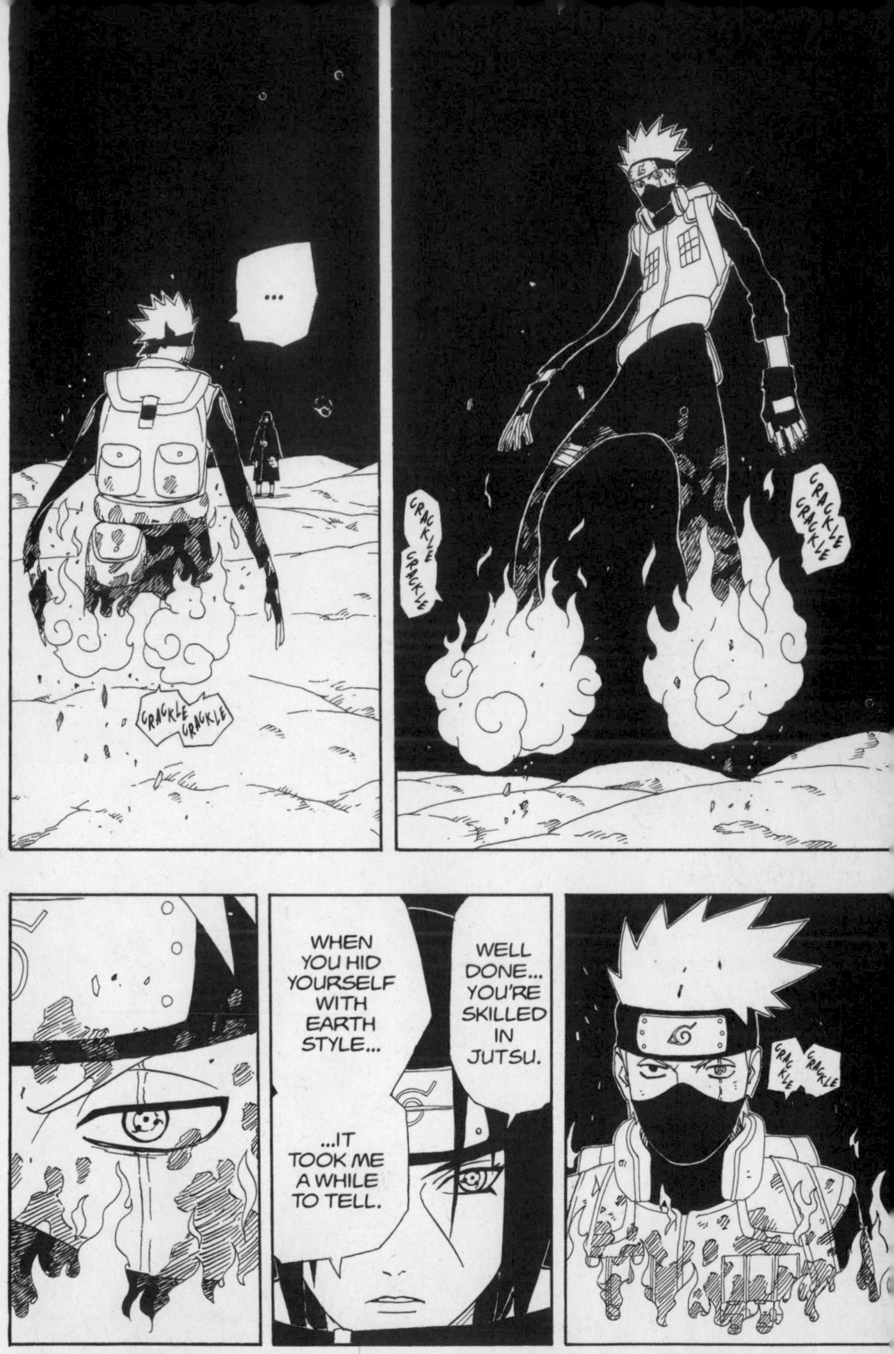
CRACKLE CRACKLE
CRACKLE CRACKLE
...
CRACKLE CRACKLE
CRACKLE CRACKLE
WELL DONE... YOU'RE SKILLED IN JUTSU.
WHEN YOU HID YOURSELF WITH EARTH STYLE...
...IT TOOK ME A WHILE TO TELL.

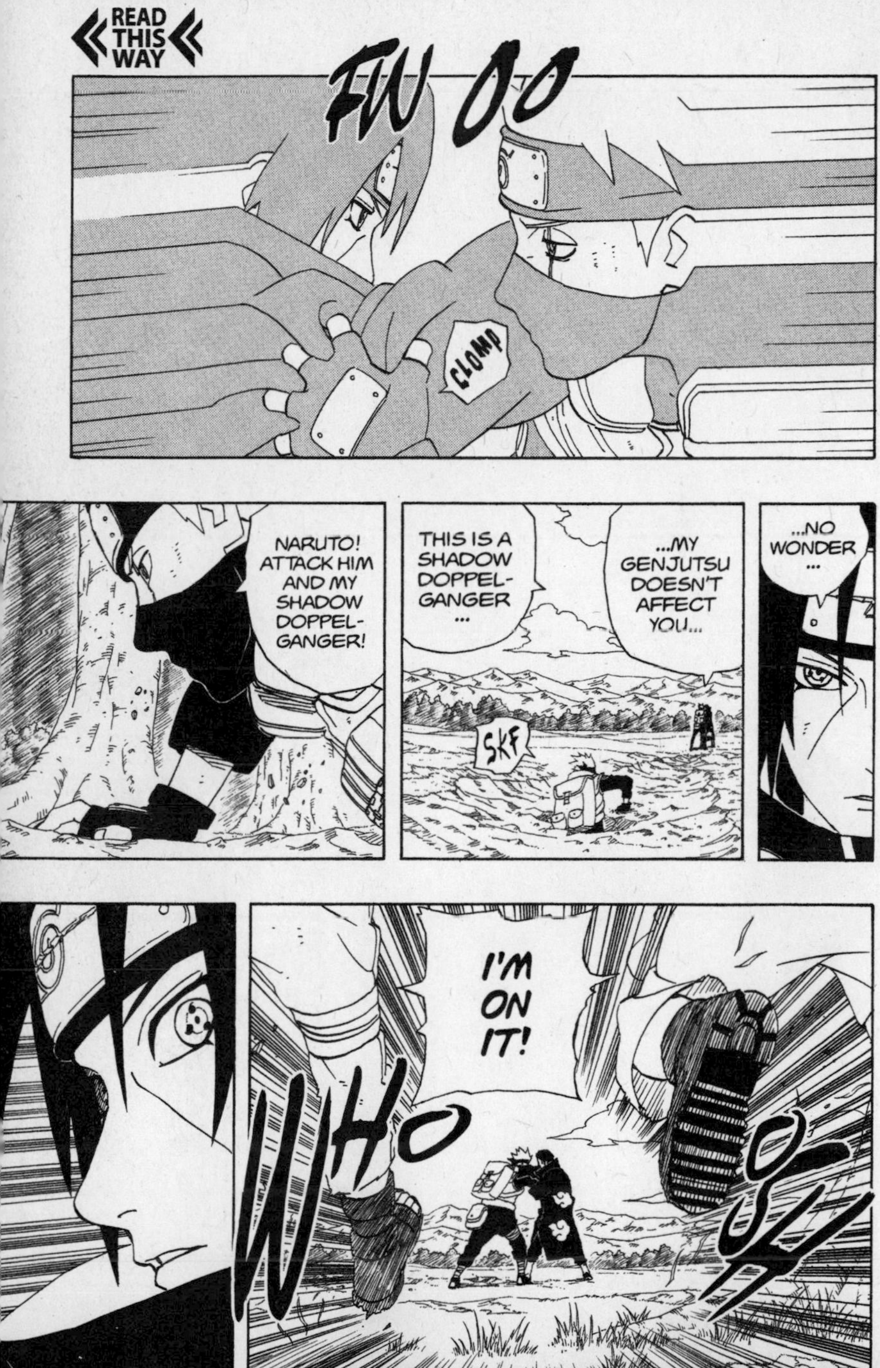
READ THIS WAY
FWOO
CLOMP
...NO WONDER ...
...MY GENJUTSU DOESN'T AFFECT YOU...
THIS IS A SHADOW DOPPEL-GANGER ...
SKF
NARUTO! ATTACK HIM AND MY SHADOW DOPPEL-GANGER!
I'M ON IT!
WHOOSH

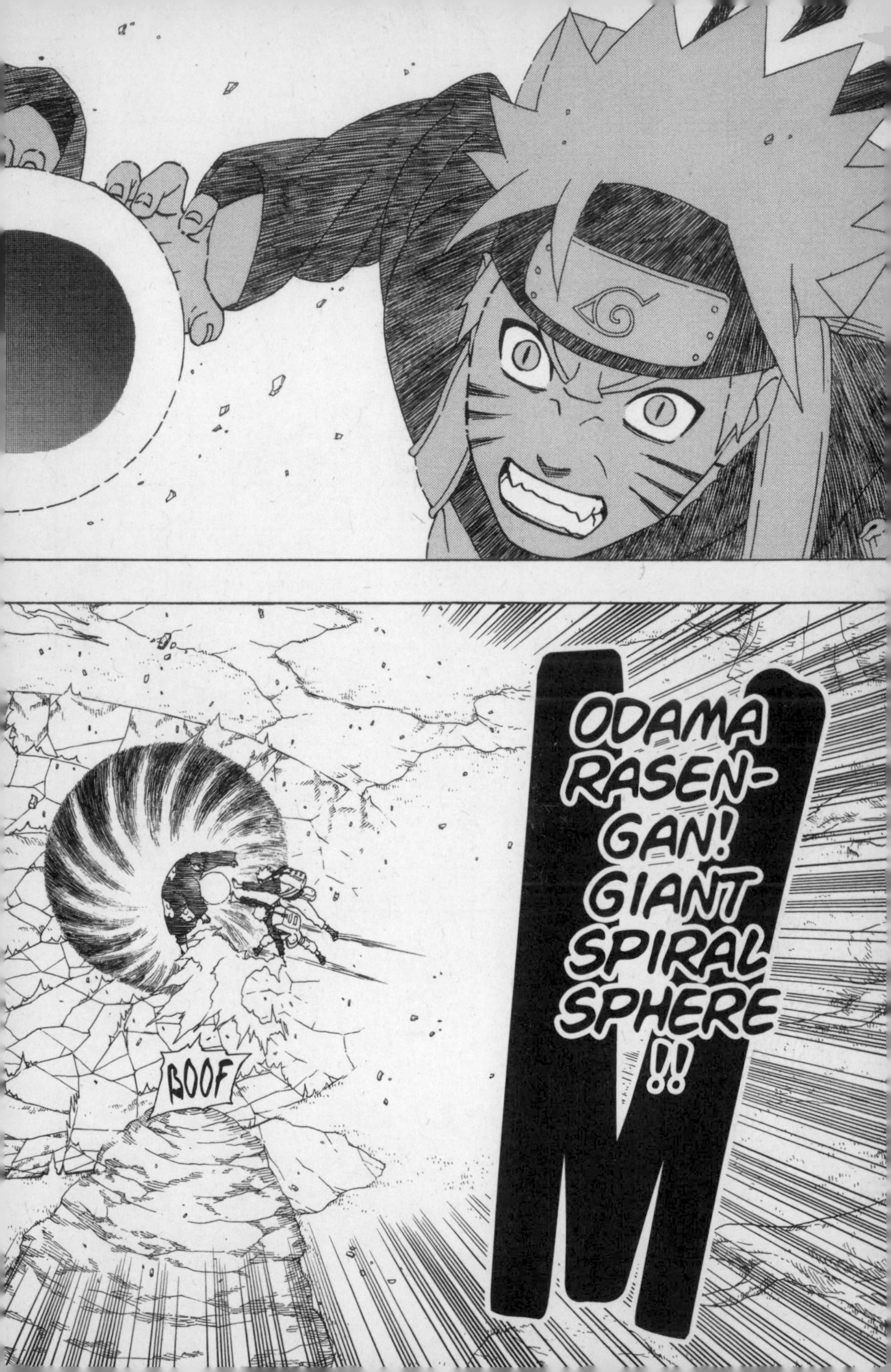
ODAMA RASEN-GAN! GIANT SPIRAL SPHERE!!
BOOF

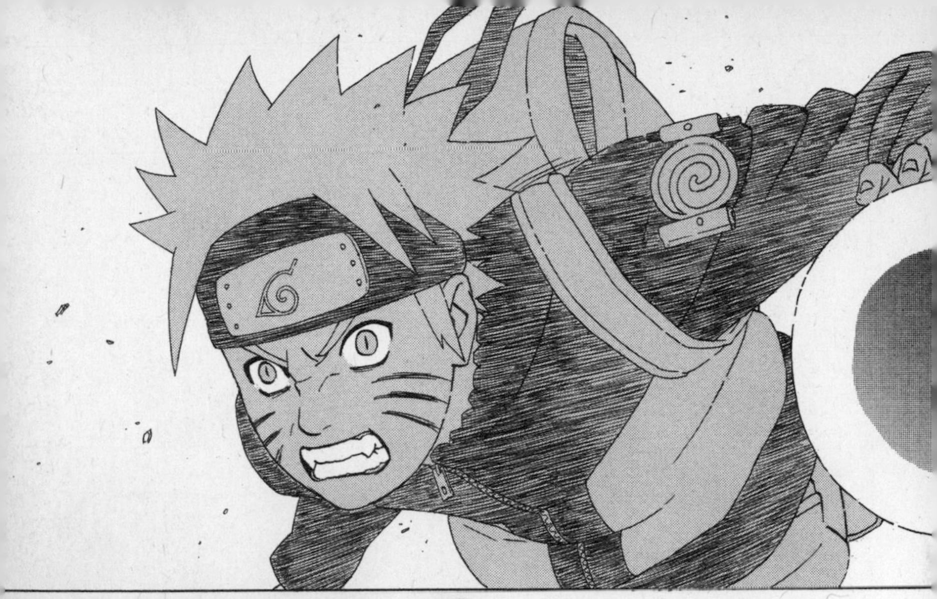

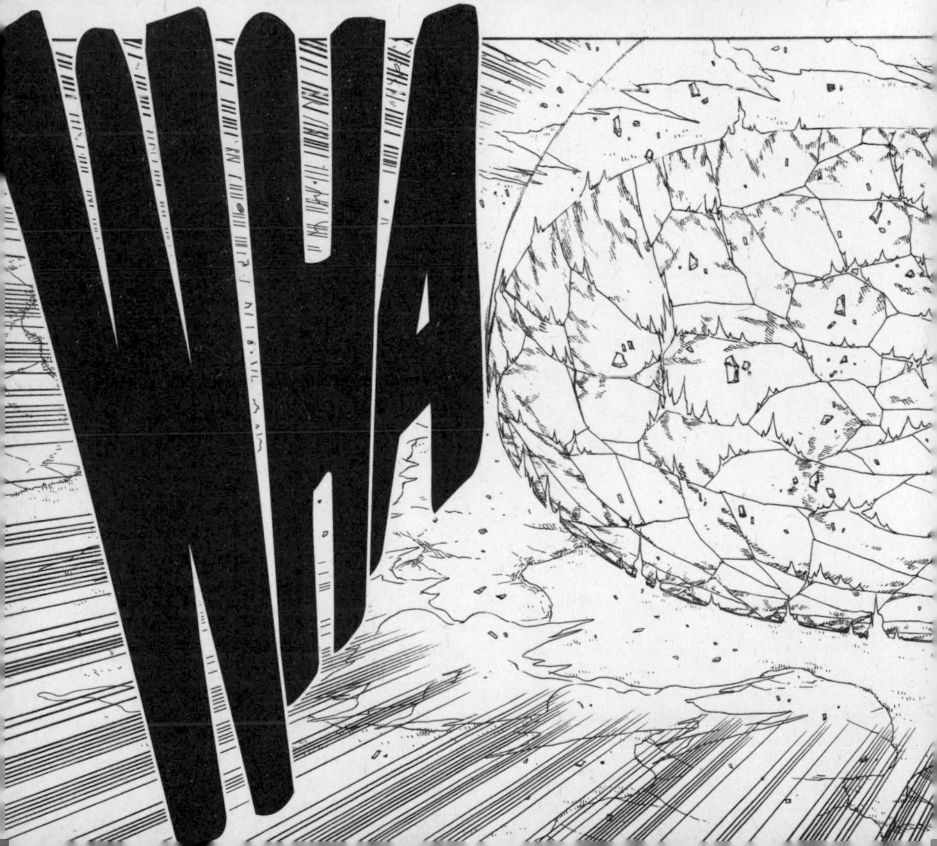
WHA

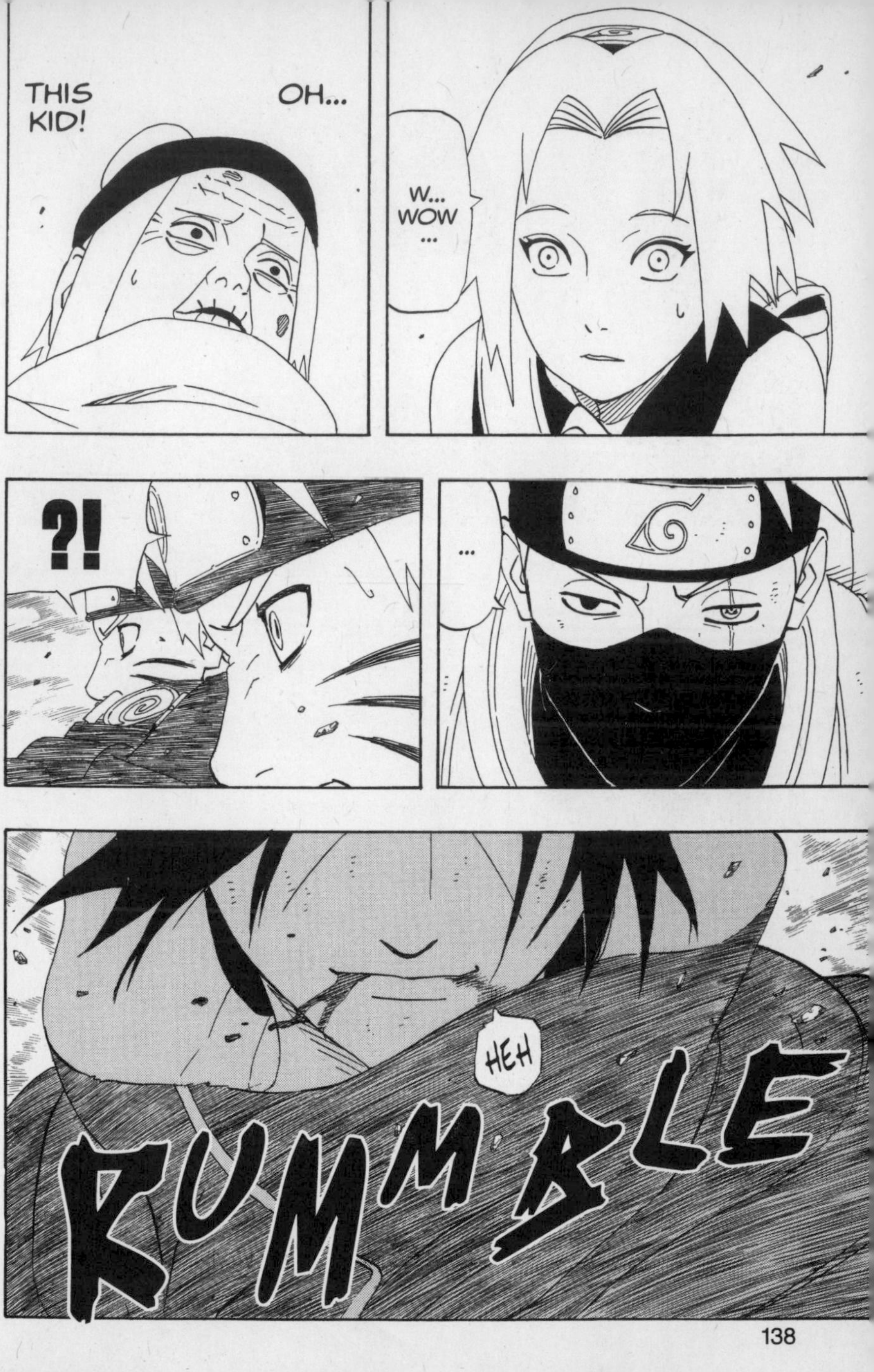
W... WOW ...
OH...
THIS KID!
...
?!
HEH
RUMMBLE

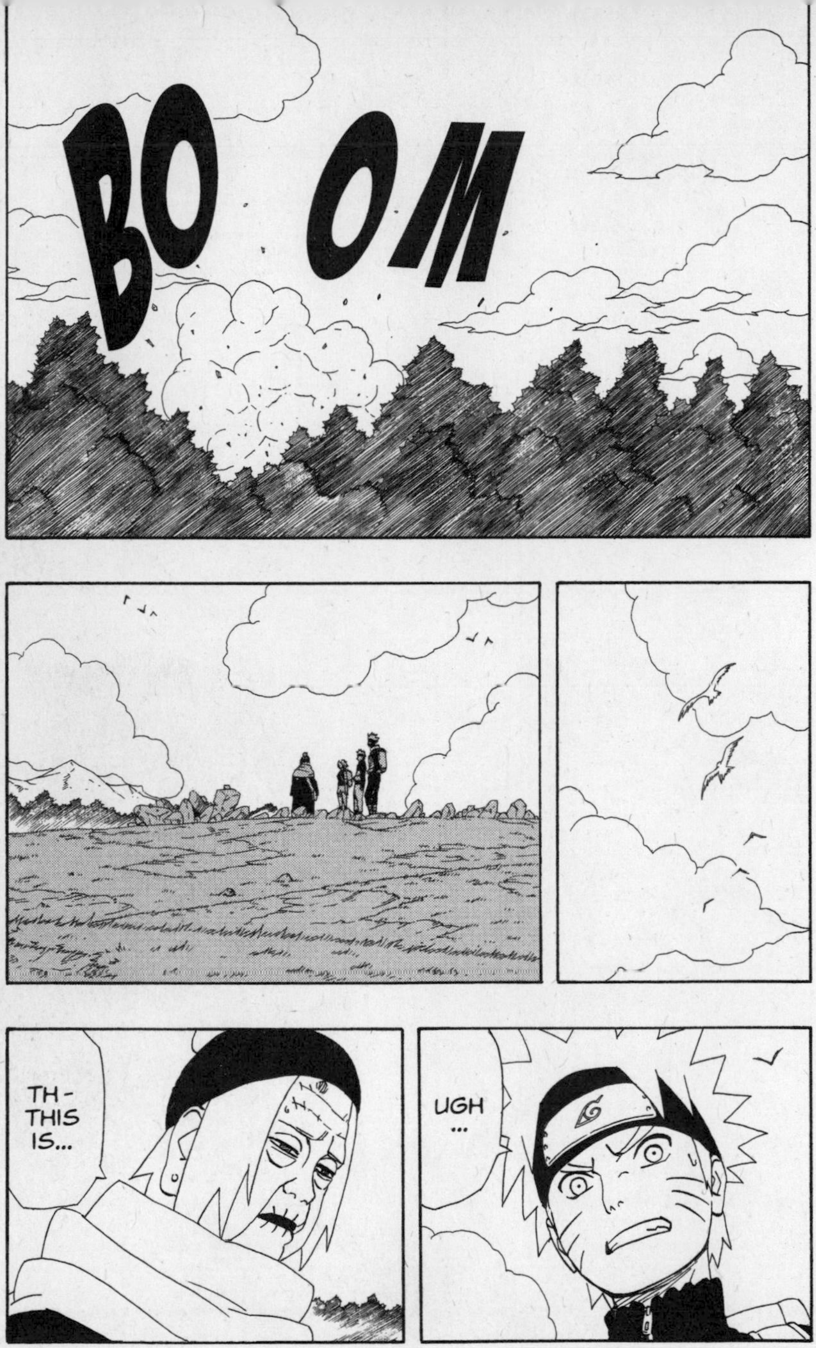
BOOM
UGH ...
TH-THIS IS...

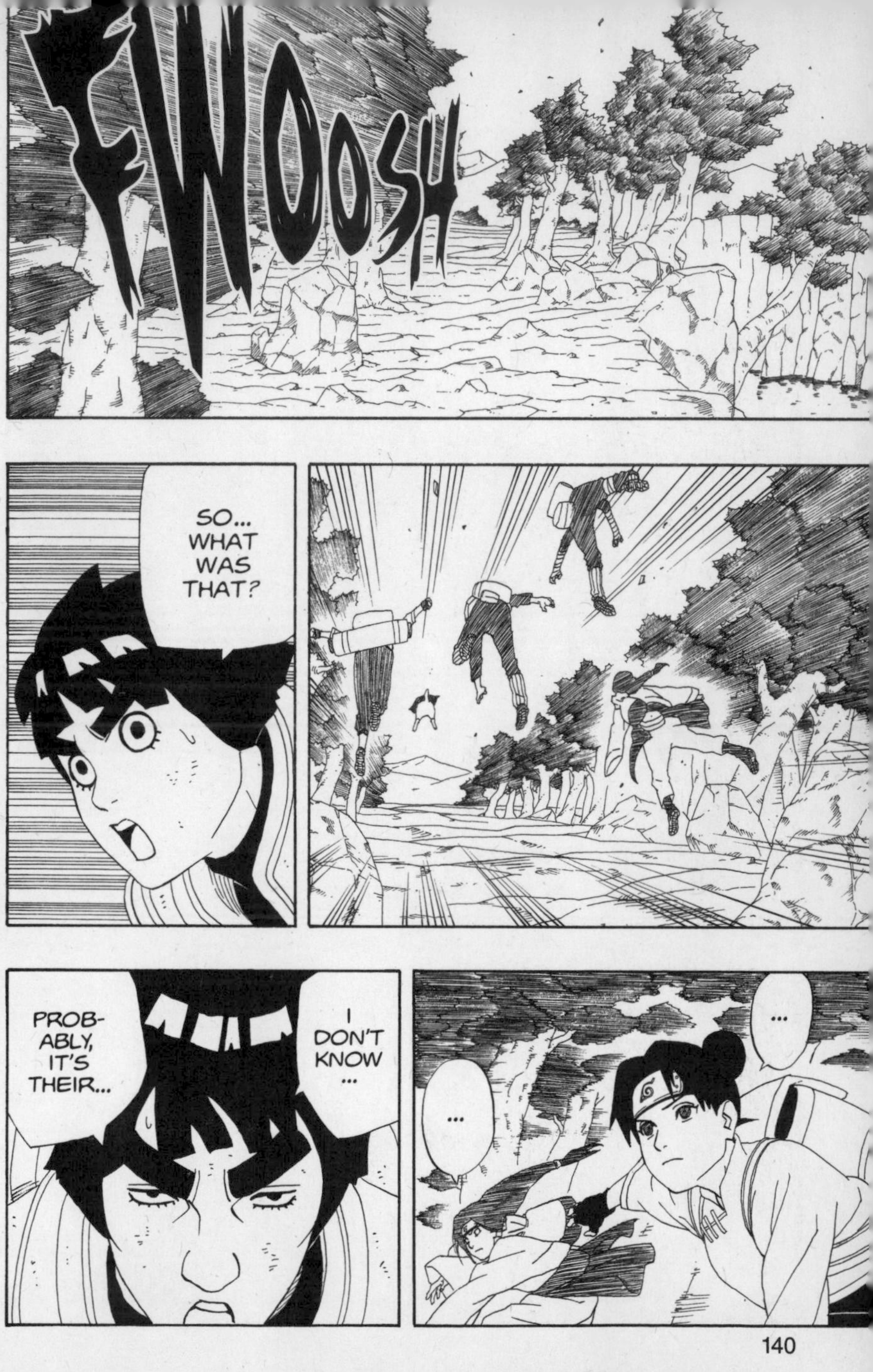
FWOOSH
SO... WHAT WAS THAT?
...
...
I DON'T KNOW ...
PROB-ABLY, IT'S THEIR...

READ THIS WAY

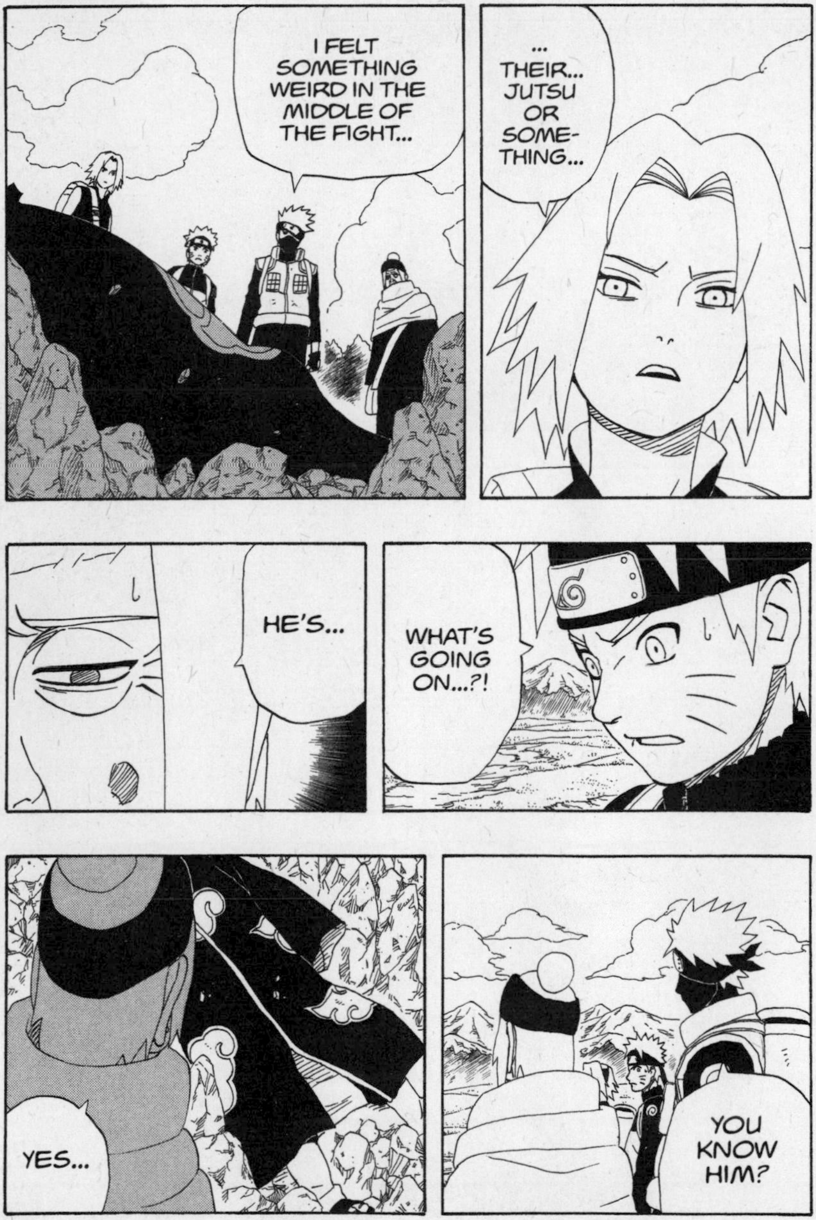

... THEIR... JUTSU OR SOME-THING...
I FELT SOMETHING WEIRD IN THE MIDDLE OF THE FIGHT...
WHAT'S GOING ON...?!
HE'S...
YOU KNOW HIM?
YES...

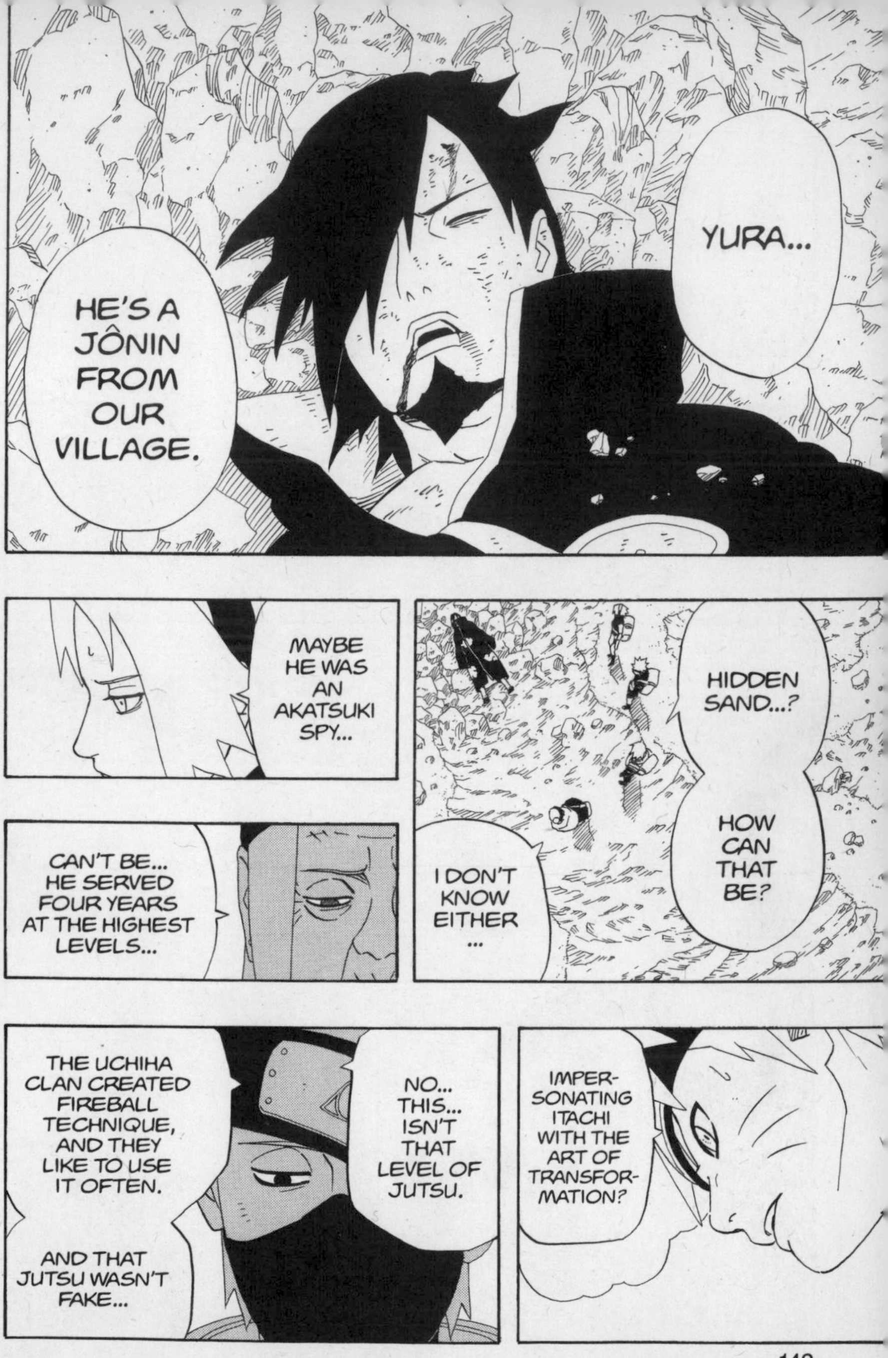
YURA...
HE'S A JÔNIN FROM OUR VILLAGE.
HIDDEN SAND...?
HOW CAN THAT BE?
I DON'T KNOW EITHER ...
MAYBE HE WAS AN AKATSUKI SPY...
CAN'T BE... HE SERVED FOUR YEARS AT THE HIGHEST LEVELS...
IMPER-SONATING ITACHI WITH THE ART OF TRANSFOR-MATION?
NO... THIS... ISN'T THAT LEVEL OF JUTSU.
THE UCHIHA CLAN CREATED FIREBALL TECHNIQUE, AND THEY LIKE TO USE IT OFTEN.
AND THAT JUTSU WASN'T FAKE...

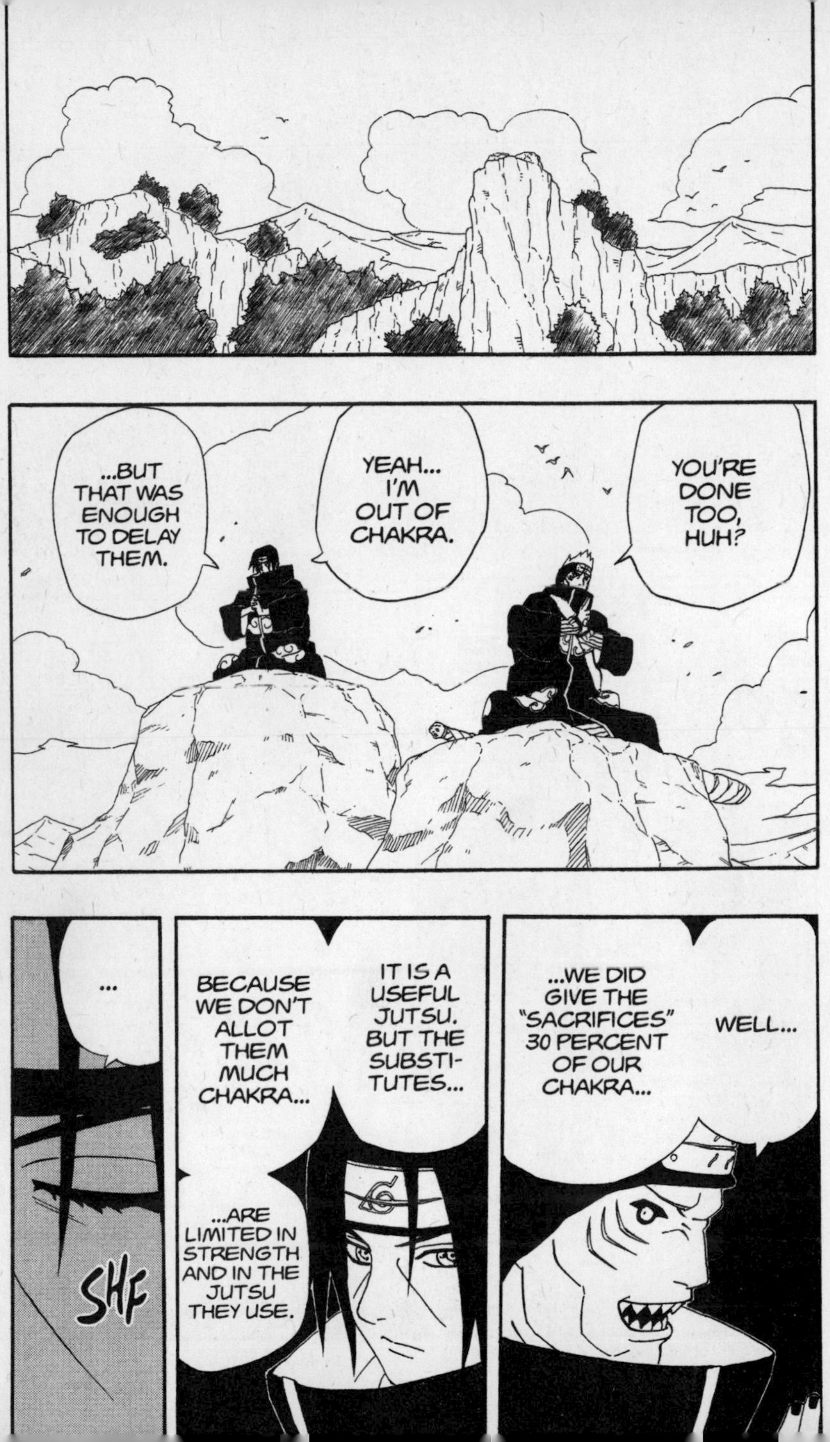
YOU'RE DONE TOO, HUH?
YEAH... I'M OUT OF CHAKRA.
...BUT THAT WAS ENOUGH TO DELAY THEM.
WELL...
...WE DID GIVE THE "SACRIFICES" 30 PERCENT OF OUR CHAKRA...
IT IS A USEFUL JUTSU. BUT THE SUBSTITUTES...
...ARE LIMITED IN STRENGTH AND IN THE JUTSU THEY USE.
BECAUSE WE DON'T ALLOT THEM MUCH CHAKRA...
...
SHF

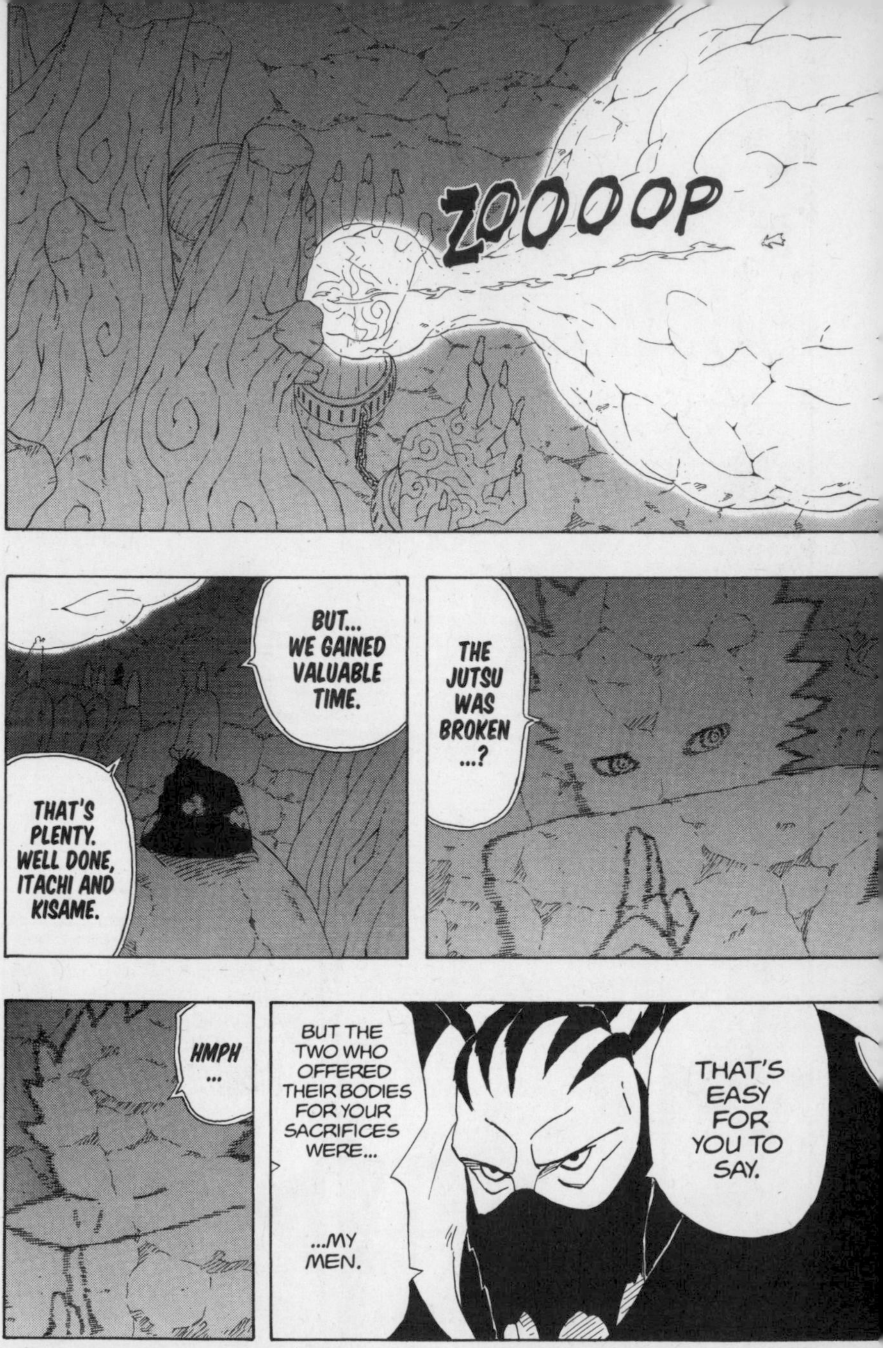
ZOOOOP
THE JUTSU WAS BROKEN ...?
BUT... WE GAINED VALUABLE TIME.
THAT'S PLENTY. WELL DONE, ITACHI AND KISAME.
THAT'S EASY FOR YOU TO SAY.
BUT THE TWO WHO OFFERED THEIR BODIES FOR YOUR SACRIFICES WERE...
...MY MEN.
HMPH ...

THEY WERE AKATSUKI MEMBERS FOR A SHORT TIME BECAUSE OF MY ART OF IMPERSONATION TECHNIQUE.

I WOULD EXPECT THEIR THANKS FOR THE PRIVILEGE...

...

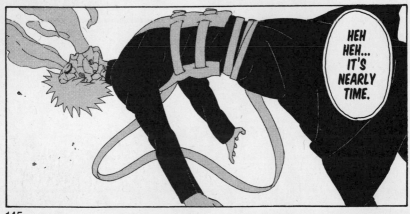

HEH HEH... IT'S NEARLY TIME.

NARUTO

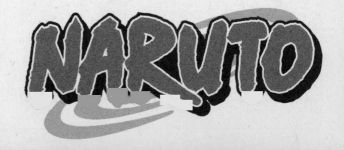

Number 261: Jinchûriki Host...!!

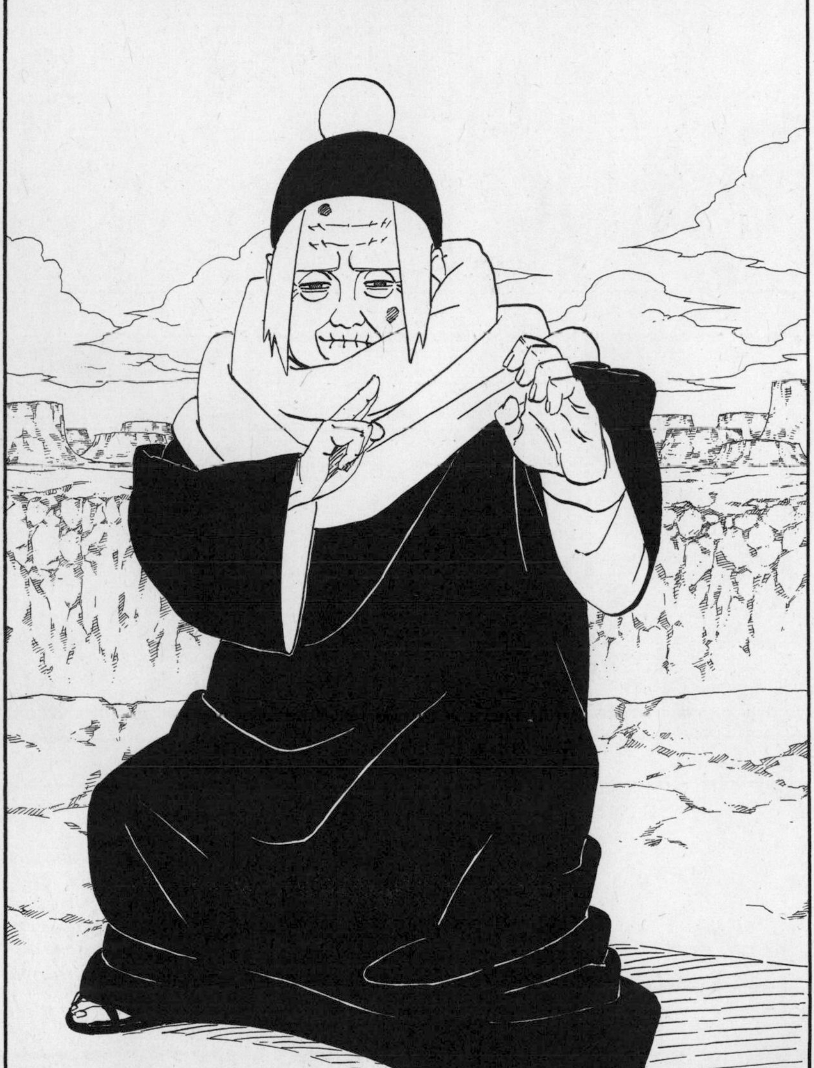

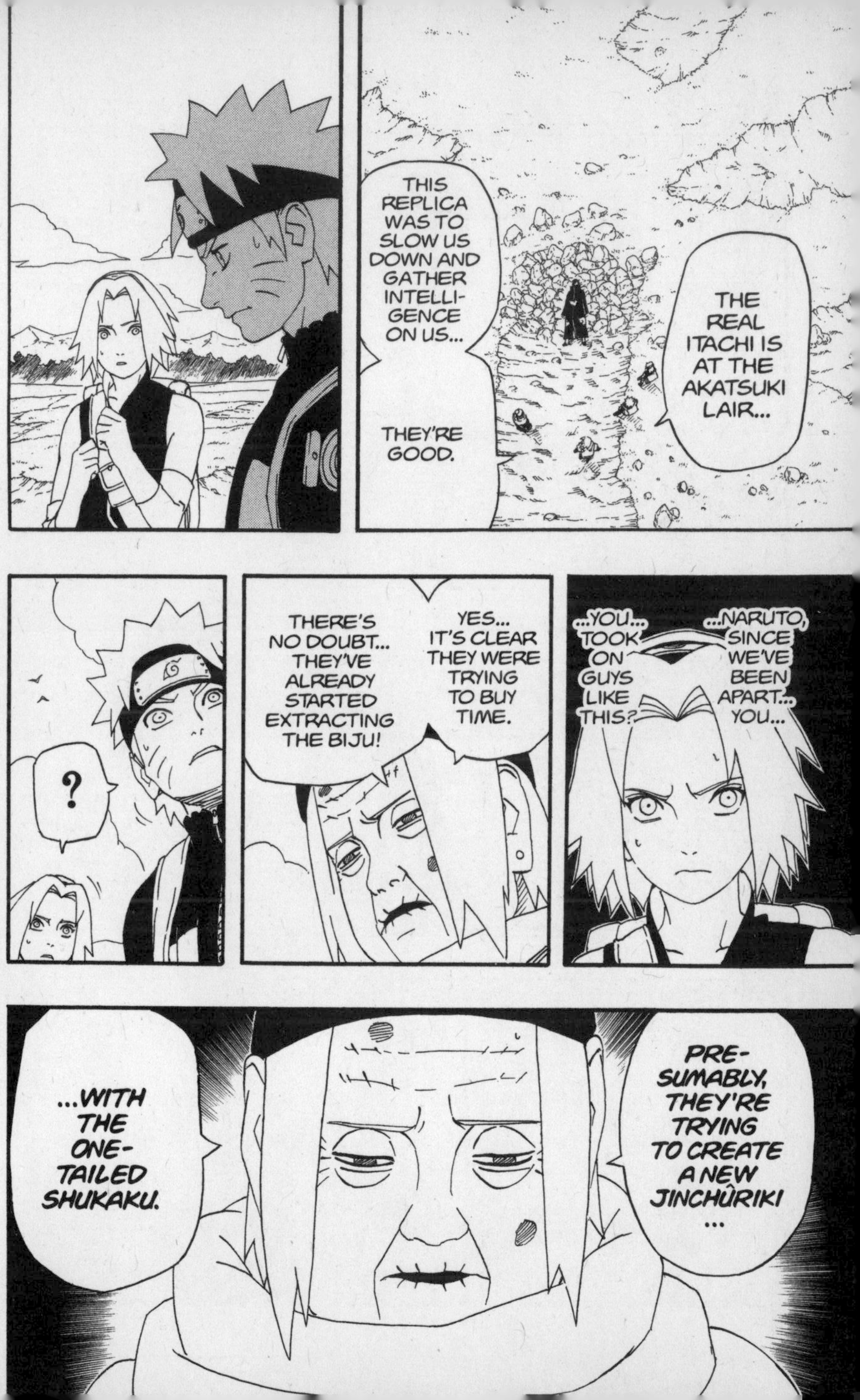
THE REAL ITACHI IS AT THE AKATSUKI LAIR...
THIS REPLICA WAS TO SLOW US DOWN AND GATHER INTELLI-GENCE ON US...
THEY'RE GOOD.
...NARUTO, SINCE WE'VE BEEN APART... YOU...
...YOU... TOOK ON GUYS LIKE THIS?
YES... IT'S CLEAR THEY WERE TRYING TO BUY TIME.
THERE'S NO DOUBT... THEY'VE ALREADY STARTED EXTRACTING THE BIJU!
?
PRE-SUMABLY, THEY'RE TRYING TO CREATE A NEW JINCHÛRIKI ...
...WITH THE ONE-TAILED SHUKAKU.

READ THIS WAY

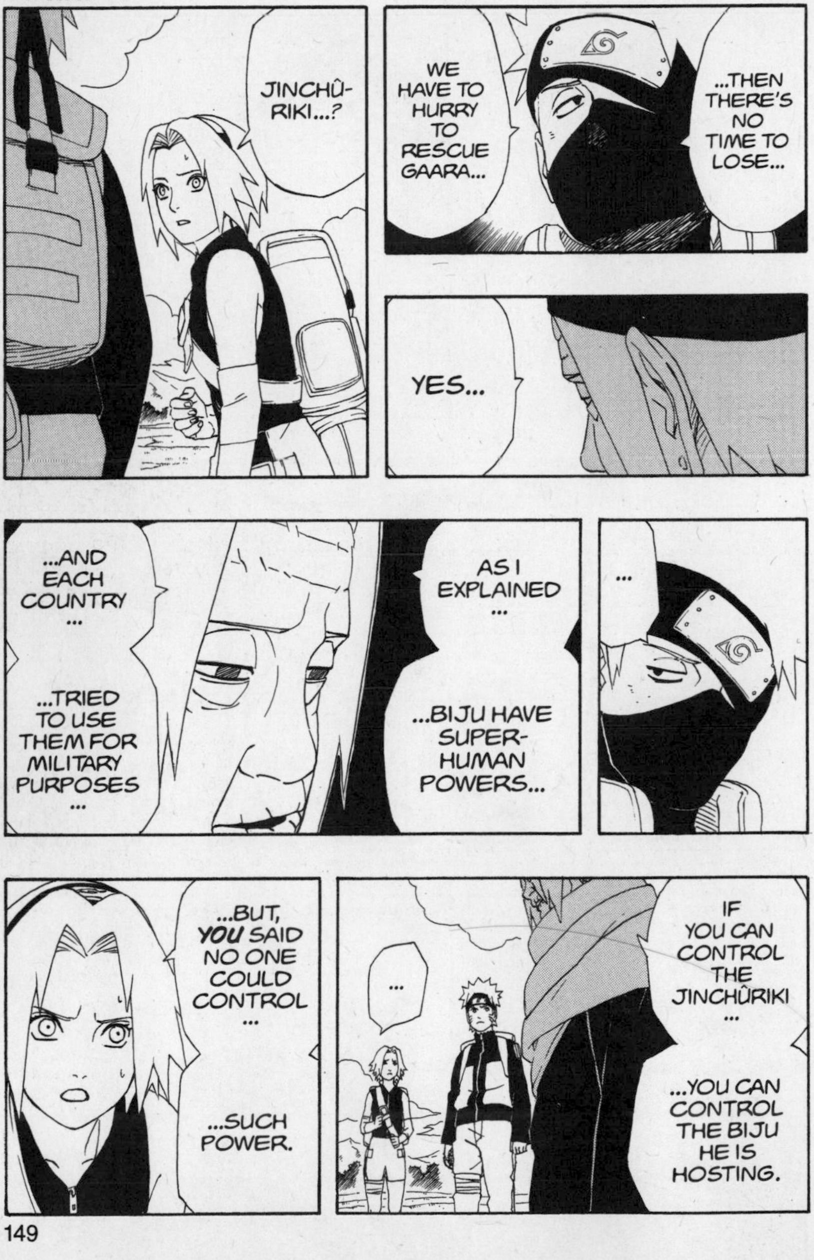

...THEN THERE'S NO TIME TO LOSE...
WE HAVE TO HURRY TO RESCUE GAARA...
YES...
JINCHÛ-RIKI...?
...
AS I EXPLAINED ...
...BIJU HAVE SUPER-HUMAN POWERS...
...AND EACH COUNTRY ...
...TRIED TO USE THEM FOR MILITARY PURPOSES ...
IF YOU CAN CONTROL THE JINCHÛRIKI ...
...YOU CAN CONTROL THE BIJU HE IS HOSTING.
...
...BUT, ***YOU*** SAID NO ONE COULD CONTROL ...
...SUCH POWER.

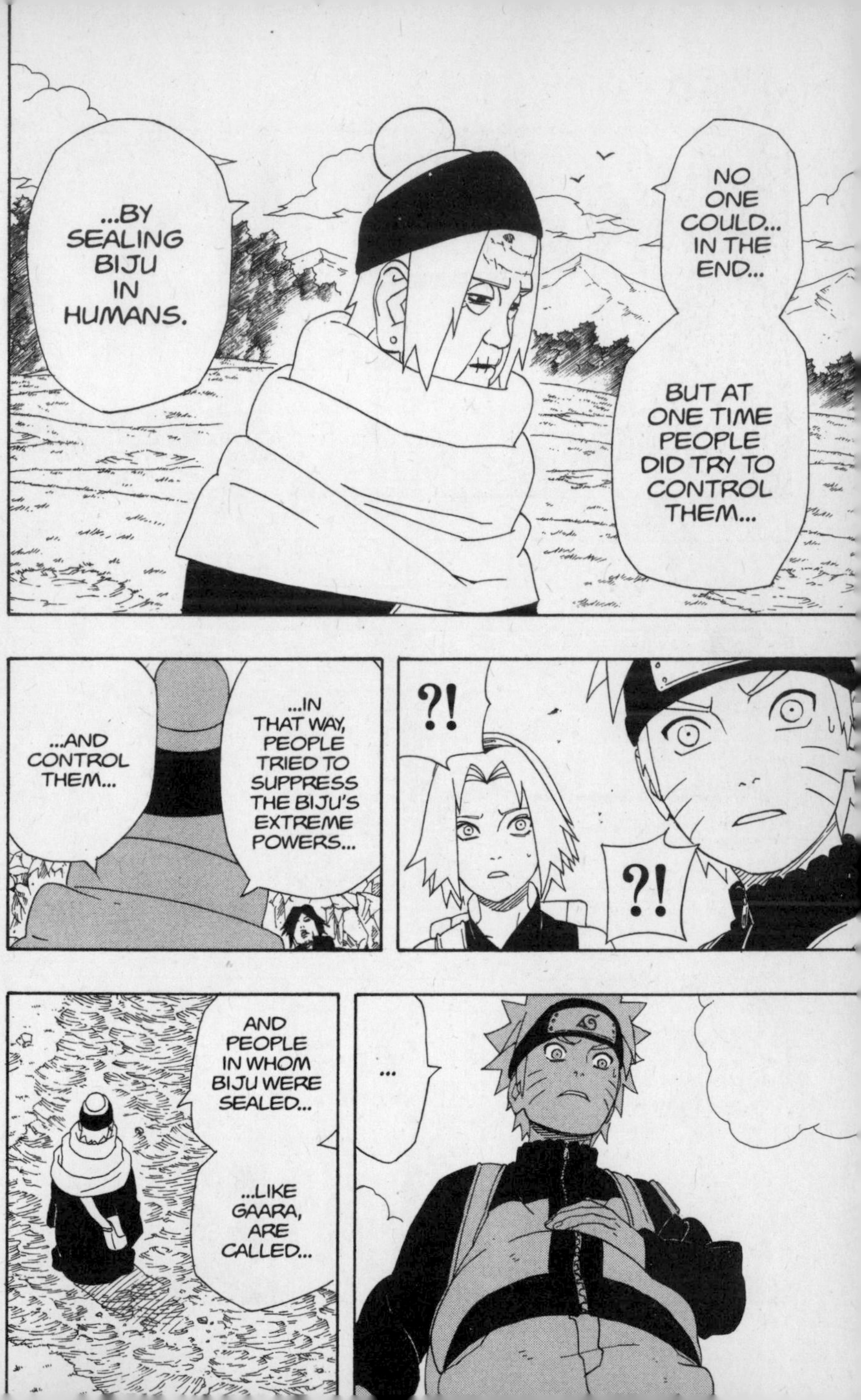
NO ONE COULD... IN THE END...
BUT AT ONE TIME PEOPLE DID TRY TO CONTROL THEM...
...BY SEALING BIJU IN HUMANS.
?!
?!
...IN THAT WAY, PEOPLE TRIED TO SUPPRESS THE BIJU'S EXTREME POWERS...
...AND CONTROL THEM...
...
AND PEOPLE IN WHOM BIJU WERE SEALED...
...LIKE GAARA, ARE CALLED...

READ THIS WAY

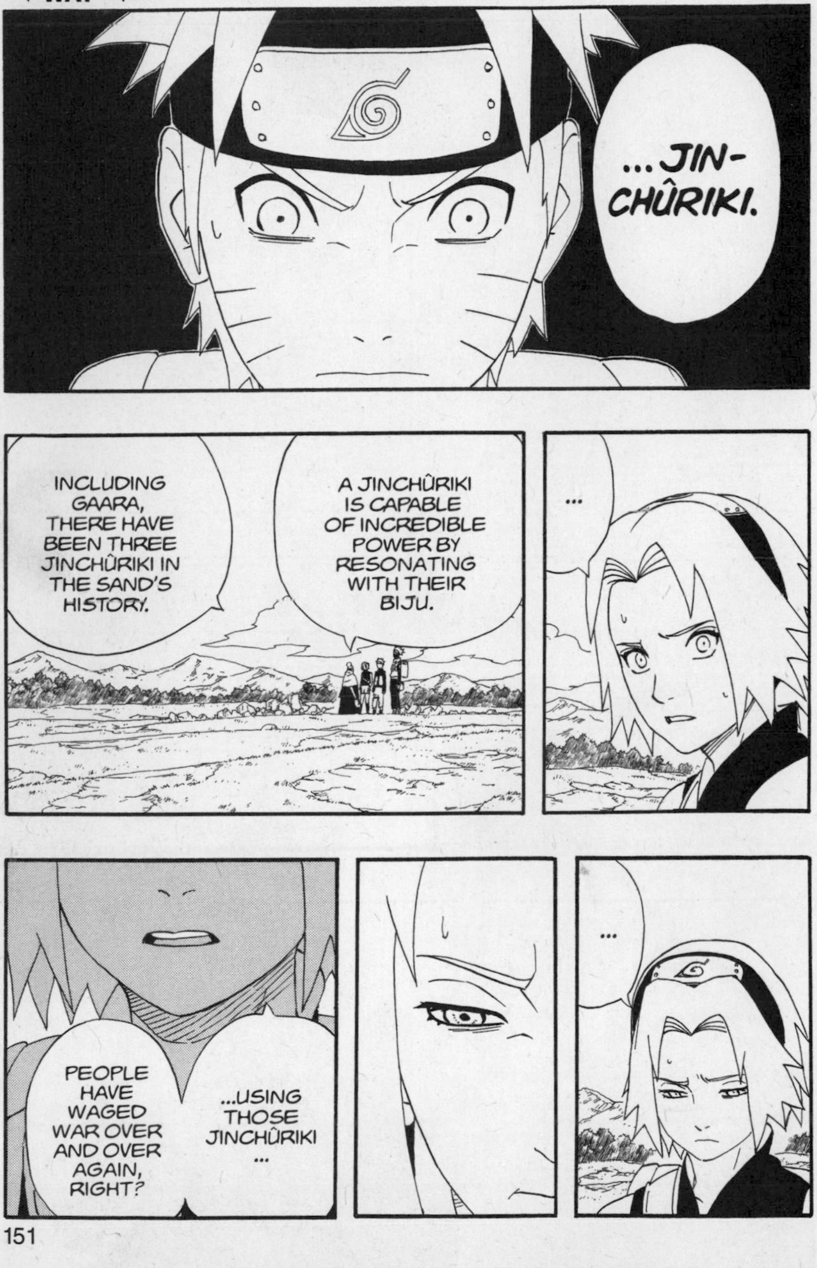

...JIN-CHÛRIKI.
...
A JINCHÛRIKI IS CAPABLE OF INCREDIBLE POWER BY RESONATING WITH THEIR BIJU.
INCLUDING GAARA, THERE HAVE BEEN THREE JINCHÛRIKI IN THE SAND'S HISTORY.
...
PEOPLE HAVE WAGED WAR OVER AND OVER AGAIN, RIGHT?
...USING THOSE JINCHÛRIKI ...

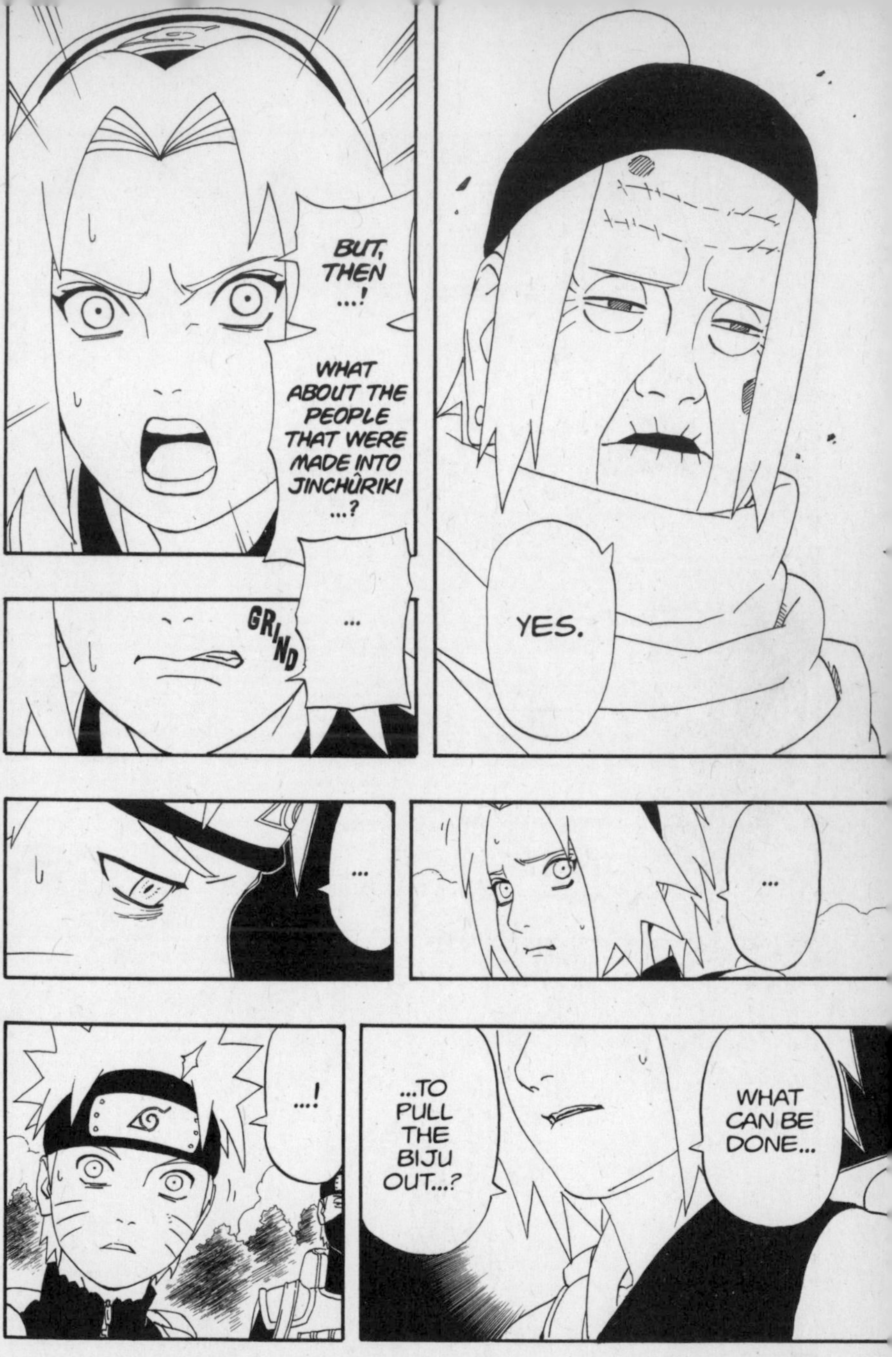
BUT, THEN ...!
WHAT ABOUT THE PEOPLE THAT WERE MADE INTO JINCHÛRIKI ...?
YES.
GRIND
...
...
...
WHAT CAN BE DONE...
...TO PULL THE BIJU OUT...?
...!

READ THIS WAY

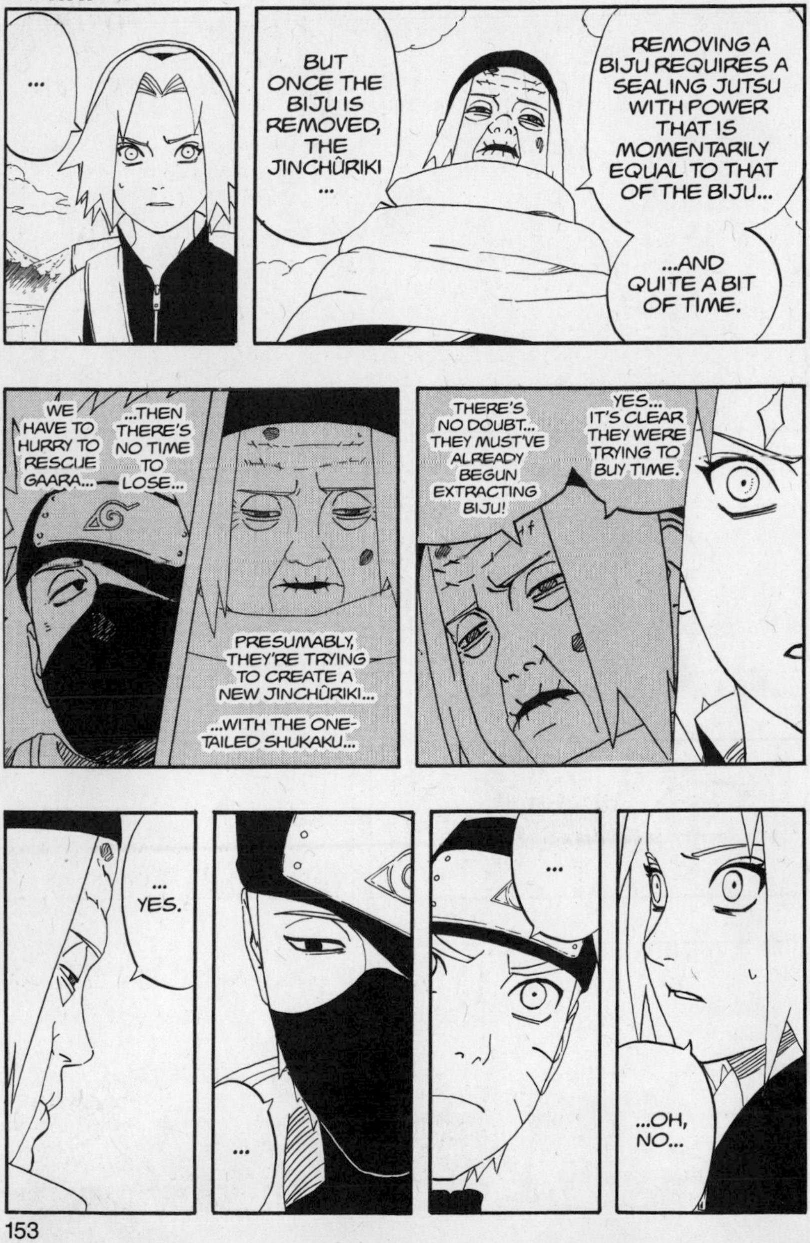
REMOVING A BIJU REQUIRES A SEALING JUTSU WITH POWER THAT IS MOMENTARILY EQUAL TO THAT OF THE BIJU...
...AND QUITE A BIT OF TIME.
BUT ONCE THE BIJU IS REMOVED, THE JINCHÛRIKI ...
...
YES... IT'S CLEAR THEY WERE TRYING TO BUY TIME.
THERE'S NO DOUBT... THEY MUST'VE ALREADY BEGUN EXTRACTING BIJU!
PRESUMABLY, THEY'RE TRYING TO CREATE A NEW JINCHÛRIKI...
...WITH THE ONE-TAILED SHUKAKU...
...THEN THERE'S NO TIME TO LOSE...
WE HAVE TO HURRY TO RESCUE GAARA...
...OH, NO...
...
...
... YES.

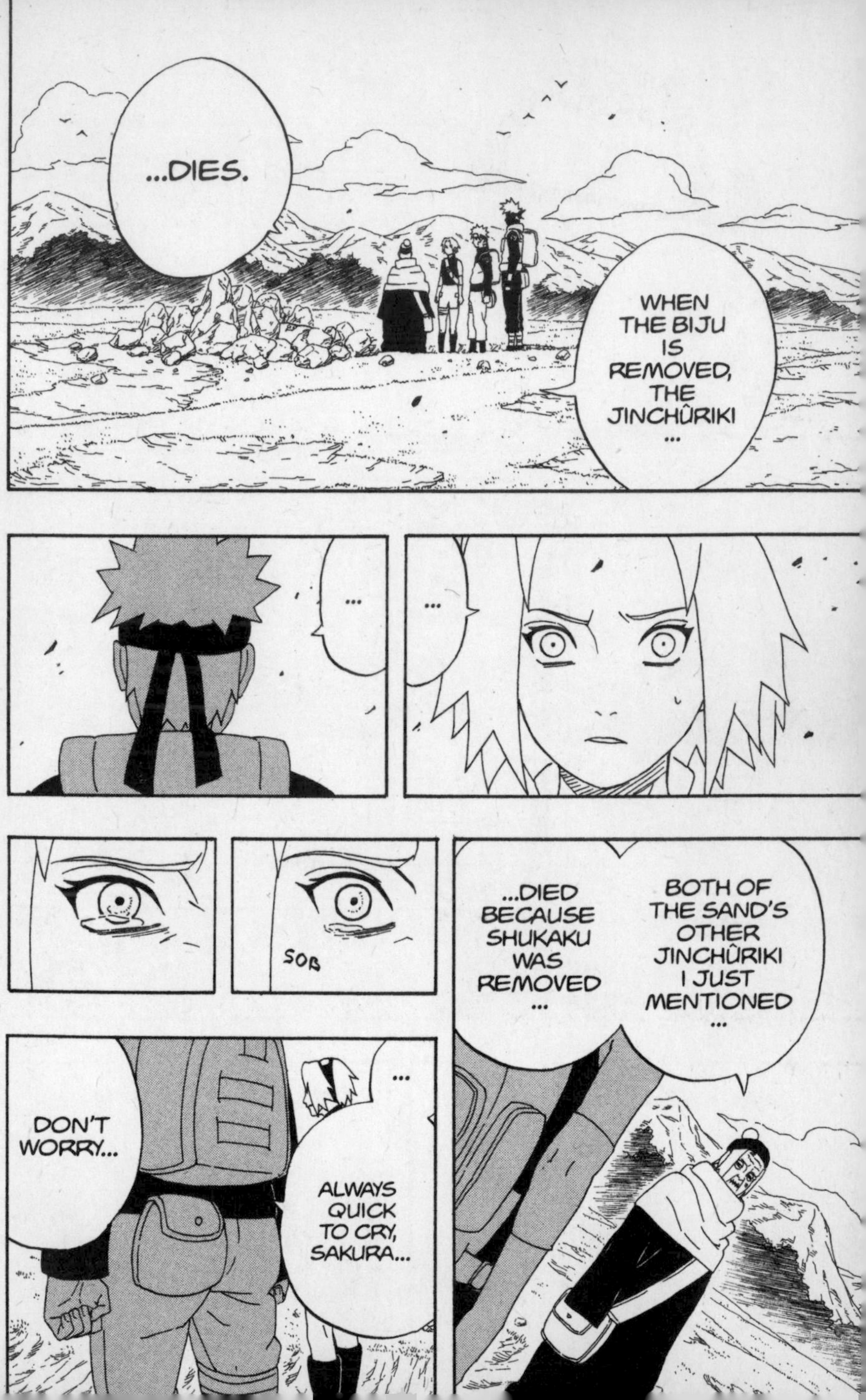
WHEN THE BIJU IS REMOVED, THE JINCHÛRIKI ...
...DIES.
...
...
BOTH OF THE SAND'S OTHER JINCHÛRIKI I JUST MENTIONED ...
...DIED BECAUSE SHUKAKU WAS REMOVED ...
SOB
...
ALWAYS QUICK TO CRY, SAKURA...
DON'T WORRY...

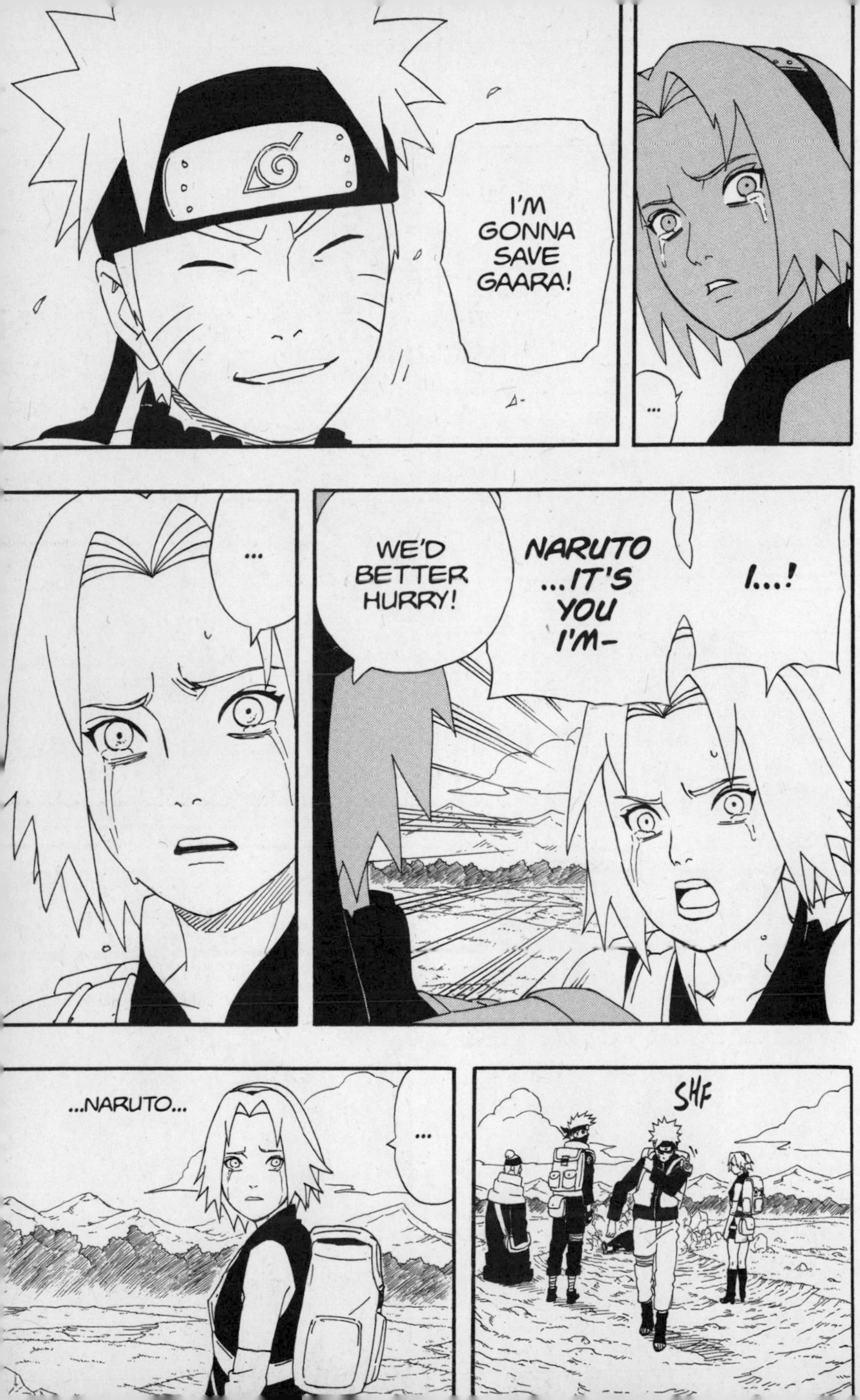
...
I'M GONNA SAVE GAARA!
I...!
NARUTO ...IT'S YOU I'M-
WE'D BETTER HURRY!
...
SHF
...
...NARUTO...

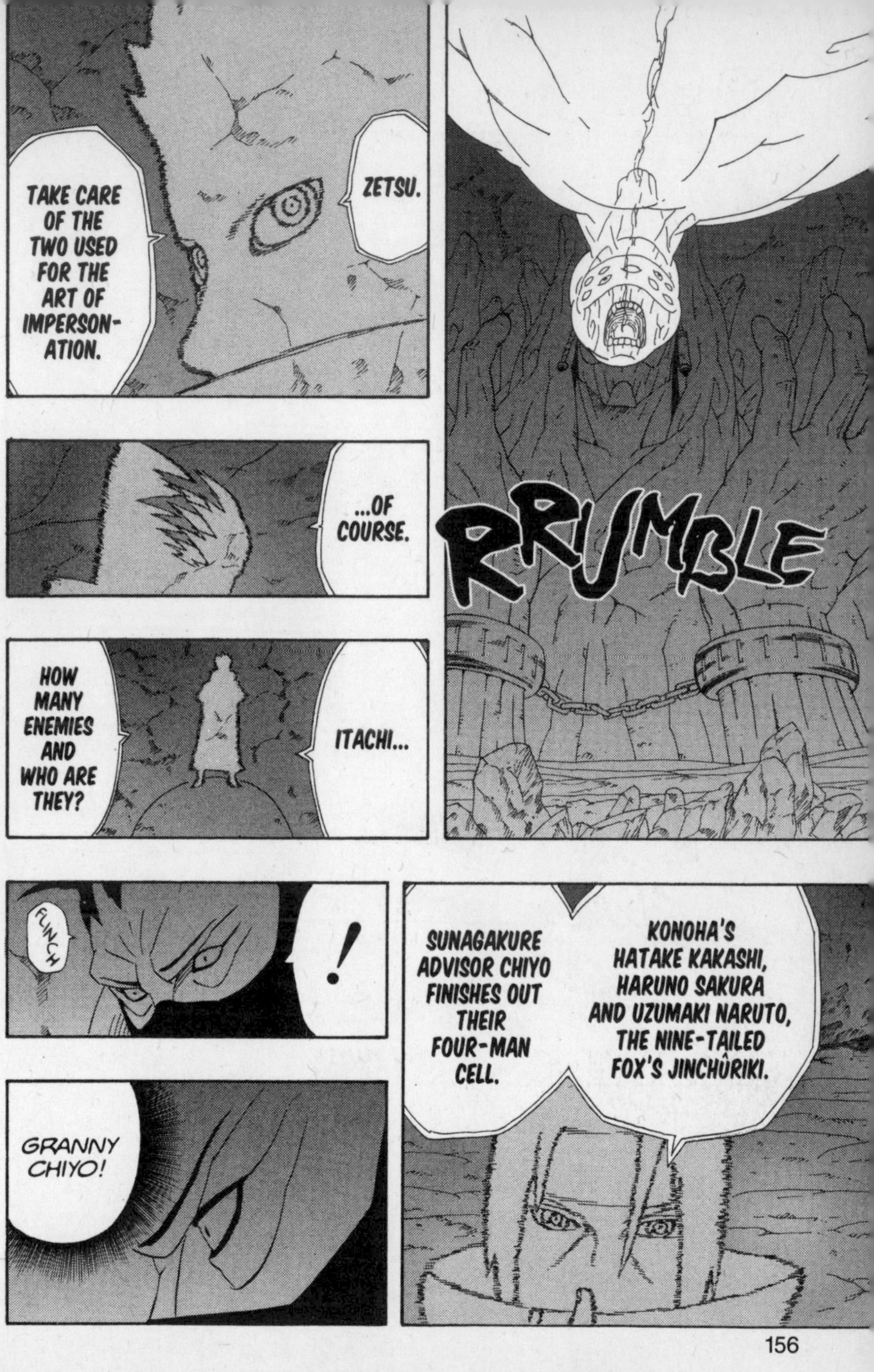
RRUMBLE
ZETSU.
TAKE CARE OF THE TWO USED FOR THE ART OF IMPERSON-ATION.
...OF COURSE.
ITACHI...
HOW MANY ENEMIES AND WHO ARE THEY?
KONOHA'S HATAKE KAKASHI, HARUNO SAKURA AND UZUMAKI NARUTO, THE NINE-TAILED FOX'S JINCHÛRIKI.
SUNAGAKURE ADVISOR CHIYO FINISHES OUT THEIR FOUR-MAN CELL.
!
FLINCH
GRANNY CHIYO!

READ THIS WAY

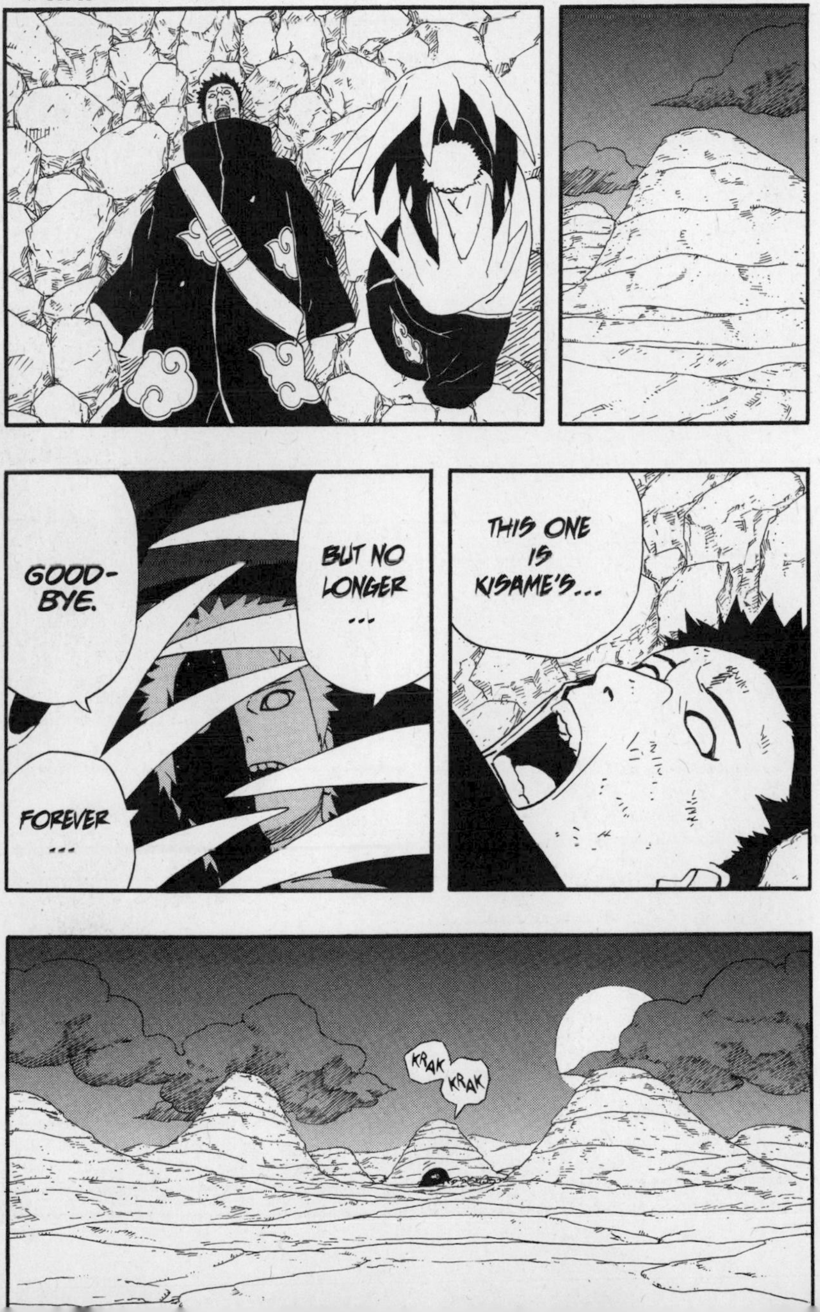
THIS ONE IS KISAME'S...
BUT NO LONGER ...
GOOD-BYE.
FOREVER ...
KRAK KRAK

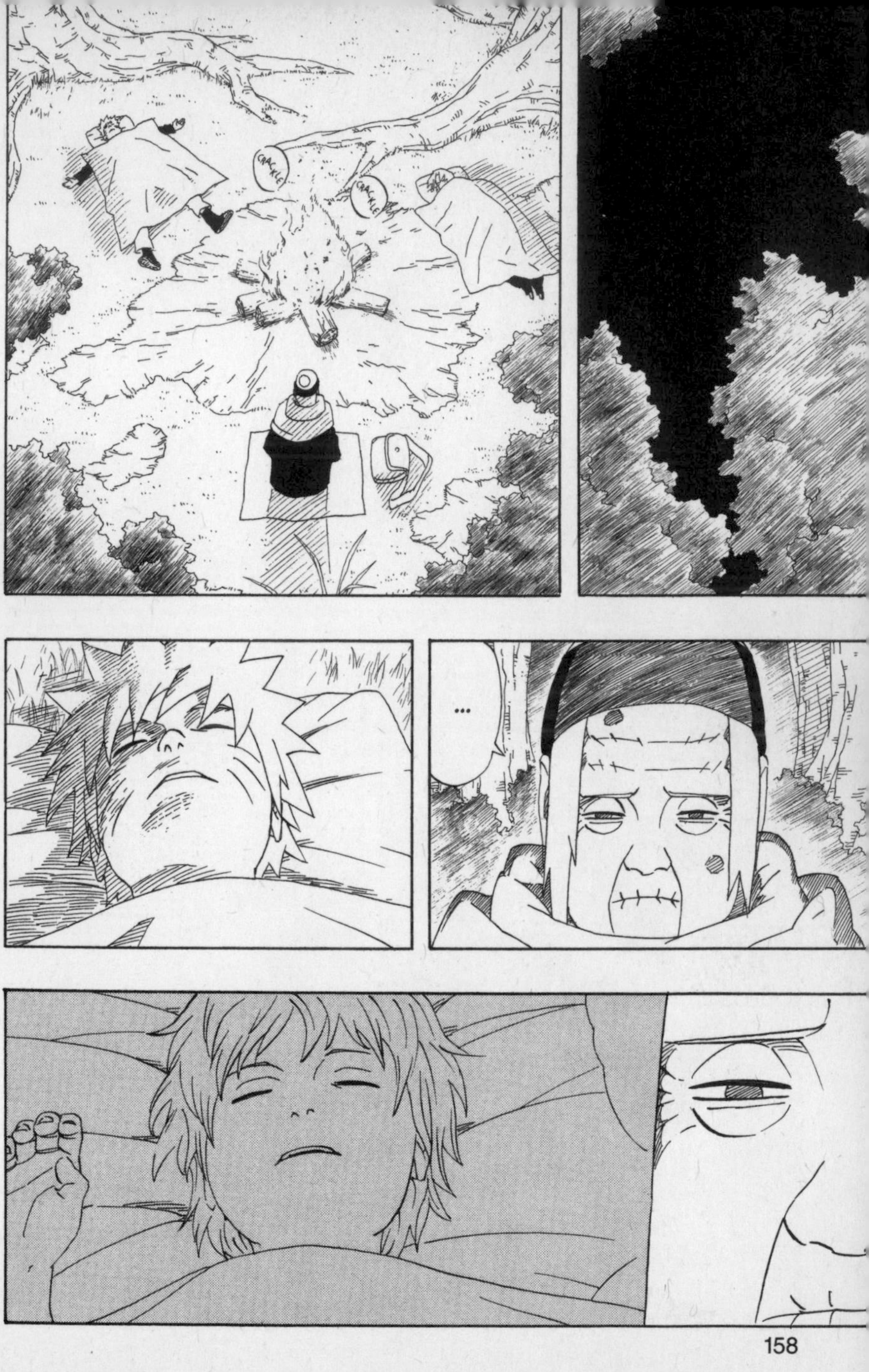
CRACKLE
CRACKLE
...

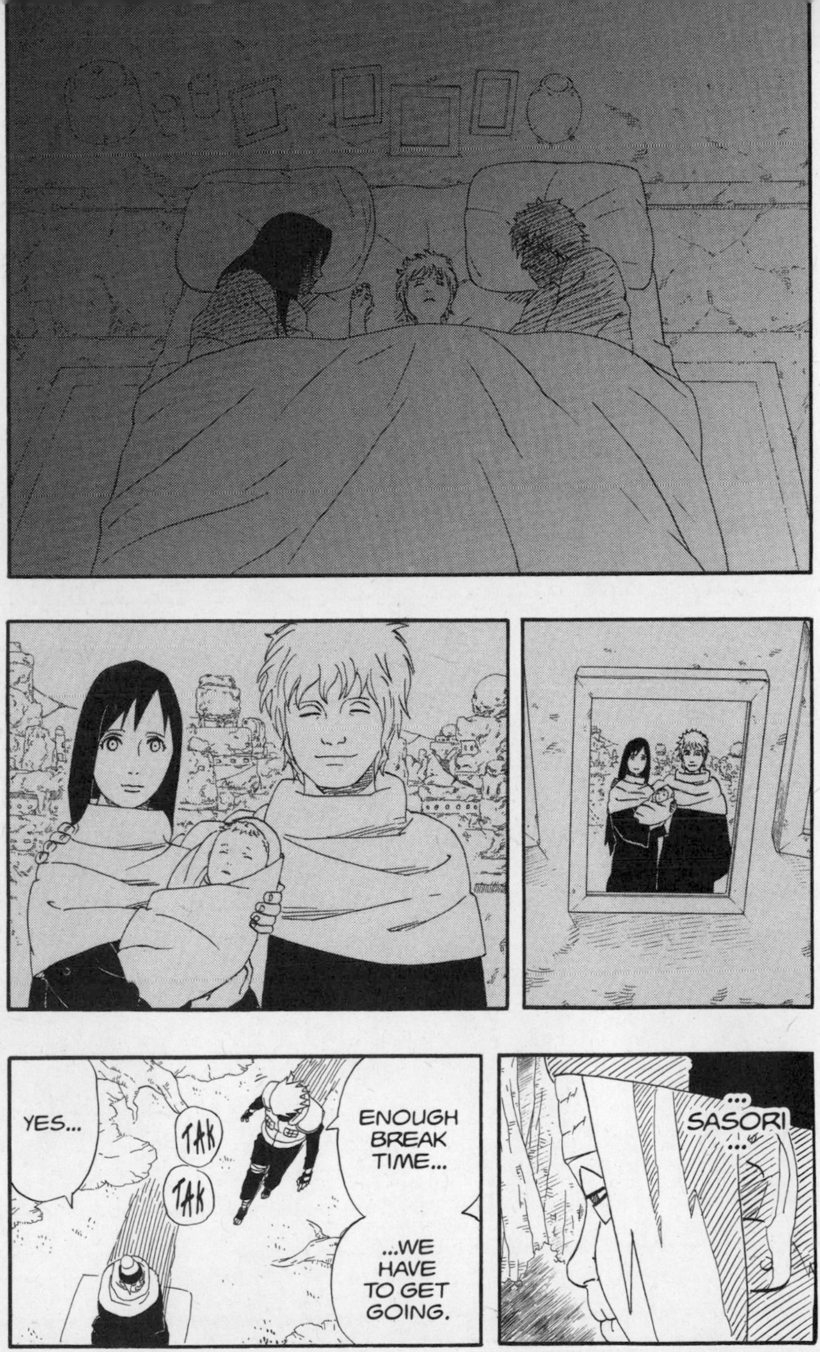
...SASORI...
ENOUGH BREAK TIME...
...WE HAVE TO GET GOING.
TAK
TAK
YES...

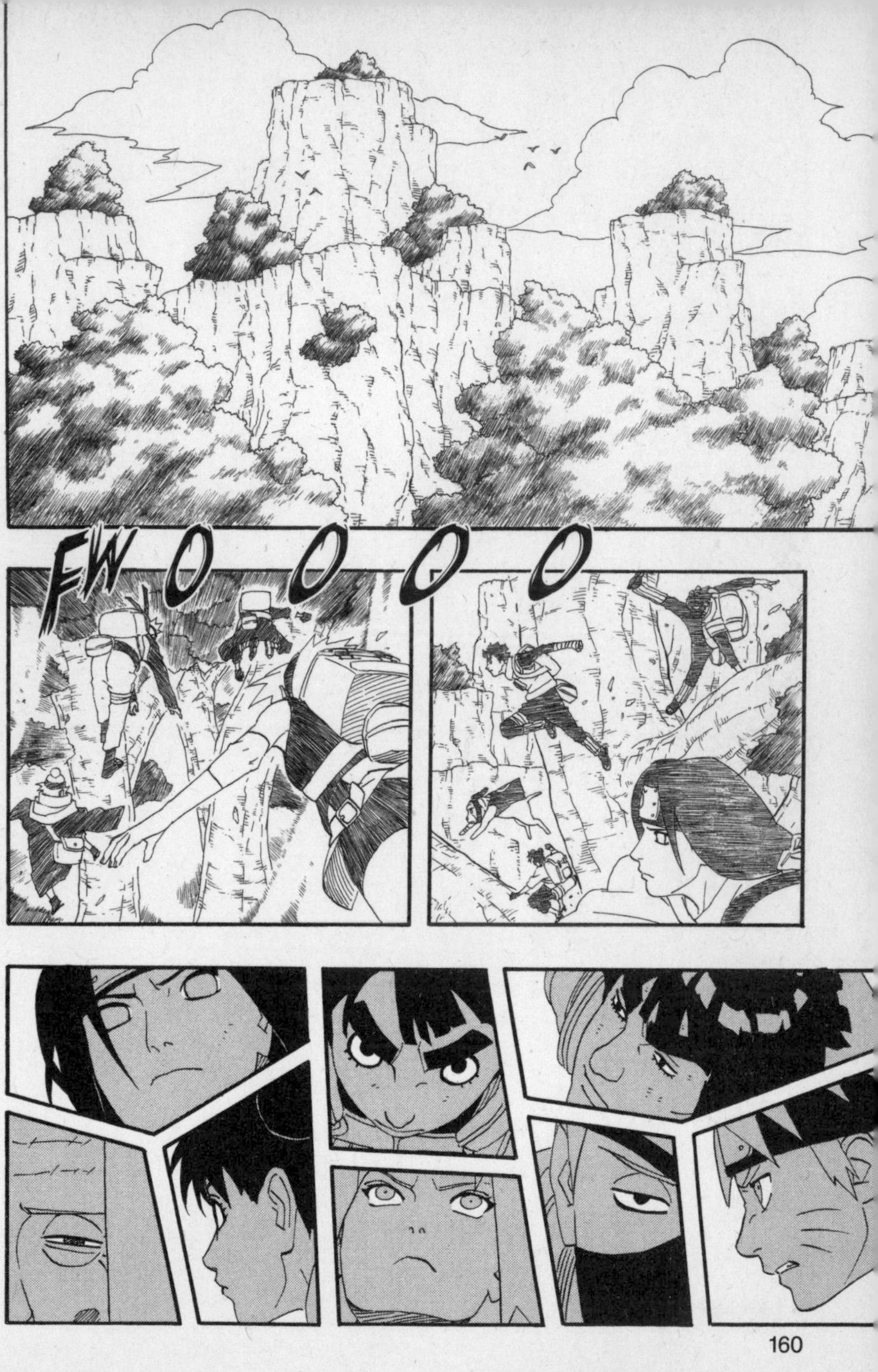
FWOOOOO

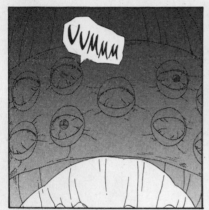

VVMMM

IT'S NEARLY COMPLETE.

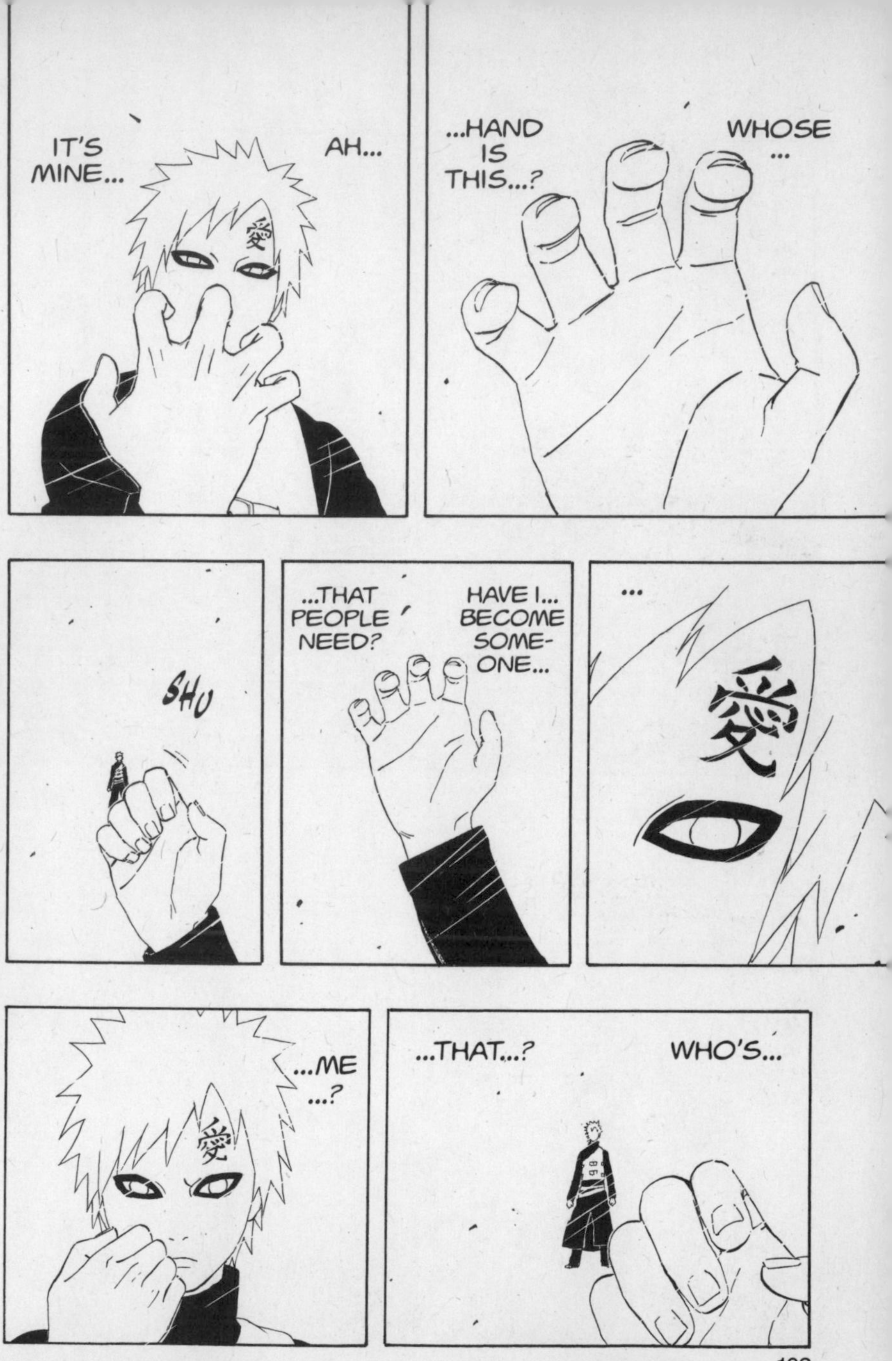
WHOSE ...
...HAND IS THIS...?
AH...
IT'S MINE...
...
HAVE I... BECOME SOME-ONE...
...THAT PEOPLE NEED?
SHU
WHO'S...
...THAT...?
...ME ...?

READ THIS WAY

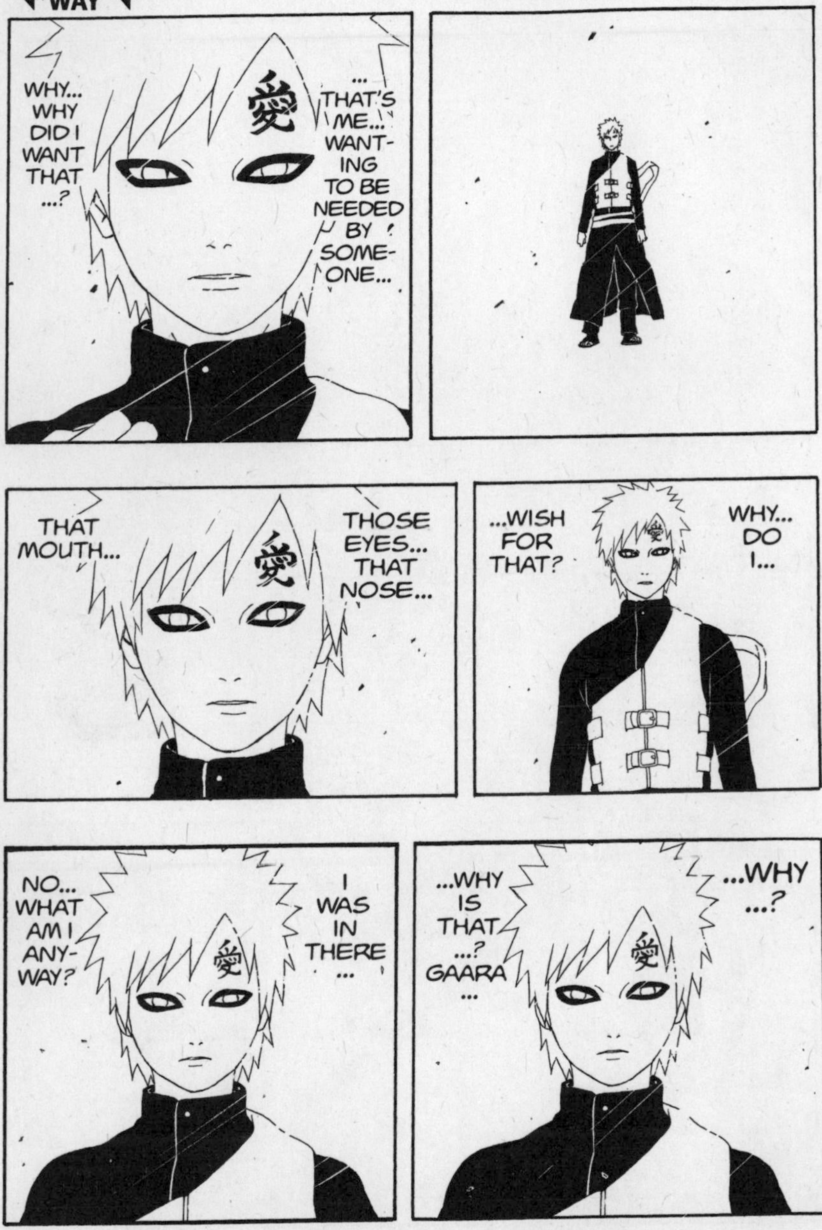
...THAT'S ME... WANTING TO BE NEEDED BY SOMEONE...
WHY... WHY DID I WANT THAT...?
WHY... DO I...
...WISH FOR THAT?
THOSE EYES... THAT NOSE...
THAT MOUTH...
...WHY...?
...WHY IS THAT...? GAARA...
I WAS IN THERE...
NO... WHAT AM I ANYWAY?

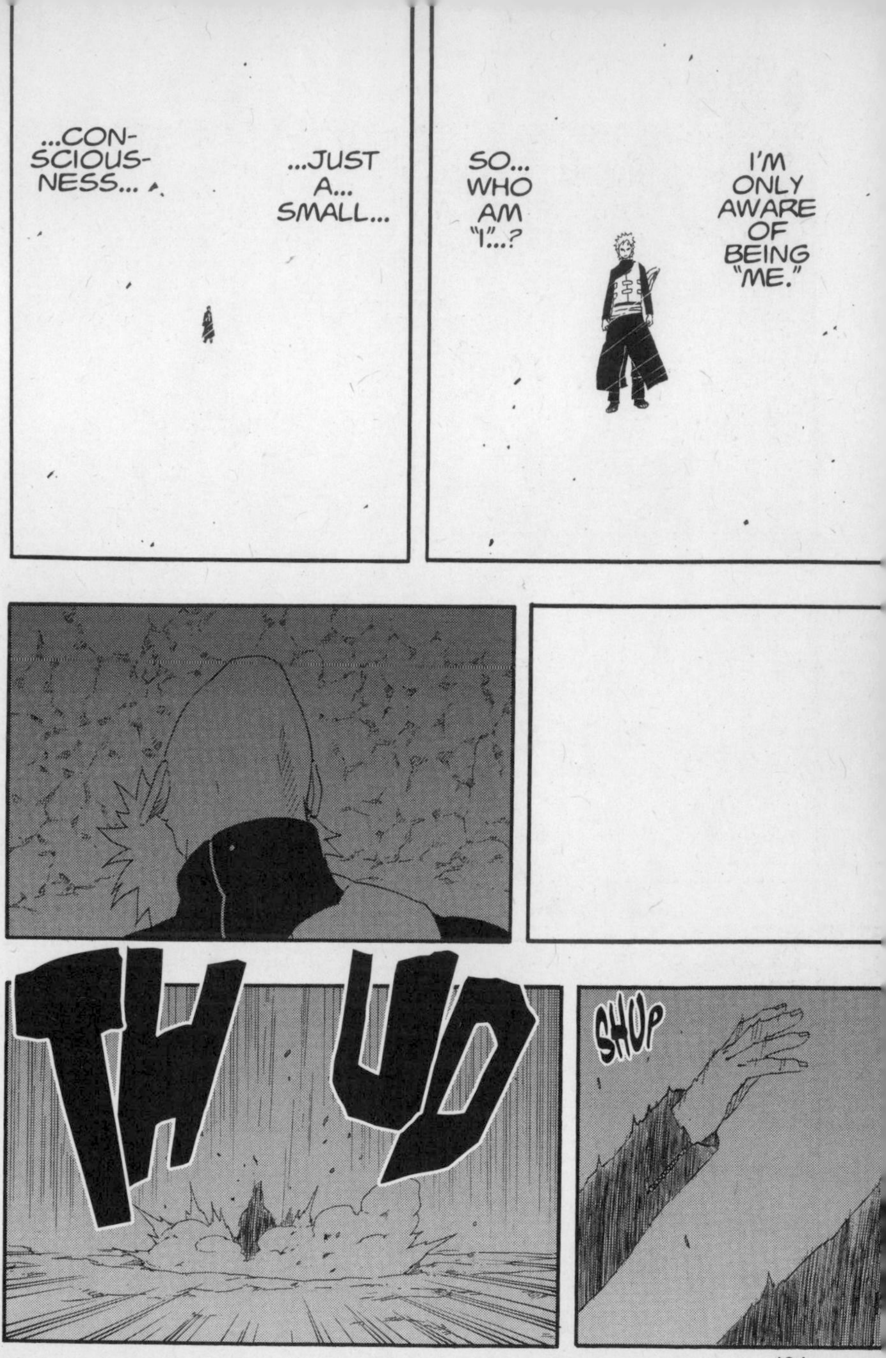
I'M ONLY AWARE OF BEING "ME."
SO... WHO AM "I"...?
...JUST A... SMALL...
...CON-SCIOUS-NESS...
SHUP
THUD

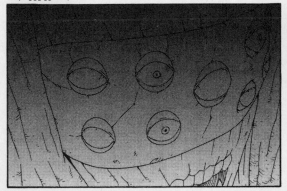

COM-
PLETE.

SHOOM

SHOOM

HERE
!!

SPLASH

NARUTO

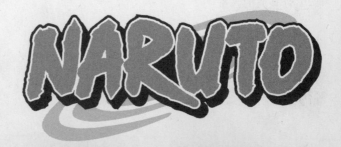

Number 262: Naruto Charges On...!!

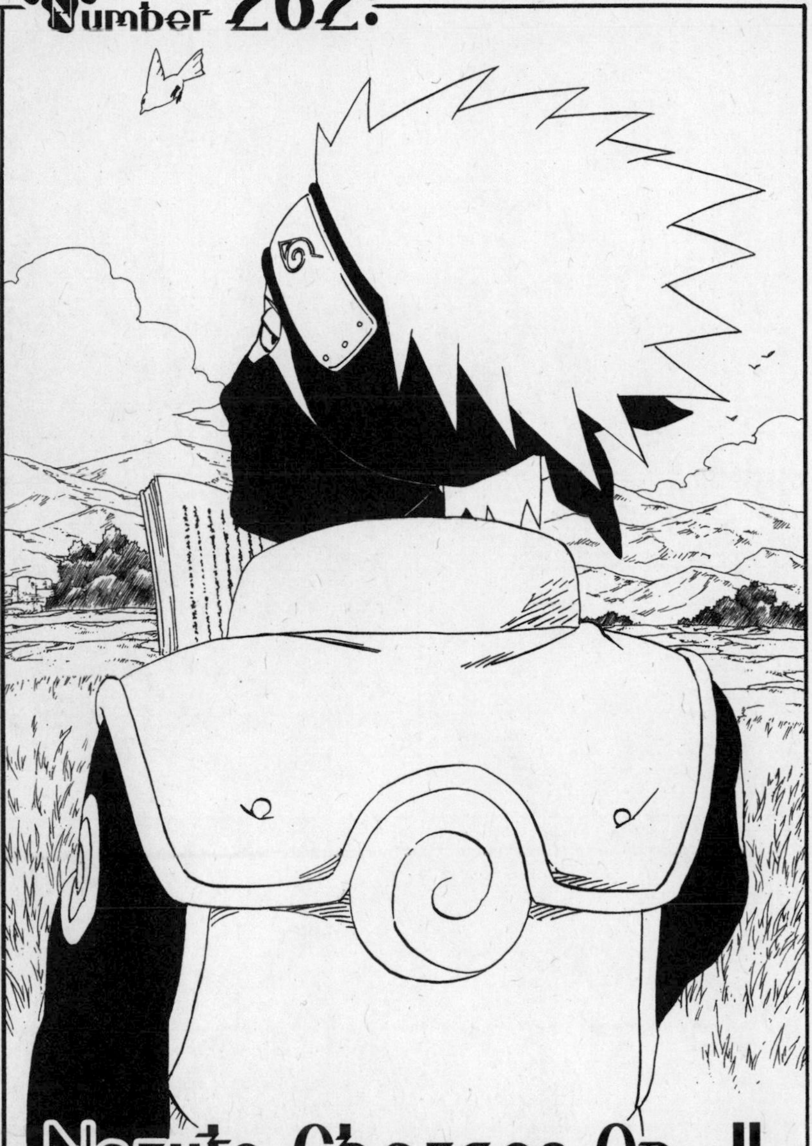

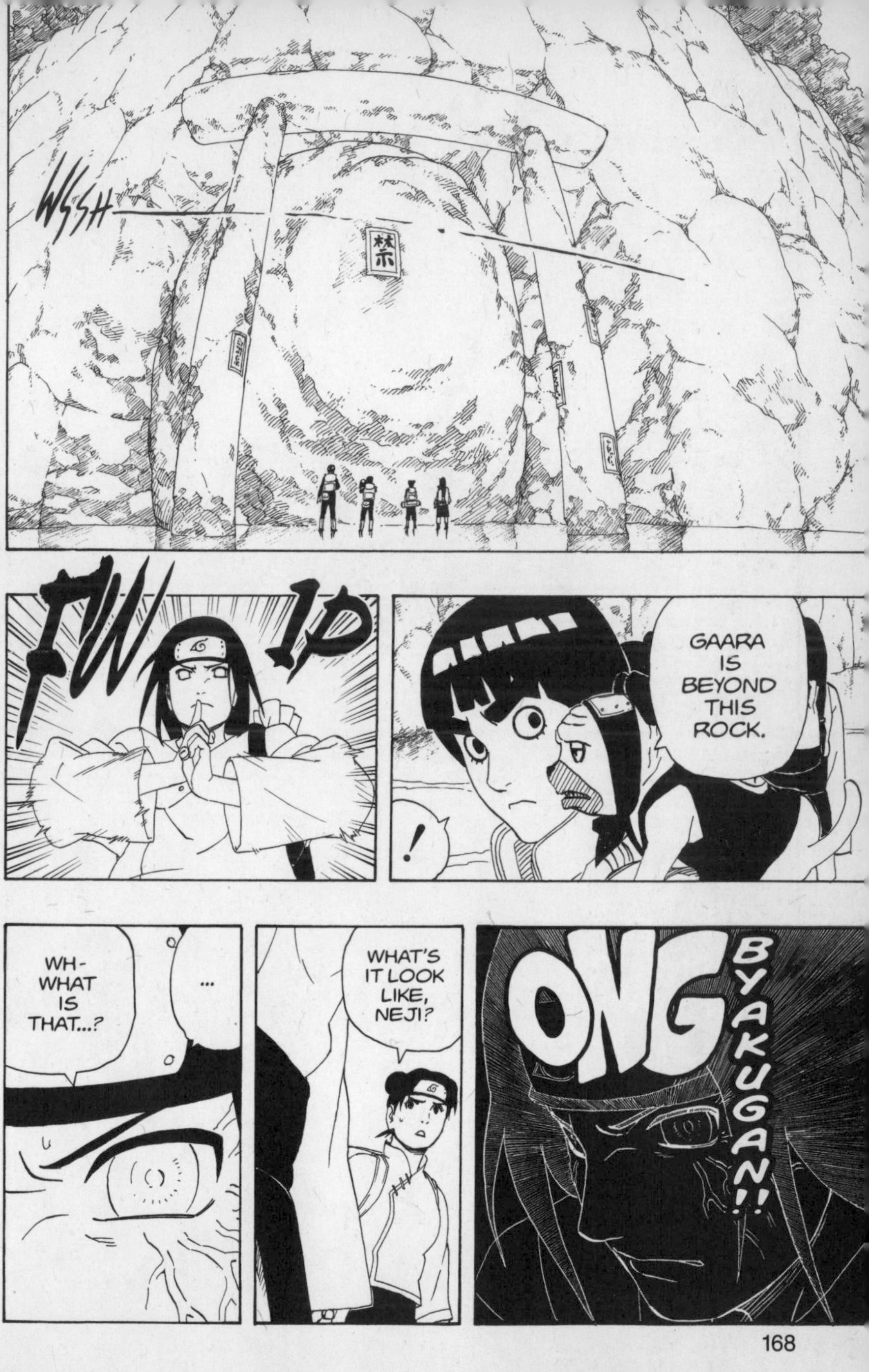
WSSH
GAARA IS BEYOND THIS ROCK.
!
FWIP
BYAKUGAN!!
ONG
WHAT'S IT LOOK LIKE, NEJI?
...
WH- WHAT IS THAT...?

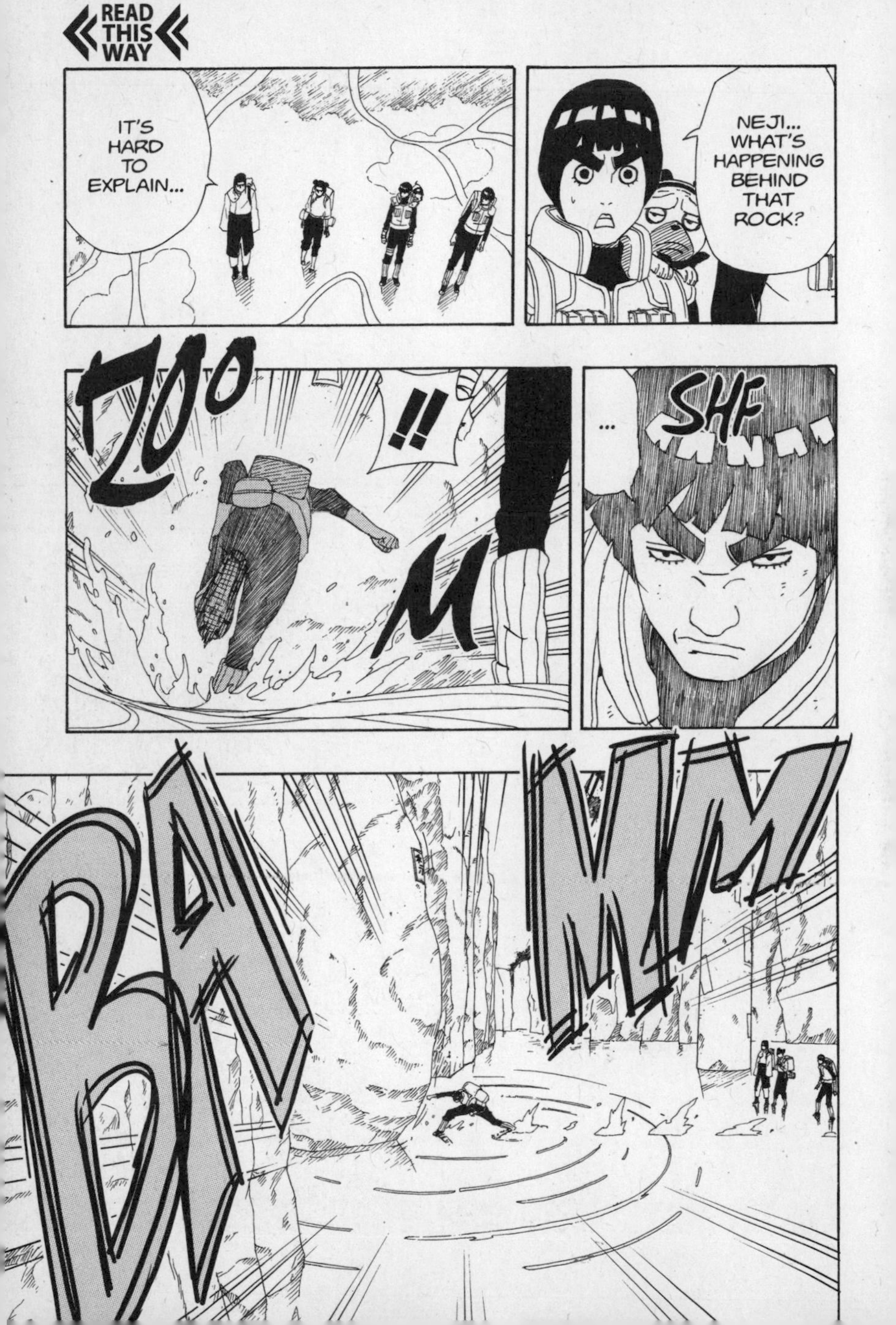
READ THIS WAY
NEJI... WHAT'S HAPPENING BEHIND THAT ROCK?
IT'S HARD TO EXPLAIN...
...
SHF
ZOOM
!!
BAMM

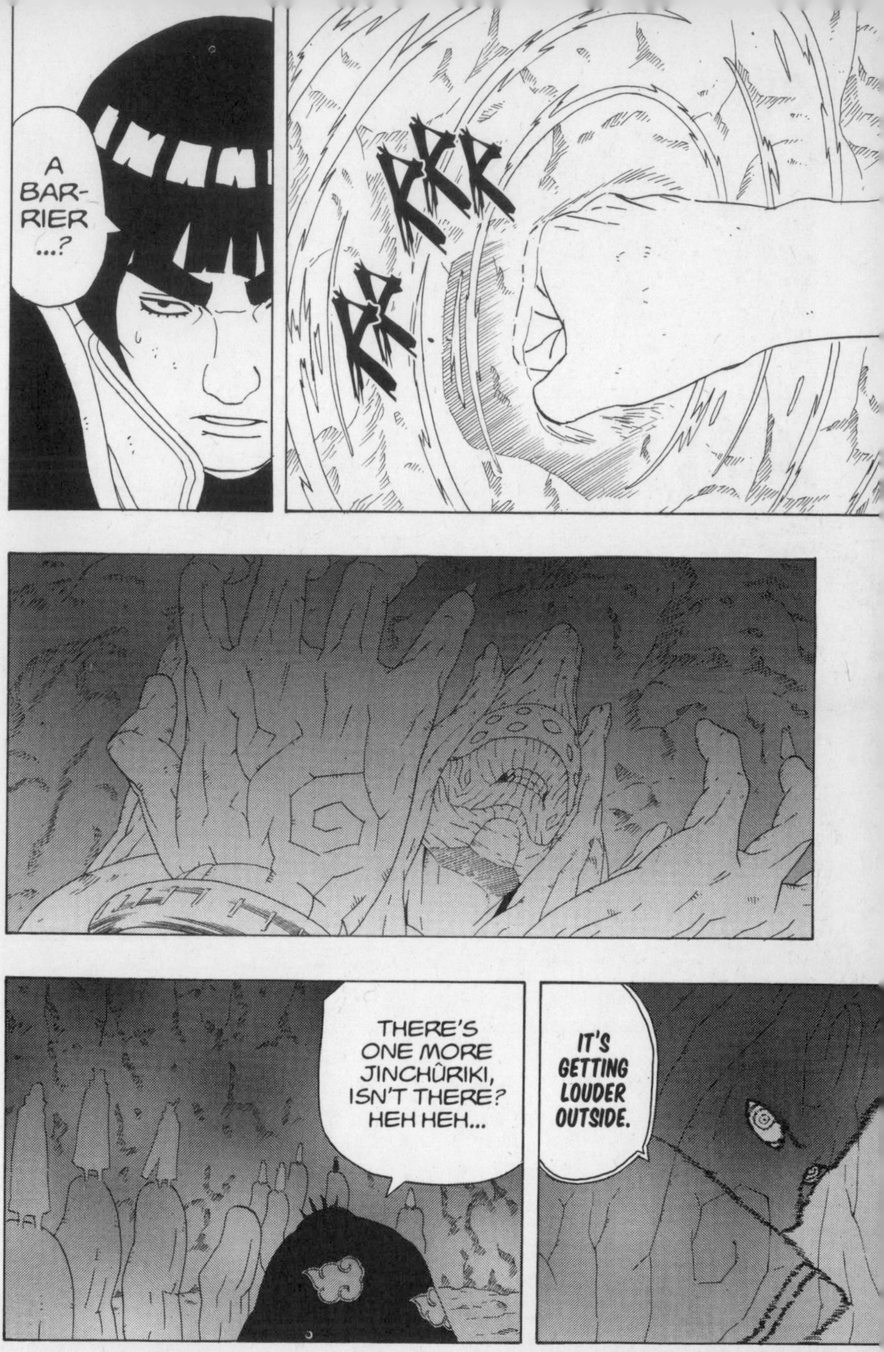
RRR
RR
A BARRIER ...?
IT'S GETTING LOUDER OUTSIDE.
THERE'S ONE MORE JINCHÛRIKI, ISN'T THERE? HEH HEH...

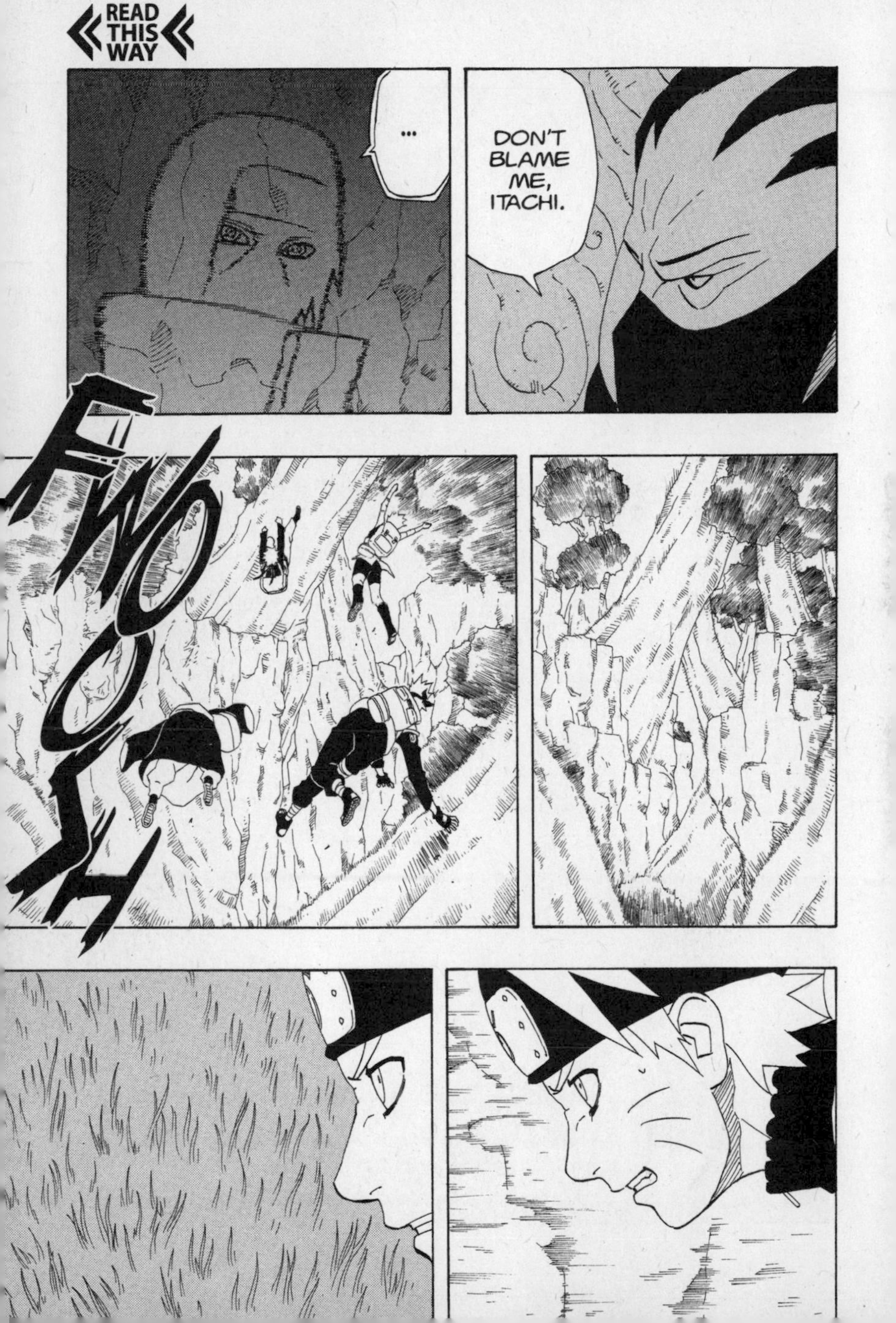
READ THIS WAY
DON'T BLAME ME, ITACHI.
...
FWOOSH

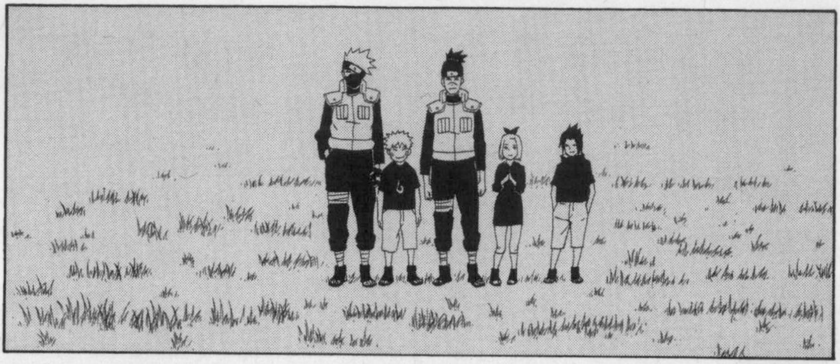
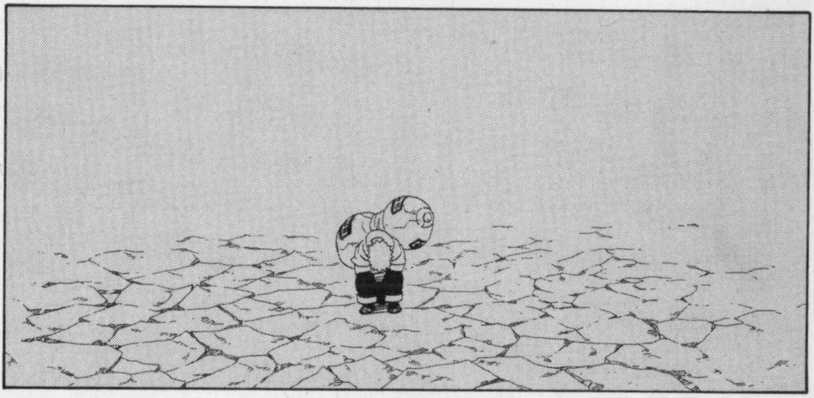
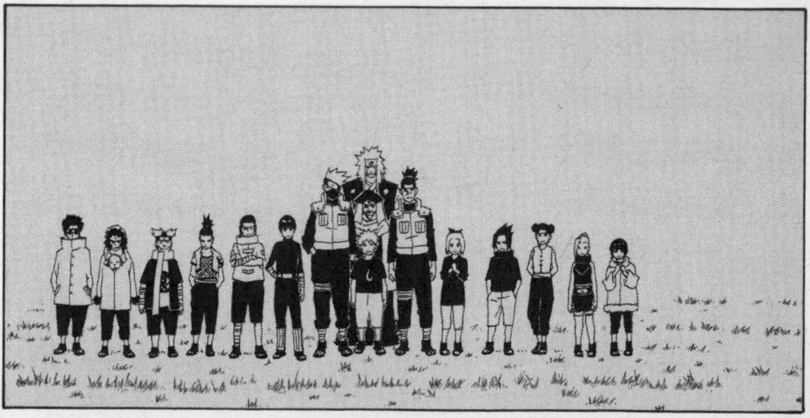

READ THIS WAY

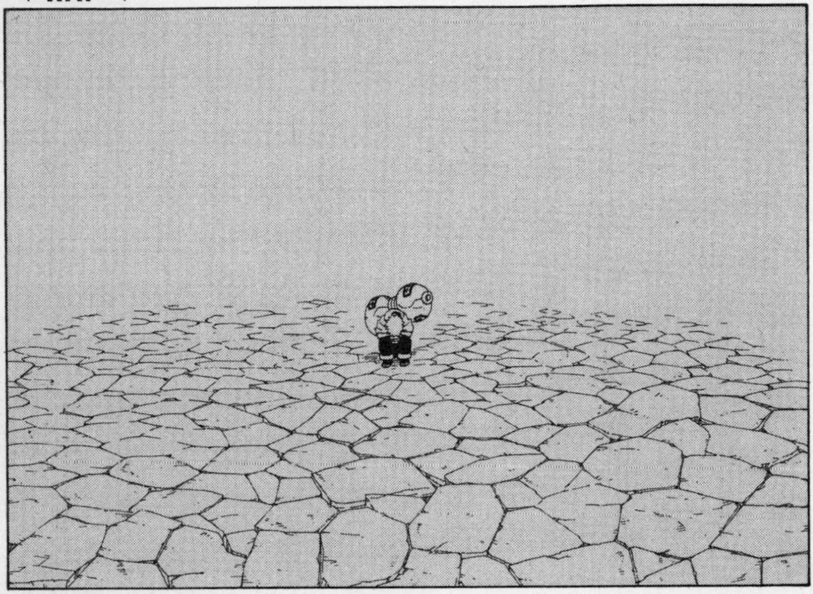

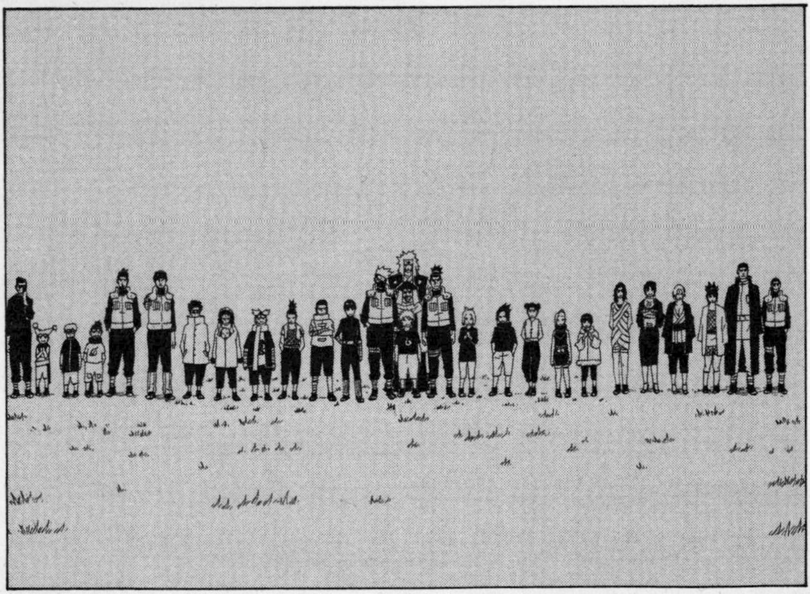

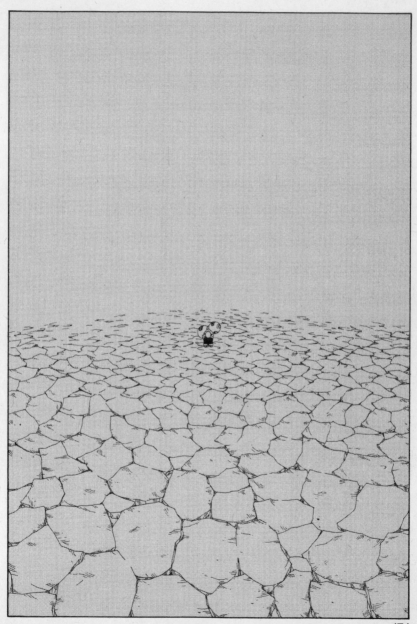

READ THIS WAY

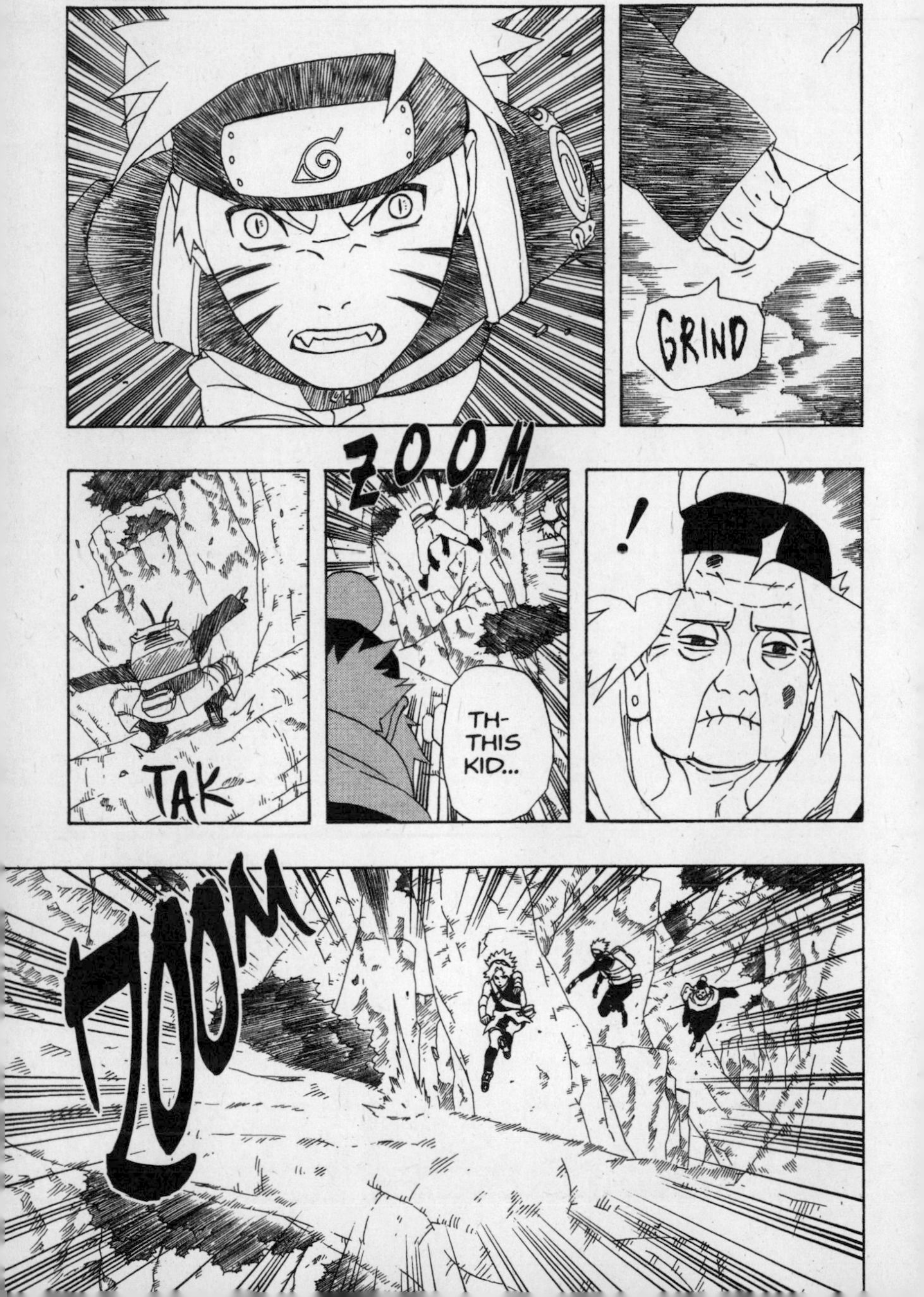
GRIND
!
ZOOM
TH- THIS KID...
TAK
ZOOM

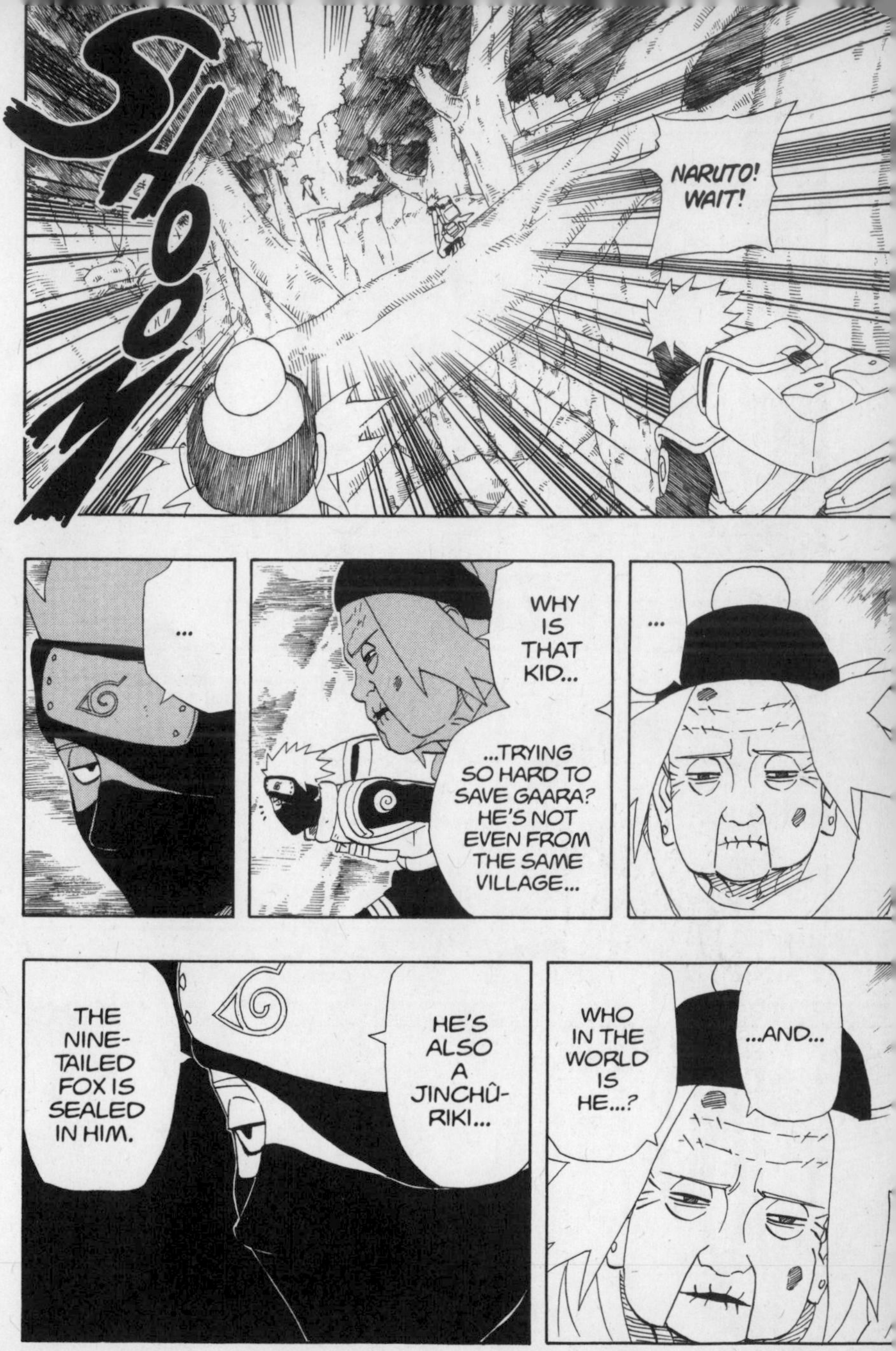
SHOOM
NARUTO! WAIT!
...
WHY IS THAT KID...
...TRYING SO HARD TO SAVE GAARA? HE'S NOT EVEN FROM THE SAME VILLAGE...
...
...AND...
WHO IN THE WORLD IS HE...?
HE'S ALSO A JINCHÛ-RIKI...
THE NINE-TAILED FOX IS SEALED IN HIM.

READ THIS WAY

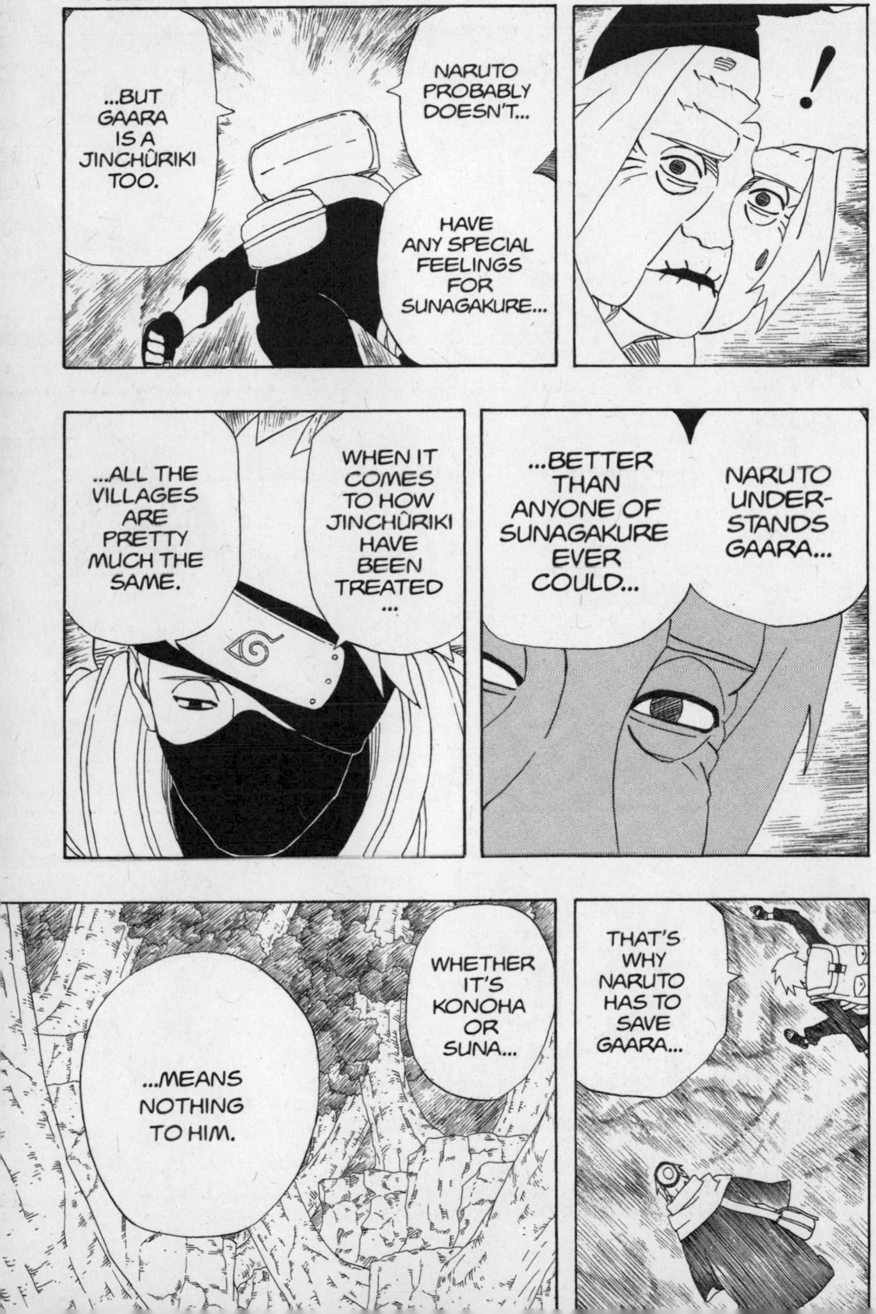
!
NARUTO PROBABLY DOESN'T...
HAVE ANY SPECIAL FEELINGS FOR SUNAGAKURE...
...BUT GAARA IS A JINCHÛRIKI TOO.
NARUTO UNDER-STANDS GAARA...
...BETTER THAN ANYONE OF SUNAGAKURE EVER COULD...
WHEN IT COMES TO HOW JINCHÛRIKI HAVE BEEN TREATED...
...ALL THE VILLAGES ARE PRETTY MUCH THE SAME.
THAT'S WHY NARUTO HAS TO SAVE GAARA...
WHETHER IT'S KONOHA OR SUNA...
...MEANS NOTHING TO HIM.

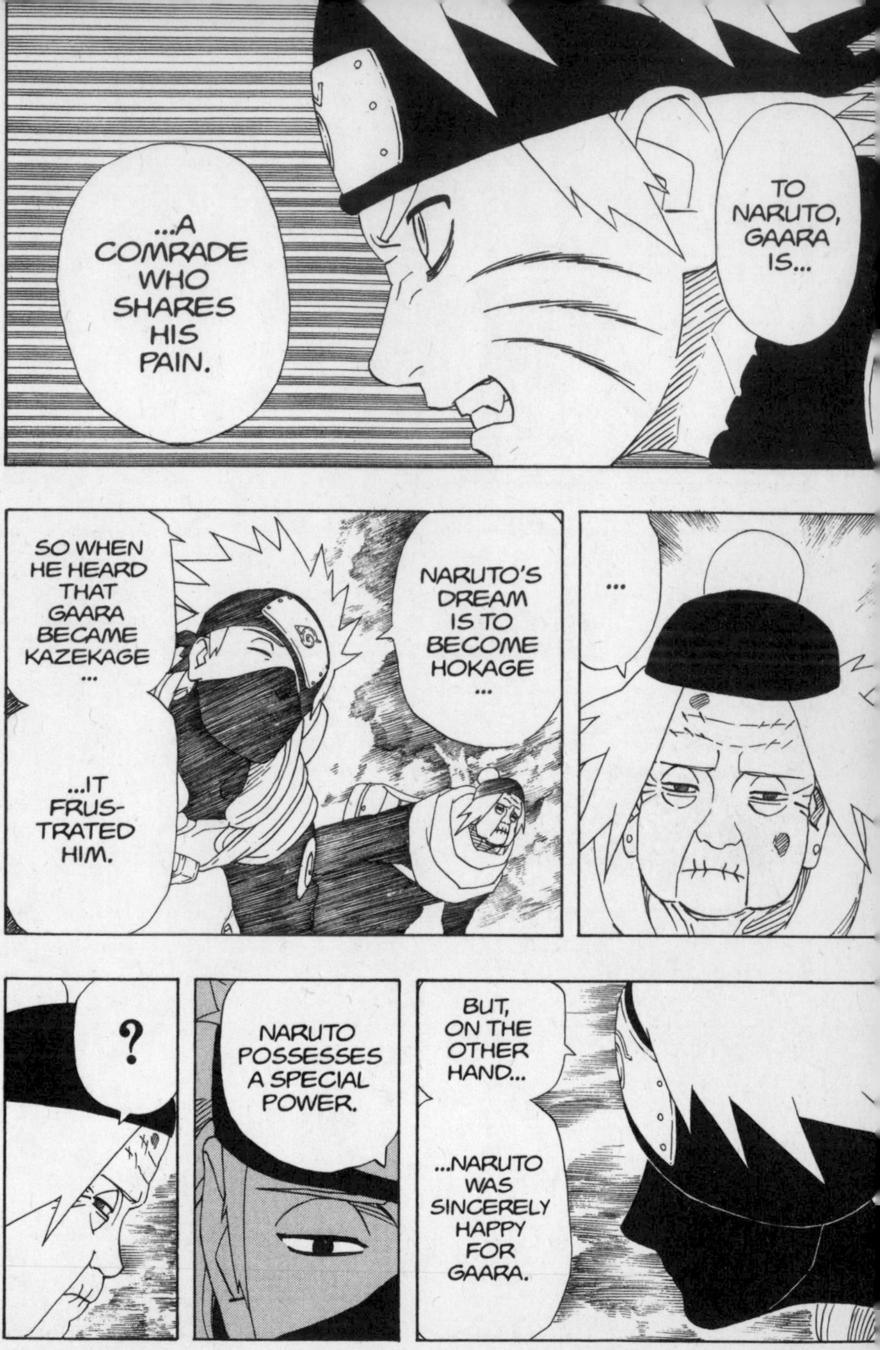
TO NARUTO, GAARA IS...
...A COMRADE WHO SHARES HIS PAIN.
...
NARUTO'S DREAM IS TO BECOME HOKAGE...
SO WHEN HE HEARD THAT GAARA BECAME KAZEKAGE...
...IT FRUSTRATED HIM.
BUT, ON THE OTHER HAND...
...NARUTO WAS SINCERELY HAPPY FOR GAARA.
NARUTO POSSESSES A SPECIAL POWER.
?

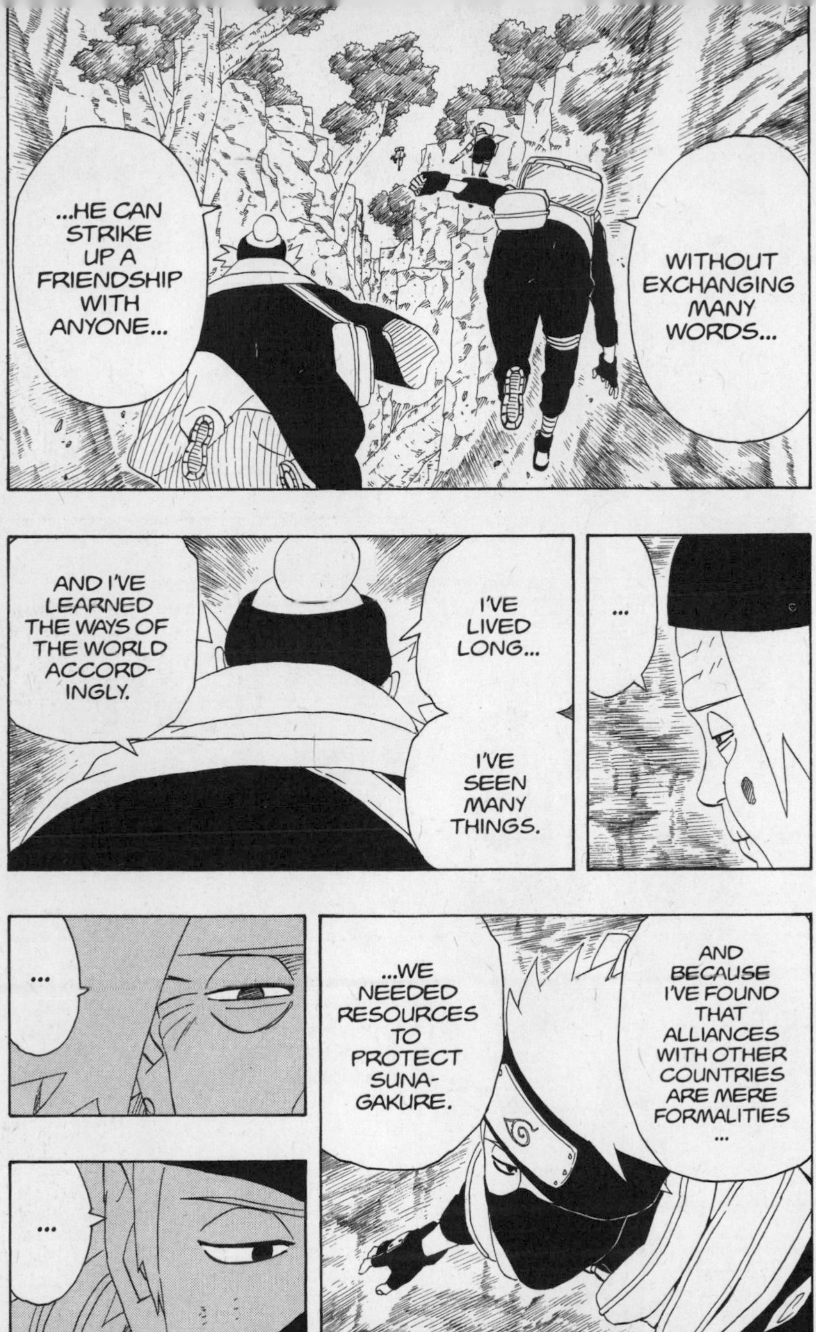
WITHOUT EXCHANGING MANY WORDS...
...HE CAN STRIKE UP A FRIENDSHIP WITH ANYONE...
...
I'VE LIVED LONG...
I'VE SEEN MANY THINGS.
AND I'VE LEARNED THE WAYS OF THE WORLD ACCORD-INGLY.
AND BECAUSE I'VE FOUND THAT ALLIANCES WITH OTHER COUNTRIES ARE MERE FORMALITIES ...
...WE NEEDED RESOURCES TO PROTECT SUNA-GAKURE.
...
...

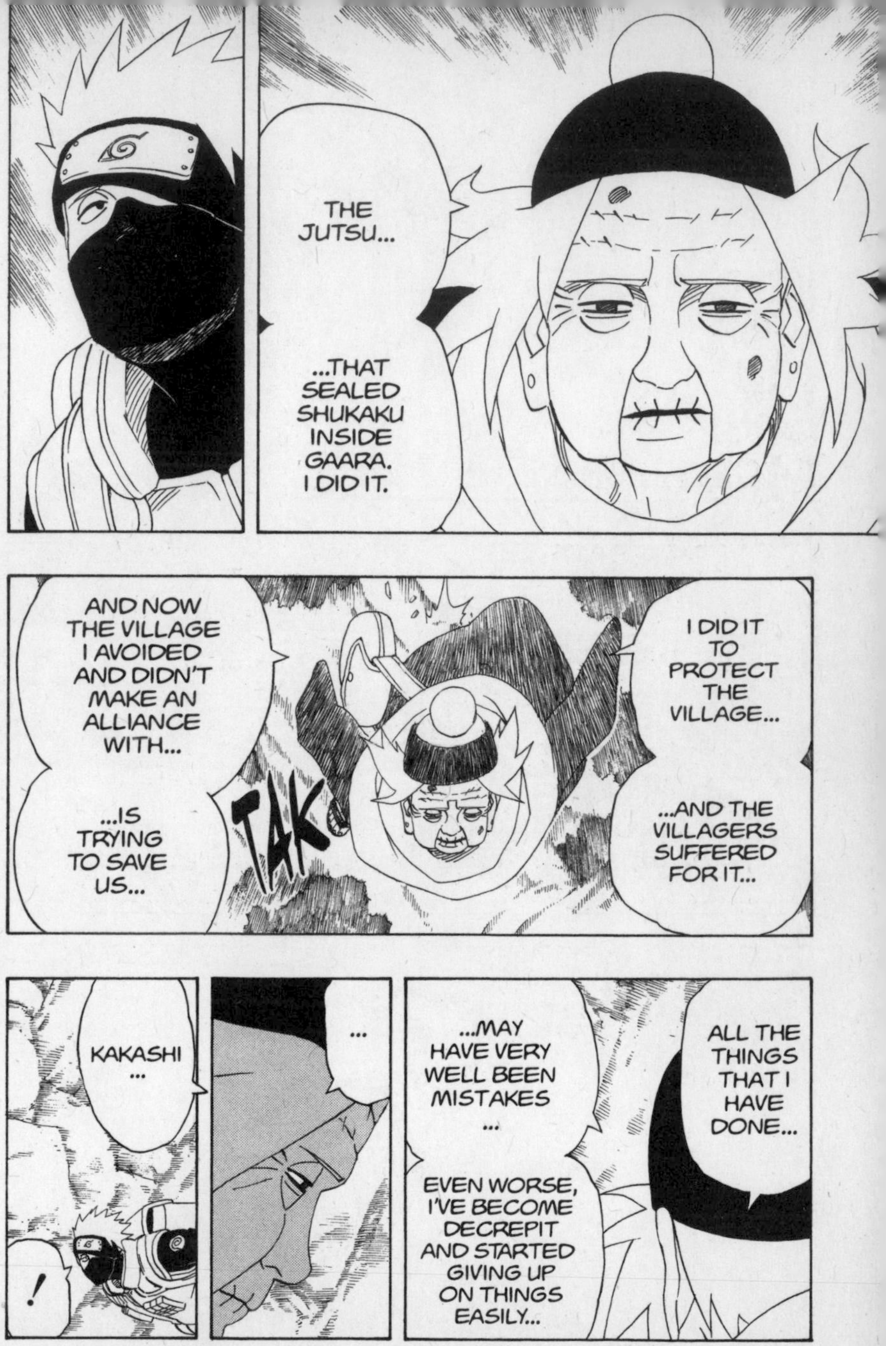
THE JUTSU...
...THAT SEALED SHUKAKU INSIDE GAARA. I DID IT.
I DID IT TO PROTECT THE VILLAGE...
...AND THE VILLAGERS SUFFERED FOR IT...
AND NOW THE VILLAGE I AVOIDED AND DIDN'T MAKE AN ALLIANCE WITH...
...IS TRYING TO SAVE US...
TAK
ALL THE THINGS THAT I HAVE DONE...
...MAY HAVE VERY WELL BEEN MISTAKES ...
EVEN WORSE, I'VE BECOME DECREPIT AND STARTED GIVING UP ON THINGS EASILY...
...
KAKASHI ...
!

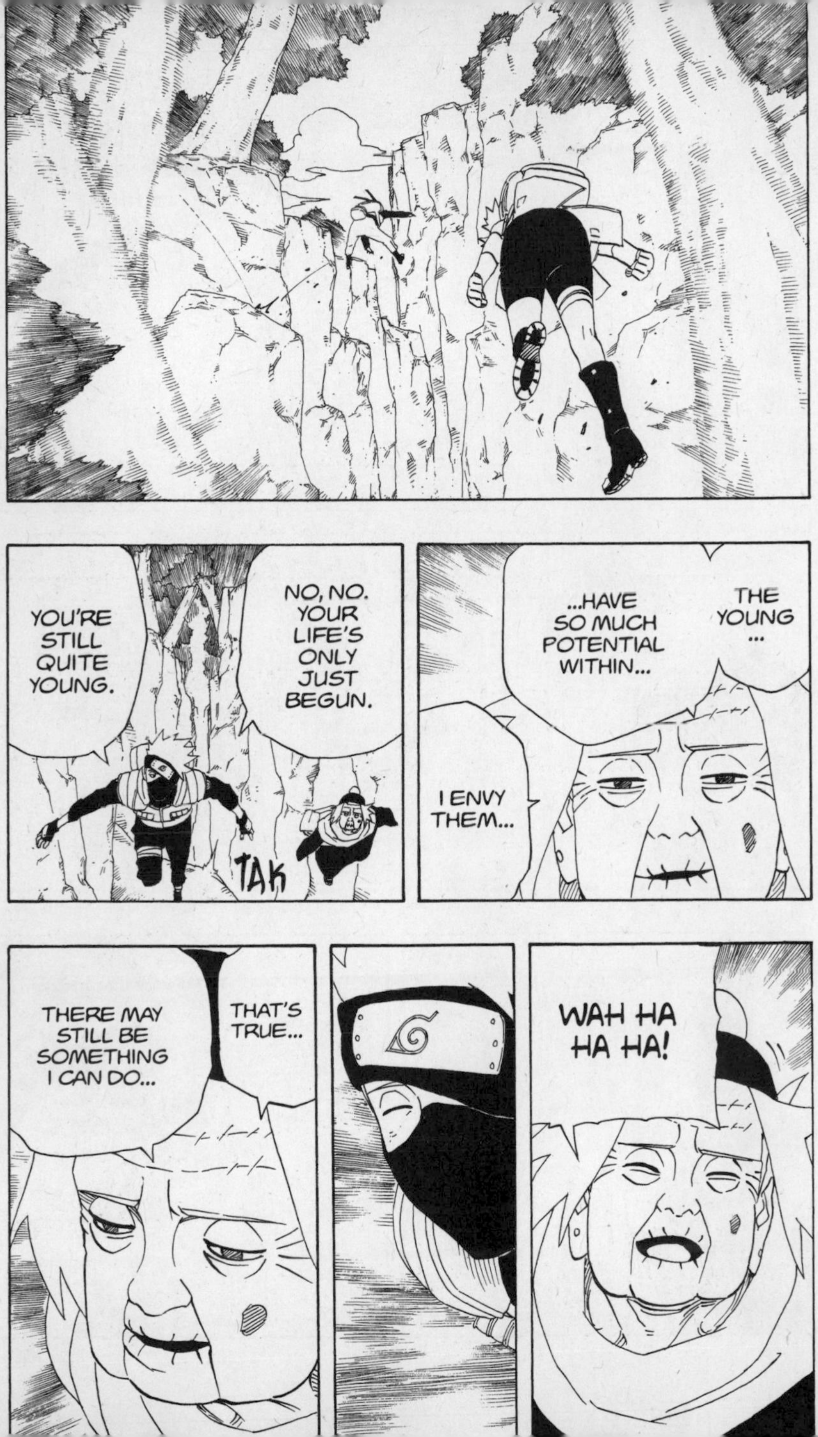
THE YOUNG ...
...HAVE SO MUCH POTENTIAL WITHIN...
I ENVY THEM...
NO, NO. YOUR LIFE'S ONLY JUST BEGUN.
YOU'RE STILL QUITE YOUNG.
TAK
WAH HA HA HA!
THAT'S TRUE...
THERE MAY STILL BE SOMETHING I CAN DO...

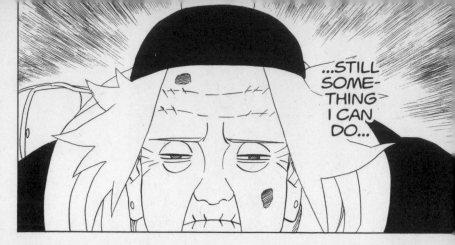

...STILL SOME-THING I CAN DO...

WHAT ARE WE GONNA DO?

BUT HOW?

FIRST WE HAVE TO BREAK THIS BARRIER!

HEY, LEE!

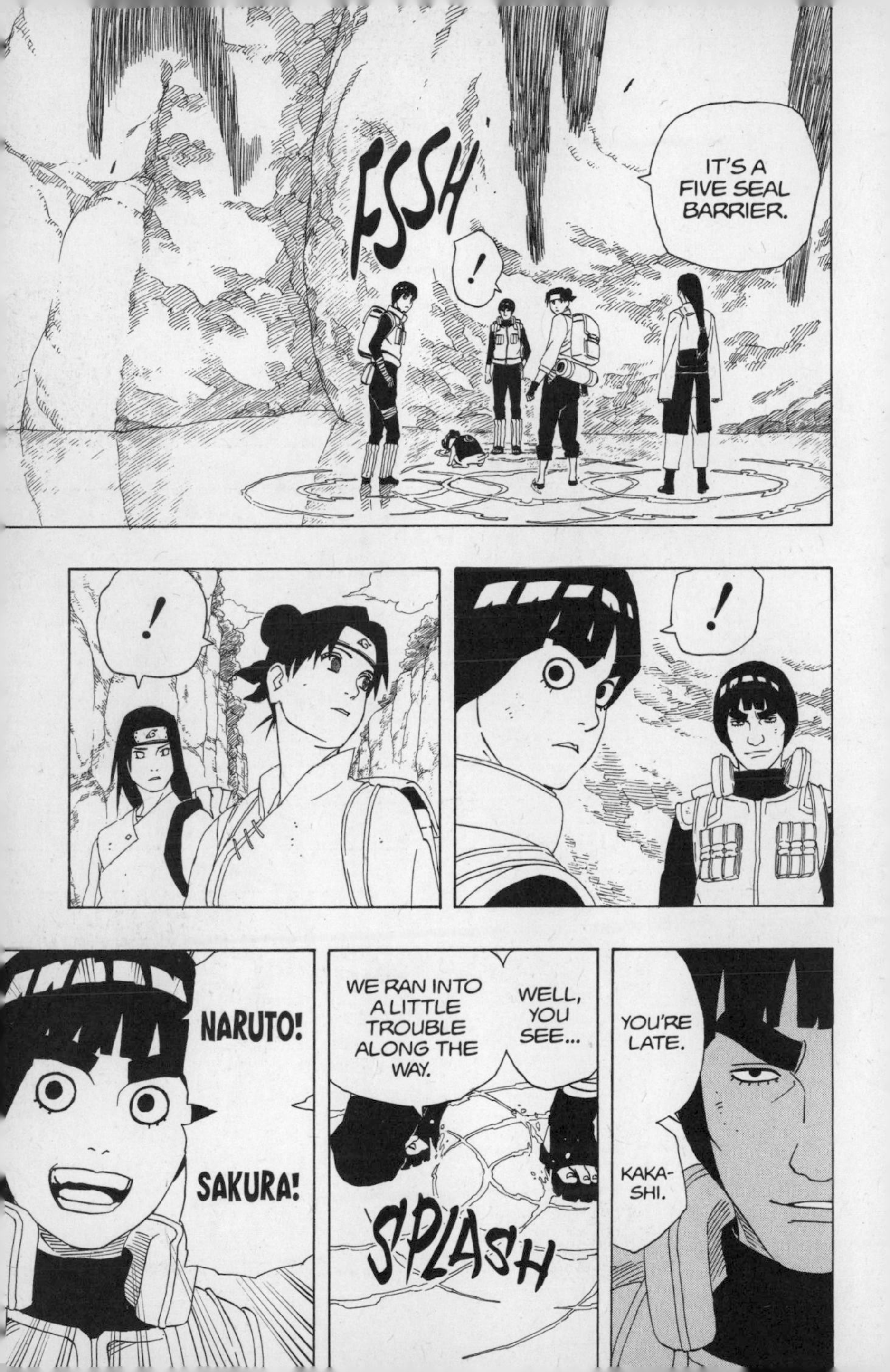
IT'S A FIVE SEAL BARRIER.
FSSH
!
!
!
YOU'RE LATE.
KAKA-SHI.
WELL, YOU SEE...
WE RAN INTO A LITTLE TROUBLE ALONG THE WAY.
SPLASH
NARUTO!
SAKURA!

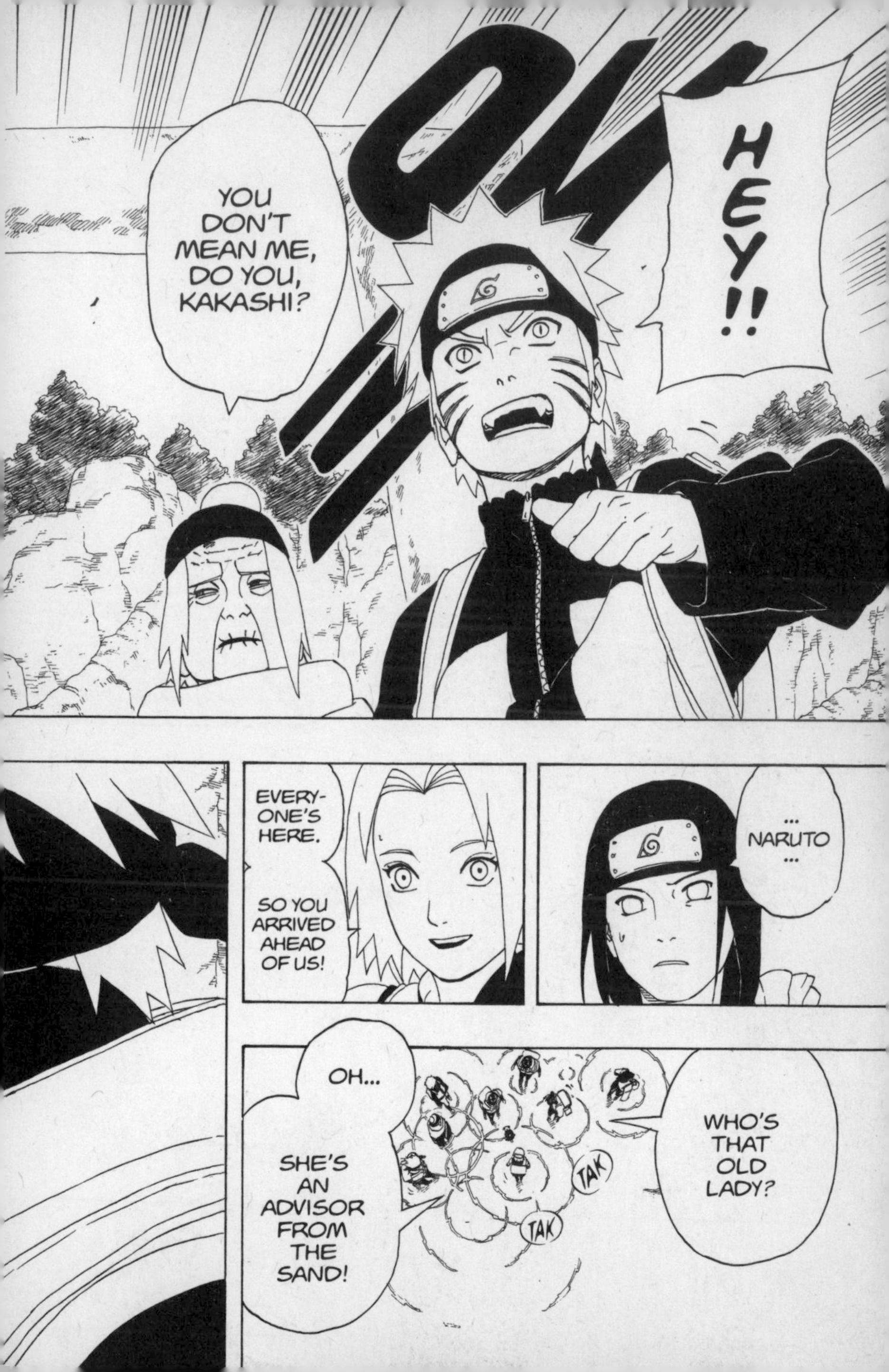
HEY!!
YOU DON'T MEAN ME, DO YOU, KAKASHI?
... NARUTO ...
EVERY-ONE'S HERE.
SO YOU ARRIVED AHEAD OF US!
WHO'S THAT OLD LADY?
TAK
TAK
OH...
SHE'S AN ADVISOR FROM THE SAND!

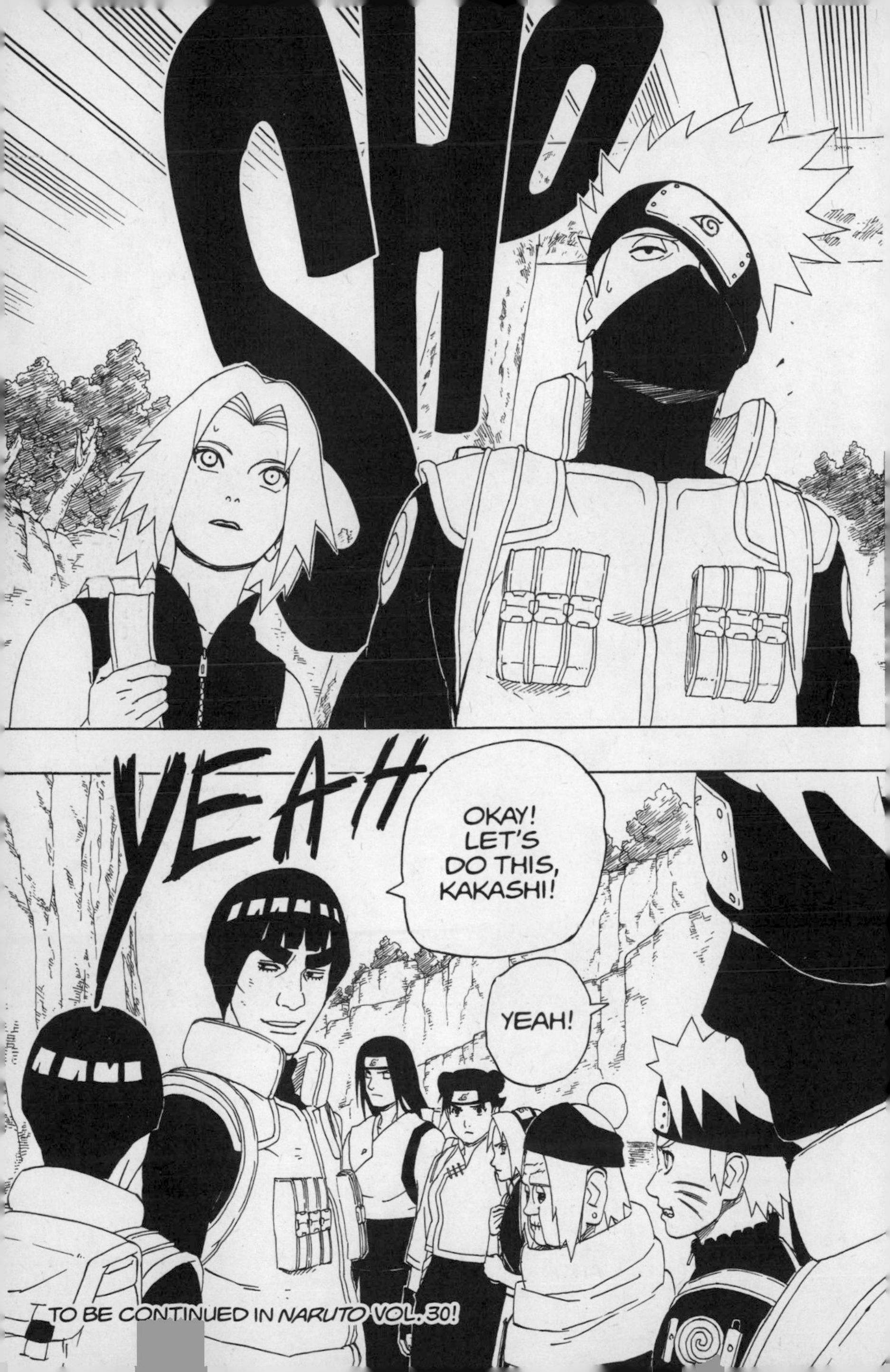
CHO
YEAH
OKAY! LET'S DO THIS, KAKASHI!
YEAH!
TO BE CONTINUED IN NARUTO VOL. 30!

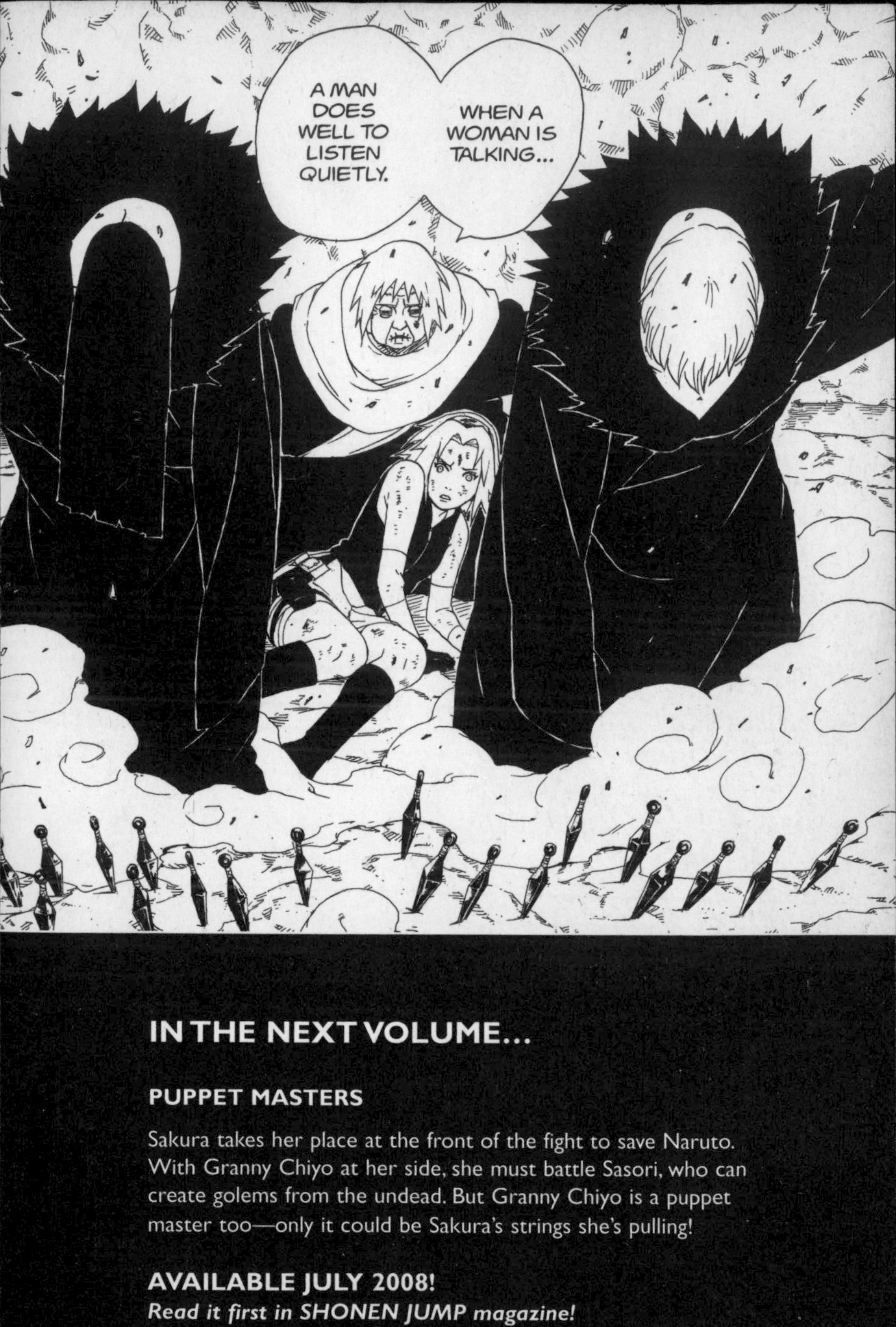
A MAN DOES WELL TO LISTEN QUIETLY.
WHEN A WOMAN IS TALKING...

IN THE NEXT VOLUME...

PUPPET MASTERS

Sakura takes her place at the front of the fight to save Naruto. With Granny Chiyo at her side, she must battle Sasori, who can create golems from the undead. But Granny Chiyo is a puppet master too—only it could be Sakura's strings she's pulling!

AVAILABLE JULY 2008!

Read it first in SHONEN JUMP magazine!

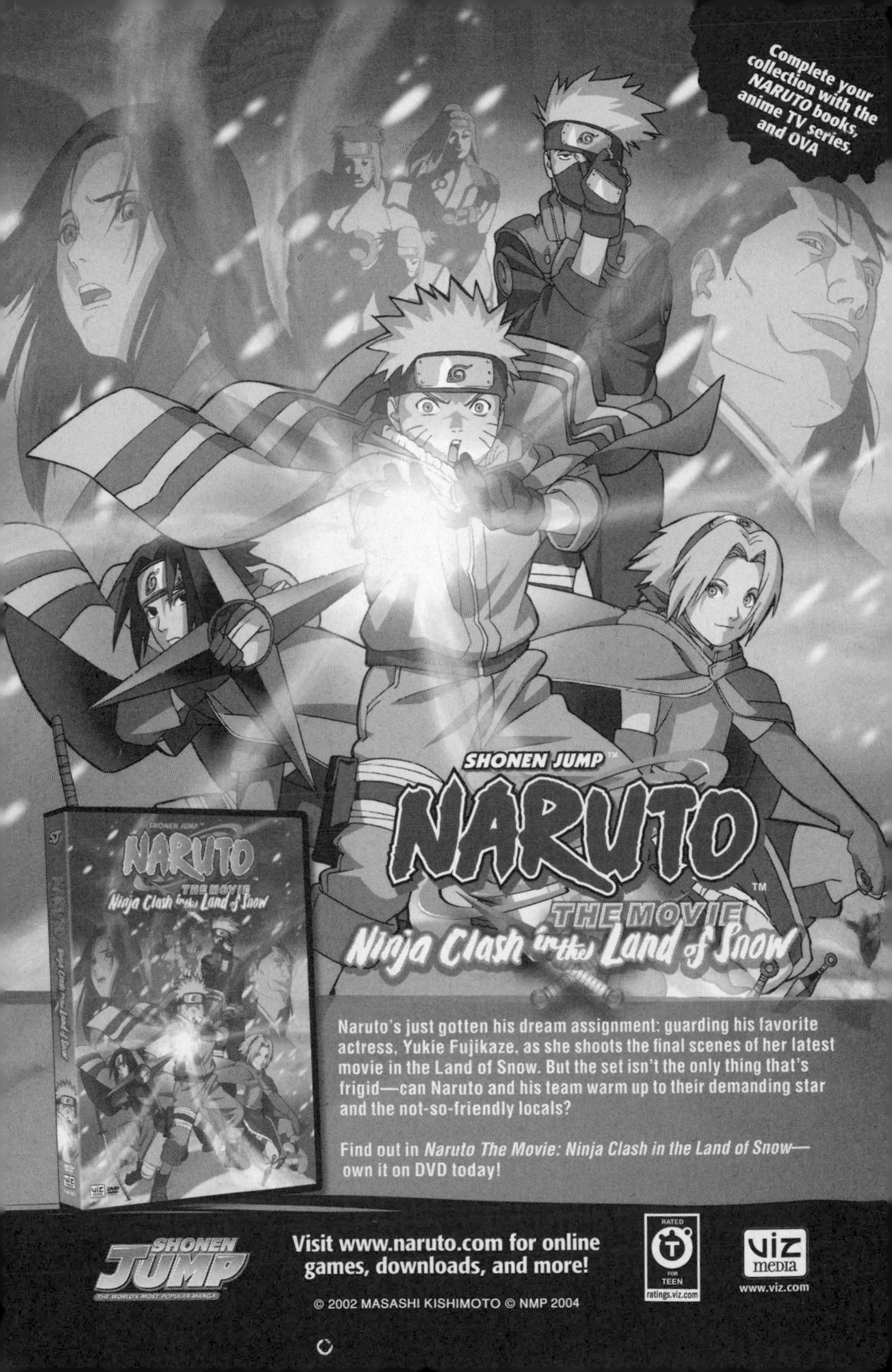

Complete your collection with the NARUTO books, anime TV series, and OVA
SHONEN JUMP™
NARUTO™
THE MOVIE
Ninja Clash in the Land of Snow
Naruto's just gotten his dream assignment: guarding his favorite actress, Yukie Fujikaze, as she shoots the final scenes of her latest movie in the Land of Snow. But the set isn't the only thing that's frigid—can Naruto and his team warm up to their demanding star and the not-so-friendly locals?
Find out in Naruto The Movie: Ninja Clash in the Land of Snow—own it on DVD today!
SHONEN JUMP
THE WORLD'S MOST POPULAR MANGA
Visit www.naruto.com for online games, downloads, and more!
RATED T FOR TEEN
ratings.viz.com
viz media
www.viz.com
© 2002 MASASHI KISHIMOTO © NMP 2004

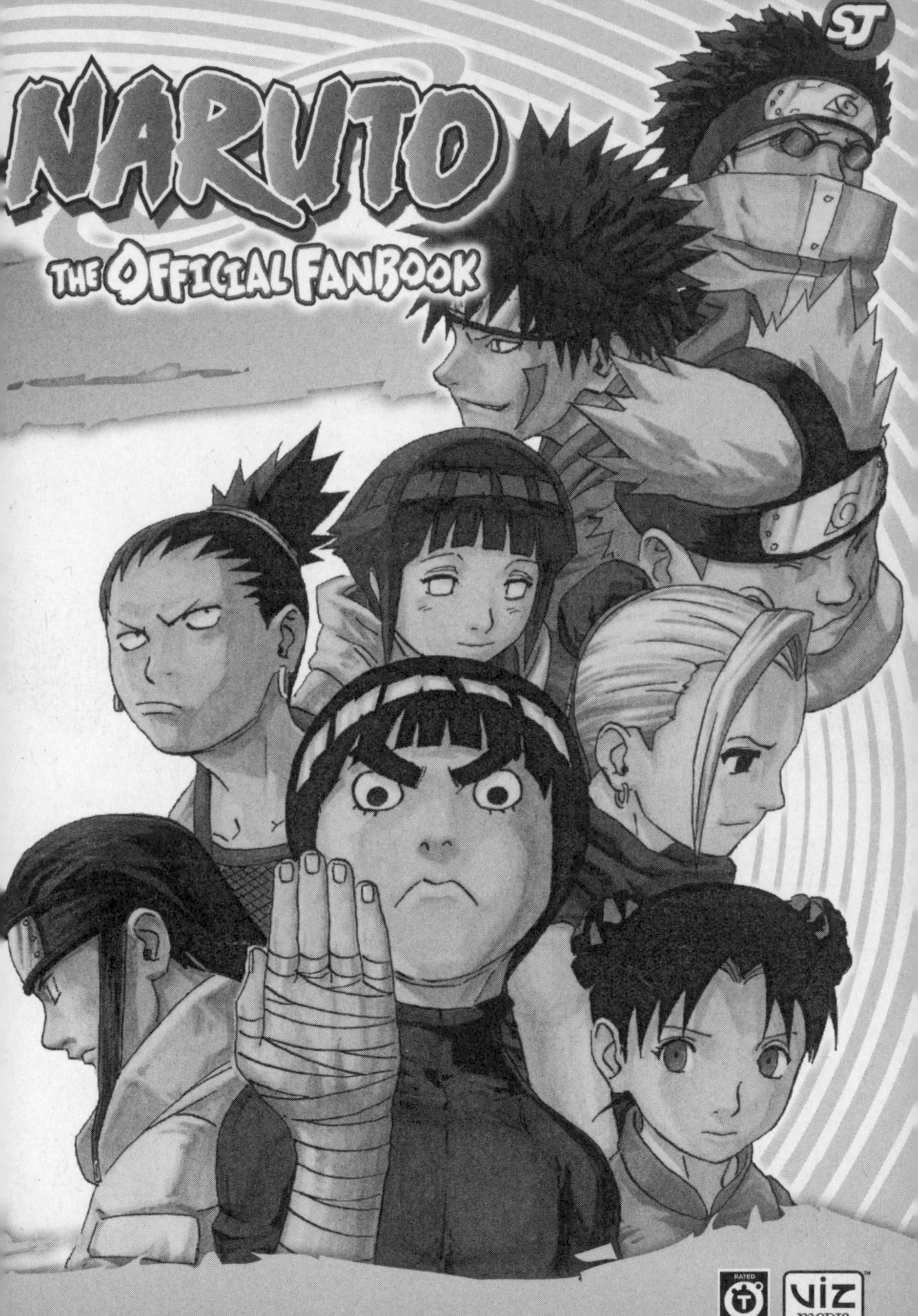
NARUTO
THE OFFICIAL FANBOOK
RATED T FOR TEEN
ratings.viz.com
VIZ media

Save **50% OFF** the cover price!

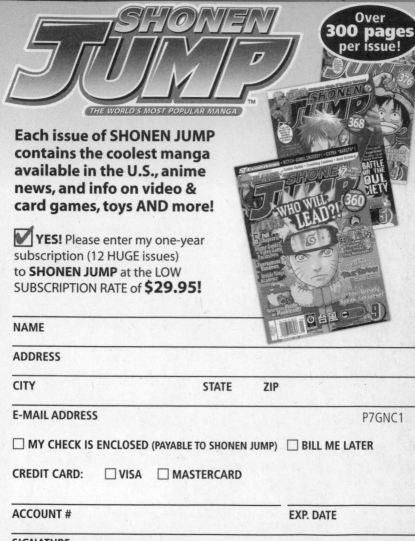

Over 300 pages per issue!

THE WORLD'S MOST POPULAR MANGA

Each issue of SHONEN JUMP contains the coolest manga available in the U.S., anime news, and info on video & card games, toys AND more!

☑ **YES!** Please enter my one-year subscription (12 HUGE issues) to **SHONEN JUMP** at the LOW SUBSCRIPTION RATE of **$29.95!**

NAME

ADDRESS

CITY   STATE   ZIP

E-MAIL ADDRESS   P7GNC1

☐ **MY CHECK IS ENCLOSED** (PAYABLE TO SHONEN JUMP)   ☐ **BILL ME LATER**

CREDIT CARD: ☐ VISA   ☐ MASTERCARD

ACCOUNT #   EXP. DATE

SIGNATURE

CLIP AND MAIL TO ➤

SHONEN JUMP
Subscriptions Service Dept.
P.O. Box 515
Mount Morris, IL 61054-0515

Make checks payable to: **SHONEN JUMP**. Canada price for 12 issues: $41.95 USD, including GST, HST and QST. US/CAN orders only. Allow 6-8 weeks for delivery.

RATED **T** FOR TEEN
ratings.viz.com

BLEACH © 2001 by Tite Kubo/SHUEISHA Inc. NARUTO © 1999 by Masashi Kishimoto/SHUEISHA Inc.
ONE PIECE © 1997 by Eiichiro Oda/SHUEISHA Inc.